W9-BUQ-762

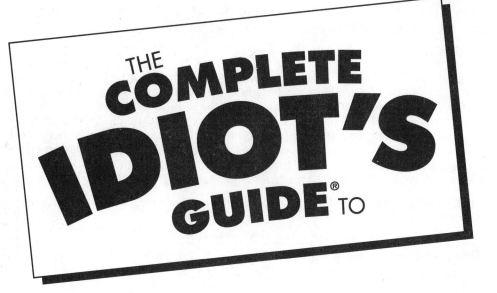

Screenwriting

by Skip Press

alpha books

Macmillan USA, Inc.
201 West 103rd Street
Indianapolis, IN 46290

A Pearson Education Company

To my family: Debbie, Haley, and Holly, the people who enable me to endure the silliness of Hollywood.

Copyright © 2001 by Skip Press

All rights reserved. No part of this book shall be reproduced, stored in a retrieval system, or transmitted by any means, electronic, mechanical, photocopying, recording, or otherwise, without written permission from the publisher. No patent liability is assumed with respect to the use of the information contained herein. Although every precaution has been taken in the preparation of this book, the publisher and author assume no responsibility for errors or omissions. Neither is any liability assumed for damages resulting from the use of information contained herein. For information, address Alpha Books, 201 West 103rd Street, Indianapolis, IN 46290.

THE COMPLETE IDIOT'S GUIDE TO and Design are registered trademarks of Macmillan USA, Inc.

International Standard Book Number: 0-02-863944-8
Library of Congress Catalog Card Number: Available upon request.

03   02   01   8   7   6   5   4   3   2   1

Interpretation of the printing code: The rightmost number of the first series of numbers is the year of the book's printing; the rightmost number of the second series of numbers is the number of the book's printing. For example, a printing code of 01-1 shows that the first printing occurred in 2001.

Printed in the United States of America

Note: This publication contains the opinions and ideas of its author. It is intended to provide helpful and informative material on the subject matter covered. It is sold with the understanding that the author and publisher are not engaged in rendering professional services in the book. If the reader requires personal assistance or advice, a competent professional should be consulted.

The author and publisher specifically disclaim any responsibility for any liability, loss, or risk, personal or otherwise, which is incurred as a consequence, directly or indirectly, of the use and application of any of the contents of this book.

Publisher
Marie Butler-Knight

Product Manager
Phil Kitchel

Managing Editor
Cari Luna

Senior Acquisitions Editor
Randy Ladenheim-Gil

Development Editor
Nancy D. Warner

Senior Production Editor
Christy Wagner

Copy Editor
Krista Hansing

Illustrator
Jody Schaeffer

Cover Designers
Mike Freeland
Kevin Spear

Book Designers
Scott Cook and Amy Adams of DesignLab

Indexer
Amy Lawrence

Layout/Proofreading
Mary Hunt
Gloria Schurick

Contents at a Glance

Contents

Foreword

I sympathize with the aspiring screenwriter. I was once there, sitting in the audience, listening to people describe how to make it. I found out firsthand how hard it can be to get started. Filmmaking is very competitive, but it all starts with the script. If you can write a great one your chances are very good.

As a producer with some decent credits like *Gettysburg, Selena,* and *Introducing Dorothy Dandridge,* I see a lot of scripts. Usually, I try to look only at material that is referred to me by a friend or associate. That way, I have at least some assurance that I might (and I emphasize *might*) have a chance of reading a decent screenplay. And every time I start reading the first page, I hope for that truly great property that everyone will love working on and watching, whether on television or in the movie theater.

Let me tell you, those screenplay gems are very rare. Why? My guess is that people don't study the basics of storytelling enough, much less the history of Hollywood and the accepted structure of good screenplays.

I've known Skip Press for several years and appeared with him on panels at the Hollywood Film Festival and Book Expo America. He might not be a household name as a screenwriter (hardly any screenwriter is, or any producer, for that matter), but he's provided quite a package here for the aspiring screenwriter. I think he feels like I do, that if he had had this book to read when he started studying screenwriting, it would have provided a very good shortcut.

There are a lot of screenplay theory books but none I know covers the ground quite like *The Complete Idiot's Guide to Screenwriting.* It outlines the complete sweep of story history and things like how psychology and the Actors Studio influenced movie-making. This book is like a mini-crash-course screenwriting degree program. It covers the structure of a TV movie, offers details about writing a Web show, and gives you tips on holding a staged reading of your screenplay (to see if what is written on the page sounds as good coming out of an actor's mouth).

Even the stuff that seems dumb to people who don't know Hollywood is in these pages. For example, you should use two brads to bind a three-hole punched script. Why? Because Hollywood people who like a script take it apart and copy it for others to read and decide on. You don't know things like that unless you're a Hollywood veteran.

With my partner, Moctesuma Esperza, I've spent a lot of time working on stories about people of ethnic backgrounds who don't have as easy a chance starting out in life as some. In Hollywood, the screenwriter often seems like a disadvantaged minority. Skip's book helps level the playing field and puts everyone who reads it a step ahead. That's why I think it's a winner.

Robert Katz, Producer

Introduction

The one movie that my entire family saw in a theater was *To Kill a Mockingbird*. We saw this Academy Award–winning film in a small East Texas town, and the racial struggle portrayed in the story was going on outside the theater doors. I remember where I was sitting and all the details of the movie.

Unfortunately, my father had problems and was no bastion of sensibility like Gregory Peck's Atticus Finch onscreen. As a child, I grew up admiring movie actors, particularly Jimmy Stewart, and stars of TV shows, such as William Shatner. More than mere actors playing roles, they were father figures who showed me the way a man should live his life.

But there was something deeper in the movies and shows that I admired. The stories etched themselves into memory, and at some point I began paying attention to who wrote those stories. When I saw *Lawrence of Arabia,* while I admired Peter O'Toole's wonderful performance, I was much more impressed by the stunning visuals, the sweeping story, and the glimpse of heroic history.

Still, I wanted to write books. I knew from a very early age that I would write, but it never occurred to me that I might some day write screenplays. When I moved to southern California, I had in mind writing the Great American Novel. I still do!

Then I won a game show and had enough money to take a half-year sabbatical to pursue my writing seriously. I lived in the shadow of the Hollywood sign at the time, and after writing my first novel, I wrote a screenplay. I met people working in "the business" and told them about another script that I wanted to write. Then they shocked me by paying me real money for my story, an "option" that was a rental of the story until they could afford to buy it and make the movie.

From that point forward, I was hooked. And every time I get a check for a script, whether it's for a kids' TV show or another option on a screenplay, I'm hooked again. The basic thought is, "Wow, they pay me to do something that's so much fun?"

Of course, it seems like fun only before the writing begins and after it is done. While the scripting is actually in progress, I can be a bear to live with--a grumpy California bear.

Thankfully, in recent years, I've grown much more congenial. That's because I've learned so much more about structure of screenplays. I no longer find it so hard to draw up the blueprints to build a new world, you see.

And that's what I've tried to give you here, in this book: a blueprint to build your own cinematic world so that someone will read your blueprint and commission the construction of something that can some day thrill us all. I hope that it helps both you and me see your name on the silver screen, and soon.

What You Will Learn in This Book

The Complete Idiot's Guide to Screenwriting is, like a Shakespearean play, divided into five parts.

Part 1, "The Evolution of Storytelling," takes us on a tour that starts with the Greek playwrights and takes us to the present, stopping to examine the discoveries of Freud, Jung, and others that have impacted cinema. We examine Shakespeare, the birth of the movies and Hollywood, and everything about filmdom, on into the current digital age.

Part 2, "What to Write," explains where to find the best movie ideas, what subjects sell, and how screenwriting differs from other writing forms, and it delves into the unique language of Hollywood that screenwriters must understand. In a few short chapters, you get an education that some writers take a decade to figure out.

Part 3, "How to Write Your Screenplay," is the nuts-and-bolts explanation of putting together a screen story, from premise to outline to completed script, with a complete step-by-step description of the best structure for your movie. And then, just when you think you're done, we cover the secrets of rewriting.

Part 4, "Post-Script Possibilities," provides a Hollywood behind-the-scenes plan for improving a screenplay when it's rewritten and tells you what happens after a script is purchased. It also explains how the film industry works and explains the nuances of writing TV movies and short films for the Internet.

Part 5, "It's All in the Details," explains the things that you learn only by working in Hollywood. For example, use two brads (not three) when binding your script. Amateur technical mistakes, screenwriting gurus, the real deal on selling scripts, and how to plan a screenwriting career are all covered.

Extras

The Complete Idiot's Guide to Screenwriting also features, sprinkled through each chapter, snippets of information in boxed sidebars. These sidebars provide you with additional tips, definitions of key terms, warnings of potential dangers, and additional information that you may find helpful or even amusing. (You *must* have a sense of humor to be a screenwriter!) We call these sidebars:

Skip's Tips

These sidebars contain useful tips on the current topic. They may fit with the flow of the page or provide an interesting counter-point to it.

It's Not for Us

When scripts are rejected, writers are often told, "It's not for us." These warnings outline potential pitfalls and mistakes that, if avoided, might help you never hear that troubling, cryptic phrase.

Script Notes

Hollywood has its own language, so you will need the definitions provided here.

Hollywood Heat

These bits provide the kind of "bet you didn't know" inside in-formation that serve to remind you that you're not the only one troubled and confused by the daunting task of embarking on a career in screenwriting in that wacky place known as Holly-wood.

Acknowledgments

Even though this is my third book of writing advice, I have no intention of being a Hollywood or writing guru. I have simply always tried to share helpful information with other writers. If I can save any other person from going through even a small trouble that I've endured, it's worth the effort.

Ironically enough, I was asked to write this book after being referred to my editor by Janet Bigham Berstel, another *Complete Idiot's Guide* author whom I met at a writers conference. I gave her free advice about Hollywood, and she remembered. And that's how Hollywood success comes about. Someone who can deliver the goods meets someone who gets that person a job. First and foremost, I would like to thank Janet for her graciousness. Next, I thank Randy Ladenheim-Gil, the Acquisitions Editor at Macmillan, who signed me up for the project and proved to be one of the most gracious and understanding editors I've worked with to date. Thanks also to editor Christy Wagner and my agent, Craig Nelson (whom I also met at a writing conference).

Ultimately, a special thanks goes to my wife, Debbie, who has endured years of back-to-back deadlines without kicking me out the door, and to my children, Haley and Holly, who have suffered the lack of my presence because of my writing. This is the last one like that, guys!

I also wanted to acknowledge every person who ever thought that I couldn't make it as a writer or screenwriter. Almost 30 books and a lot of sold scripts later, I know who these unmentionables are, even if they don't.

And that's why I last want to acknowledge every hopeful writer out there whom I'm able to help in any way. I'm glad to do it, folks. It's giving back to people who helped me in the beginning. Keep those great stories coming, and never, ever give up!

Special Thanks to the Technical Reviewer

The Complete Idiot's Guide to Screenwriting was reviewed by an expert who double-checked the accuracy of what you'll learn here, to help us ensure that this book gives you everything you need to know about screenwriting. Special thanks are extended to Arthur Taussig.

Arthur Taussig is an internationally recognized authority on the psychology and sociology of film who teaches and lectures on film in Southern California. He is the originator of the multiple prize winning Web site, FilmValues.com, which provides film reviews for responsible parents. He has been professor of film at Orange Coast College for over 20 years and is adjunct curator of film at the Orange County Museum of Art. Holding degrees from both UCLA and UC Berkeley, he is in great demand for lectures and workshops around the world.

Trademarks

All terms mentioned in this book that are known to be or are suspected of being trademarks or service marks have been appropriately capitalized. Alpha Books and Macmillan USA, Inc., cannot attest to the accuracy of this information. Use of a term in this book should not be regarded as affecting the validity of any trademark or service mark.

Part 1

The Evolution of Storytelling

Get on the Movietown Bus as we tour through the centuries, starting with the Greek playwrights. There are fascinating stops along the way as we examine the discoveries of Freud, Jung, and others whom you might not suspect have impacted cinema. You'll meet William Shakespeare, attend the birth of the movies in Europe and in Hollywood, and learn how filmdom is driving headlong into the current digital age. Warning! Your driver's name is Oedipus!

Chapter 1

History Lessons Make Better Writers

In This Chapter

➤ The hero with a thousand faces

➤ What the Greeks gave us

➤ Aristotle still makes the rules

➤ Give me your Romans, Christians, and Italians

➤ Classic stories live forever

➤ Our stories and our minds

➤ Mentors of the mind

➤ The impact of Jung

➤ Joseph Campbell's powerful myths

Some of the best screenplays are based on historical events. You probably know the story of Adam and Eve from the Book of Genesis, but how about the story of the beginning of life found in the *Brihadaranyaka Upanishad?* Written around 700 B.C.E., this tale from India describes how the original Self divided himself into two parts because he "lacked delight." With his new female half, conflict began! In Western and Eastern civilization, writers have been devising plots for more than 26 centuries. That fact alone is reason enough to look into history for screenplay ideas.

Script Notes

When writing a screenplay, **conflict** doesn't have to mean violence. *Webster's New Collegiate Dictionary* offers this definition: "The opposition of persons or forces that gives rise to the dramatic action in a drama or fiction." In action movies, however, some producers, want something blown up every 10 minutes.

Hollywood Heat

In 1924, Joseph Campbell met Indian philosopher J. Krishnamurti on a boat trip to Europe and became interested in Hinduism and Buddhism. Later, he worked with Swami Nikhilananda to translate Indian holy texts. He also spent time with the great American author John Steinbeck. No ivory tower scholar, Campbell wrote about stories and authors he knew first-hand.

Don't Miss the Myths: *The Hero with a Thousand Faces*

In almost any screenwriting class, you will hear discussions about the importance of *conflict:* good guy vs. bad guy, good vs. evil, or youth vs. tradition. It's really the dual nature of the universe. Remember this: The "villain" of any film is the "hero" of his own movie.

Author and teacher Joseph Campbell spent his lifetime studying the great stories of the Earth and noticed a pattern in the conflicts the stories described. The great stories of mankind, he realized, all had a similar pattern, which he called a "myth structure." He taught this story blueprint in classes at Sarah Lawrence College in Bronxville, New York, and then codified it with the publication of *Hero with a Thousand Faces* in 1949. Thirty years later, Hollywood caught on.

One of those influenced by Campbell's book was screenwriter and director George Lucas, who told the National Arts Club, "It's possible that if I had not run across [Campbell], I would still be writing *Star Wars* today."

The Greeks Made the Rules

It is believed that the Greek poet Thespis founded the art of drama about 600 B.C.E. Plays before his time did not feature an actor who spoke independently of the Greek chorus. Thespis created monologues for actors and also gave them dialogues with the leader of the chorus. The birth of drama is generally dated from this innovation. It was also Thespis's idea to use masks and makeup, so it's no wonder that an actor is also known as a "thespian."

The Greek dramatist Aeschylus introduced a second actor, as well as the idea of costumes and scenery. Sophocles added a third actor and made intricate plots possible, and is usually considered to be the greatest of the Greek playwrights. His contemporary, Euripides, was an equally important playwright whose works influenced many writers who followed, but Euripides received great criticism from the comedy writers of the day. As one example, Aristophanes, himself a great playwright, satirized Euripides in the play *The Frogs*. Other Greek dramatists didn't like Euripides because he bucked the system, writing about the ordinary person and using more natural dialogue than his contemporaries, who preferred to write about moral and religious themes.

Think about it: In Western civilization, writers have been devising plots for more than 26 centuries. That fact alone is reason enough to look into history for screenplay ideas.

Aristotle and the Three-Act Structure

If you've ever wondered why we have three acts in modern screenplays, look no further than Aristotle. He studied with Plato and was the tutor of Alexander the Great of Macedonia, the first Western conqueror of the known world. Aristotle wrote many things, but his *Poetics* is still heavily influential among writers today. Here's what he said about the construction of a dramatic work:

> "... the plot manifestly ought, as in a tragedy, to be constructed on dramatic principles. It should have for its subject a single action, whole and complete, with a beginning, a middle, and an end."

Aristotle also held that the plot of a story was "the first principle, and, as it were, the soul of a tragedy" and that "*character* holds the second place." He asserted, "A similar fact is seen in painting. The most beautiful colors, laid on confusedly, will not give as much pleasure as the chalk outline of a portrait."

Other Aristotelian observations are particularly applicable to screenwriting: He coined the terms "Reversal of the Situation," defined as "a change by which the action veers round to its opposite," and "Recognition," defined as "a change from ignorance to knowledge." Aristotle then pulled the two together for a general conclusion: "Two parts, then, of the Plot, Reversal of the Situation and Recognition, turn upon surprises."

It's Not for Us

A fortune-teller predicts that a king will kill his father and marry his mother. Abandoned in the woods by his father, the boy survives, grows up, meets a king, kills him, and then marries the king's widow. He later discovers that his new wife is also his mother! She commits suicide, and the king blinds himself. That's *Oedipus Rex*, by Sophocles, which the philosopher Aristotle thought was perfect.

Script Notes

Aristotle defined **character** as "that which reveals moral purpose, showing what kind of things a man chooses or avoids." He went on to say, "Speeches, therefore, which do not make this manifest, or in which the speaker does not choose or avoid anything whatever, are not expressive of character."

Consider Bruce Willis's heroic character in the movie *Die Hard,* and you'll see continuous reversals and recognitions. The classic *Casablanca,* starring Humphrey Bogart, delivers them, too.

Romans, Christians, and Italians

Writers in ancient Rome were poets first and playwrights second. The Romans contributed few works that are still performed today, but they provided the preservation of old stories. Because the seat of the Christian church was in Rome, Latin became its language, and Christian monks preserved the past during the Dark Ages by writing things out in Latin. In fact, the Bible translated by Saint Jerome is the Latin Bible in use today.

Hollywood Heat

For 10 centuries after the fall of Rome, miracle, morality, and mystery plays illustrated Christian principles. In 1210, however, the Pope ruled that priests could no longer appear on public stages. This caused two major changes: trade guild members took the place of the clergy as actors, and playwrights began writing comedic scenes between plays.

Unless you were a nobleman in Rome, you could not speak freely, and this early censorship continued for centuries after the fall of Rome, thanks to the Catholic church. In medieval times, the only plays that were performed in public were those with religious themes, usually staged during church services. Starting in 1487, a work could be printed and distributed only after church authorities had approved it. We've come a long way, baby!

Classic Stories Are Immortal

As the art of storytelling evolved, epic poets propagated great feats and legends. An epic was a long poem that celebrated the feats of a legendary hero. You may have studied them in school, with *The Iliad* or *The Odyssey*. If you haven't read either, I can't blame you. My copy of *The Iliad* runs 594 pages, and my copy of *The Odyssey* is 426 pages.

How do such classics apply to writing movies? Well, *The Iliad,* set in the tenth and final year of the Greek siege of the city of Troy, has been described as one of the greatest war stories of all time. What if a clever screenwriter changed the setting to a city in space, being attacked by an invader force, and now young men who were barely of school age when the siege began have to take over the battle from their dying fathers?

The Odyssey is the story of Odysseus, a weary warrior who simply wants to sail back home to his wife and son. The barriers and struggles that Odysseus and his men overcome could also be transferred to a science fiction setting, couldn't they?

Stories from mythology have long been popular with film audiences. *Jason and the Argonauts,* the 2,500-year-old story of the quest for the legendary Golden Fleece, was filmed in 1963 by Columbia Pictures and remade by Hallmark Entertainment in 2000.

And let's not forget *Beowulf,* the Anglo-Saxon epic about battles with demons and dragons dating back to the sixth century. A newly translated book version by Irish Nobel laureate Seamus Heaney was awarded Britain's prestigious Whitbread Prize, while in 1999 a consortium of four companies made a movie titled *Beowulf* that was—you guessed it—a science-fiction update of the classic tale.

Sometimes modern movie epics work, and sometimes they do not. *Waterworld,* starring Kevin Costner, was a very expensive film that barely made a profit, whereas *Star Wars: Episode 1—The Phantom Menace* was a box office smash. George Lucas has drawn from many stories and legends in creating his films. Perhaps that has something to do with the popularity of the *Star Wars* films.

Millions of stories around the world have not yet been dramatized on film. How about this one? In a world that is a constant struggle between good and evil, a messiah returns to wage a final battle, after which the leader of darkness is defeated and the Kingdom of God is established on Earth. That's the plot of the 1999 movie *The Omega Code,* where ancient codes hidden within the Torah reveal the secrets of global events. It's also a story that comes from the Persian Zoroaster, approximately 3,000 years old.

To write an epic screenplay, study history and mythology, or even your own family history. You might find an undiscovered classic.

Story and the Mind

Movies provide dream fulfillment. A person buys a ticket, sits in a darkened space, and for an extended length of time lives vicariously. As a screenwriter, it is easy enough to learn basic structure, passable dialogue, and clever tricks. The more difficult task is to create a story that will stand the test of the ages, such as a Greek classic or a Shakespearean play.

In the late nineteenth century, intellectuals began to examine, more freely than ever before, what makes people tick, their dreams, ambitions, and motivations. This opened the Pandora's box of the human mind and changed storytelling forever.

Skip's Tips

Playwrights who adapt their work for the screen must learn proper screenplay format. Most screenwriting software programs will reformat text automatically, and formatting is discussed later in this book (refer to Part 3, "How to Write Your Screenplay"). The next thing playwrights need to do is turn as many speeches as possible into visuals. Moving pictures, remember?

Hegel, Freud, Sex, and Stanislavski

German philosopher Georg Wilhelm Friedrich Hegel developed the argument that self-development results from the conflict of opposites. He proposed that any thesis has an incompleteness that causes its own antithesis, or opposition, to arise. When the synthesis of the thesis and antithesis, or third point of view, comes about, the conflict is resolved at a higher level of truth. Then, he said, comes a new thesis and resulting antithesis.

Skip's Tips

If you have trouble developing a character, ask yourself what the character wants. This will help you plot behavior scene to scene. For example, the alien in *E.T.* simply wanted to go home.

Let's use the *Star Wars* movies as an example. Both thesis and theme come from the same Greek work meaning "something laid down." In other words, an idea proposed. An antithesis would be a force against this, and the synthesis would be what results from these opposing forces. The word *premise* comes from the Latin meaning "to place ahead," so basically it has the same meaning as *theme*. Luke Skywalker (thesis) at first questions "the Force" (antithesis) and then learns to use it to advantage (synthesis at a higher level of truth). More broadly, the rebel forces (who propose the thesis that people should live freely) use the Force to fight the Galactic Empire and "the dark side" (antithesis). The rebels ultimately win, resulting in a more stable peace (synthesis), and Luke is revealed as a "royal" Jedi (higher level of truth).

In *The Philosophy of History,* Hegel said, "The first glance at History convinces us that the actions of men proceed from their needs, their passions, their characters and talents; and impresses us with the belief that such needs, passions, and interests are the sole spring of actions." Apply that to your characters.

And now to Sigmund Freud, who loved mythology and Greek gods. Athena, the goddess of war and wisdom, was particularly significant to him. Remember Aristotle's favorite play, Oedipus Rex? Freud felt that society creates mechanisms for the social control of human instincts and that, at the base of these controlling mechanisms, is a prohibition against incest. Guilt, he said, arose from the symbolic murder of a patriarch by sons ruled by their father's commands even when he is dead. Freud also wrote repeatedly about the biblical stories of Joseph and of Moses, both of whom had troubled family backgrounds.

Freud called the wish to push aside guilt repression, the act of which instantly creates in the mind conflict, that concept so loved by Hollywood. Freud was absorbed with sex and was obsessed with the "Oedipus complex." He believed that people were bisexual and that individuals have death drives that conflict with their sex drives. Sound like Hollywood, where people often seem obsessed with shattering taboos. Freud believed that all groups prohibit only those things that individuals actually desire.

Freud formed the nucleus of his opinions early in his career. In 1927, Freud said, "In my youth I felt an overpowering need to understand something of the riddles of the world in which we live and perhaps even to contribute something to their solution."

This brings us to Russian actor-producer Konstantin Stanislavski, the founder of the Moscow Art Theater and the creator of the Method style of acting. Stanislavski, who produced the first successful performance of Anton Chekhov's famous play *The Seagull,* put great emphasis of the psychological motivation of an actor.

Stanislavski discovered that, by recalling old, troubled feelings or traumatic experiences while doing a scene, actors could affect a more believable performance. Let's say that you are doing a scene about your character's grandmother's funeral, yet your own grandmothers are still alive. You could simply create the emotion freshly, or using Stanislavski's technique, you could substitute the death of a loved one, thinking of it while saying your lines.

With Stanislavski, the actor's emotional mind-set during a scene was all-important. Here's how his Method affected Hollywood and, as a result, screenwriting. The Actors Studio, a rehearsal group for professional actors founded in New York in 1947 by writer/director Elia Kazan, became the hotbed for the Method. It was the calling card of the Studio's director, Lee Strasberg, who joined in 1948. Many screen legends studied at the Actor's Studio or with Strasberg, including Marlon Brando, James Dean, and Marilyn Monroe. Given the life problems of famous Method actors, you might wonder why no one considered the possibility of lasting, deleterious mental effects from using the technique. But, because they emoted so well on-screen, we've had Method actors ever since.

Skip's Tips

In Hollywood, when a screenplay or property is being considered for purchase or has been purchased, and a number of in-demand actors or directors want to be a part of the project, it is said to have heat. The term implies sexual tension, and that's Hollywood.

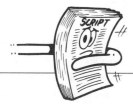

It's Not for Us

It's a well-known Hollywood cliché for an actor to ask, "What's my motivation?" As a writer, however, you're better off *not* sharing the psychoanalysis of your characters with people whom you want to buy your script. They won't matter to a script reader.

Carl Jung and the Symbolic World

And now to Carl Jung, Freud's most famous associate. In 1909, accompanied by devotees whom he called "The Committee," Freud traveled to Massachusetts to lecture on psychoanalysis. Following this visit, he formed the International Psychoanalytic

Association and chose Carl Jung as his successor. Unlike Freud, Jung did not concentrate so heavily on sexuality. He was the founder of analytical psychology, which dictates that mental aberrations represent an attempt by a person to find spiritual wholeness.

If you've ever seen a movie in which a doctor and a patient are doing "word association," that is a Jungian technique. Jung also coined the terms "extrovert" and "introvert" in his 1921 book, *Psychological Types*. He believed that repressed thought and feelings had great impact on individuals, but he also held that a "collective unconscious" existed that contained "archetypes" symbolically manifested in the great stories of the world.

This becomes interesting when we consider what Jung thought about films in general. "The cinema," he said in 1944, "like the detective story, makes it possible to experience without danger all the excitement, passion, and desirousness which must be repressed in a humanitarian ordering of life." What do you think?

Hollywood Heat

Carl Jung believed that men had feminine inner personalities, while women had a submerged animus, or inner masculinity. Similarly, great movie heroes have an inner struggle to overcome that is as important as their outward struggle. In *Raiders of the Lost Ark*, Indiana Jones battles to keep the Ark of the Covenant away from the evil Nazis. And he has a deathly fear of snakes. That's interesting because, in the Book of Genesis, evil (or forbidden knowledge, depending on your interpretation) is represented as a snake.

Here are some excerpts from Jung's "On the Nature of Dreams," first published as "Vom Wesen der Traume" in 1945, in which he discusses a procedure that he calls "taking up the context."

> "... the dream begins with a STATEMENT OF PLACE. ... Next comes a statement about the PROTAGONISTS. ... I call this phase of the dream the EXPOSITION. It indicates the scene of action, the people involved, and often the initial situation of the dreamer."

> "In the second phase comes the DEVELOPMENT of the plot. ..."

> "The third phase brings the CULMINATION of peripeteia [a sudden change of events or reversal of circumstances]. Here something decisive happens or something changes completely. ..."

"The fourth and last phase is the lysis, the SOLUTION or RESULT produced by the dream-work. ... This division into four phases can be applied without much difficulty to the majority of dreams met with in practice—an indication that dreams generally have a 'dramatic' structure."

To a seasoned screenwriter, Jung's four phrases of a dream could easily be akin to the three acts of a screenplay, with his "lysis" comparable to the denouement (events following the climax).

Jung observed that the incest theme was found in numerous myths and philosophies of Earth. Whereas Freud concentrated on incest fantasies in the years before the age of six, Jung dealt with the incestuous wishes of adulthood. Jung also felt that every person has a personal unconscious called "the shadow," a primitive, untamed threat. Sounds like the "dark side" in *Star Wars*.

Jung also said, "Eternal truth needs a human language that alters with the spirit of the times." I don't know about you, but to me, that language could very well be motion pictures.

To further illustrate the connection between screenplays and psychology, consider *Eyes Wide Shut,* the last film of the acclaimed director Stanley Kubrick. It was adapted from the novel *Traumnovelle* by Arthur Schnitzler, an Austrian who corresponded with Sigmund Freud. The plot of *Eyes Wide Shut* follows the "myth" structure outlined by Joseph Campbell: We see a couple living an ordinary life descend into an underworld of sorts (taboo sex), and then make a return from which they emerge transformed.

Hollywood Heat

Film professor Arthur Taussig, author of *Film Values/Family Values: A Parents' Guide,* compares the 1997 movie *Men in Black* to the "36 Righteous Men," a Jewish folk legend about hidden saints responsible for the fate of the universe. Says Taussig, "*Men in Black* may be the first totally Jewish movie that has not a single obvious Jew in it."

Skip's Tips

The film Kubrick was planning when he died was *A.I.* (for "artificial intelligence"). Director Steven Spielberg picked it up for his next project and even wrote the script. And before we forget, what did the great Spielberg name the studio that he formed with David Geffen and Jeffrey Katzenberg? DreamWorks!

Joseph Campbell and the Power of Myth

While doing European graduate study in the Holy Grail legends of Arthurian mythology, Campbell discovered the work of Freud and Jung. This helped him see the parallels between myths, legends, and dreams. A couple years later, in 1931, Campbell went to California, met then unknown novelist John Steinbeck, and got to know marine biologist Ed "Doc" Ricketts, a friend of Steinbeck's who was the model for main characters in *Cannery Row* and *Sweet Thursday*. On a coastal journey to Alaska collecting intertidal specimens, Ricketts mentored Campbell in Jungian philosophy. Finally, in 1954, Campbell and his wife Jean met Jung and his wife at Bollingen, Jung's castle on a lake near Zurich.

Joseph Campbell's work gained a foothold in Hollywood partially due to filmmakers such as George Lucas and Dr. George Miller (an Australian Campbell devotee whose *Mad Max* movies made a star of Mel Gibson). The person perhaps most responsible for the respect given Campbell, however, is Christopher Vogler, who discovered Campbell while studying at the University of Southern California film school (where George Lucas was also a student).

Skip's Tips

For storytelling purposes, Joseph Campbell defines a hero as one who goes on an adventure and brings back the message (Campbell's "elixir") that gives life and vitality to his community. For what it's worth, the real Hero was a first-century scientist who invented water-driven and steam-driven machines and devised a formula for determining the area of a triangle.

When Vogler began working as a story analyst for movie studios, he found that the hero's journey gave him a reliable set of tools for diagnosing story problems. He wrote a memo titled "A Practical Guide to *The Hero with a Thousand Faces*," which convinced Jeffrey Katzenberg, then running Disney, that every project that the studio took on should be compared against "myth" structure. Vogler later wrote *The Writer's Journey* (see www.writersjourney.com for details). Campbell's *Hero with a Thousand Faces* and Vogler's *The Writer's Journey* are an unbeatable duo.

Isn't it funny that, in 10,000 years of recorded history, a certain kind of story seems to work over and over again? In a way, it makes you feel kind of good about humankind.

The Least You Need to Know

➤ Read *The Hero with a Thousand Faces* by Joseph Campbell and *The Writer's Journey* by Christopher Vogler to understand the story structure most favored by Hollywood today.

➤ The three-act structure outlined by Aristotle in *Poetics* (beginning, middle, and end) is still the standard very commonly used.

➤ Hollywood's preoccupation with sex and violence reflects *Oedipus Rex*, Sigmund Freud, and Carl Jung.

➤ Stanislavski's "Method," in which actors mentally dredge up old traumas while performing, has had more influence on film actors than any other acting style.

➤ Some of the most successful movies of recent years have been derived from ancient tales.

That Fellow Shakespeare

One writer has had a greater influence on motion pictures than any other, yet he has been dead for almost four centuries. As new celebrated actors arrive on the scene, it seems almost inevitable that they will film new versions of William Shakespeare's *Hamlet,* attempting to offer the world some new vision of the moody Prince of Denmark that it has not yet managed to see.

Shakespeare is as current today as he was 500 years ago, and you may have seen a movie based on his work without even knowing it. For example, *10 Things I Hate About You,* starring Julia Stiles, was based on *The Taming of the Shrew.* Actress Stiles must like Shakespeare because she went on to star in *O,* a modern *Othello* set in a high school, as well as a year 2000 version of *Hamlet* opposite actor Ethan Hawke. Five centuries after his heyday, William Shakespeare is still thrilling actors and audiences.

Skip's Tips

You could do a lot worse than basing your screenplay on Shake-spearean stories or structure. More than 400 dramatizations, variations, and inspirations from the works of William Shakespeare have been put onscreen, beginning with the filming of *King John* in 1899.

Shakespeare in Love

The Bard of Avon generates stories even today. The most notable recent example was 1999's *Shakespeare in Love,* a romantic comedy by Marc Norman and Tom Stoppard that won the Academy Award for Best Writing, Screenplay Written Directly for the Screen. In the script, young Will Shakespeare is broke, has a terrible love life, and has not delivered a promised play, *Romeo and Ethel, the Sea Pirate's Daughter.*

The situation looks hopeless, but things start to turn around when he meets the fictional Viola de Lesseps, a young and beautiful noblewoman who is desperate to be an actor at a time when women were not allowed upon the stage. Love at first sight leaps to inspiration and, mostly due to Shakespeare's clandestine affair with the soon-to-wed Viola, the Bard of Avon changes his play into a tragedy called *Romeo and Juliet,* which, to his surprise, entertains even the great Elizabeth herself, Queen of England.

Hollywood Heat

The *Shakespeare in Love* screenplay won the major cinematic awards in Brazil and Germany and was nominated for the top honor at the British Academy Awards. The Broadcast Film Critics, the Chicago Film Critics, the Florida Film Critics, the New York Film Critics, the Online Film Critics Society, the Southeastern Film Critics Association, the Writers Guild of America (WGA), and the Foreign Press Association in Los Angeles (Golden Globes) all gave writers Norman and Stoppard their top award for screenwriting for *Shakespeare in Love.*

Using Shakespeare

Shakespeare in Love was great for obvious reasons: The story was clever, the dialogue was delicious, and one of the most popular plays of all time was woven into the plot. Less conspicuous is the fact that William Shakespeare is the most famous writer of all time, yet little is known about him personally. Therefore, we have at the least a subconscious desire to know.

Any school child can identify the source of the quote, "O Romeo, Romeo! wherefore art thou Romeo?" or perhaps even tell you that it comes from Act II, Scene II of the play *Romeo and Juliet,* but how many people know that Shakespeare was born on April 23 and likely died on the same day? You might know that his wife, Anne Hathaway, was eight years his senior and that their marriage came about due to pregnancy, but can you lay to rest the endless speculation of who his infamous "Dark Lady of the Sonnets" might have been, or why his will stipulated that his wife receive his second-best bed? It is precisely our lack of information about the great playwright that makes him an intriguing lead character.

Shakespeare in Love's concocted character Viola (wonderfully portrayed by Gwyneth Paltrow, who won the Best Actress Oscar) is a plausible explanation of a barely known aspect of Shakespeare's life. She is also his muse, the inspiration for Shakespeare's Juliet, and a blonde. (The "Dark Lady" a blonde? Shocking!)

In the script, the writers use Shakespeare's very words, play upon his mystery, and use a Shakespearean plot device. Historical characters, very well-known, real life people, are dramatized in a manner that makes us think yet entertains, stirs the blood yet offers laughs, and touches deep passions while commenting on the recurring need to change antiquated societal conventions, even when it means risking everything in the attempt.

Shakespeare's Secret

The secret of Shakespeare's lasting appeal is that *he writes for everyone on a scale bigger than normal life.* When he examines the ordinary, he does so in a fearless yet poetic way that offers a perspective heretofore unnoticed. He takes us to places we have not been and into ideas that we have not examined and that speak to the great questions of humankind throughout the ages.

Writing in a time when actors were looked upon with little more regard than beggars in the street, and when criticism of a monarch or members of the ruling class could result in death, Shakespeare knew that writing about larger-than-life characters would fascinate royalty and commoners alike. He made his own legends.

Queen Elizabeth was a living legend, but no playwright could dramatize the Virgin Queen and survive. This left other royals as subjects for high

Skip's Tips

Before you start a screenplay based on a Shakespearean play, do some research. Search the Internet Movie Database at www.imdb.com with the keyword phrase "William Shakespeare," and see what comes up. Even when modern screenwriters adapt his work, the Bard is given credit, such is the respect for his writing.

drama, but many contemporary members of the court were less levelheaded and more thin-skinned than their queen. So, Shakespeare drew from history and myth, weaving in characters from his own fertile imagination who, mixed with legendary real people, displayed lusts and lamentations, fears and rejoicings as human as any-one in the audience, regardless of social station. He examined common, deep human passions on tableaus broader than common, everyday life.

Hollywood Heat

Shakespeare drew from ancient stories, so why can't you? In 1999, screenwriters Mark Leahy's and David Chappe's science-fiction update of the famous sixth-century poem *Beowulf* was made into a film by director Graham Baker. Meanwhile, Irish poet Seamus Heaney did a new translation of the 1,100-year-old tale, which won Britain's top book award, the Whitbread Prize. And the Miramax film studio had yet another adaptation planned, a film "inspired" by the *Beowulf* story with French actor Christopher Lambert in the title role. All this even though Penguin Books's three different editions of *Beowulf* sell 70,000 copies annually.

Pages from History

Many of the greatest movies drew from real-life historical events. Modern examples are Oscar-winning *L.A. Confidential* (from 1950s Hollywood tabloid magazine stories) and the 1970s film generally accepted as the greatest screenplay of a generation, *Chinatown* (loosely based around the life of engineer William Mulholland).

Here's an example of Shakespeare technique: There may be no more deathly story than *Macbeth,* drawn from Raphael Holinshed's *Chronicle of the Reigns of Duncan and Macbeth (1034–1057).* This dramatization of real historical events commented heavily upon Shakespeare's time, without pointing fingers. The real-life corollary? Queen Elizabeth's struggle with her own cousin, Mary Stuart, better known as Mary, Queen of Scots, who was beheaded in 1587 on charges of sedition against the English crown.

How could a playwright in London dramatize great and bitter royal struggles and keep his neck intact? *Macbeth* was likely written in 1606, but even two decades after Mary's death, no one had forgotten her beheading. Shakespeare could, however, safely write about a royal death match set in Scotland 600 years before. Blood lust, the struggle for power, witchcraft, and the psychology of evil are all woven into the mix of this great tragedy, a play that casts its own legendary shadow over thespians today.

The Screenplay's the Thing

So much for history, theater, and speculation. What does all this have to do with putting your own words into a screenplay that will inspire actors to heights of ecstasy and impel directors, producers, and others who write checks to beg to work with you?

Skip's Tips

Your screenplay is your property until you sell it. When it's sold, your book or story is referred to as a property. This is in contrast to the theater, where a property is any physical thing used during the play.

Take a hint from Shakespeare, who knew that when an audience has too much of one thing for too long, you've lost them. Swords and daggers and knives and poisons appear in profusion amongst his great words. People fight and die. They go mad, see ghosts, and hold the skulls of fallen comrades in their hands. They battle for kingdoms, wear disguises, and embark on great follies. "Action!" shouts the movie director. Know that word first. You may be in love with dialogue, but if you put too much in a screenplay, you most likely will never see that screenplay filmed.

In Shakespeare's time, theaters had two types of patrons. The upper class sat in balconies, while the lower classes stood in front of the stage on a bare dirt floor, and were referred to as "groundlings." The upper class understood the clever turns of phrase and the use of languages other than English, while the groundlings who could not read or write thrilled to the action. Today, the overall level of education of any given movie-going audience is almost impossible to gauge, but one thing is certain: Action movies do well around the world.

Skip's Tips

Movies are moving pictures. Beginning screenwriters forget that and write too much stage play-like dialogue. Try this exercise:

➤ Write a three-minute scene with all the dialogue you want.

➤ Write the same scene, this time without words. Just describe the action.

➤ Reread both and decide which one you would be more interested in watching in a movie theater.

That includes action comedies. Italian star Roberto Begnini's English might have been broken as he accepted his Academy Award for *Life Is Beautiful,* but everyone who saw that Oscar telecast remembers how Begnini stepped on the back of director Steven Spielberg's seat in his rush of enthusiasm to reach the stage.

Movies are moving pictures. Smart movie actors have used that maxim from the days of silents. Charlie Chaplin, with his "Little Tramp" character, could convey a universe of pathos with the twitch of a mustache. Buster Keaton, with his ever-mournful face, could hand you a belly laugh and a gasp in the same instant, when he took a step forward and narrowly escaped being flattened by the front of a falling building.

Think of your screenplay as moving pictures first. You'll write better screenplays.

Shakespeare's plays have always been popular sources for film material. Using 1927 (the advent of "talkies") as a cut-off date, we find nearly 100 films of Shakespearean plays or those inspired by his works. For example, *The Real Thing at Last* was a 1916 English satire on American films derived from *Macbeth*. Story credit for the film goes to Sir James M. Barrie, the creator of *Peter Pan*. Is it a stretch to assume that the immortal character Peter Pan was inspired by Puck in Shakespeare's *A Midsummer Night's Dream?* The notion is not too far-fetched; Barrie co-wrote the 1936 film version of *As You Like It* and seemed to have a fondness for Shakespearean themes in his copious screen work.

It's Not for Us

If you utter the word "Macbeth" in a theater, the superstition among actors is that it will curse the production. Some actors feel the same way on a film set, so watch your Macmouth.

Shakespeare's Continuing Influence

Like the Avon River whose banks he knew so well, Shakespeare as a source seems to never run dry. When Akira Kurosawa, arguably the greatest Japanese filmmaker of all time, released his epic battle film *Ran* in 1985, he readily acknowledged that it was based on *King Lear*. Some critics believe that Orson Welles' *Chimes at Midnight* is the greatest *Lear* adaptation, but who is to say?

In recent years, English actor Kenneth Branagh has made a virtual career of Shakespeare. In 1999, audiences were presented with the visually stunning *Titus,* a derivation of *Titus Andronicus*, starring Jessica Lange and Sir Anthony Hopkins. This was the second film from director Julie Taymor, her first being a version of *The Tempest* in 1986. And, of course, you might have seen director Paul Mazursky's 1982 modern-day adaptation of the play entitled *Tempest*. But who's counting? That play in various incarnations has been dramatized in several languages almost two dozen times, including the science-fiction thriller classic *Forbidden Planet* in 1956, starring Leslie "Naked Gun" Nielsen.

You can't kill Shakespeare.

No matter how many versions of any one Shakespearean play have been done, if you as a screenwriter can come up with a different way of presenting it, that's a screenplay you might sell.

Stealing from Shakespeare

Top writers do it all the time. Have you ever seen *West Side Story?* It was a huge hit on Broadway before becoming a classic film. It's simply *Romeo and Juliet* all over again. Want to write the gangsta rap version of the same play? Who's stopping you?

That reminds me of an old Shakespeare joke. The great actor Richard Burbage was starring in *Richard the Third,* and a lady patron was enamored of him. She invited him to her chambers, advising him to identify himself as "Richard the Third."

Skip's Tips

If you have written plays or acted in them, you're used to stage directions stage right and stage left. Don't use those in a screenplay. The first film actors were from the stage, but screenwriting has its own rules. One big one is that actors and directors don't like the writer telling them where to go.

Shakespeare overheard the invitation and went to entertain the lady first. When the actor knocked and said Richard the Third was at the door, Shakespeare left, after explaining to the startled Burbage that William the Conqueror came before Richard the Third.

Shakespeare's Log Lines

When you are asked to describe your screenplay, you will be asked for the "high concept" or (more likely) the *log line*. This means, can you describe what your movie is about in 25 words or less? Generally, if you can't lay out your story in a few sentences, you probably don't have your plot well-conceived. This is one reason why, during the 1990s, it became common practice to combine two well-known movies in describing a new property. For example, "It's *Forrest Gump* meets *Godzilla*." Or, the venue of a successful movie could simply be changed. *Under Siege* is simply *Die Hard* on a boat.

By and large, adaptation from other sources is how many films come about. Someone compares a plot to some successful film and the person who can "green light" the picture (that is, approve the financing) decides that lightning is most likely to strike again in a similar place. They want it to be original, just not too original. The box-office receipts (they think) depend on it.

The following list shows my interpretation of some Shakespeare's plays, expressed in *log line* terms. One of them might help you come up with your own saleable variation or spark a new idea altogether, such as *Two Gentlemen of Venus,* perhaps, or (if you like

Script Notes

Why do they call it a **log line**? Traditionally, when screenplays or other properties are received at a studio or production company, an entry about each is entered in a log, with a short description of what the story is about, often on a single line.

It's Not for Us

Writing for the screen can be substantially different from writing a stage play. Shakespearean speeches are wordy, often conveying complex thoughts and amplified examinations of situations, but they are meant for the stage, where talk is king. Just remember, his dialogue is interspersed with lots of action.

horror) *Thirteenth Night.* It can't hurt to study the plays; people have successfully stolen from Shakespeare for ages.

➤ *The Two Gentlemen of Verona.* Two friends, Valentine and Proteus, fall in love with the same woman, Silvia. Proteus' love, Julia, disguised as a boy, follows them from Verona to Milan. In the end, weighing friendship over love, Valentine offers Silvia to Proteus.

➤ *The Taming of the Shrew.* Against a backdrop of social intrigues, a fortune-hunter named Petruccio woos and wins the extremely difficult beauty Katherine.

➤ *Richard III.* This play's dark examination of greed and power is based on historical facts of the cutthroat, bloody rise to the throne by a man absorbed in his own insanity.

➤ *Venus and Adonis.* This erotic comedy verse play was drawn from Ovid's Metamorphoses, about a teenage boy and Venus, the goddess of love. Her unrelenting adoration of him drives him to go off hunting, with fatal consequences.

➤ *Love's Labour Lost.* Four men, a king and three friends, vow to spend three years improving themselves while avoiding female relationships. The arrival of the Princess of France with three of her beautiful ladies complicates this decision in comedic fashion.

➤ *A Midsummer Night's Dream.* As the Duke of Athens prepares to wed the Queen of the Amazons, two young men fall in love with the same girl, complicated by another girl jilted by one of the men. Into this mix is a quarrel between the King and Queen of the Fairies.

➤ *King John.* A study in the futility of war and the price that a country and a family can pay over struggles for the throne. Most interesting is Richard the Lionhearted's bastard son, Philip Falconbridge, who is prevented from ruling because of his illegitimate birth.

➤ *The Merchant of Venice.* Love is more valuable than worldly things in this tale of a suitor of a young woman required by her father's will either to choose correctly between love and caskets of gold, lead, and silver.

➤ *The Merry Wives of Windsor.* In this look at love and lust, a nobleman, Sir John, unsuccessfully attempts to seduce two women, only to be frightened out of his lecherous ways in a forest at midnight.

➤ *Julius Caesar.* This study of the assassination of a great leader and the motivations of the conspirators involved was based on histories of the famous Roman general and ruler.

➤ *As You Like It.* This contrast between courtly life and country living centers on two royal maidens, Rosalind (disguised as a boy) and her cousin, Celia, who fall in love with unexpected suitors.

➤ *Hamlet.* To revenge his father's murder by his uncle, a prince feigns madness and kills his uncle's adviser. Caught and banished to England, he alters a letter ordering his execution, resulting in his captors' death instead; then he returns and kills his uncle.

All this brings us once again to the movie *Shakespeare in Love.* At the close of the film, young Will Shakespeare has lost his lover, Viola, after unexpectedly winning the favor of the Queen of England, with much thanks to Viola's efforts. As he says his goodbye to Viola, they discuss his next, unwritten play.

When Viola de Lesseps is gone, Shakespeare picks up a pen and begins to write scenes that we see onscreen: A ship goes down and all are lost but one girl, who makes it to shore and walks alone across a wide beach toward a waiting forest. Then we see young Will's handwriting as he gives the heroine of his new play, *Twelfth Night,* the name Viola.

In the actual play, Viola disguises herself as a boy, just as the character Rosalind disguises herself in *As You Like It.* In *Shakespeare in Love,* Viola de Lesseps also disguises herself as a boy for the sake of her passion, namely acting the part of Juliet at a time when women were forbidden from the stage.

William Shakespeare drew from many sources to create his great works: other plays, legends, folk tales, and real history. If you aspire to write winning screenplays, it might be greatly beneficial to read Shakespeare and study his plots; it is highly unlikely that any writer will ever be more successful.

The Least You Need to Know

➤ More than 400 films have been drawn from the works of the Bard, so don't be afraid to steal from Shakespeare.

➤ An unexplored facet of any famous person's life is ripe material for a screen-play, á la *Shakespeare in Love*.

➤ Do thorough research before starting a fact-based screenplay, using resources such as the Internet Movie Database at www.imdb.com and www.biography.com.

➤ If someone else has drawn from the source material that you have in mind, that doesn't mean that you can't also.

➤ Movies are moving pictures, so in most cases, be sparing on the dialogue and concentrate on the action.

➤ When you can describe your movie in 25 words or less (also known as a "high concept" or a "log line"), you probably have a well-conceived plot and can write a much better screenplay.

Birth of the Movies

In 1980, I first heard about *The Gods Must Be Crazy* in which Xixo, a bushman in the Kalahari, sees a Coke bottle dropped from a passing airplane. He thinks it is a gift from the gods and takes it back to his tribe. They fight over the mysterious object, so Xixo decides to return it to the gods or throw it over the edge of the Earth. The bottle is his first encounter with western "civilization," and to him the outside world seems insane.

The Gods Must Be Crazy won the 1981 Grand Prix at the Festival International du Film de Comedy Vevey and was voted Most Popular Film at the Montreal World Film Festival. It enjoyed three years of showings in the United States and made more than $50 million. Even more amazing was the fact Xixo, the bushman in the lead role, had no contact with modern civilization before being cast in the movie, and the white characters spoke Afrikaans.

Skip's Tips

Audiences love to see characters undergo a catharsis, a term Aristotle used to describe purification or purging. When characters undergo a transformation in which egocentric notions are shattered and they restructure their lives, it can result in a classic.

Hollywood Heat

More than 600 years after the death of William Wallace, Randall Wallace's script *Braveheart* resulted in a movie that won several Oscars, including Best Writing, Screenplay Written Directly for the Screen. The epic tale of a thirteenth-century Scottish warrior won awards around the world and took in more than $200 million. Who says "period pieces" don't sell?

Great film stories can come from anywhere in the world, and the world loves movies. I often tell people the story of a Tunisian filmmaker who went into a Masai warrior's mud hut. He saw no modern furnishings, but prominently displayed was a *Saturday Night Fever* movie poster of John Travolta in a white disco suit.

The Worldwide Storytelling Tradition

The Australian aborigines believe in "dreamtime," a spiritual dimension that surrounds all things and creates the reality that we live in. They believe that the creators of the dreamtime project their dream onto our physical dimension, and their dream is our reality. Before writing existed, such stories of origin were passed orally from generation to generation. And that's the great thing about great stories. They can be centuries old and yet, made into a film, enthrall audiences around the world.

Influences of the Great Playwrights

For purposes of their influence on movies, the work of several playwrights is worth noting. Let's start with Moliere, France's greatest comic dramatist. His satirical plays dealt with serious themes and paved the way for experimental theater. Perhaps his most famous play is *Le Tartuffe*, written in 1664. It dealt with religious hypocrisy and got banned from the stage because of the Roman Catholic Church's influence.

Tartuffe is five-act play in verse, about a scoundrel masquerading as a holy man who is taken in by a rich family. Tartuffe's real intent is to have an affair with his benefactor's wife and snatch his fortune. Did you see Paul Mazursky's *Down and Out in Beverly Hills* (1986)? It was a remake of Jean Renoir's *Boudu Saved from Drowning* (1932), which came from a René Fauchois play. It seems rather obvious what inspired the play, particularly because Moliere is recognized as the father of French comedic theater.

During the Renaissance and into the nineteenth century, writers rarely specialized. Johann Wolfgang von Goethe was an eighteenth-century German dramatist, novelist, poet, and scientist whose work may have been more influential on early German film than any other. His great dramatic poem *Faust* is about a German doctor who sold his soul to the devil in exchange for knowledge, youth, and magic powers. *Faust* continues to fascinate audiences and has been filmed several times, the latest on Swedish TV in 1996.

As serious dramatists go, however, Norwegian Henrik Ibsen was likely the most influential playwright of his time. One drama researcher claimed that all modern drama owed homage to Ibsen. Perhaps Ibsen's work has had lasting influence because he wrote often about characters who feel that they are missing out on life to such a degree that they feel they are in a living death. The sentiment speaks to why millions watch movies in the first place.

Ibsen's play *A Doll's House* was first put to film in 1911, and several other dramatizations of the play followed, with the latest being a TV movie in 1991. In *Hedda Gabler,* Ibsen shows us people who trample others to reach their own goals. He creates such deep psychological portraits that he became know as the "Freud of the theater." In fact, Freud himself used Ibsen's character Rebekka West to draw a psychological portrait of a victim of incest.

There's that Oedipus complex again! You can't get away from it. Voltaire, one of the great French writers, wrote his first major play, *Oedipe*, while in prison in 1717. Guess what it was about.

The most influential Russian playwright in pre-cinema days was Anton Pavlovich Chekhov. (Yes, the character in the original *Star Trek* TV series was named after him.) Like Ibsen, Chekhov's plots deal with loneliness and wasted lives. He also concentrated heavily on internal conflict, an innovation that had worldwide influence. Almost every serious actor has performed in a production of *The Seagull, Uncle Vanya,* or *The Cherry Orchard.* And we shouldn't neglect to mention an earlier influential Russian, Alexander Pushkin, author of *Boris Godunov* and other works. Two centuries before the world saw the award-winning movie *Amadeus,* Pushkin told the story in *Mozart and Salieri.*

It's Not for Us

Beginning screenwriters *must* learn the differences in format of stage plays and screenplays. Unless you are submitting a stage play to a movie production company for consideration, your work will likely not even be read unless it is presented in accepted screenplay style (covered later in this book).

Skip's Tips

Chekhov believed that if you had a gun hanging over a fireplace, the gun should be used during the play. If it is not used, don't write it in. Such attention to detail goes a long way in writing screenplays.

Many influential playwrights were also novelists. Victor Hugo, recognized as the most important French Romantic writer of the nineteenth century, gave us *The Hunchback of Notre Dame* and *Les Miserables,* but how many people can name one of his plays?

The reverse is true for Scottish playwright Sir James Matthew Barrie. Certainly you've seen a movie of his play *Peter Pan,* about the boy who refuses to grow up. Did you know he also wrote popular novels such as *The Little Minister* (also written as a play)?

Hollywood Heat

When I interviewed Steven Spielberg for *Boy's Life* magazine in 1991, I was surprised to learn that he was ready to go into production on a different Peter Pan script when he read *Hook* by James V. Hart. Hart must like nineteenth-century writers because he co-produced *Frankenstein* (Robert De Niro as the monster) in 1994, wrote and co-produced Francis Ford Coppola's version of *Dracula* in 1992, and penned *Muppet Treasure Island* (based on the Robert Louis Stevenson classic) in 1996.

Last but not least, it's reasonable to say that cinema was influenced by British writer W. S. Gilbert. His comic operas with composer Sir Arthur Seymour Sullivan such as *H.M.S. Pinafore, The Pirates of Penzance,* and *The Mikado* were the precursors of movie musicals. They continue to impress; the 1999 movie *Topsy-Turvy,* an improvisation about a strained relationship between the duo, resulted in numerous awards and accolades, including a nomination for an Oscar for Best Writing, Screenplay Written Directly for the Screen, for writer/director Mike Leigh.

Skip's Tips

A creative work no longer covered by copyright is "in the public domain." It can be used in any way. If you want to adapt an older work, check with an attorney. You can also get substantial information from the U.S. Copyright Office Web site at www.loc.gov/copyright.

Authors from Centuries Past: The Great Storytellers

Hollywood never tires of classics. A major film from Turner Network Television in 2000 was *Don Quixote,* starring John Lithgow. That didn't stop director Terry Gilliam from planning *The Man Who Killed Don Quixote* later in the year, with Johnny Depp starring as Sancho Panza. Miguel de Cervantes wrote the classic book from which these films were derived 400 years ago!

The remainder of this section deals with eighteenth and nineteenth-century American and European writers who influenced the beginnings of film. Let's start with the author of a book whose theme is by far the most popular in Hollywood. This probably has Freudian implications because the subject is vampires! (After meeting a few Hollywood producers, you'll understand ...)

Bram Stoker, the author of *Dracula,* held a number of jobs and was published often before *Dracula* emerged in 1897. It was a worldwide success. Although the author met many famous people, including American presidents and Mark Twain, his name did not gain equal recognition. Perhaps Francis Ford Coppola took that into consideration when he made *Bram Stoker's Dracula* in 1992.

More movies have been made about vampires than any other subject. A search of the Internet Movie Database (www.imdb.com) reveals more than 200 matches that have the word "vampire" in the title. Roughly 600 vampire films have been made worldwide.

Ah, but the movies love all monsters, such as Mary Shelley's *Frankenstein,* a novel inspired by a party game. The Frankenstein monster has been the subject of many successful films, but vampire movies are a better bet. For example, the 1994 *Frankenstein* starring Robert De Niro was a box office disappointment.

Even though Jane Austen died in 1817, her novels have been adapted into several miniseries from the British Broadcasting Company (BBC) and films from American movie studios. *Clueless,* the breakthrough movie for Alicia Silverstone, was based on the Austen novel *Emma.* Austen's social intrigues were so popular that she was listed in *People* magazine's "Most Intriguing People" in 1996.

A contemporary of Austen, Scottish writer Sir Walter Scott, is generally regarded as the progenitor of historical novels. His *Ivanhoe,* published in 1819, is a repeatedly popular movie subject. Scott's *Rob Roy* (1818) inspired a 1995 film of the same name.

Skip's Tips

Think you'd like to try adapting a classic novel into a screenplay? You can freely download the full text of many classic books, thanks to Project Gutenberg, at promo.net/pg. You can also download the e-texts via File Transfer Protocol (ftp) at ftp.etext.org.

It's Not for Us

Just because many other writers have used vampires as the subject of screenplays doesn't mean that you should not. A search of the Internet Movie Database shows more than 100 entries with the word "Dracula" alone, including the TV series "Mr. and Mrs. Dracula."

The great Scott must have anticipated Hollywood studio accounting methods when he penned these lines: "O, what a tangled web we weave, when first we practice to deceive!"

Stories from famous authors of the eighteenth or nineteenth century continually resurface on film. Director Tim Burton created a gory visual masterpiece with *Sleepy Hollow* in 1999, based on Washington Irving's *The Legend of Sleepy Hollow*. Walt Disney's earlier animated version fascinated Burton as a child. Similarly, although Herman Melville's *Moby Dick* became a classic film directed by John Huston, it was remade as a 1999 TNT cable movie.

Nathaniel Hawthorne's *The Scarlet Letter* has been a film seven times, mostly recently in 1995. Irish writer Oscar Wilde's 1891 horror novel *The Picture of Dorian Gray,* about a corrupt but beautiful young man who remains young and handsome through the years as his portrait becomes ugly, has been filmed seven times, with another one planned by New Line. Louisa May Alcott's *Little Women* has been filmed eight times and been a TV series twice.

In the 1960s, producer Roger Corman made a mini-industry of films based on Edgar Allan Poe works, such as *The Raven* (1963). Poe's works have been put to film more than 70 times.

One author gave rise to a virtual film studio of material. Sir Arthur Conan Doyle was the author of more than 50 books, not all of them featuring his greatest creation, Sherlock Holmes. The 1905 film *Adventures of Sherlock Holmes* helped establish the detective genre of film, and more than 70 Sherlock Holmes movies and TV series have been made. Holmes is always interesting.

Skip's Tips

Film tastes constantly evolve, and you must keep up. As Oscar Wilde said in *Soul of Man Under Socialism,* "The only thing that one really knows about human nature is that it changes. The systems that fail are those that rely on the permanency of human nature, and not its growth and development."

Before reading all the descriptions of great books turned into movies, you may have felt that the classics are what Mark Twain said they are: "Something that everybody wants to have read and nobody wants to read." Almost 60 of Twain's works have been set to film. His *Huckleberry Finn* has appeared in films almost 20 times, about the same number of appearances as Huck's buddy Tom Sawyer.

The most filmed author who wrote in English is Charles Dickens, with more than 100 novel and story adaptations. His *A Christmas Carol* has been seen on-screen more than 30 times. Much of Dickens's work deals with children in dire circumstances. Paralleling his own life, Dickens's self-made characters triumph over meager beginnings, and his novels offer poignant commentary on society.

The work of other English authors contributed greatly to film because they were works of high adventure that adapted well. The works of Robert Louis Stevenson, author of *Treasure Island,* have been filmed almost 80 times. Stevenson's *The Strange Case of Dr. Jekyll and Mr. Hyde,* first filmed in 1908, has inspired more than 20 films, including the Julia Roberts movie *Mary Reilly.*

Rudyard Kipling, an Englishman born in Bombay, India, had an Indian nurse in his youth who taught him the language and folklore of India. Kipling shared these stories with the world and inspired the massive Indian film industry, known affectionately on the subcontinent as "Bollywood." Kipling's characters have appeared in almost 30 films, including a new *Gunga Din* in 2000. Remember the most popular subject for films? The first Kipling property filmed was *The Vampire,* in 1910.

In the adventure vein, several French authors were influential on early films and have continued influence. The works of Victor Hugo have been put to film almost 50 times, most noticeably his *The Hunchback of Notre Dame.* Even more successful is Alexandre Dumas pere. (His son, known as Alexandre Dumas fils, gave us *The Lady of the Camelias,* a.k.a. *Camille,* which has been filmed more than 20 times in several different languages.) Alexandre Dumas the father is perhaps most popular for *The Count of Monte Cristo* and *The Three Musketeers.* More than 70 films have been made from the elder Dumas's works; not surprisingly, yet another *Count of Monte Cristo* will have reached movie theaters by the time you read this.

H. G. Wells produced more than more than 80 books, including science-fantasy novels that became films, including *The Time Machine* and *The Invisible Man.* More interesting as far as Hollywood is concerned is his 1898 novel *The War of the Worlds.* When it was dramatized on radio in 1938, a panic was created on the United States' east coast when thousands believed that an alien attack was actually occurring. The incident propelled producer, director, and writer Orson Welles into a Hollywood contract.

Hollywood Heat

The team of director James Ivory, producer Ismail Merchant, and screenwriter Ruth Prawer Jhabvala has created remarkable movies from classics. From Henry James came *The Europeans* and *The Bostonians.* From E. M. Forster, they got *Maurice, A Room with a View,* and *Howard's End,* which won three Oscars.

Skip's Tips

Science fiction will likely be "hot" for a long time. Of the top 10 U.S. domestic grossing films of all time, six are science fiction. Number 2: *Star Wars.* Number 3: *Star Wars: The Phantom Menace.* Number 4: *E.T., the Extra-Terrestrial.* Number 5: *Jurassic Park.* Number 8: *Return of the Jedi.* And number 9: *Independence Day.*

Speaking of science fiction, let's "cut" back to France. More than 50 movies have been based on the works of Jules Verne, who is the father of the genre. You're probably familiar with his *Journey to the Center of the Earth* or *20,000 Leagues Under the Sea*. Both have been filmed more than once. You may know his *Around the World in 80 Days* or *Mysterious Island*, but how about *Le Voyage dans la Lune (A Trip to the Moon)*? This 14-minute 1902 short, directed by fellow Frenchman Georges Melies, came from a Verne novel about a group of men who travel to the moon in a capsule shot from a giant cannon. That film marked the birth of "special effects."

European Originals: The Brothers Lumiere and Other Lights

Who invented "the movies"? Well, the experience might have begun on December 28, 1895, in a basement in Paris, France, that held an audience of 35 people. This is where two brothers, Auguste and Louis Lumiere, debuted the Lumiere Cinemato-graph, the first machine to combine the functions of camera and projector in one, allowing the projection of film onto a screen. Ten short films, all less than a minute, were screened for the unsuspecting first movie patrons. The first film seen was *The Shift Ends at the Lumiere Factory in Lyon,* and the last was *La Mer (The Sea)*. In two years, the Lumieres made more than 1,000 such documentaries.

Skip's Tips

Don't be satisfied with a thimble-size version of film history. To learn more about the Lumieres and their other inventions such as 3D cinema, contact:

> Institut Lumiere
> 25 rue du 1er Film
> 69008 Lyon
> France
> Phone: (33) 4 78 78 18 95
> Fax: (33) 4 78 01 36 62
> www.lumiere.org (in French)

Perhaps the most important person that the Lumieres impressed in 1895 was a professional magician who fell in love with the new "moving pictures." As Georges Melies began filming he discovered, by accident, moviemaking techniques such as dissolve, fade-in, and fade-out, and special effects such as double exposure and superimposition. This helped the documentary style give way to narrative films. Melies, who was trained in classic eighteenth century theater and so composed his films in scene form, made more than 500 films that influenced filmmakers around the world. Charlie Chaplin called Melies "the alchemist of light," while the most important of early American directors, D. W. Griffith, said that he owed Melies "everything." In 1931, France recognized Melies with the Legion of Honor medal and a rent-free apartment in Paris, where he and his actress wife, Jeanne, lived happily ever after.

Pathe, one of France's first film companies, was initially formed by Charles Pathe and his brothers Emile, Jacques, and Theophile to sell phonographs. Charles began producing short films in 1901, and by 1902 he had an assembly style movie studio. By 1908, the company had facilities in Budapest, Calcutta, Kiev, and Singapore and was selling twice as many films in the United States as all the American companies combined. Although the 1953 American movie *Houdini* starring Tony Curtis was a hit, we know what the real master of escape looked like in action thanks to *Houdini, the Handcuff King and Prison Breaker,* a Pathe film. The Pathe brothers also created the world's first weekly newsreel.

Skip's Tips

If you have children, you're probably familiar with Nickelodeon, the cable network for kids of all ages. But do you know where it got its name? The channel was named for early movie theaters (odeons, music halls) that charged 5¢ (a nickel) for admission.

Thomas Edison and the Monopoly That Didn't Work

"I am experimenting upon an instrument which does for the eye what the phonograph does for the ear, which is the recording and reproduction of things in motion," said Thomas Alva Edison in 1888. But did he really invent the medium of film?

We read mentions of early projectors such as Skladanowsky's bioscope and the Eidoloscope (developed by Dickson, Lauste, and Rector, used for paying audiences in Chicago four months before the initial Lumiere screening in Paris). Thomas Edison's laboratory was responsible for the Kinetograph motion picture camera and the Kinetoscope motion picture viewer, with Edison's assistant William Dickson doing the most work. But that's like saying that Mickey Mouse became popular worldwide thanks to someone other than the Mouse's originator, Walt Disney.

Dickson also constructed the "Black Maria," a tar paper-sealed studio structure with a large skylight that sat on a revolving track to follow available sunlight. In West Orange, New Jersey, The Edison Manufacturing Company built the machines and produced films that set the world standard. The studio was the first to use the 35mm film from George Eastman with four perforations on each side of each frame, still in use today. Lastly, with regard to the question of "first," a Library of Congress "American Memory" collection of Edison films includes a camera test made in 1891.

Edison was early to realize the drawing power of celebrity. One early film made at his Long Island estate featured Mark Twain, but the first famous person he put on film was strongman Eugene Sandow in 1894. Edison filmed Native Americans performers from Buffalo Bill Cody's "Wild West Show" and a famous pair of boxing sisters. His company made what may have been the first commercial, for Admiral Cigarettes in 1897. Edison's portable camera made it possible to film action scenes and news events, such as the first war films covering the Spanish-American war that made Theodore Roosevelt and his Rough Riders famous. Edison also first brought film into the home with his Home Projecting Kinetoscope in 1911.

When the public appetite for narrative films grew, Edison's assistant, Edwin S. Porter (the first American studio director), gave the company the classic *The Great Train Robbery* (1903) and other dramas. Under Porter's guidance, when foreign films began flooding the American market, The Edison Company concentrated on American stories such as *Uncle Tom's Cabin* and kept actors busy. Porter's contributions are as important as any. For example, he gave us the close-up and pioneered film editing techniques.

Production companies in the early days often specialized; for example, the special effects "trick" movies came from Vitagraph. Edison, who held more than 1,200 patents, could not dominate the film business. The competition was fierce, and by 1909, Edwin S. Porter was out of a job, mostly because Edison and some others made a big mistake, one that led to the birth of Hollywood.

Skip's Tips

The earliest films were brief partially because people simply put a camera in place and turned it on. Georges Melies innovated by stopping a camera in mid-shot and rearranging a scene before continuing, or cranking back the film a few feet before the next shot (making a dissolve). Thus, film storytelling was possible, and the silent film "one-reelers" were born.

A Place Called Hollywood: How Tinseltown Was Born

In 1909, Edison and several other companies formed the Motion Picture Patents Company trust to thwart independent producers. This resulted in a government antitrust action that broke up the monopoly in 1917. The Edison Company went out of business. One company that survived the monopoly's pressures was owned by William Selig of Chicago. In 1909, Selig faked a film about President Theodore Roosevelt's safari to Africa and released a film of "Teddy" killing a lion that coincided with news of the real event in newspapers. Selig also gave us animated cartoons, Westerns with early cowboy movie star Tom Mix, and the first movie serial, *The Adventures of Kathlyn*. In 1907, he moved part of his company to Hollywood, and in 1909, opened the first L.A. studio.

The words *Hollywood* and *film* are synonymous, however, due to Cecil B. DeMille. In 1913, DeMille planned to shoot *The Squaw Man,* from a Western novel, in Phoenix, Arizona. The snow-capped mountains there didn't fit the story, so DeMille and his co-director, Oscar C. Appel, took the train west. The line ended in Hollywood. When they got off, a legend got going.

The Least You Need to Know

➤ Great film stories can come from anywhere in the world.

➤ Mythologies of indigenous peoples and tales of ancient history can be the source for highly successful films.

➤ The most popular subject of movies is the vampire.

➤ The works of eighteenth- and nineteenth-century playwrights and authors offer a seemingly endless supply of movie source material.

➤ Science-fiction films hold the majority in all-time box office bonanza movies, a trend that may not end soon.

➤ No one is truly certain who invented the movies, but we do know how Hollywood was born.

Chapter 4

From Scenario to Screenplay

In This Chapter

➤ Scenarios before screenplays

➤ Women writers once ruled Hollywood

➤ When sound came

➤ Everyone moves to Hollywood

➤ The genre evolution

➤ Hollywood's greatest year

On Highland Avenue in Hollywood, across from the Hollywood Bowl, sits a historical landmark, the studio used by Jesse L. Lasky, Cecil B. DeMille, and Samuel Goldfish (Samuel Goldwyn) when they made *The Squaw Man*. Down at the corner of Highland Avenue and Hollywood Boulevard, the new Academy of Motion Pictures Arts and Sciences is being built. Across the way is Disney's refurbished El Capitan movie theater, and further along is the Roosevelt Hotel; the first Academy Awards were held in the hotel's Blossom Room.

Hollywood takes itself seriously these days, with a billion dollars being spent on renovation. It has its own major film festival now, begun on a shoestring in 1996 by Carlos de Abreu. The state of mind known as Hollywood is getting its glamour back.

Hollywood Heat

Deida Wilcox and her husband divided their southern California ranch into parcels, and in 1903, a village was incorporated under the ranch's name, Hollywood. The Hollywood sign, however, was not their doing. Reading "Hollywoodland," it was built to advertise a real estate development. When a despondent actress committed suicide by jumping from the final D (the thirteenth letter), the last four letters were torn down. And that's the story of Hollywood and its sign.

The Scenarists: How Screenwriting Began

Before silent films, crank-operated machines called mutoscopes used the same eye-tricking principle employed by flip books. A customer dropped a nickel in a slot, turned the crank, and photographs mounted on an axis turned, giving the illusion of motion. They lasted about a minute. A manufacturer of the devices, The American Mutoscope and Biograph Company, was an early antagonist of Thomas Edison when he refused them a regular supply of film, but they later joined him in the Motion Picture Patents Company that was broken up by government antitrust actions.

W. K. L. Dickson, so instrumental in Edison's success, joined the American Mutoscope and Biograph Company in 1896, and the New York company became a spawning ground for silent film greats. Dickson helped develop the company's American Biograph, which used non-perforated film of a larger size than was customary, resulting in a sharper image. This drew talent to the studio that included director D. W. Griffith, director/producer Mack Sennett, actress Mary Pickford, and many others.

Skip's Tips

When you outline the scenes of your screenplay, write only the action, as if you were writing a silent movie. You'll end up with a dialogue–light, less amateurish screenplay. It's an old Hollywood trick.

In 1920, seven years after DeMille made his first film there, Hollywood turned out 800 films a year. Because of the difficulties in handling nonperforated film, the most important person in those days was the camera/projector operator. What mattered most was the filming and handling of the film, a series of scenes on a "one-reeler" that averaged about 10 minutes. It wasn't until 1911 that directors began pushing for two-reel films.

When writers were employed, they described the scenes and were known as "scenarists." Other duties included composing snips of dialogue or description that was displayed on cards interspersed in the film. The writer wasn't that important. Of course, producers and more directors these days say the same thing!

Women Writers Ruled: Frances Marion and the Scenario Queens

Women screenwriters often complain about a lack of opportunity in a business whose main consumers are purported to be males aged 18 to 34. The demographic is debatable, but what is not debatable is the fact that, in early Hollywood, women screenwriters ruled.

Cecil B. DeMille has been called "the most successful filmmaker of them all." He knew what stirred emotions. This "founder of Hollywood" discovered stars such as Gary Cooper, Paulette Goddard, Gloria Swanson, and Charlton Heston. Remember Swanson's "I'm ready for my close-up, Mr. DeMille!" from *Sunset Boulevard?* DeMille's films are legendary, but did you know about his "harem"? Every important creative person on DeMille's production staff was a woman. Actress/scenarist Jeanie Macpherson was known as DeMille's "write hand." DeMille hired her as his stenographer, but it wasn't long before they co-wrote a script, *The Captive* (1915). They collaborated for 30 years, through silent epics such as his first (silent) *The Ten Commandments* in 1923 and into the sound era.

If Cecil B. DeMille was the founder of Hollywood, Alice Guy Blaché was the Mother of Cinema. She was the first female producer and the first woman film director. Some believe she, not Georges Melies, directed the first narrative film. Blaché was involved in almost 700 films, 400 in Europe and 300 in the United States. Her first, a one-minute fairy tale called *La Fee Aux Choux* (*The Cabbage Fairy*), was apparently made a few months before Melies' first.

Blaché got into film early, working for the Gaumont organization as a secretary. Seeking funding, Louis Lumiere introduced his motion picture camera to Gaumont,

Skip's Tips

Julia Roberts is the world's most popular star, as Mary Pickford was in the silent era. Roberts's biggest complaint is that it is very hard to find a good script with strong women characters! Interested?

Skip's Tips

Hollywood has terms for everything. You might think that *Return to Me* was simply a great movie, or you might call it a "date movie," but chances are good that Hollywood movie executives would call a funny, touching movie like that one a "chick flick."

Skip's Tips

If you find women screenwriters fascinating, read the memoirs of Frances Marion, *Off with Their Heads! A Serio-Comic Tale of Hollywood* (Macmillan, 1972). Another great read is *Without Lying Down: Frances Marion and the Powerful Women of Early Hollywood* (Lisa Drew Books/ Scribner, 1997), by Cari Beauchamp. And don't miss the great Web site at www.reelwomen.com.

but Blaché was the only staff member who could see any use for the gadget. Her first film was popular, and she became *the* filmmaker for Gaumont, developing many "trick" film techniques. By 1912, she had moved to the United States and formed the Solax Company, which turned out more than 300 films. Blaché left the United States and went back to France in 1922. With no copies of her films, she had trouble working in Europe. When Blaché was almost 80, France recognized her as the first woman filmmaker and gave her the French Legion of Honor.

As writers go, Anita Loos was Hollywood's first golden girl. After she wrote a hit for actress Mary Pickford, director D. W. Griffith assigned Loos to silent star Douglas Fairbanks. She wrote a number of hits for Fairbanks. In 1925, she wrote *Gentlemen Prefer Blondes*, a hit novel about a "flapper" party girl. A stage version and the script for a Paramount movie followed. When "talkies" began, Loos wrote memorable films such as *San Francisco,* starring Clark Gable, and Jean Harlow's last film, *Saratoga*. Her last script was a 1953 musical remake of *Gentlemen Prefer Blondes*.

Someone with similar sentiments but who was more important to film history was writer/director Lois Weber. She made sensational films such as *Hypocrites* (1914), which featured a nude woman as "Naked Truth." Some think that Weber is the most important American woman filmmaker in history because of tackling controversial subjects. If a movie had no moral point, Weber wasn't interested. She was the first woman to write, produce, direct, and star in a major feature. She mentored many filmmakers, including director John Ford. Unfortunately, she finished her career as a script doctor.

Frances Marion was the most prolific screenwriter of all time. Introduced to films by Lois Weber in 1915, Marion became a close friend of superstar Mary Pickford and wrote 10 Pickford movies, including *Rebecca of Sunnybrook Farm* (1917). She may have written as many as 200 films, but we don't know for sure because she wrote under pseudonyms. Marion wrote silent classics such as *The Wind* (1928), starring Lillian Gish. When sound arrived, she penned the Garbo starrer *Anna Christie* (1930) and won Academy Awards for writing *The Big House* (1930) and *The Champ* (1931). Frances Marion wrote 137 produced screenplays. For a long time, she was the highest-paid screenwriter in history. It is almost certain that no screenwriter will surpass her credits.

What the Transition to Sound Did

Al Jolson made a name for himself wearing "blackface" makeup (meant to look like an African-American but, in reality, a slur). He starred in a number of Broadway musicals and was a popular radio performer and recording artist. Warner Brothers hired him to sing three songs in the experimental sound film *April Showers* and then again in *The Jazz Singer* in 1927 (the first feature film with synchronized sound). When he began speaking onscreen, audiences gasped. Jolson's phrase "You ain't seen nothin' yet!" became the popular slogan of the day. Stunned by "talkies," one screenwriter remarked that the "international language" of silent films was dead. The advent of sound caused a lot of trauma in Hollywood!

Charlie Chaplin, known worldwide as "The Little Tramp," hated talkies. In 1929, Chaplin said: "Talkies are ... ruining the great beauty of silence. They are defeating the meaning of the screen." Chaplin, who made his first film for Mack Sennett in 1913, was so opposed to sound films that he didn't make one until 1940, when he gave us *The Great Dictator*. Playwright George Bernard Shaw called Chaplin "the only genius developed in motion pictures," but Buster Keaton and even Harold Lloyd were equally inventive.

After Chaplin died, his fourth wife, Oona, revealed that her husband had rehearsed all his bits on film before shooting them "officially." It was the precursor of training by video playback. Chaplin scrupulously preserved all his films, including the rehearsals and outtakes. Any writer wanting to write comedy would be wise to study Chaplin's short films for Keystone or Essanay, and his features for First National and United Artists.

Understanding film history is imperative to good writing. At one time, the "hats" of stars, directors, and producers could be one and the same. With the advent of inexpensive digital filmmaking, that day has to some degree returned. Study the classics of early stars, and you'll write better films, no matter who shoots them.

Skip's Tips

If you want to write an action comedy, study Charlie Chaplin, Buster Keaton, and Harold Lloyd, who all methodically planned their stunts. Turn on a camera, act out a scene, and then play it back with the sound off. If you don't laugh, it might not be funny.

Script Notes

A **montage** is a series of images without dialogue. Russian Sergei Eisenstein used his "montage of attractions" to elicit emotions on several levels. To him, the clash of two images resulted in an unseen third emotion (such as thesis, antithesis, synthesis). Because beginning screenwriters rarely understand montage, they're better off leaving them out.

Here are some examples of film history you might not know. Ever heard of Tay Garnett? How about Mack Sennett, the master of sight gags who called himself "The King of Comedy," gave us the Keystone Kops, and helped Chaplin get started? You may know Sennett's rival, Hal Roach, a producer who emphasized story and structure over pratfalls, made Harold Lloyd a star, got Will Rogers and Laurel and Hardy started, and gave us the *Our Gang* comedies. Tay Garnett worked as a gag writer with both men. One of his writing partners was Frank Capra (*It's a Wonderful Life*). Garnett directed and produced such memorable films as *The Postman Always Rings Twice* (1946) and Mark Twain's *A Connecticut Yankee in King Arthur's Court* (1949). Perhaps because both of those movies came from famous books, few people remember who directed them, much less who wrote the screenplays (not Garnett).

These days, like early Hollywood, you get more notice if you do more than write screenplays. Beginning writers rarely look at history to see that long careers happened because of flexibility and a thorough knowledge of the entire moviemaking process.

Hollywood has a tendency to remember people for only one thing. We know Raoul Walsh as a director who made films in the silent era (including *The Thief of Baghdad,* with Douglas Fairbanks [1924]) and after sound (including *They Drive by Night,* starring Humphrey Bogart [1940]). Walsh was also a writer, producer, and actor. He played John Wilkes Booth, the villainous assassin in D. W. Griffith's *The Birth of a Nation* (1915). You may have seen a movie that Walsh directed and wrote, *Sadie Thompson* (1928), starring Gloria Swanson in one of her best roles, but how about *The Delta Factor* (1971)? Walsh wrote it with Tay Garnett, who also directed it. Ah, screenwriting. It's just not as glamorous, is it?

Perhaps the greatest director who ever lived, John Ford, made more than 600 films. He was also a director, producer, and writer, but when he first came to Hollywood, he toiled as a cameraman and a film editor, and even did stunts. Classic Ford films include *Stagecoach* (1939), starring John Wayne; *The Grapes of Wrath* (1940), starring Henry Fonda; and *The Quiet Man* (1952), also starring John Wayne. The last script credit Ford received was for *3 Bad Men* (1926). Ford must have seen the writing in the sand. After 1926, he mostly directed and produced. Like Raoul Walsh, Tay

Skip's Tips

Many common terms originated in Hollywood. The word "corny" was coined in the pages of *Variety*. To better understand Hollywood expressions, see the "Slanguage" dictionary at www.variety.com.

Hollywood Heat

Hollywood filmmakers continually rework old scenes into new scripts. Remember the sequence in *The Untouchables* (1987) when a baby in a carriage goes jolting down a flight of steps during a shootout? It's Eisenstein's classic "Odessa Steps" scene from *Bronenosets Potyomkin* (*The Battleship Potemkin*, 1925).

Garnett, and Frank Capra, Ford made a smooth transition from silents to sound by being flexible *and* talented. Others, such as Chaplin, did not fare well because they were convinced that the art of film should not be sullied by synchronized sound. Now, with digital filmmaking and movies shown on the Internet, inflexible writers unwilling to learn new media may not survive.

Hollywood, the World, and Migrating Writers

As the movie industry grew in Hollywood, Germans made silent classics such as the vampire thriller *Nosferatu,* by F. W. Murnau (1922), and the futuristic *Metropolis,* by Fritz Lang (1926). European filmmakers experimented with techniques that pushed their American counterparts to higher levels. In France, director Abel Gance worked with a 103-year-old collaborator named Simon Feldman to craft his masterpiece, *Napoleon* (1927). Having had the pleasure of seeing a restored *Napoleon* in its complete, 17-reel, triple-screen "Polyvision" accompanied by a full symphony orchestra, I can tell you personally that it has held up magnificently.

Like France and the United States, India's movie industry began in the 19th century. Audiences in India saw silent movies to live Indian music, perhaps because dancing often fit into the film's story. Like today, love stories were very popular, and kissing scenes were allowed. Today they're taboo. Did talkies do that?

Scandinavian filmmakers gave us moody lighting from Hamlet's home, Denmark. Swedish filmmakers, perhaps influenced by their Norwegian neighbor Henrik Ibsen, made socially conscious movies, which influenced the young director-to-be, Ingmar Bergman.

Musicals, comedies, gangster flicks, and horror movies dominated U.S. screens in the 1930s under the "star system" of actors on contract with U.S. movie studios. In Europe, influential filmmakers fell under the domination of political tyrants. Adolf Hitler used Leni Riefenstahl's *Triumph of the Will* (1935) to glorify the Nazi Party, while Sergei Eisenstein exalted Russian communism under the iron fist of dictator Joseph Stalin. A mass migration of European talent fled to the United States. Brave French filmmaker Jean Renoir made the antiwar *Grand Illusion* (1937), while English directors turned out documentaries, sharing with the world the mounting troubles on the continent.

Great American writers migrated to Hollywood to cash in on easy money. Broadway playwrights and working journalists made the journey west and struck gold. One of the most successful was Ben Hecht. In 1925, he began turning out screenplays

Hollywood Heat

Ben Hecht on producers in his *A Child of the Century:* "Half of the large sum paid me for writing a movie script was in payment for listening to the producer and obeying him. ... The movies pay as much for obedience as for creative work. An able writer is paid a larger sum than a man of small talent. But he is paid this added money not to use his superior talents."

Skip's Tips

In the days before air conditioning, transom windows were built over office doors for air circulation on hot days. These windows were left open when doors were locked. Aspiring writers would throw scripts over the transom. Scripts from unknowns are still occasionally referred to as "coming in over the transom."

It's Not for Us

Before you adapt a famous work into a screenplay, do some research. I know one writer who wrote an updated version of Fitzgerald's *The Great Gatsby*. His timing was unfortunate: A new production was already in progress, scheduled to air on a cable channel.

for Paramount every two to eight weeks, at $50,000 to $125,000 a script. Like Fitzgerald, he worked on *Gone with the Wind* (Hecht got $5,000). Hecht also won the Best Original Story Oscar at the first Academy Awards in 1927 for *Underworld,* but maybe he was just in it for the money. In his 1954 book *A Child of the Century,* he said, "Hollywood held this double lure for me, tremendous sums of money for work that required no more effort than a game of pinochle."

Hecht's frequent co-writing partner, Charles MacArthur, also started as a journalist and later wrote plays. One of their most notable collaborations was *Twentieth Century* (1934), directed by Howard Hawks. One of the unaccredited writers on *Twentieth Century* was Preston Sturges, a former playwright whose name is synonymous with the term "screwball comedy." More on that in a minute.

One great American writer notably did *not* go to Hollywood. Eugene O'Neill is regarded as the father of modern American drama. He won the Nobel Prize for literature in 1936, and four of his plays won Pulitzer Prizes. Hollywood liked him immediately. O'Neill's play *Anna Christie* (1922) was made into a film in 1923 and again in 1930 with Greta Garbo starring. Perhaps O'Neill was simply too thoughtful a writer to work in Hollywood, or he might have stayed away because his daughter, Oona, married Charlie Chaplin!

After the Depression, Hollywood hit a boom that some refer to as its Golden Age. Primary among famous authors who arrived at this time was William Faulkner, winner of two Pulitzer Prizes and the Nobel Prize for Literature. Faulkner worked on many films, including five with director Howard Hawks. Their most interesting project was derived from the Ernest Hemingway novel *To Have and Have Not.* This 1944 film marks the only time in history that two Nobel Prize–winning authors had their name onscreen in the same picture. The screenplay came about when Hawks bet Hemingway that he could make a good film out of Hemingway's worst novel.

Like William Faulkner, F. Scott Fitzgerald could not support himself with stories and novels. Much of Fitzgerald's Hollywood work went uncredited. For example, he was paid $2,904 for work on *Gone with the Wind* (1939). Fitzgerald detested Hollywood "like poison with a sincere hatred." Maybe he felt mistreated? One thing we know for sure; great writers might not have always liked Hollywood, but they certainly liked its money.

How Genres Evolved: What's a Screwball Comedy, Anyway?

In 1935, when money was scarce, Hollywood studios that owned their own chains of theaters offered double bills with "A" (the feature) and "B" films (cheaply made with lesser-known stars). Former President Ronald Reagan was referred to as a B movie actor by detractors because he starred in B films. Some independent studios specialized in B's; Republic Pictures was famous for B Westerns. Any script that could be shot with a minimal amount of locations and costume changes might make a B movie, and the B's were a godsend to writers. Writing them was easy; competence was expected, not genius, and working writers didn't complain.

The screwball comedy was named after a baseball pitch that breaks the opposite direction of a curve ball. This type of 1930s picture had slapstick physical humor, sarcastic barbed dialogue, and wacky romance between the hero and the leading lady, who loathe each other in the beginning. Writer/director Preston Sturges, credited with films such as *Sullivan's Travels* (1941), is considered the screwball master. Post-Depression America loved seeing acerbic dialogue duels between stars, like William Powell and Myrna Loy in *The Thin Man* (1934), a B movie that turned into a giant hit, prompting several sequels and elevating its stars to A status. When World War II began, however, the world grew too serious for the screwball comedy, and it fell out of favor.

Skip's Tips

Are the recent *El Mariachi*, *Reservoir Dogs*, or *Clerks* B movies? Most filmmakers would say yes. These days, $5,000 buys you the equipment to make and edit a digital feature. Independents are today's B films.

The Impact of 1939, Possibly Hollywood's Greatest Year

No year epitomizes Hollywood's Golden Age like 1939. There was a World's Fair in New York that year, showcasing new wonders of television. At the movies, some of our greatest films were playing. The Academy Awards of 1940 did not limit its Best Picture category to five, so there will never be another lineup quite as great as the choices of 1939. In a ceremony hosted by Bob Hope in Los Angeles, the Best Picture category included these nominees:

Picture	Producer
Gone with the Wind	David O. Selznick
Dark Victory	David Lewis
Goodbye, Mr. Chips	Victor Saville
Love Affair	Leo McCarey
Mr. Smith Goes to Washington	Frank Capra
Ninotchka	Sidney Franklin
Of Mice and Men	Lewis Milestone
Stagecoach	Walter Wanger
The Wizard of Oz	Mervyn LeRoy
Wuthering Heights	Samuel Goldwyn

Gone with the Wind, set against the American Civil War, won Best Picture and seven other statuettes, including Best Writing, Screenplay. But to get there, producer Selznick went through 3 directors and 15 screenwriters!

But all things must pass. World War II was beginning, and the world would never again be the same. Writers from all over the world had helped create the Golden Age, but it was quickly gone.

The Least You Need to Know

➤ Compose your scenes as if they were for a silent movie. You'll get stronger action.

➤ The most successful screenwriter of all time was a woman, Frances Marion.

➤ People in Hollywood who have the longest and happiest careers are those who can adapt to changes.

➤ Hollywood's Golden Age owed much to the infusion of ideas from talented authors, journalists, and playwrights.

➤ 1939 is generally regarded as Hollywood's greatest year.

Chapter 5

From the Big Screen to the Computer Screen

In This Chapter

➤ Post World War II: worldwide changes

➤ Television transforms Hollywood

➤ *I Love Lucy* and the situation comedy

➤ Antiheroes and oddities

➤ Genres don't change but outlets do

➤ Hollywood in the digital age

In 1999, the American Film Institute published "America's 100 Greatest Movies." The top two films were made while America was fighting World War II, but only one had a wartime setting. Number one was *Citizen Kane* (1941), the Orson Welles masterpiece based on the life of newspaper magnate William Randolph Hearst. *Casablanca* (1942) was number two. Written by twins Philip and Julius Epstein, with Howard Koch, the Academy Award–winning film was directed by Michael Curtiz and produced by Hal Wallis, who would make Elvis Presley a movie star. *Casablanca* was based on an unpublished play, *Everybody Comes to Rick's,* by Murray Burnett and Joan Alison. Burnett and Alison made $20,000, but have you ever seen another movie with their names on it? How easily Hollywood forgets.

To understand how screenwriting has evolved, it is important to realize Hollywood changes over the past 50 years. If the change from silent films to sound was a great leap, the evolution that began after 1939 was the equivalent of jumping the Grand Canyon.

It's Not for Us

World War II audiences saw classic movie musicals such as *Yankee Doodle Dandy* (1942), with James Cagney; the all-black *Cabin in the Sky* (1943); and *Meet Me in St. Louis* (1944), with Judy Garland. Live action musicals today, even when based on Broadway successes, have been box office disappointments. Writing and selling an original movie musical today is very difficult.

Skip's Tips

Film noir makes stars. With its femme fatales, "hard-boiled" detectives, 1920s German lighting techniques, and 1930s gangster movie plots, the "black film" genre never dies. *The Maltese Falcon* (1941) made a star of Humphrey Bogart, as did *Chinatown* (1974) for Jack Nicholson, *Body Heat* (1981) for Kathleen Turner, and *L.A. Confidential* (1997) for Russell Crowe.

Hollywood pitched in heavily during World War II. Movie star Jimmy Stewart flew real-life bomber missions over Europe. Clark Gable and other stars joined the service, while Hollywood directors made training films and documentaries. Germany lost more than just the war. Universum-Film AG (UFA), the Berlin studio where classics such as *Metropolis* and *The Blue Angel* were made, saw an exodus of talent that included all-time great writer/director Billy Wilder.

The year 1946 rivaled 1939 for classic films. *The Big Sleep, Gilda, Henry V* (starring Laurence Olivier), *It's a Wonderful Life*, and *The Postman Always Rings Twice* debuted in 1946. Americans wanted more realistic stories, which is why Frank Capra's *It's a Wonderful Life* was dismissed by moviegoers as overly sentimental "Capra-corn." William Wyler's *The Best Years of Our Lives*, about three GIs who have trouble adjusting to postwar life, won a number of Oscars, including Best Picture and Best Director.

Movies After World War II; the Whole World Changed

After the war, wholesome films such as *The Bells of St. Mary's* (1946), with Bing Crosby, were popular, but so was "film noir" fare such as *Key Largo* (1948), with Edward G. Robinson and *Treausre of the Sierra Madre* (1948), with Humphrey Bogart playing a man driven crazy by greed. And Bette Davis in *Now, Voyager* (1942) represented resilient women who had worked men's jobs in factories during the war and liked their new freedom.

Minority roles also began to change. Other than all-black "race movies" by Oscar Micheaux and other independents, black roles in films were few. When Bill Robinson had tapped out rhythms on a staircase with Shirley Temple in *The Little Colonel* (1935), he did so as a servant. Buckwheat in Hal Roach's *Our Gang* comedies was an equal, and so was Eddie "Rochester" Anderson on the popular Jack Benny radio show, but otherwise, black people were unequal. In 1949, director Stanley Kramer bravely broached the subject of military race bias in *Home of the Brave*, much as Elia

Kazan tackled anti-Semitism in *Gentlemen's Agreement* (1947). Hollywood was about to become the focal point for national problems.

Everyone in Hollywood shared a common enemy in the Hays Office. The Hollywood Production Code was devised in 1922 by Will Hays to make sure that movies did not anger government censors. The code was not always logical; a man and a woman could lay on a bed together, as long as there was no nudity and they kept one foot on the floor. The code was tolerated until director Howard Hawks made *Scarface* in 1931. Hawks refused to comply with Hays's editing demands. Only the intervention of producer Howard Hughes allowed the picture to go forward. The film angered citizen groups, causing studios to cut down on violence and emphasize sex. This prompted the Catholic Church to form the Legion of Decency and threaten boycotts. In 1934, a strict Roman Catholic named Joe Breen took over for Hays and even rewrote scripts if he thought it was warranted. Although it sounds odd today, some have speculated that Breen's efforts helped bring about the Golden Year of 1939.

In 1943, Howard Hughes pushed the morality envelope again with *The Outlaw*, which starred the amply endowed Jane Russell. Had we not been at war, Hughes might not have been able to release the film (lonely GIs loved it). Alcoholism, mental illness, and rape were also written about. Then, in 1947, the masters of morality zeroed in on Hollywood. With Stalin in power in Russia and Mao in China, communism was a world threat, and the House Un-American Activities Committee (HUAC) wanted to ferret out communist operatives in Tinseltown. The hearings led by Senator Joseph McCarthy resulted in a polarization of the country. Were there communists in Hollywood? Well, actors studying at the Actor's Lab, behind world-famous Schwab's Drugstore, sang the Communist anthem "Le internationale" in the parking lot after classes.

A screenwriter, John Howard Lawson, probably sealed the fate of the accused when he chastised HUAC members. The "Hollywood Ten" (directors, producers, and screenwriters who refused to answer questions) were held in contempt of Congress and were blacklisted from working in the industry by Louis B. Mayer and 49 other film executives. More than 200 people in the movie business had their careers ruined.

Resourceful screenwriters simply wrote under pseudonyms. Hollywood Ten member Dalton Trumbo won Best Original Screenplay for *The Brave One* at the 1957 Academy Awards under the name "Robert Rich." In 1960, in open defiance of the blacklist, actor/executive producer Kirk Douglas hired Trumbo to write *Spartacus* under his own name, and that served to break the blacklist.

Hollywood Heat

The films of the 1930s and 1940s have often been favorites for remakes. *Here's Comes Mr. Jordan* (1941), starring Robert Montgomery, became Warren Beatty's *Heaven Can Wait* (1978) and received several Oscar nominations, including Best Picture. Conversely, Steven Spielberg's *Always* (1989) was a remake of *A Guy Named Joe* (1943), but was a box-office disappointment.

There were other postwar changes. A 1945 union strike raised the price of making films, and as television caught on, movies had less appeal. By 1948, one out of every eight American families owned a television. Even more threatening to Hollywood was a 1947 Supreme Court decision against the five major and three minor studios, which forced them to sell off theater chains. The antimonopoly "Paramount Case" ruling stated that controlling both production and exhibition gave studios an unfair monopoly. Marketing their films on a theater-by-theater basis meant cost-cutting and the end of B pictures and serials. Signing actors and writers to long-term contracts didn't make economic sense.

In October 1948, the five majors were again ordered to give up their interests in more than 1,400 movie theaters. Howard Hughes caved in first, declaring RKO would sell its almost 250 theaters within a year. Other studios fell in line, and the vast studio system was dead. Did the government do the right thing? Maybe not. The bulk of the films in the American Film Institute's Top 100 were produced by major studios during the Golden Age of Hollywood.

How Television Transformed Hollywood

In 1946, 80 million people went to the movies each week. By 1948, that was down to 60 million. Moviegoing offered less "bang for the buck" without B pictures and serials, and TV shows were free. People stopped going to the movies, and Hollywood paid the price.

Variety shows were popular on early TV. The writers turned out skits and jokes that hearkened back to vaudeville. The best of the variety breed was Sid Caesar's *Your Show of Shows,* from New York. It debuted in 1949 as the *Admiral Broadway Revue.* (Admiral was the name of the sponsor.) Writers now recognized as Hollywood superstars, including Mel Brooks, Neil Simon, Woody Allen, and Larry Gelbart (or *M*A*S*H*), were staff writers for Caesar.

Advertiser-supported television brought about censorship called "Standards and Practices." Sponsors knew that if a show offended, the all-powerful consumer could boycott products. Where Hollywood writers had to write scripts that conformed only to the Production Code, TV writers toed a tighter line. As television expanded into a writer-consuming behemoth, supporting 80 percent of the registered members of the Writers Guild of America, TV writing was regulated by moral standards that gave us shows such as *Leave It to Beaver,* which celebrated the status quo rather than challenging it.

I Love Lucy: **The Power Shifter**

Lucille Ball and Desi Arnaz did more to change television history than anyone else. Lucy was almost 40 when she was approached about moving her hit CBS Radio *situation comedy My Favorite Husband* to television. She agreed, but she refused to move to New York. The network agreed to let her film it in Los Angeles and caved in to her demand that her Cuban bandleader husband, Desi Arnaz, play her show husband. Using comedy moves that she had learned from Buster Keaton at MGM and the Marx Brothers at RKO, Ball mugged for the camera and took pratfalls before a live audience. Housewives loved her plucky adventures, and the 1951 show was an immediate hit. Within six months, more than 30 million Americans tuned in each Monday night to watch the number 1 hit *I Love Lucy* on CBS.

Instead of doing the show live, Lucy and Desi wanted to film it, which cost a lot more. The cigarette company Philip Morris was the only sponsor that went for it. The couple took less money in exchange for producing the show and keeping the negatives. This was before anyone had conceived of reruns; poor quality kinescopes (film recordings made from television pictures) were the only record of most TV shows. By filming, reruns could be aired across the country, and the shows could be dubbed in other languages. Eventually, *I Love Lucy* was seen in over 80 countries.

Script Notes

A **situation comedy,** or **sitcom,** about characters caught in comedic situations, is structured like any other story. With a beginning, middle, and end, characters struggle to reach goals, encountering obstacles and conflict. The solutions that they devise result in even more complicated, funny situations.

Desilu Productions developed a major TV innovation. Working with Academy Award–winning cinematographer Karl Freund, Desi devised the three-camera filming technique to allow for better editing. It became the standard for all TV sitcoms. Other shows from New York opted for three cameras and the more pleasant climate of southern California, and Hollywood's television industry was born.

The Birth of the Antihero and the Death of Feel Good

In October 1947, the Actors Studio was founded in New York by Cheryl Crawford, Elia Kazan, and Robert Lewis. Two years later, Lee Strasberg joined this bastion of Method acting, which was derived from Konstantin Stanislavski, author of *My Life in Art*. Strasberg learned Stanislavski's "System" from Richard Boleslavski, a defected member of the Moscow Art Theatre. When the Actors Studio began, the founders invited 50 young actors to join the company and recruited teachers such as Kazan and Sanford Meisner, who went on to great success teaching Hollywood.

Twenty films from the 1950s were in the American Film Institute's "Top 100" film list, making the 1950s the movies' most influential decade. The only actor to star in two of the top 10 films is Marlon Brando, who studied at the Actors Studio. Number 8 on the list, *On the Waterfront* (1954), starred Brando and was directed by Elia Kazan. Number 14, *Some Like It Hot* (1959), starred Marilyn Monroe, a Studio alum. The

Studio also had a Playwrights Wing, and one of that group's founding members, Tennessee Williams, wrote number 45 on the list, *A Streetcar Named Desire* (1951), perhaps Brando's greatest role. Studio alumnus James Dean starred in two movies on the AFI list: number 59, *Rebel Without a Cause* (1955), and number 82, *Giant* (1956). Studio members also included Paul Newman and Joanne Woodward. The Studio's influence on Hollywood is in enormous.

When the Korean War was over, even though the atomic bomb and communism were real threats, life in America was peaceful. Young men who didn't have to go to war idolized rebellious movie characters such as those played by Brando, James Dean, and Paul Newman. These "antiheroes" challenged middle class values. They talked tough, looked cool, and, in James Dean's case, died young.

Studios still made plenty of "family fare" movies during the 1950s, of course, with great musicals such as Gene Kelly and Stanley Donen's *Singin' in the Rain* (1952). When rock 'n' roll exploded mid-decade, however, it was inevitable that music stars such as Elvis Presley would appear in films, most definitely not in the traditional musical. No musical ever made had a sequence as electrifying or overtly sexual as the title scene in Presley's *Jailhouse Rock* (1957). Presley films produced by Hal Wallis went on to influence movies for decades.

With B movies and serials gone, film stars moved to TV. Gene Autry, the original singing cowboy, got his own series, as did "The King of the Cowboys," Roy Rogers. Their success motivated Warner Brothers to produce a number of made-for-TV Westerns, the most popular being *Maverick* (1957), starring James Garner. Other studios followed suit, making their own shows for the new medium.

Skip's Tips

Ride your modem on over to www.cowboypal.com, pardner. You'll find Western comics, B Westerns, and Warner Brothers TV series. You can watch the "Double Trouble" episode from the *Cisco Kid* TV series, learn about *Zorro* serials, or listen to a *Hopalong Cassidy* (William Boyd) radio show. See ya there, buckaroo!

As television climbed and film declined, studios fought back with sweeping epics and gimmicks such as Cinemascope and 3D. Filmmakers took chances by putting previously taboo content in movies. *A Streetcar Named Desire* (1951) pushed the limits of the Production Code and was condemned by the Legion of Decency. Two years later, Otto Preminger's *The Moon Is Blue* was deliberately released without the Production Code seal of approval and was condemned by the Legion. When Preminger made *The Man with the Golden Arm* (1955), starring Frank Sinatra, the film was denied a production seal because it dealt with heroin addiction. This prompted United Artists to resign from the association of studios that upheld the Code, and set in motion a Hollywood rebellion. The film that brought the confrontation to a head was Elia Kazan's *Baby Doll* (1956), written by Kazan's friend Tennessee Williams. The openly sexual content caused the film to be banned by the Legion.

Code-challenging director Otto Preminger was notorious for having little patience with actors, but he worked with writers repeatedly. Ben Hecht was credited on *Where the Sidewalk Ends* (1950) and uncredited on *Angel Face* (1952), *The Man with the Golden Arm* (1955), and *The Court-Martial of Billy Mitchell* (1955). Dalton Trumbo worked without credit on *The Court-Martial of Billy Mitchell*. Birds of a feather flock together in Hollywood.

With the studio system broken, some productions went overseas for cheaper labor. Additionally, movie theaters in major cities began importing and exhibiting foreign films that had great impact on young filmmakers. No foreign moviemaker was more influential than Japanese writer/director Akira Kurosawa. *The Magnificent Seven* was an American remake of Kurosawa's *The Seven Samurai* (1954), and Kurosawa's favorite American director was John Ford, who made many great Westerns. Kurosawa's heroes were often antiheroes, particularly when his favorite, Toshiro Mifune, starred. If you've ever seen a *Star Wars* movie in which the existing scene is wiped away by the next, that's Kurosawa. *Star Wars* is based on Kurosawa's *The Hidden Fortress* (1958).

Hollywood Heat

In the January 1954 issue of *Cahiers du Cinema*, French critic Francois Truffaut held that the director was the *auteur* (author) of a film because he controls the mise–en–scene ("placing of the scene"). Truffaut loved mainstream American directors, B pictures, and English director Alfred Hitchcock (he married Hitchcock's daughter, Patricia). Truffaut also directed the Oscar-winning *Day for Night* (Best Foreign Film, 1973). In homage to the author of *auteur*, Steven Spielberg cast Truffaut in *Close Encounters of the Third Kind* (1979). That's right. The "A Film By [Director]" in the opening credits is all Truffaut's fault.

Hollywood Genres Don't Change, but the Outlet Does

Another influence on young filmmakers in the 1950s was the plethora of classic science-fiction films as *The Day the Earth Stood Still* (1951) and *Forbidden Planet* (1956). Many films mused on horrors resulting from atomic bomb tests. In Japan, where atomic explosions had destroyed cities, audiences loved the mutated giant lizard *Godzilla*, and other atomic mutant films followed. Roger "King of the B's" Corman got his start during this time with low-budget knockoffs such as *Not of This Earth*

(1957). Perhaps too many science-fiction films were made in the 1950s because, by the mid-1960s, the genre was relatively dead. For the most part, films during the 1960s were about social issues, not the future dreams of science fiction. Which is odd, given the 1960s American race to put a man on the moon in that decade.

In 1968, Stanley Kubrick made perhaps his best film from a book by science-fiction futurist Arthur C. Clarke. In reality, Kubrick's *2001: A Space Odyssey* was a social drama about a machine as Frankenstein monster, with technology defeating its creators.

Hollywood grasped for substance and meaning in the 1960s, a time of turbulence, confusion, and changing mores that resulted from the appearance of the birth control pill. In an attempt to get a grasp on public desires, Hollywood adopted a new film rating code almost identical to the one we have today. There was not yet a PG-13, and X was reserved for films suitable to viewers 16 years and older. That is precisely how *Midnight Cowboy* (1969), starring Jon Voight and Dustin Hoffman, became the first (and likely the last) X-rated film to win the Oscar for Best Picture.

When Baby Boomers came of age, most Hollywood studios were slow to pick up on their rebellious tastes. Boomers loved movies with music that weren't really traditional musicals. That truly became evident when Columbia took a chance on an independently made low-budget film called *Easy Rider* (1969). The box office results and soundtrack album sales quickly opened everyone's eyes.

Almost all remnants of the studio system were gone by the end of the 1960s. Most of the participants in Hollywood's Golden Age had either died or retired. Actors worked independently, not on contract, a trend that had begun when Jimmy Stewart took a cut in pay for a share in the profits of two films that he made in 1950.

Skip's Tips

No matter how permissive we have become in today's society, there is still a very clear line between X-rated films and other ratings. If a feature film is given an X rating due to excessive violence, explicit sex, or other reasons, it's basically a box office kiss of death. X-rated films are a different industry.

When the Baby Boomers began making feature films, Steven Spielberg and George Lucas quickly moved to the forefront. College dropout Spielberg sold a co-written feature in 1973 (*Ace Eli and Rodger of the Skies*) and wasn't happy with the filmed result. So, he directed his next feature, *Sugarland Express* (1974). After winning several awards in film school at the University of Southern California, Lucas became the protégé of Francis Ford Coppola and directed his first feature, *THX 1138*, in 1971. His next feature was *American Graffiti* in 1973. Its box office success helped him get financing for his next film, *Star Wars*. Lucas got rich largely due to retaining most of the merchandising rights on items from that movie. These Boomers well-remembered their Hollywood lessons. When Spielberg and Lucas teamed up to do the *Indiana Jones* films, they did so in homage to the great serial films.

Most aspiring screenwriters do not realize that top filmmakers today, just as in the beginning of

Hollywood, impressed people with their stories when they first started. Check the film credits of Spielberg and Lucas. You'll find dozens of writing mentions, even if they are only story credits. This should tell the beginning screenwriter that the people who often make the biggest impact with their scripts are those who can also film them.

Spielberg and Lucas contributed to the field of screenwriting in other ways. Spielberg's third acts tend to be longer than usual, while Lucas support of the myth story structure outlined by Joseph Campbell has resulted in a paradigm shift in Hollywood stories.

A Hollywood World in the Digital Age

"Experts" predicted that both the Cable News Network (CNN) and Music Television (MTV) would fail. Independent filmmakers offer similar surprises. Low-budget films with big impact include: John Sayles's *Return of the Secaucus 7* (1980); Louis Malle's *My Dinner With Andre* (1981); the Coen brothers' *Blood Simple* (1984); Spike Lee's *She's Gotta Have It* (1986); John Singleton's *Boyz N The Hood* (1991); Quentin Tarantino's *Reservoir Dogs* (1992); Robert Rodriguez' *El Mariachi* (1992); Kevin Smith's *Clerks* (1994); Edward Burns' *The Brothers McMullen* (1995); Neil LaBute's controversial *In the Company of Men* (1997); and, last but in first place, Daniel Myrick and Eduardo Sanchez' *The Blair Witch Project* (1999). *The Blair Witch Project* initially cost around $8,000. After improvements were added and an ingenious Internet marketing campaign put it on the map, the film made more than $140 million in the United States alone. Ever consider shooting your own script?

Screenwriting and filmmaking have come a long way in 100 years, and now we have Internet distribution. For writers, there are more outlets and opportunities than ever before. It helps if you know some history and are willing to adapt to suit the changing tastes of the public. And now that you have some idea of what has come before you, let's get into how to get you where you want to go.

Skip's Tips

HDTV is an abbreviation for High-Definition Television. Video may someday replace 35mm film in making movies, but getting a true "film look" from video cameras has not been easy. Now, with George Lucas using a Panavision-modified HD video camera from Sony to shoot the live action scenes of *Star Wars: Episode II*, video's day may have finally arrived.

The Least You Need to Know

➤ Although they were popular for decades, selling an original movie musical today is next to impossible.

➤ Movies after World War II movies reflected a desire for equality of women and minorities who had contributed to the war effort.

➤ For decades, unknown actors in film noir movies have become stars; a first script in that genre is a good idea.

➤ Positive results from attempted censorship of Hollywood movies and creative people is a highly debatable issue.

➤ Lucille Ball and Desi Arnaz are responsible for the television industry being centered in southern California and the three-camera situation comedy format.

➤ In the past decade, the success of inexpensive independent films such as *The Blair Witch Project* have made it more attractive than ever before for writers to become successful filmmakers.

Part 2
What to Write

Great ideas and how to sell them, writing forms and other oddities are all explained here as you learn that unique language of Hollywood that screenwriters must master to succeed. In a few short chapters, you'll get an education that some writers take a decade to figure out (the ones that don't give up, that is). The shortcuts and the detours are mapped out here in full.

Chapter 6

Sources for Movie Ideas That Will Sell

> ### In This Chapter
>
> ➤ The newspaper as story source
>
> ➤ Old movies make new movies
>
> ➤ Scripting true stories
>
> ➤ Qualifying original ideas
>
> ➤ TV shows as movie inspiration
>
> ➤ Understanding movie demographics

When I was a freelance journalist, I either came up with story ideas that editors would buy, or I didn't get paid. The first time I made money on a story that I hoped would be a movie, I had no idea what would sell to Hollywood. I knew only that I had pleased the two producers who *optioned* my story. Thankfully, I learned what types of stories I could write best. And because I learned the power of networking, I never hesitated in passing a good story that was unsuitable for me to someone I thought could use it.

One day I came across the story of a psychiatrist in Australia who drugged patients and raped them. I passed it on to Michael Rymer, a then-unproduced Australian screenwriter living in Los Angeles. He didn't know about the true story, and it intrigued him. He wrote a screenplay and sold it to Village Roadshow; he even gave me a finder's fee. His movie *Dead Sleep* was a thriller starring Karen Black and Linda Blair. And, as I write, he is preparing to direct the movie of Anne Rice's *Queen of the Damned*.

Script Notes

When a production company thinks that your property would make a good movie, they make an **option** deal. You're paid something now (usually 10 percent of the total price) or nothing, if you allow it, and the rest when the movie is made. Usually, the remainder is due on the first day of principal photography.

It's Not for Us

Unless you live in Hollywood or near a movie studio *and* are an accomplished writer with credits (so why are you reading this book?) or can write a competent script very quickly, forget writing to exploit a current trend. Get a good story and script it well; if your screenplay is good, its time will come.

Reading the Newspaper Like a Screenwriter

Showbiz veterans develop a sense of good movie stories, and one of the best sources is the newspaper. Any newspaper. Writer/producer Mary Sweeney was reading *The New York Times* one day in 1994 when she came across the story of Alvin Straight, a 73-year-old man from Laurens, Iowa. When he found out that his estranged brother in Mt. Zion, Wisconsin was ill, Straight, who no longer qualified for a driver's license, rode his lawn mower to see his brother. Sweeney found the story "very American." She clipped out the article and faxed it to her friend John Roach, who also loved it. When Sweeney looked into optioning the story, however, highly successful producer Ray Stark had already grabbed it, with Larry Gelbart, of *M*A*S*H*, set to script it.

Nevertheless, Sweeney didn't forget the story. When Alvin Straight died in 1996, she contacted his children and found out that the *option* had lapsed. She made a deal with them for the story and then verified with Ray Stark's lawyers that the option had indeed lapsed. She and Roach retraced Straight's route by car and met some of the people Straight had met. They wrote (and rewrote) a screenplay, and then Sweeney gave it to director David Lynch, her partner in the Los Angeles production company, The Picture Factory. Lynch loved it and suggested that they recruit acclaimed actor Richard Farnsworth to play Alvin Straight. Farnsworth liked the script so much that he came out of retirement to do the part. Filming of *The Straight Story* began in Iowa in September 1998 and finished that October. And in 1999, Richard Farnsworth received a Best Actor Oscar nomination. All because a smart writer/producer saw an interesting story in a newspaper and followed up.

Read your local newspaper. Is something unusual happening? Can you get the film rights? Dig up famous local stories. If they were covered in the newspaper, look them up in old editions at your library or at the paper itself. A story doesn't have to be in *The New York Times* to make it to Hollywood. Remember, *The Blair Witch Project* was inspired by a local legend of Burkittsville, Maryland.

Hollywood Heat

After Robert Katz and Moctesuma Esparza made the highly successful movie *Gettysburg* with Turner Network Television, TNT owner Ted Turner asked what they would like to do next. Katz suggested the story of Teddy Roosevelt and the Rough Riders during the Spanish-American War. Turner agreed. When Katz met with the head of the network, he was reminded that TNT liked to do movies based on books. So, they began researching and found that no one had written a definitive book on the subject. Finally, they settled on Roosevelt's campaign diary as a reference source, a document that was in the public domain (freely available to anyone).

Recycling Old Movies

As the story goes, George Lucas, who loved the old serial movies, wanted to do a remake of *Flash Gordon*. Unfortunately, producer Dino De Laurentiis had already secured the rights. So, Lucas wrote *Star Wars*. People who grew up loving a film or TV show often think of new twists. Producer David Permut was flipping back and forth between cable TV channels one night and saw Dan Ackroyd in an old movie and then Jack Webb in an old *Dragnet* TV show. Ackroyd. Webb. The next day he called Ackroyd's manager and pitched his idea for a new, comic *Dragnet* feature. The manager signed on, and Permut made the quickest deal of his life with the president of Universal. Chances are, you're not a producer with access to stars and studio heads. That doesn't mean that you can't find an old movie that has lapsed into the public domain that you can rewrite.

Script Notes

When a production company wants to make a movie, it acquires a property and puts it **in development.** That means that the company will hire the original writer(s) to rewrite it, or hire another writer or writers to further develop the project to make it the best script possible. When that process is taking seemingly forever, it's called "development hell."

How do you ascertain whether someone in Hollywood is already doing the remake you've picked? In recent years top Hollywood Web sites have begun listing films *"in development."* For a monthly fee to www.hcdonline.com, inhollywood.com, or www.showbizdata.com, you can get all the Hollywood contacts you need and read development listings. Just remember Mary Sweeney's story, and stay vigilant.

Skip's Tips

Veteran screenwriters can rattle off any number of films whose plot resembles *Shane* (1953). In my opinion, Kevin Costner's *Waterworld* was *Shane*. Even if you can't get the rights to an old film, you could still parallel the plot in a new setting.

It's Not for Us

If you write the screenplay of a true story and sell it, don't be surprised if the producer hires other screenwriters for rewrites and they get credit. A story credit can substantially boost your career, but if you think you've been cheated, you can ask for an arbitration by the Writers Guild of America, *if the producer is signatory to the Guild.*

True Stories: How to Secure the Rights and Where to Sell Them

I'm not a lawyer, and I don't play one on TV. I don't intend to offer you legal advice or to try. But I will give you some tips:

➤ You cannot write a screenplay based on a true story of a living person or persons unless you secure the rights from one of the involved parties. Use legal representation to help you with finalizing any agreement(s).

➤ You can write a screenplay based on documents in the public record, such as a trial transcript.

➤ You can base a screenplay on a true story if the parties involved are no longer living, unless they have descendants whose interests might be infringed. Consult an attorney.

For entertainment business legal advice, I recommend *Business and Legal Forms for Authors and Self-Publishers*, by attorney and publisher Tad Crawford (Allworth Press), and *The Writer Got Screwed (but didn't have to): A Guide to the Legal and Business Practices of Writing for the Entertainment Industry*, by Brooke A. Wharton (HarperPerennial). Both are excellent resources.

If you secure the rights and decide for some reason that you do not want to write a screenplay, some producers may be interested in obtaining the rights from you. One of the most active is Robert "Pitch King" Kosberg at www.moviepitch.com (sorry, non-Webbers, that's how he's doing business these days). Kosberg will take fictional ideas as well, and you don't even need to have true story rights secured to contact him about a movie idea.

Another possible route is Industry R&D, Inc. (R&D stands for research and development), if you have "caught on camera" video of the critical event that makes a story newsworthy. This company brought to national attention the real-life story that became the Sony movie *Fly Away Home*. You can reach the company at …

Tom Colbert, President
Industry R&D, Inc.
23945 Calabasas Road, Suite 207
Calabasas, CA 91302
Phone: 1-800-995-6808
Fax: 1-800-995-7978
E-mail: tcolbert@IndustryRandD.com

If a true story is something that you find in the media (newspapers, magazines, radio, TV, or the Internet) chances are good that someone else will have seen it, too. Do your research and learn how to legally secure rights before you start looking, and then move quickly as soon as you decide that a story is good. How much should you pay to secure the rights? That is entirely between you and the person(s) with the story. You could pay as little as $1 in some states to make an agreement legal. Just make sure that you have a signed, legally binding agreement.

If you have the financial means, or if you're simply a good salesperson, you might be able to secure the rights of a hot true story even when many other people want it. American Billy Hayes was caught attempting to smuggle drugs out of Turkey and was put in prison. After Hayes made a daring escape and returned to the United States, one of the first things he did was acquire a literary agent. He had been home only a few days when producer Peter Guber (who had read the national newspaper story, like dozens of other eager producers) flew to Long Island, New York, to meet with Hayes and his parents. Hayes told me that Guber made an offer that he would have been a fool to refuse:

> "And when he flew me out to LA first class to meet with the Columbia brass, he pulled up in front of the hotel with a shiny new Mercedes and a lightning bolt with the word "FLASH" emblazoned across the front of his sweater. I was impressed. Of course, I'd been

Skip's Tips

When you contact a producer about a story, you might be asked to come in and pitch, as in "sales pitch." You meet with the producer or the producer's development person and tell the story. The most effective pitches are succinct and easily described, as in, "It's the true story of the first lady pirate."

Skip's Tips

If you're serious about selling screenplays, keep up with what is being sold. Get a subscription to either *Daily Variety* or *The Hollywood Reporter* or both. You can read portions of each magazine free online at www.variety.com or www.hollywoodreporter.com, or you can subscribe to the complete versions online. The site www.scriptsales.com also tracks recent sales.

in jail for five years, so I was easily impressed. But I knew Peter was going places, and his driving energy got my movie made, and made well, so I have nothing but good things to say about Peter. I even took his producer/class at UCLA one year, when he used *Midnight Express* as the model deal discussed that semester. Made for fascinating view of my project from the other side."

The critically acclaimed *Midnight Express* was one of the hits of 1978. If you're as creative a producer as Guber and are willing to go the extra several thousand miles, you might be able to secure the rights to an equally compelling story.

How to Know If You're Original Idea Is Truly Original

In 1981, I co-wrote a screenplay called *Fair Game*. It was an action film about a man seeking revenge on modern-day pirates who kill his wife while stealing his yacht. "Fair game" referred to a law of the sea that states that you are within your rights to kill someone who attacks you on waters outside the territorial limits of seaside nations. Not long after we wrote the script, it was optioned by a successful producing duo. Not long after that, we learned of a movie starring Gary Busey that sounded very much like our story. We hired a detective, who got a copy of the script before the movie finished production. He concluded that the scripts were different. Since that time, there have been at least four other *Fair Game* movies: a TV thriller in 1985, another TV movie in 1989, another TV movie in 1994, and the disappointing feature film with Cindy Crawford in 1995. None of these movies came from our original script; we later changed its name to *South China Sea* and sold it to a producer living in Thailand.

Hollywood Heat

Return to Me, one of the better movies of 2000, came from the original script *Distance Calls* by Andrew Stern and Samantha Goodman. Actress Bonnie Hunt read the script with the intention of directing it. When she and writing partner Don Lake changed the story and rewrote the screenplay, what remained from *Distance Calls* was the core idea of a man who loses his wife in an accident, only to later fall in love with the female recipient of his late wife's donated heart. The story got changed drastically. That's Hollywood.

You can't copyright a title. If you wrote a screen-play called *Star Wars,* though, you might be in trouble. The term is trademarked, and the George Lucas franchise is firmly established. (Confused? The "All About Trademarks" page at www.ggmark. com is a good place to begin learning about trade-mark law.) You can also read a lot about what can and cannot be copyrighted at the U.S. Copyright Office home page at www.loc.gov/copyright.

Here's another example of matching titles. I was in a video store in 1988 when I happened across a video titled *Fatal Attraction,* starring Sally Keller-man. The movie was about sex fantasies and bizarre games between consenting adults. Say what? It starred Glenn Close, not Sally Kellerman? No, that was the *other Fatal Attraction,* which came out in 1987 and was a hit for Close and Michael Douglas. The one I saw in the video store was made in 1980 in Canada and originally was titled *Head On.* It was retitled *Fatal Attraction* when re-leased in the United States in 1985, two years be-fore the release of the more famous *Fatal Attraction.*

Skip's Tips

Time after time, I've seen Holly-wood folks get interested in an idea and say, verbatim, "Hey! Nobody's ever done a movie about [insert idea here]." If you're musing over possible screenplay ideas, it might help to use, "Nobody's ever done a movie about ..." as a starting point. Into copycat movies? How about this: Has anyone ever done *Die Hard* on a spaceship?

How do you know if your movie idea is truly original? You don't. You simply have to do the best research you can. Check the Internet Movie Database at www.imdb.com. You can search by keywords there; it's a fairly complete database, but it's not perfect. There are also many books covering every movie ever made. A long-time favorite of mine was *Videohound's Golden Movie Retriever* (Invisible Ink Press).

If you really want to be a successful screenwriter, you need to watch a lot of movies. Successful screenwriters can rattle off lines and scenes and obscure bits of film trivia (which is precisely why I can write this book). They know the medium.

No matter how much research you do or how many movies you watch, you can't be sure that your idea is truly original. World civilizations have been keeping records for at least 10,000 years. Who knows how many stories there have been? You simply have to exercise what attorneys call "due diligence." That is, put forth the effort that an average, sincere, energetic person would exhibit. I can guarantee you this: If you come up with a well-written script with a truly original story in a recognized movie genre, you might be surprised how well you'll do with it.

It's Not for Us

Mum's the word. When you've decided on a story for your screenplay, don't discuss it with anyone except a professional. Amateurs often offer comments based only on emotion and not story structure. Or, you might receive too much praise and stop writing. Really.

Movies to TV and Back Again to Movies

Filmmakers often do remakes of things that made a strong impression on them in their youth. For young males in the Unites States, perhaps nothing makes a stronger impression than comic books (and now video games). Superman debuted in a comic book, and that's where he stayed for years. In 1941, the first animated Superman cartoon by Dave Fleischer debuted. (There were several others.) *The Mad Scientist* featured the Man of Steel fighting a mad scientist intent on destroying Metropolis with an energy cannon styled on the legendary "death ray" supposedly invented by Nikola Tesla. Bud Collyer voiced Clark Kent and Superman in the cartoon, while Joan Alexander was the voice of Lois Lane.

The first time an actor played Superman on film was in 1948, in serials featuring Kirk Alyn as Clark Kent/Superman and Noel Neill as Lois Lane. Another 15-chapter serial was made in 1950. *Atom Man vs. Superman* also featured Alyn and Neill. When the *Adventures of Superman* TV series began in 1953, with George Reeves as our favorite man from Krypton, Neill once again played Lois Lane.

And then came Christopher Reeve as Superman with a number of movies in the 1970s. And just when we thought that was the last of it, *Lois and Clark: The New Adventures of Superman* was a hit on ABC starting in 1993. There have been recent rumblings about a very different Superman on the big screen once again, with Nicolas Cage as the Man of Steel. Will it happen? Who knows? It seems like nothing can really kill Superman.

Can you think of another character who first appeared in movies, then on television, and then back again to film? This one began in novels: Tarzan of the Jungle, from the original books by Edgar Rice Burroughs. As popular as Superman is, with almost 50 onscreen portrayals, Tarzan doubles that count. Tarzan rules!

Are you picking up a pattern here? The lone hero, with special powers or abilities far beyond that of the normal man, follows an ethical code, either acknowledged or innate. Would that describe Superman and Tarzan? How about some others like these two? Batman, certainly. How about Hercules? And let's not forget the swashbuckling Zorro, first seen in the silent *Don Q Son of Zorro* (1925), with silent film superstar Douglas Fairbanks as Don Cesar de Vega/Zorro. Through many movies and several TV series, including the popular Disney series in 1957, Zorro keeps coming back even better, if the excellent *The Mask of Zorro* (1998) with Antonio Banderas as the masked avenger was any index. All told, Zorro also has been onscreen more often that Superman!

Take a cue from these characters. A solitary hero, with superhuman skill or abilities, who follows an inner ethical code and can be played by any number of handsome actors, is a winner time after time in many mediums. And all these characters have one more thing in common: Either their family structure was heavily threatened, or they were orphaned at a very early age.

How we interpret that I'll leave up to you. To me, it's too reminiscent of the Oedipus story, and utterly Freudian!

Anything Males Eighteen to Thirty-Four Like

You've probably never heard of the *Statistical Abstract of the United States,* a reference book of vital U.S. statistics compiled by the Bureau of the Census in the Department of Commerce. It comes out annually and is available to anyone via the U.S. Government Printing Office. I doubt that anyone in Hollywood ever read it, but from somewhere, the idea of males between the ages of 18 to 34 keeps coming up. Supposedly, that is the number-one demographic movie audience, the one that screenwriters should strive to please as their core audience.

Skip's Tips

One script element that *must* be present in an adventure is the character arc. While fighting a villain equal in power to his own, the hero changes inside while changing the world outside. This transformation of inner nature during the story is his character arc. The villain, on the other hand, does not change and, by keeping static, remains a villain.

That could be true, if the amount of money that every Adam Sandler movie makes is any indication. You could research the demographics of the American population online, at www.census.gov if you want. I clicked "Projections" under "People" and found some interesting things, including a pyramid graph showing the number of males by age group, in five-year segments. Interestingly enough, there are more men between the ages of 40 and 44 than any other male group. But maybe they don't see as many movies.

Let's think about it. In the United States, young men become adults in the eyes of the law at age 18. At 18, U.S. citizens can vote. In some states, they can drink alcoholic beverages. By the time they're 34, these males are usually married, have usually finished college, and have been earning a living (we hope) for a number of years. If they are not yet married, their families are worried about them because where's that next generation coming from? And best of all, they have the most disposable income!

Movies are where young men most often take their dates. If they're traveling in packs, they might even go to the movies (even though some of them might feel funny sitting right next to each other). Thus, the magic age group of moviegoers that you hear about in Hollywood over and over is 18 to 34. That continues with new media. When I created an original animated cartoon series for the Web, the core demographic target was males 18 to 34. What do males 18 to 34 most have in common? Ummm ... testosterone? That'll do. Now let's take the top 10 grossing movies of all time. See if you think they are the kind of movies that males 18 to 34 would love.

1. *Titanic*
2. *Star Wars*
3. *Star Wars: The Phantom Menace*
4. *E.T., the Extra-Terrestrial*
5. *Jurassic Park*
6. *Forrest Gump*
7. *The Lion King*
8. *Return of the Jedi*
9. *Independence Day*
10. *The Sixth Sense*

I'd say *Titanic* easily qualifies as a "date movie," but I also know that my elementary school-age daughter insisted on seeing it several times, and it was the same with her friends.

The two *Star Wars* movies, *E.T.*, and *Jurassic Park*, also seem to me to have more appeal for children and families. Hmmm ....

Hollywood Heat

When producer Jennie Lew Tugend read *Free Willy*, she was crying as she read the last page. Tugend had a long and successful track record at Warner Brothers at the time, having worked with director/producer Richard Donner on all the muy macho *Lethal Weapon* movies, among other things. When she presented the script to executives at the studio, they wanted a part written in for a macho male star such as, oh, Mel Gibson. She argued, "Guys! You don't understand. The whale is the star!" Eventually, Tugend got her way, and three *Free Willy* movies and hundreds of millions of dollars in revenues later, she's still smiling.

The same thing goes for every other movie in the top 10, except the Baby Boomers favorite *Forrest Gump* and *The Sixth Sense*.

Gee whiz, what's wrong here?

I'll tell you what's wrong later in the book, but you need to know this: The "conventional wisdom" of Hollywood is that males ages 18 to 34 are the core moviegoers. Keep that in mind when you're picking out a story for your next screenplay that you hope will thrill a development executive, who will recommend it to his boss the producer to buy. In case I didn't mention it, the majority of the development executives I've met are males. Aged 18 to 34.

The Least You Need to Know

➤ A story in your local newspaper, if well-scripted and filmed, might make a movie good enough to earn Oscar attention.

➤ Recycling old movies into modern scripts is best left to established producers, but sometimes you can get lucky.

➤ The basic plot of a classic movie can easily be adapted to a different time or setting to form a new screenplay.

➤ Before writing someone else's true story, see a lawyer.

➤ The right kind of heroic character could turn into a franchise, resulting in dozens of movies and TV series.

➤ Males aged 18 to 34 are considered to be the primary moviegoing audience. Whether or not they really are, male movie development executives *do* fit that demographic.

Chapter 7

Movies Are Not Books or Plays

In This Chapter

➤ Screenplays are not stage plays

➤ Book are more flexible than scripts

➤ Television and movie scripts are different

➤ Screenwriting points to remember

A sculptor I know, Chuck Johanasen, often raved about *The Natural Way to Draw,* by Nicolaides. I read it because I knew Robert Redford was a talented artist who painted in Europe before coming home to Hollywood. Redford sketched out scenes before directing people. I thought some day I'd like to be able to do that, too, so I read through Nicolaides' book and discovered he insisted you practice drawing six hours a day, until technique becomes effortless. I got the point. With any art, you have to learn the basics of the form, or you will always be handicapped.

Beginning screenwriters need to read scripts, particularly those of recent movies. You can download scripts at these sites:

➤ screentalk.org/moviescripts.htm

➤ simplyscripts.com

➤ www.dailyscript.com

➤ www.script-o-rama.com

If you live in southern California, it's easy to get copies of TV show and feature film scripts at a number of stores. Newmarket Press has a Shooting Script Series that includes supplementary notes, still photos, and credits of scripts from recent movies such as *American Beauty, Magnolia, Man on the Moon,* and *Snow Falling on Cedars.* The first one is *The Shawshank Redemption,* written by Frank Darabont from a story by Stephen King.

Skip's Tips

Busy producers send projects "out for coverage," meaning someone they trust does the initial reading. The reader provides a synopsis of the story, along with a "pass," "consider," or "recommend." A "recommend" is rare. The reader's job could be on the line if they recommend and the movie flops.

Hollywood Heat

Real heat! Recently, Hollywood movie stars have taken off for and taken it off on the London stage. When Nicole Kidman did *The Blue Room* in London, performances were sold out because she appeared *au naturel*. More recently, sultry Kathleen Turner wowed audiences with an in-the-buff exhibition as Mrs. Robinson in a stage version of *The Graduate*.

We'll get into formats later, but keep this in mind: The script that you want to submit for consideration will not be a shooting script. A shooting script is a specially formatted script with numbered scenes and is not the "master scene" script that you will write. Scripts written by those who also direct the film, however, can look very different than a normal script. For example, John Milius's *The Wind and the Lion* (1975) has the scene descriptions in *past* tense, like a novel, rather than standard present tense.

Why You Don't Write a Screenplay Like a Stage Play

Hollywood owes a great debt to Broadway. Unique connections still exist between playwriting and screenwriting, with a number of notable playwrights making a mark in Hollywood in recent years. If you attempt to write a screenplay like a stage play, however, you should never expect to quit your day job.

In the theater, the playwright is god. The words are performed as written. Changes in the script are made only in the presence of the playwright, with the permission of the playwright, or *by* the playwright, who also has final say on casting. Changes are rarely made after the play has opened, with the exception of preview performances in some place other than New York (and, these days, in London, where New York stage hits increasingly originate).

In moviemaking, the prevailing rule is that the film director is god, the *auteur* of the movie. Often enough, if the screenwriter and the director are still speaking by the time the film wraps, chances are the screenwriter is also producing the picture. Catch the difference? Writer for the stage = god. Writer for Hollywood = not even a demigod. Not terribly encouraging, is it?

And now to format. Unless you're one of those exceedingly talented souls who can capture people's attention whether you write on napkins or fine stationery, you must learn the proper format of screenplays. Don't turn in a stage play expecting the reader to transpose it in the mind to "see" the movie version. There are simply too many properly formatted scripts submitted each day.

Below you will find a short example of the difference in an opening of a script, both in stage version and screenplay. This script started as my stage play *Fourth World*. Its premise is that a true love may happen when you least expect it.

After writing the play, I submitted it to national competitions. The play was a finalist in two and a semifinalist two others. People who read it, however, kept telling me that it would be better as a movie. So, after two people in one week said it should be a movie, I wrote the screenplay, which I titled *Walking After Midnight* (inspired by the great country music hit). The great actor Ben Johnson wanted to play one of the main roles and was telling other top actors about it before he died. Later, a neophyte producer optioned the screenplay for a sizable sum, but then the producer had family troubles and abandoned the project. So that's why you've never heard of the play or movie.

Here's how my play opened. Note the format, which is the standard recommended by the Dramatists Guild of America. If you are not familiar with it, the "AT RISE" means "at the curtain rise":

Skip's Tips

If you're about to write a screenplay that you hope to film as a low-budget or microbudget independent film, do yourself a favor and write the play first. It's easy to find actors to do readings with you, and if you stage it, you might work out things that you wouldn't think of when writing the script.

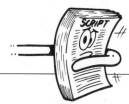

It's Not for Us

Checkov's rule that objects on a stage must perform a function does not always hold true in a screenplay. Unless a specific object will be used, you need to only roughly describe the environment in a screenplay, such as "A family room like we see in *The Simpsons*."

<u>ACT I</u>

<u>SETTING:</u> We are in a small diner just outside Gallup, New Mexico. The counter features stools with red vinyl seats. Stage right are two booths with Formica table tops and overstuffed red vinyl seats. This place saw its best day 30 years ago, but it is well kept, clean, and functional, a sparse statement of the desert Southwest.

A clock on the wall has simple, big hands. It reads 12:30. Between the booths and to the left of the counter is a door with a "RESTROOMS" sign. A window in the wall features an order ticket carousel, with the kitchen beyond.

The entrance to the diner is stage left. A bell on the door jingles when someone enters. An ancient coat rack stands next to the counter, near the door. On a back shelf, behind the counter, is a half-empty display of handmade turquoise and silver Indian jewelry. To the side of the jewelry is a tiny crystal unicorn.

The diner has the necessary accouterments: a malt and shake mixer, glasses, menus, a John Deere tractor calendar behind the counter, and a pay phone near the door leading to the restrooms, where the counter joins the wall. Sometimes people sit at the counter and talk on the pay phone. High on the back wall are two fairly modern-looking speakers that serve both the radio and the old Wurlitzer jukebox positioned in a corner.

<u>AT RISE:</u> There is no music. Sitting in a booth, drinking a cup of coffee, is an older African-American man, JAKE PARSONS. Jake is trying to read a newspaper.

Behind the counter is MIRABELLE FLOWERS, known to all her friends and most of her customers as "MIRA." She inherited the diner from her mother and is working the graveyard shift while trying to figure out her life. Tonight is Mira's 30th birthday. She may not look 30, but she's feeling it.

Using the mirror in her compact, Mira puts on lipstick, humming along to herself. She takes one final look, smacks her lips loudly and faces Jake, who grins a drunken grin.

                    MIRA

          (Hopeful)

How do I look, Jake?

                    JAKE

          (Slowly, kind of drunk)

Not bad, for a woman turnin' 30.

                    MIRA

Jake, it's never hard to find an asshole with an opinion.

                    JAKE

Don't start with me, Mirabelle. You know the spiritual turmoil I'm goin' through.

Imagine that the preceding was being seen by a theater audience. How much of the play would they see? They wouldn't dwell on the meticulous detail. All they would notice as the curtain opened would be the general layout of the stage and the two main characters. They would notice Mira with her compact and lipstick, and Jake with his coffee and newspaper. And they would listen to the spoken lines, all of which would take about 20 seconds.

Now let's look at the opening of the screenplay, which was rewritten from the opening scene of the play. Again, note the format and see if you can guess how much time elapses.

It's Not for Us

Cut the "CUT TO." In some books on screenwriting, you will be advised to insert "CUT TO:" on the right side of the page at the end of a scene, signifying a switch in location. The majority of people who make movies no longer see a need for it. So cut it out.

FADE IN:

EXT. DINER - NIGHT

MUSIC OVER, on a lonely New Mexico highway. There's a light wind kicking up dust and a piece of paper. To Patsy Cline's "Walking After Midnight," the paper dances in the air toward a small diner.

     PATSY CLINE (V.O., singing)
     I go out walking, after midnight
     Out in the moonlight
     Just like we used to do
     I'm always walking, after midnight
     Searching for you …

```
INT. DINER - NIGHT

CAMERA PANS ACROSS a place which saw its best days 30 years ago,
but is a clean, sparse statement of the desert Southwest. An an-
cient coat rack is near the door. The counter stools have red
vinyl seats, and booths with matching benches and Formica table
tops are against a wall. A clock reads 12:01. An opening in the
wall behind the counter features an order ticket carousel with no
orders. On a back shelf is a half-empty display of turquoise and
silver Indian jewelry. Near the jewelry is a tiny crystal unicorn.
There's a John Deere tractor calendar on the wall, a pay phone
near the restrooms door. High on the back wall are two speakers
that serve the radio and the old Wurlitzer jukebox.

Sitting in a booth, holding a cup of coffee, is an old black man,
JAKE PARSONS, eyes closed, HUMMING ALONG.

ON THE DOOR as the bell JINGLES and we see the diner owner,
MIRABELLE FLOWERS, known to friends and customers as "MIRA." She
leans against the doorjamb, standing neither in nor out, looking
outside. When the piece of paper floats by, Mira grabs it.

INSERT on fortune from a fortune cookie.

                    MIRA (O.S., reading)
            "You have a deep inner beauty."

                      ON MIRA

                    MIRA (cont.)

        You believe in fortunes, Jake?

                       JAKE
                    (kind of drunk)
            Don't know, Mira. Never had one.
```

How much time did you guesstimate? Two minutes? Roughly, a general rule of screenplays is one minute per page.

If you have any trouble following any of the camera moves above, I'll explain them. An "INSERT" is a close-up of something that a character is looking at; in this case, a fortune cookie fortune. Because you can't count on a viewer being able to read written things on a screen, we have our female lead, Mira, read what it says. "CAMERA PANS ACROSS" means that the camera starts in one place and then slowly moves to the left or right so that the viewer can see the things described. "ON MIRA" merely means that the camera is now tighter on Mira in the scene than it was when we first saw her. I could have written "RESUME SCENE" because a potential director might think I'm writing camera direction. After all, I'm not the author, am I? I might have also left out the "CAMERA PANS ACROSS," but I felt that it was important.

"O.S." means offscreen. We don't see Mira on the screen as she reads the fortune, but she is present in the scene. If she were not present in the scene and was describing what we were seeing onscreen (as in the opening of To Kill a Mockingbird, which is narrated by the character Scout), I would have used the term "V.O.," for "voice over," but then the composition of the scene would have been much different. "(cont.)" means "continued" and is used to show that no one else speaks between the cut from the insert of the fortune to resuming the scene with Mira and Jake.

Although theater patrons would not notice much that is described on the page, moviegoer *will* see most of what is written on the screenplay page, with the exception of song lyrics. I added those in case the reader of my screenplay was unfamiliar with the song and would not get the intended mood. I ended the quote from the song on "Searching for you" because it's relevant to the plot.

Compare stage plays that have been made into films to screenplays of the movies. For example, David Mamet's *Glengarry Ross,* a play about New York real estate salesmen, was a hit on Broadway. Mamet wrote both the play and the screenplay. With most successful stage plays that have been made into movies, the playwright usually writes the screenplay alone or participates in its writing. As I was saying earlier, in the theater, the playwright is god, a sentiment that is respected even in Hollywood.

What a Book Can Do That a Movie Cannot

Great novels are movies on paper. By triggering mental pictures in our minds, they stimulate senses that a film may not. We can taste the chocolate, smell the frangipani, feel the delicate warmth of an aroused sexual partner, and be privy to something difficult to portray onscreen. Namely, a character's thoughts.

Skip's Tips

Just as some directors believe that they are responsible for all aspects of a film, actors and actresses like to think of themselves and their characters in the highest regard. When describing the male or female lead, go for the ego. Use descriptions such as "the lusciously beautiful MIRABELLE FLOWERS."

It's Not for Us

Don't cheat a script. Some screenplay formatting programs offer you the option of "cheating" a script, or squeezing the space between lines and letters so that, for example, what should be a 130-page screenplay looks like 120. Don't do it, because it breeds distrust. They'll find out sooner or later.

I remember seeing the promotional spots for the TV series *Ally McBeal*. When a man Ally admired revealed he was spoken for, arrows thudded into her chest. Her thoughts were literalized in a very clever way, a difficult thing for a screenwriter to do. Even an adequate novelist could simply describe how she felt.

Several years ago, I remember a top agent being all a-twitter about *The Blue Train,* a novel by Richard Manton. According to her, "everyone" in Hollywood wanted to make a movie from this story of eroticism in perversely luxurious train cars where beautiful young women are willing and unwilling prisoners. Trouble was, no one could figure out how to convert the novel into a good screenplay. I haven't seen the movie; I suppose no one ever figured it out.

The same fate was suffered by *I, Robot,* the science-fiction classic by Isaac Asimov about robot behavior. Even though Asimov is a master of science fiction and the genre remains highly popular, the book was very mental. For example, how do you show a robot reading a human mind in an entertaining fashion?

Hollywood Heat

In Hollywood, the first "gatekeeper" is a reader, more formally known as a "story analyst." Readers once had their own union, established in 1954. The International Alliance of Theatrical Stage Employees (IATSE) Story Analysts Local 854 had 180 members on May 1, 2000, when they merged into IATSE Editors Local 700. Local 700 was not for print editors. Formed in September 1998, when members of Editors Local 776 in Los Angeles and Editors Local 771 in New York merged to form a joint local, its editors were film editors, sound editors, music editors, their assistants, and other postproduction workers.

Thought-heavy books can be filmatically problematic, but books dealing with mental patients often make compelling films. That's because we see outward behavior, not what goes on inside heads. A great recent example is *Girl, Interrupted* (1999) from the book of essays by Susanna Kaysen about her own 18-month stay at a mental hospital in 1967. The movie is the latest in a long heritage of films set in mental hospitals. My personal favorite is *One Flew over the Cuckoo's Nest* (1975), from the book by Ken Kesey, which is now one of Penguin's "Great Books of the 20th Century." While Kaysen's book was about her own stay at a mental hospital, Kesey derived his novel from his experiences on staff at an institution in San Jose, California. The film was the first since Frank Capra's *It Happened One Night* (1934) to win the five top Oscars: Best Picture, Best Director, Best Actor, Best Actress, and Best Screenplay (Bo Goldman and Lawrence Hauben).

I hope these examples give you some idea of why some great books are made into films and some are not. Characters in novels are not limited. There is no consideration of cost or difficulty in staging the scenes described. A whole chapter can dwell on a character's thought processes and hold our attention, if the writer is deft enough, craft-wise. But try showing those chapter-long thought processes on film, and it becomes difficult.

As you begin to outline a big story, you should ask yourself whether you want any of the principal characters to do a lot of important thinking on the page. If you do, you have a novel.

The Differences in Television and Movie Scripts

Unless you are an established screenwriter, it is difficult to sell a Movie of the Week script that will air on a major network. It's easier than it used to be to get a movie on television, though, because of the proliferation of cable. When a cable channel has been profitable for a while, it starts making its own movies. MTV is in the movie business now, as is VH-1, the History Channel, the Science Fiction Channel, and many others. If you write for kids, The Disney Channel is great. I know a previously unproduced writer living in New England whose manager arranged a script sale to the Disney Channel, and the manager doesn't even live in the Los Angeles area. That's television today.

I often hear from beginning screenwriters who ask me how the structure of television movies differs from features. If you don't live in southern California or have a good, established agent here, it's better to concentrate on writing the best script possible, without trying to tailor it to meet what you think are the needs of any given network. Although there are formatting differences, movies are movies. Films made for American TV (movies, not miniseries) are generally filmed for $3 million or less. By its nature, this limits the amount and types of locations, special effects, costumes, and other things.

Skip's Tips

Don't confuse a "log line" with a "tag line." The former is a *TV Guide* description of a screenplay, a one- or two-sentence summary. Tag lines are advertising "teasers" often seen on movie posters. The tag line for *Girl, Interrupted* listed on the Internet Movie Database (www.imdb.com) is: "Sometimes the only way to stay sane is to go a little crazy."

Script Notes

You might hear about **TV queue,** referring to actors so popular TV audiences would form a queue (line) to see them. If an actor with sufficient queue wants to do a project, the network may green-light it. Networks also keep lists of "approved" writers. Neither type of list is supposed to exist, yet they do.

TV movies also have a seven-act structure instead of the normal three-act structure, but that is easily explained. How often do commercials air during a two-hour TV movie, leaving out the commercials before the movie begins and after it concludes? Let's say that we see a commercial break every 15 minutes.

Did you count seven breaks? Hey, you're a genius! You can write for Hollywood! And after you've had a movie made, you're much more likely to be acceptable as a writer for a network movie.

You can find TV movie scripts in the same places that you find feature movie scripts, except they're not as much in demand. Why? Well, how many TV movies can you name, compared to features? And if a TV movie budget rarely goes over $3 million, with the writer getting 5 percent of the production budget, that's only $60,000. A studio feature writer generally makes a lot more money.

Hollywood Heat

As this book is written, the production of the feature version of the *Charlie's Angels* TV series is plagued with rumors of problems. Have there really been 15 screenwriters? (Could it be another *Gone with the Wind?* Just kidding.) Why do they make these remakes? Familiarity and numbers. The feature of *The Brady Bunch* cost only about $12 million to make and produced a nice profit. It required less advertising because fans of the TV series already knew what it was about.

Elements to Remember When Writing a Movie

Let's review. If you want to tell a story about deep philosophical discussions between friends, in a confined space with two main characters, would you write a stage play or a movie?

A movie. Specifically, the Louis Malle–directed *My Dinner with Andre* (1981), written by Andre Gregory and Wallace Shawn, who play themselves discussing life and living over dinner. The movie still plays on cable and cost next to nothing to make. Because the late director was known for hit films such as *Atlantic City* (1980) and *Pretty Baby* (1978), his participation in the project encouraged low-budget and microbudget moviemakers worldwide.

Now let's say something is written that is an examination of the viewpoints of four different people involved in an incident, their reflections and perceptions. Mental.

Ah, a book! Let me give you another clue. The incident is a rape and murder in which all four were involved. It must be a play! No, it's the classic *Rashomon* (1950). With writing credits to Ryunosuke Akutagawa (the stories *Rashomon* and *In a Grove*), Shinobu Hashimoto, and the director, Akira Kurosawa, this film about different viewpoints of people involved in the very same incident was an international hit.

As you may have noticed, neither of the directors I just mentioned were native Americans. Malle was from France, and Kurosawa was the pride of Japanese cinema. Filmmakers in other countries often have very different attitudes toward what makes an interesting film.

What elements should you remember when writing a movie? I can't tell you because I don't know what you like. That's the main secret. You should write something that you would dearly love to see onscreen. I've heard that from famous filmmakers time after time. When they reach a point where they can make their choice of scripts, they film the ones that they want to see or the ones they think they can make better than anyone else can, as Nora Ephron did with *Michael* in 1996 (five writers, including sister Delia).

If you decide that your story idea should definitely be a screenplay, before you commit yourself to weeks, months, or years perfecting it on paper, first ask yourself this question:

> Do I *really* want to see this movie?

The Least You Need to Know

➤ It is essential that you perfect the basics of any art before you attempt to deviate from established norms, but breaking the rules could make you famous.

➤ For beginning screenwriters, it is wise to read as many scripts as possible, particularly scripts of recent movies.

➤ Writers for the stage are treated like gods; writers for Hollywood are often treated like hell.

➤ Stage plays and screenplays have distinctly different formats and approaches to dialogue; if you like long, eloquent speeches, you're probably better off as a playwright, or a politician.

➤ If you want to spend much time revealing a character's thoughts, you're better off writing a novel.

➤ The format of TV movie scripts and feature films is not that dissimilar, but it's generally very difficult as a first-timer to make a TV movie sale.

Chapter 8

What Your Audience Really Wants to See

In This Chapter

➤ What sex and violence really mean

➤ Escape from reality

➤ Genre success

➤ Writing for the world

➤ The kids have it

Writers for television sooner or later realize that certain types of programs repeatedly get on the air. One-hour cop shows and one-hour medical dramas will most likely be with us, for the foreseeable future. It's pretty much the same year after year. Family comedies—even if the "family" is a group of friends who hang together in a coffee shop—were a staple of early television and still work today. But how about features?

As a screenwriter, you should basically write a story that *you* want to see onscreen. Nevertheless, to remain ignorant of established genres, box office successes, and market preferences is screenwriting suicide. Do yourself a favor and study what has done well, with an eye toward what may remain popular in the future. When you've mastered the basics, it's easier to innovate.

Hollywood Heat

Here's the Billion Dollar Club of box office stars from 1996 to date (data from IMDb.com and ShowBizData.com): (1) Will Smith—*Enemy of the State, Independence Day, Men in Black, Wild Wild West*—$1.86 billion; (2) Bruce Willis—*Armageddon, The Fifth Element, The Sixth Sense*—$1.48 billion; (3) Tom Hanks—*The Green Mile, Saving Private Ryan, Toy Story 2, You've Got Mail*—$1.46 billion; (4) Nicolas Cage—*City of Angels, Con Air, Face/Off, The Rock*—$1.11 billion; (5) Julia Roberts—*Erin Brockovich, My Best Friend's Wedding, Notting Hill, Runaway Bride*—$1.1 billion. (All movies are not listed; figures given are of the date of this writing.)

There will always be artists and intellectuals in any art form. They'll whine about commercialism and bemoan the low tastes of the masses. History has a keener eye. Often enough, some of the most popular works of entertainment manage to become classics. The most successful screenplays and films remind me of Mark Twain's comparison of his writing to more literary works. The others were like fine wine, he said, while his books were like water—and a lot more people drank water. They still do.

Sex and Violence Sell: What That Really Means

I never cared much for horror movies, but I once dated a girl who loved them. Which is why I found myself one day watching George C. Scott in *The Changeling* (1980). The movie was about a man who loses his family in a road accident and then moves into a haunted mansion and begins experiencing supernatural phenomena. Nancy, the girl I was dating, was a beautiful dancer, so I didn't mind indulging her movie preferences. I'm glad I did, because I noticed something that day that I'd never before realized. Like me, Nancy lived in southern California, but unlike me, she was frustrated in her profession and was apathetic about chances for advancement. Being scared by horror movies made her feel better!

You don't have to be an intellectual to get scared. That day I saw why so many people like the horror genre. A lot of people lead humdrum lives. They work at jobs they don't like. They don't live in southern California, like I do, where seeing or meeting a Hollywood celebrity is not uncommon in certain geographical areas. The thrill of horror made them feel better.

For a long time, movie people had told me that "sex and violence sell." They never qualified it much, and I had trouble with the idea. Did I have to write bloodily violent films or push the bounds of sexual content in scripts to get noticed? Having grown up admiring Walt Disney movies and with Jimmy Stewart as my favorite movie star, I've felt that I would be betraying my heritage in writing overly salacious and grossly violent movies.

Don't get me wrong. I love Clint Eastwood films, particularly the Dirty Harry stories. I'm not a regular viewer of porno, but I've seen a few. I just wasn't inclined to write either type of material. So how did I use the "sex and violence sell" dictum?

That day with Nancy left me crawling with inspiration. I suddenly realized that my Hollywood mentors were talking about an *increased sense of living* comparable to the increased blood flow necessary for sex. Your heart races, your senses are enhanced, and you breathe more deeply. Hopefully, when it's over, you're left with a memorable emotional experience, and you simply feel more alive. Has anything similar ever happened to you, watching a movie?

Now let's look at violence. Have you ever been in a fight or been attacked? Your heart races, your senses are enhanced, and you breathe more deeply. When it's over, you're left with a memorable emotional experience, whether it's positive or negative.

In terms of Hollywood movies, sex and violence can be metaphorical. What is sex but attraction and interaction between potential sexual partners? What is violence but conflict between two opposing forces? You could even say that each can be a dance of life or death, and there are degrees to each. On a scale from 1 to 10, an interested flash in a girl's eye might be a 1, with an actual sexual act between her and the object of the flash a 10. Think of the first time Michael Douglas sees Sharon Stone in *Basic Instinct* (1992), then compare it with their last scene together. That's a highly charged sexual arc. But that's a pretty graphically sexual film, isn't it?

Skip's Tips

Ah, the "sexy" opening. Starting a script with a sexual or violent scene will likely grab a reader's attention and get them past the first few pages, but you should ask yourself two questions: First, is this incident a major turning point in your main character's life? Second, does it immediately propel your main character into the heart of the story?

It's Not for Us

Thinking that I was very clever, I once began a feature script with a weightless sex scene in space. Six months later, I discovered that someone had already filmed one—in a porno movie. Never write a scene merely for the "wow" factor. Besides, if it doesn't fit the flow of the story, you may jar the reader or viewer out of getting through your script.

So let's knock it down a number of degrees and use the example of *Gone with the Wind* (1939), for a long time the all-time box office champion. There was never a more sexually charged relationship onscreen than that of Rhett Butler (Clark Gable) and Scarlett O'Hara (Vivien Leigh). We never see them naked, together or alone, but a lot of people prefer that movie over *Basic Instinct*.

In any number of Clint Eastwood films, someone is brutally victimized by a very evil person or a pack of evil people. Eastwood's character suffers through many travails to finally wreak even greater revenge on the bad guys at the end of the film.

That's graphic violence, so how about a lesser arc of violence? Let's take the suffering of Gary Cooper's character in *High Noon* (1952). We don't see much graphic violence in that movie, but Cooper suffers wound after emotional wound as the townspeople cowardly refuse to help him defend the town against approaching thugs. And, at the end, just as in the much more violent Eastwood films, there is great relief as we experience a sense that rightness has prevailed and that justice has once again won out in our world. Don't take my word on this. See which movie you find more appealing, Eastwood's *Unforgiven* (1992) or *High Noon*.

Sex in Hollywood does not have to equal sweat and skin. Beautiful leading ladies and handsome leading men help us live vicariously and fulfill our fantasies. When movies are truly entertaining, they make us feel better, more alive. Similarly, bad guys who live by violence only respect a stronger force, in real life and in the movies. If you cannot combat them, an onscreen hero who smashes thugs into oblivion helps fulfill a desire for justice.

You don't have to write graphic sex and violence to sell. If a movie engages your intellect, makes your blood race, and leaves you feeling better or more thoughtful when it's over, you've done your job as a screenwriter. Sex and violence are simply terms describing normal human activity, and different people like varying degrees of each. The real test is whether the movie makes someone feel more alive. And here's one more tip—both words, sex and violence, denote *action*. In a business built around "moving pictures," they imply a connection and movement between opposites and an interesting story moving forward.

Skip's Tips

Most scripts begin with "FADE IN:" (note the colon). This means that a picture gradually appears from a black screen. Scripts end with the opposite, "FADE OUT." (note the period). Think of these editing actions in terms of being born and dying, with varying shades of sex and violence in between.

Helping Your Viewer Escape from Reality

I'd like you to do something different. If you are around a shopping mall with a multiplex movie theater, spend some time there, but don't watch a movie.

Sit outside and watch the people. Or try a video store. Go browse the hundreds of videos, but don't rent anything. Watch the other people who are renting. Don't discriminate by age. Watch the teenagers, the working adults, the parents with kids, the couples on a date, and the seniors, too. Try and figure out what they're spending their money on.

How good are you at reading people? Can you read faces? Do you know when someone is overworked? Can you tell when someone's eyes are sad, even though they're smiling? See if you notice a change in their demeanor, perhaps a quickening in their step, after their ticket is purchased or their video is selected.

If you live in a city where live theater, opera, or more expensive entertainment is available, take another trip. Watch the people outside the venue, and compare them to the people you saw at the movie theater and the video store.

Yes, you should do all of these. Now, let me guess. Except perhaps in dress, all the audiences discussed varied greatly in emotional levels, but you did often see a distinct lightening of manner when they made their selection or entered the theater.

It's Not for Us

In *Adventures in the Screen Trade: A Personal View of Hollywood and Screenwriting* (Warner Books, 1983), screenwriter William Goldman offered a single axiom about Hollywood: "Nobody knows anything." This gets misinterpreted to mean that you can break any rule at will. What Goldman really meant is that someone always comes along who successfully defies conventional film wisdom. But those mavericks know the rules they break. Learn the rules, and then amaze us.

Why do you suppose that is? I don't know about you, but for the time I'm watching a video, a movie, or a theatrical or musical performance, I forget about my cares and escape from reality.

That's the great thing about the movies—they provide this escape for anyone, anywhere, no matter what their social station or location. If you saw the delighted young Dalai Lama in *Seven Years in Tibet* (1997), you know what I mean. Even a spiritual leader needs relief from life. Long before that movie was made, Preston Sturges emphasized this very point in his *Sullivan's Travels* (1942), about a disheartened "fluff" movie director who thinks that his work is meaningless. Dressed as a hobo, he sets off to research a socially relevant movie called *O Brother, Where Art Thou?* and, through a series of circumstances, ends up on a criminal chain gang in the South, where life seems very bleak. Then, on a Saturday night, the hardened criminals are treated to a Hollywood movie, projected with rudimentary equipment. As he watches the delighted laughs of his fellow chain gang members, the director realizes the true service that he provides his fellow human beings by creating escapist entertainment. He realizes that, for a while, his movies help relieve a harsh reality. With that epiphany, the director turns his life around.

If you've never seen *Sullivan's Travels,* I highly recommend it. If your screenplay is made, you have no idea who will see it. It may be the Dalai Lama or a man on a chain gang. They both have their everyday burdens, and each equally welcomes the escape that a good movie provides. That starts with you, the screenwriter. For your script to be made (unless you film it yourself), you will have to please, at minimum, a producer, a director, and someone who finances the filming of your script. Just don't get lost in trying to be too "Hollywood" and writing for a sophisticated audience.

Remember the story about Shakespeare, who had to please the commoner "groundlings" as well as the royals in the balconies? Things haven't changed in 500 years. The ultimate recipient of your work may be a girl working for minimum wage at McDonald's, or the CEO of the worldwide corporation. For a little over an hour, maybe two or even more, you have a chance to be important in all sorts of lives and help each person gain relief from the rigors of existence. The words of screenwriters may someday live in the heavens, but not until they pass the high test of the common man.

Pick a Genre and Pick Success

In the first class on writing that I ever taught at the Extension Writer's Program at the University of California at Los Angeles (UCLA), I had my students go to a bookstore and report on all the categories they found. At first they thought it was dumb, but then I asked them where the manuscript they would work on in class would be filed. As the light dawned in their eyes, I explained that *when* (not if, when) they sold their work, the first thing they would be asked about was the genre of the piece.

Script Notes

Because of the dynamic nature of the World Wide Web, you can find more up-to-date information there than anywhere else, as long as you know where to look. For a very thorough listing of top movies by genre, do some browsing at us.imdb.com/Charts/. It's an education in itself on what has succeeded in Hollywood.

It's the same way with screenplays, and if you took that trip to the video store that I just mentioned, you probably noticed that, as in a bookstore, the titles are filed by category. Did you notice the size of each category? Were there more dramas or comedies? How many were classics, and how many were horror? What does that tell you? At the very least, it should give you a general idea about what has been popular in the past few years. Will those tastes continue? Generally, yes. Anomalies such as *The Blair Witch Project* come along, but there is no category for "Unexpected Success."

Many authors attempt to distill plot lines into repeating formulas. Eugene Polti's *Thirty-Six Dramatic Situations* is one of the oldest. Genres and subgenres are covered in Robert McKee's excellent *Story* (Regan Books, 1997), but not exactly in the type of classification that you see at a video store. In this book, I'd rather list genres as you would hear them mentioned by Hollywood development executives and producers, and also give you some indication of how popular they are currently. This is a primer, alphabetically listed shorthand, with examples from recent years. If you think I've left out any important genres, let me know.

➤ **Action.** This is most often a cross-genre description. A crime drama such as *The Untouchables* might be considered action by some, but epic historical dramas such as *Braveheart* or *Gladiator* are also action movies. In definite action movies, monumental forces clash in an almost continuous and unrelenting fashion. Examples are *Air Force One,* the *Die Hard* series, *Face/Off,* and the *Lethal Weapon* series. Action movies usually involve big stars.

➤ **Adventure.** Anyone who favors the Joseph Campbell myth structure is a fan of adventure movies. The main character almost always deals with some kind of new and amazing world. Any of the *Indiana Jones* movies fit this genre, which can also be referred to as epic or myth, due to the Campbell influence. Again, we're talking big stars.

➤ **Animation.** With the advent of computer animation with *Toy Story,* this genre is very sophisticated. Disney's *Dinosaur* in 2000 is an example. It's a hard genre to break into, but it's not impossible.

➤ **Comedy.** This is a very broad genre that in recent years has skewed toward the bizarre, with the successes of Jim Carrey, Adam Sandler, and the Farrelly Brothers (*There's Something About Mary*). A maxim in Hollywood is: Drama is easy, comedy is hard. If you have the talent to write broad comedy such as *Austin Powers* or family comedy like *Honey, I Shrunk the Kids,* go for it. You'll get rich.

Hollywood Heat

Jennie Lew Tugend had worked on a number of the *Lethal Weapon* films when she found *Free Willy.* The powers-that-be at Warner Brothers liked the script, but they suggested that it be rewritten to accommodate an action star such as Mel Gibson. In a desire to make "cutting edge" controversial material, many producers would have overlooked this family favorite, but Tugend insisted that the star was the whale and convinced Warner to fund the movie. The original cost $10 million to make, grossed $100 million, and was followed by two sequels. Not bad for an unknown cetacean.

It's Not for Us

If you find it hard to pin your script down to one genre, don't worry. Just don't use more than a couple genres to describe it, and use popular genres in the description, if possible. For example, a "mystery musical comedy" is certain to get your script tossed, unless you are an established writer/director.

Skip's Tips

In today's movie atmosphere, absolutely anything can be put on film. The gods of computer-generated images have deemed it so. The more special effects the better, as long as they're great effects such as those in *The Matrix*, not clunky effects such as those in *Battlefield Earth*. Let your imagination run wild on the page—thanks to computers, it's a great time to be a screenwriter.

➤ **Coming of age.** Also known as "rites of passage," this genre is a reflective drama requiring skillful and insightful writing. When it works, it works big, as in *Cider House Rules*. When it doesn't work, it is maudlin. If you aspire to win an Oscar, this could be your genre. Starting with *To Kill a Mockingbird* and moving through *The Graduate, The Last Picture Show, Saturday Night Fever, American Graffiti,* and *Forrest Gump,* this one's often a classic.

➤ **Crime/detective.** This once prolific genre has been largely hijacked by television. Crime features now are usually cross-genre thrillers, as in *L.A. Confidential,* or are mixed with love stories, as in *Ghost.* Many people list courtroom dramas as a separate genre, but to me it's all legal. One recently neglected subgenre is the "caper" film, but an upcoming remake of *Ocean's Eleven* with an all-star cast might change that. If you are clever enough to create great crime dramas, you should think about writing a book first—I guarantee that you'll make a lot more money that way.

➤ **Drama.** These days, this very broad category is generally used to refer to a story about some social issue or struggle, as in *Philadelphia* or *Schindler's List.* If you're intent on sending a message in a script, this is your genre. If you can do it without preaching, you might attract big stars because this type of film most often results in nominations come Oscar time.

➤ **Dramedy.** Rapidly becoming its own genre is this combination of drama and comedy in which serious issues are dealt with in a comedic fashion in various parts of the film. More often than not, the movie revolves around family or coming of age stories, as in *Dead Poet's Society* or *My Dog Skip.* Usually, a comedian who wants to prove serious acting ability stars, such as Robin Williams or his pal Billy Crystal.

➤ **Ensemble.** This type of drama is usually made by first-time or experienced directors who also write. Examples are *The Big Chill, Diner, Metropolitan, Parenthood,* and *Sex, Lies & Videotape.* The emphasis is on a central issue, not a central character. You must be able to write interesting dialogue to make this one work.

➤ **Fantasy.** This genre is generally reserved for young audiences and so has again been co-opted by children's television. When we do see fantasy features these days, they are usually animated. If you expect to sell one, it had better be *very* different, such as *Princess Mononoke* or *Who Killed Roger Rabbit?*

➤ **Film noir.** This stylized crime drama is great for launching a career or even *making* a career. The Coen Brothers broke in with *Blood Simple,* while *Chinatown* was considered for a long time to be the greatest script of the latter twentieth century. *L.A. Confidential* won an Academy Award. If the guy gets the girl, she comes with plenty of trouble, and he rapidly gets embroiled in some kind of conspiracy. Does that sound like you?

➤ **Horror.** This one seems easy, but you need a twist, such as *The Blair Witch Project* (promoted on the Internet in a way that made it initially seem like real people died on camera). If you are original, you'll get rich because horror movies can be made with unknowns, and a hit calls for sequel after sequel.

➤ **Independent.** Yes, it's a genre. If you don't understand it, just read up on the Sundance Film Festival or watch a lot of movies on The Sundance Channel on cable TV. These films, formerly known as "art films," involve quirky subjects and low budgets, and can be a fine way to launch a career. *Clerks* is a great example of this type of movie.

➤ **Musical.** Ye gads! When is the last time anyone made one that wasn't animated? When Broadway hits such as *Evita* appear onscreen with international superstars like Madonna and then *bomb*, Hollywood forgets musicals. This might mean that it's wide open for success.

➤ **Mystery.** It's sad to say, but this genre seems like a remnant of another age. Was *The Usual Suspects* a mystery, a crime drama, or a thriller? These days, mysteries mostly work on television (*Murder, She Wrote* and *Diagnosis, Murder*). If you aspire to make your own movie, however, mysteries are relatively inexpensive to shoot.

➤ **Outdoors/wildlife.** Most beginning screenwriters don't consider this genre, but a good script of this type is comparatively easy to sell. *Homeward Bound* and *Babe* are good examples. If you have one in which kids interact with animals, such as *Free Willy,* you usually can get it read, if it's any kind of script at all. This type of film is visually rich and usually inexpensive to make, and if the actors are unknowns, family audiences generally don't care.

➤ **Romance.** There aren't enough good romances around, so if you can write a good "date movie," you're in luck. Just don't flinch when someone calls it a "chick flick." Great recent examples are *As Good as It Gets, Pretty Woman,* and *Return to Me.*

➤ **Romantic comedy.** Also known as "romcom," this is a completely separate genre from comedy. Think Julia Roberts or Andie McDowell: *Four Weddings and a Funeral, Groundhog Day, My Best Friend's Wedding,* and *Notting Hill.* Awfully close to the romance genre, aren't they? Here's the catch: In the former, there's more drama than comedy. In the latter, it's reversed, and the way the couple fumbles toward their inevitable union is hilarious. To write either of these genres successfully, you'd better know women and relationships well, and also have a great sense of humor.

➤ **Sci-fi.** No one in Hollywood calls it science fiction, but that's what it is. This genre needs no explanation, and with computer-generated film technology and the megasuccess of movies such as *The Matrix,* there's no better genre, if you can make it work. Take a look at the top 10 moneymakers of all time, and you'll see a lot of sci-fi titles. If you want to write a blockbuster, this could be you.

➤ **Thriller.** Alfred Hitchcock virtually invented this genre. To master it, see all his films. Usually, the hero is an innocent and the enemy is seemingly unbeatable. *Silence of the Lambs* is a great example, as is *The Firm.* Authors of thrillers make big bucks, and movies of their novels draw big stars and big box office success.

It's Not for Us

Don't force trying to write for a certain genre just because you like it. Sometimes the proper genre finds you. Stephen King has had more books, stories, and scripts made into films than any other living writer, but the King of Horror started out wanting to be a great Western writer like Louis L'Amour!

➤ **War.** For some reason (looming mortality, perhaps) the Baby Boom generation has rediscovered the war movie. Unfortunately for fans of the genre, only *Saving Private Ryan* was much of a success. War movies are expensive, usually not good for beginner writers, and wide open to criticism, as with 2000's hit submarine movie *U-571.*

➤ **Western.** A long-time Hollywood staple, this genre has been mostly unsuccessful in recent years unless done by veterans such as Clint Eastwood. If you have some Western variation that we haven't seen before, you could have hit material, as Kevin Costner learned when he made *Dances with Wolves* and Tom Selleck proved when *Last Stand at Saber River* was Turner Network Television's top movie of 1997.

I've listed only fictional genres here. Documentaries are worthy of another book and generally are not as profitable. Whatever genre you pick, remember that people who are genre-savvy mix them in description all the time. For example, *Ace Ventura, Pet Detective* can be described as an action comedy mixed with outdoor/wildlife. I hope that you find a genre or two at which you excel.

Writing for the Worldwide Audience

To get an introduction to the tastes of audiences worldwide, remember this word—*action*. Wordy movies are generally not popular overseas. People understand moving characters; moving lips that don't speak your language are harder to understand. Roberto Begnini understood this well when he made *Life Is Beautiful* in his native Italian; Begnini's onscreen characterizations and pratfalls are right out of silent Buster Keaton films.

For more insight into non-American, international tastes, pay close attention to the yearly Golden Globe winners selected by the Hollywood Foreign Press Association. The HFPA is an association of journalists in southern California who write for foreign media. HFPA members tend to like rebels and those who challenge the societies in which they live, at least when they select the Best Screenplay. Winners in the last decade include *Shakespeare in Love, Good Will Hunting, The People vs. Larry Flynt, Pulp Fiction, Schindler's List, Thelma & Louise,* and *Dances with Wolves.*

Curiously, in previous decades the Golden Globe for Best Screenplay usually went to more traditional, emotional, even epic films—*Born On the Fourth of July* (1988); *The Last Emperor* (1986); *Amadeus* (1984); *Terms of Endearment* (1983); *Gandhi* (1982); *On Golden Pond* (1981); *Kramer vs. Kramer* (1979); and *The Goodbye Girl* (1977). At first glance, you might assume that tastes of the HFPA have simply changed. The truth, however, is that there have been many complaints in recent years, particularly in Europe, that American movies are adversely impacting foreign film culture.

A fledgling screenwriter is generally happy just to sell any script at all, and the tastes of worldwide audiences are often not a consideration. On the other hand, if you want to write for an international audience, think action, watch the Golden Globes, and pay attention to events at the annual Cannes Film Festival. And don't forget—a truly great story appeals to people across time and culture. Remember the earlier story about the international South African success, *The Gods Must Be Crazy?* It still applies.

Skip's Tips

In the United States, the paper standard is 8½ × 11 inches. That's not so in Europe and the United Kingdom, where measurements are mostly metric. If you are ever in contact with British writers trying to sell to Hollywood, you'll learn about the A4 paper they use. Don't be surprised when they ask you to help them acquire some three-hole punched 8½ × 11 sheets!

The Kids Have It: Write with Children in Mind and Win

While researching this book, I did a study on the top-grossing movies of all time and discovered something that amazed me. Rather than any particular genre being dominant, it seemed that the most money has been made in the movie business based around a kid factor. That has particularly been true in the past decade.

Hollywood Heat

The most successful cable television network is Nickelodeon, thanks to "Nick at Nite" reruns of Baby Boomers' favorite old shows and new animated programs such as *Rugrats*, which spawned two animated features. Nickelodeon wasn't the only studio or network scrambling to serve the animation boom. The amount of Hollywood animation was so enormous that it generated a foreign reaction against animation. What foreign exhibitors have been hungry for recently are live-action films and programming for younger viewers. Does this mean that we'll see a *Mary Poppins* remake with rap music, or simply more good shows and films with actual live people? Count on the latter and increased opportunities for screenwriters who write for kids.

The kids have it. Starting with a breakdown of the 250 top all-time box office leaders (using gross domestic box office only), I broke down successful elements of these films into some very interesting categories. I did not pay attention to the conventional wisdom that movies should generally be geared to the 18 to 34 male age group demographic, nor did I pay any attention to movie ratings (G, PG, PG-13, and so on). I listed the top 250 movies in categories that I developed (listed alphabetically, not by importance) as follows:

A	Action
CH	Childlike main character(s)/learning like a child
CA	College-age character(s)
E	Epic/grand in scope
GC	Group situation, comedy, or caper
K	Prominent kid character

KL	Kids love it
L	Love/matters of the heart
NH	Strong animal or nonhuman character
S/T	Suspense/thriller
T	Teen character(s)/coming of age
YP	Young professionals in lead roles

I found that the most important element, by far, of highly successful movies is a kid connection. Whether it is simply that "kids love it," that there is a childlike main character (which Tom Hanks has excelled at playing), or that it includes nonhuman characters that children love, real box office success more often than not derives from one or more elements in a film that all add up into *something that kids love*. Often these films are not those that you would suspect small children would love, such as *Titanic,* which my (then) six-year-old daughter wanted to see repeatedly because of the love story. Naturally, movies with a prominent kid character appeal to young children, but other successful films with a youth element reach viewers of an age much *less* than the conventional wisdom 18 to 34 demographic.

Having published a number of novels and nonfiction books for young adults (generally considered to be ages 12 to 18), I know that if you write a 12-year-old main character, that character will normally appeal most to kids who are two to three years younger. If you write high school kids in the lead (as I did with three "You Solve It Mystery" novels that were optioned for film), junior high students find them appealing. If movies have teen characters in the lead roles, that means they will not only appeal to teen moviegoers, but also strongly to kids as young as nine. Similarly, if movies have a young professional in the lead role, teens strongly identify with them. Again, this means that the appeal is much younger than 18 to 34. The same would hold true with the college-age category.

Script Notes

I have a 19-page breakdown on my notes about "kids love it," focusing on the primary quality(s) and secondary quality(s) of the top 250 movies of all time. If you would like a copy, e-mail me at skip_press@excite.com for details.

Six of these 12 categories listed relate to kids. Kids want to emulate the actions of older people with whom they can identify. With a little bit of child in all of us and the childhood years so formative in our minds, it is little wonder that a main character with childlike qualities is so popular. *Forrest Gump* is a good example. Of the top 12 movies of all time, all but 1 have the main quality of "kids love it." This means that a family can take the kids to see these movies, and these films get a lot of repeat business (kids like to see things over and over). Only *Forrest Gump* does not fit in, but the main character is very childlike. We first see him as a kid, and his visit with his own young son late in the film is perhaps the movie's most touching moment.

Out of the top 20 all-time films, only *Beverly Hills Cop* out of the top 20 domestic box office successes does not fit the "kids love it" category, although many would argue that the main character, Axel Foley (played by Eddie Murphy) is very childlike.

Thirty out of the top 50 all-time domestic box office successes have the predominant quality of "kids love it"—even movies such as *Austin Powers: The Spy Who Shagged Me*, which is not geared to appeal to them. Again, many of the films whose predominant quality is not "kids love it" might arguably fit because of their amazing action sequences (consider movies with Tom Cruise, for example). A number of movies also have a main character who acts like a child, such as Dustin Hoffman's role in *Tootsie*.

At the movies, the kids have it, and something tells me they'll keep it.

The Least You Need to Know

➤ "Sex and violence sells" is really about the manner in which movies provide the viewer with an increased sense of living.

➤ The screenwriter's number-one job is to write a movie that will, at least for a time, help the viewer escape everyday reality.

➤ Writers who do not fully understand movie genres are greatly handicapped and may overlook success opportunities.

➤ A truly great story with lots of action is guaranteed to appeal to movie audiences across time and culture.

➤ In recent years, movies about rebels who challenge the societies in which they live have been popular worldwide.

➤ The predominant element, by far, of the majority of highly successful movies can be simply qualified as "kids love it."

Chapter 9

Defining Your Movie

In This Chapter

➤ Premises first

➤ Messages are for e-mail

➤ Pre-script documents

➤ The movie's basic idea

➤ What a "log line" means

New screenwriters ask the same questions and inevitably get confused because the definitions and "rules" in the movie world change whimsically. There is no Hollywood dictionary that defines terms for everyone, and every screenwriting teacher tries to come up with something different to make his or her philosophy stand out. That's why, when someone produces a standard, logical observation that defines something about the business, it is adopted in choke-hold fashion. That's what happened with Syd Field's "paradigm" of screenplay structure after his book *Screenplay* burst upon the scene. Hollywood readers would check scripts to see if each act and plot point ended where Field said it should, and some development people actually rejected a script if it didn't match the Field schematic. The practice was maddening to writers.

As you think through the story line of a script, what page an act turns on should not be much of a consideration. You start with an idea, or maybe a dozen ideas, and then settle on one that you think is most viable. Then you determine what you're really trying to say, and you outline the scenes. And sometimes you throw it all away and start over. You really must be willing to do that. Now let's talk about how to shape a movie story.

Skip's Tips

It costs two people in my neighborhood $25 to go to a first-run movie theater and buy popcorn and sodas. Would you spend the $25 on your idea? Would the poster of your movie prompt you to commit the next hour or two of your life? When I'm selecting possible ideas, I pop the $25 question.

First, a Premise

The root definition of *premise* is "to place (or send) ahead." In *Webster's New Collegiate Dictionary,* one pertinent definition is "to set forth beforehand as an introduction or postulate." What's a *postulate?* The word comes from a very ancient root, *prcchati,* a word from perhaps the most ancient language of Earth, Sanskrit. It means, "he asks." A postulate is a question asked, a "what if?" You could also say it's a prayer (that your script will be bought!).

Here's another definition of premise: "to presuppose or imply as pre-existent." What would that mean in a screenplay story? It means that within our pages, we want to create a world that, even if it reflects a familiar reality, envelopes viewers so that they feel as if the world onscreen has always existed. They get to live in that world, experiencing a gamut of emotions and perhaps sights that they may never have a chance to know in real life.

Watching great films, we are in an elevated experience. You can walk the streets of Philadelphia pictured in *The Sixth Sense,* but if you were actually outside a location from that movie, would you have a tendency to try to see if you could "see dead people"? I would. I don't know how you feel about *Star Wars: Episode I—The Phantom Menace* as a movie, but if you're like me, the idea of living on a planet like Naboo was a thrilling idea.

Hollywood Heat

Writers and writing teachers borrow from each other all the time—and sometimes forget that they've borrowed. That might have happened with Irwin R. Blacker when he wrote *The Elements of Screenwriting: A Guide for Film and Television Writing* (Macmillan, 1986). In Chapter 2, he defines *premise* as the basis of the conflict and then gives examples of *King Lear* and *Macbeth* that are almost word for word the premises given by Lajos Egri in *The Art of Dramatic Writing.* I advise writers to read all these books—you may get some duplication, but everyone comes up with something new. And some things are just plain true for everyone.

When you're imagining a good movie, you're creating a world that we should feel has always been there, as if it exists in its own separate universe. That's particularly true in science-fiction films such as *Blade Runner, The Fifth Element,* or *The Matrix.*

It's a daunting task to create a world. According to the Bible, it took God six days to accomplish the task, and then He rested. If you spend a week thinking about the premise of your movie, you're right on schedule. Unless you're God, the script takes longer.

In *The Art of Dramatic Writing,* Lajos Egri (writing mostly about playwriting) says there is a premise for every life, every second of every day. To him, a premise is a basis of argument, something proposed that will lead to a logical conclusion. A number of writers I know object to Egri's proposition because they think he is telling the writer to start with a message and then make the story prove it. I wonder if they've read the entire book.

Skip's Tips

Pitching a screenplay or screenplay idea goes on in Hollywood all the time. Proven screenwriters (those with a track record or whose writing is respected by readers and producers) are frequently invited to "come in and pitch." That's when you need to be able to easily describe what your movie is about.

Shortly after Egri gives his definition, he lists other writers who talk about things such as theme, root idea, goal, subject, thesis, and other things. All of them, Egri says, are talking about the premise.

Let's examine this premise business with some movies that you may have seen. Adam Sandler's *Happy Gilmore,* perhaps? *What if* a hockey player took up professional golf? Don't you instantly see some of the scenes, such as Sandler putting with a hockey stick, or the way he stepped up and slammed the club into the teed-up ball, using a hockey stroke? Or the fight on the golf course? We instantly have what Lajos Egri called the "unity of opposites"—namely, the rowdiness and raw power of hockey pitted against the gentility and precision of professional golf. Conflict is inevitable on many levels. And that's why *Happy Gilmore* was a good idea and a very funny movie. It started with a great premise.

A great premise immediately sets up the conflict to come. Does it apply in all genres? Well, let's see. In the romantic comedy *Return to Me,* David Duchovny's character loses his wife in a car accident, only to unknowingly fall in love a year later with a beautiful young woman (played by Minnie Driver) who was the recipient of his wife's donor heart. Even if you haven't seen the film, I'm sure you can see what might happen when Duchovny found out the truth, and imagine Minnie Driver's reactions as well.

What about *Men in Black?* How about this: "What if the outrageous tabloid stories were true, and there have been aliens living on Earth for decades, with a special government force that monitors them, and a new alien arrives that threatens the fate of the entire galaxy?" Does that premise work for you?

Later in this book, we'll discuss pitching your screenplay to producers and writing effective query letters. If you start out with a premise like I've described here, it will be much easier to tell people what your movie is about, and I think you'll find that your screenplay will be easier to write.

Both Lajos Egri and Irwin R. Blacker define the premise of Shakespeare's *The Tragedy of King Lear* as "Blind trust leads to destruction." If you don't know the story, it's about a monarch who turns everything over to his three daughters, with disastrous results. Let's describe it this way: "What if an angry patriarch turns over the family farm to his three daughters and their husbands, prompting the family's dark past to boil over?"

Family farm? A king on a farm? Sort of. I just described the plot of *A Thousand Acres* (1997), starring Michelle Pfeiffer, Jessica Lange, and Jennifer Jason Leigh as the Cook sisters, and Jason Robards as their father, Larry Cook. It's a tragedy, and it's also *King Lear* set on a farm in Iowa. If you were searching for screenplay ideas, you could say, "What if *King Lear* took place on a farm?" After that, it's merely adaptation from Shakespeare. You'd also have a pitch for a movie, provided that the person listening knew *King Lear*. But if you tried to sell someone on "Blind trust leads to destruction." you would hear, "Okay, so what's the story?"

I prefer the "What if?" approach. Everyone understands that. If you want to look deeper into your story, you might find a *theme*. That isn't the same as a premise, really, unless you're talking about an Egri premise. You can use a theme as a guidepost or a landmark as you write your story. Think of Indiana Jones chopping through a jungle with a machete to get to the top of a mountain always visible above the jungle canopy. There's a cave in the mountain full of golden treasure. Let's say that his theme is "Persistence on a straight path leads to wealth." He can always look up and see whether he's getting closer. Then a new character pops up, a beautiful temptress who beckons him to a river barge. If he strays to one side, pursuing some theme such as "Beauty has its own reward," he'll never reach that cave, will he? He has to stick to his original theme to do that.

You could define the theme of *Men in Black* as "Alien contact does not come without a price." The alien handlers, the Men in Black, must have all vestiges of their former lives erased when they begin their career. If they choose to give up their job, as Tommy Lee Jones' character does at the end of the movie, all memory of the job is removed from their memory. Jones goes back to the woman he longs for, sacrificing all memory of his exciting career. The *Men in Black* theme I just described would most likely prove true in real life, just as *King Lear*'s blind trust would usually lead to destruction in real life. But my *Men in Black* theme could also apply to *Close Encounters of the Third Kind* or *E.T.* A premise that is actually a theme is problematic. It does not define the story well enough, and you may find yourself trying to prove your point throughout the writing of the script. Then, instead of discovering your story as you write, you're a slave to a theme.

"What if?" does define the story and is true to the original "he asks" definition of the root word of *premise* itself. When you come up with the right "What if?" question, it can have magical results. When a Hollywood executive, who is usually knowledgeable of movies and TV shows of at least the last five years, hears the right "What if?" the reaction is predictable. "Wow!" this executive will say, with his face lit up. "No one's ever done *that* before!" (Take my word for it, Hollywood executives are big on "No one's ever done *that* before.") Even when you're simply putting *King Lear* on a farm, if no one's done it, someone will probably be interested.

When you think you have your premise in good shape, try it out on a friend you can trust. Remember, this person is the ultimate recipient of your script, in the form of a movie, and it has to be sold to similar folks by the people who make your movie. For example, you might say, "What if a hockey player went on the pro golf tour?"

"It's been done," they'll say. "Didn't you see *Happy Gilmore?*"

It's Not for Us

Don't waste time in arguments with other writers about how to "properly" write a screenplay. Everyone goes about necessary tasks in their own way. As author and UCLA Screenwriting Program professor Richard Walter says, all that matters is the script.

If You Want to Send a Message, Use E-Mail

There probably never will be a more colorful Hollywood character than producer Samuel Goldwyn. He was one of the Hollywood originals, the Goldwyn in Metro Goldwyn Mayer (MGM), and notorious for his nutty statements such as "Gentlemen, include me out," and "A verbal agreement isn't worth the paper it's written on." You could spend a day laughing at Goldwynisms and have a good time, but one of his statements is particularly true with regard to writing movies. "Pictures are for entertainment," Goldwyn said. "Messages should be delivered by Western Union."

You've probably never sent a message by Western Union. You might not even know what a telegraph was, and you might not ever have had anyone wire you money to a Western Union office. In Goldwyn's day, however, telegraphs were sent all over the world, in a time when international phone connections were often chancy.

These days, you can send a written message around the world immediately, via e-mail. If Goldwyn was alive, his statement might be "If you want to send a message, use e-mail."

When I think of movies of great social conscience that I've admired, I think of films such as *Ghandi,* Sir Richard Attenborough's great triumph. Well, guess what? Mahatma Ghandi changed the world. With nonviolent methods, he got the British to give up their colony in India, and he freed his country. He fought racism and spread peace, and he was assassinated for his efforts. Even so, it took Attenborough as a highly experienced director and show business veteran 25 years to bring this story to the screen.

One of my favorite screenwriters, Robert Bolt, thrilled me with *Lawrence of Arabia, A Man for All Seasons,* and *Dr. Zhivago.* He turned great true stories into works of art. But then, aren't all great lives themselves works of art? Compared to the rest of us, aren't they elevated lives? All the movies that I've just mentioned are based on true stories on a world stage, in times of great social change, but I'm not sure that Bolt or anyone else who writes movies like these sets out to send a message to the world. I think, rather, that they tell the story and let it pose questions.

The great Greek philosopher Socrates asked questions to elevate consciousness. By posing the proper questions and having people answer them (known as the Socratic method), he led them to conclusions, but they discovered those conclusions on their own.

Hollywood Heat

Screenwriter Robert Bolt was one of my favorites, so when my agent of the time, Sherri Mann, told me that Bolt was working on a remake of *Mutiny on the Bounty,* I was thrilled. (Sherri was the ex-wife of director Daniel Mann, whom she said was going to direct the film, but in the end Roger Donaldson helmed the picture.) Unfortunately, *Bounty* (1984) with Mel Gibson as Fletcher Christian bored me, and it didn't do well at the box office. I puzzled about it until I realized that Bolt was best at writing original scripts from history, *not* remakes. It was another lesson to me of the importance of doing what you do best.

Did you ever see *Blade Runner* (1982)? The scene where Rutger Hauer's android dies in the rain in front of his enemy, an executioner of escaped replicants (android slaves) played by Harrison Ford, is one of the most dynamic in screen history. We do not have a message dictated to us—androids have a right to life and freedom, too—but we are left debating the morality of giving life to androids in the first place (a scientific possibility), much less enslaving them. The movie came from a Philip K. Dick novel entitled *Do Androids Dream of Electric Sheep?* Within that title, you have the theme of the film: Are androids—with real cells and real blood—automatons who think like, and of, machines only, or are they alive like us, with basic rights?

If you absolutely must say in a screenplay, use a feather, not a hammer. If you hit people over the head with an idea, they won't appreciate it. If you use a feather to tickle their imagination, they'll be pleasantly stimulated. Don't send a message—get your viewer to ask a question. If you're not willing to do that, you're probably better off writing and filming documentaries, but even then you must learn subtlety and persuasion, letting the movie speak.

Outlines, Synopses, and Treatments

You may feel confused when you start asking about "treatments" in Hollywood because you'll run into so many differing opinions. Some folks will tell you that you can never sell a treatment, but they're sold every year. At least 10 times as many pitches are sold, however, which should tell you something about the importance of relationships in Hollywood. If your work is known and respected—which almost always comes only from completed screenplays—you can pitch a story and get paid to write a treatment—or perhaps a synopsis first and then a treatment.

What is a treatment, anyway? Let's start with a synopsis first, just to give you a taste of the Hollywood runaround. When you mail someone a completed "spec" screenplay—meaning that it was not written as a paid assignment, but on the speculation that you would sell it—that person gets it "covered." That works like this: Someone is paid to read your work and comment in writing. This reader might do only a "top sheet," which is one page. Most likely, the reader also will do full coverage, which runs two to three pages. The description of your work will be a synopsis. Should you provide one? No. These people want to write that themselves.

Skip's Tips

If you want to fully understand the process of coverage, read *Reading for a Living: How to be a Professional Story Analyst for Film and Television,* by T. L. Katahn (Blue Arrow Books, 1991). It's a how-to book that includes coverage samples.

In doing coverage, the reader describes what the story is about and offers one of the following recommendations: recommend, consider, or pass. The first thing the reader is interested in is the commercial potential of the material (after all, it is show *business*). If it's commercial, you'll likely get a consider vote. Recommends are rarely given. What if the reader recommends your script, the producer or studio makes the movie, and it bombs? Who gets the blame? The reader is the lowest person on the production company totem pole and the easiest to fire.

The reader might also recommend a consider vote just because he or she likes the quality of your work, so don't fret if you don't think that you write material that would readily be considered commercial.

You can write a synopsis if you want, but I would advise you to not ever show it to anyone unless you're asked to do so. You might be doing the reader's work for them,

Script Notes

You go to a pitch meeting hoping to sell something to the company where you're auditioning. If the company is interested, sometimes you'll be asked if you have a "leave-behind." That usually means a two- to three-page synopsis, or a one-pager. But pitch kings will tell you to never, ever leave anything behind. If they can't remember your story, that's a problem.

It's Not for Us

Gatekeepers are there for a reason. Don't think of readers and development executives as someone to get around to reach the real decision-makers. These people are hired because producers, production companies, and studio heads trust their taste in material. If you find them to be cranky, they might just be overworked. Treat them with respect, and they'll likely do the same with you.

and if that person is in a hurry, he or she might just rewrite your synopsis and not read your script. Sounds unethical, I know, but when you get paid by the script ….

Now to treatments. If you've ever written a book, or if you had a good composition teacher in school, you probably learned to outline a story. Think of an outline as the skeleton of a treatment. It describes what Hollywood veterans called the "beats" of the story. A real "treatment" is a *tool* that studios, production companies, and screenwriters have used for years. It is simply a description, scene by scene, of the movie, minus most or all the dialogue. If you were writing *Casablanca* and wanted to include the importance of some dialogue in a scene, you might include Bogart's line about "Of all the gin joints in all the world, she has to come in this one." Any strong line that illustrates a crucial part of the story might be included.

Sometimes these days, people (particularly development executives) think of a treatment as 10 to 25 pages (or more) that describes the story. I've heard a development exec say that if he's pressed for time but interested in an idea, he'd rather read the treatment to see if he wants to read the script.

My advice is to use a treatment as a tool for telling yourself what your screenplay is about, scene by scene. That's what I do with them. I don't show them to anyone much anymore, unless I'm thinking of collaborating with someone on the script, or want to get feedback about a script. I've had treatments optioned, and there was a time when treatments sold regularly, but I discovered that producers generally got burned with this practice. They saw a good story on paper but didn't get the goods delivered when the screenplay was done. Maybe the writers thought they'd made easy money and got sloppy.

If you're not a known quantity, don't try to sell a treatment or get hired to write a screenplay based on a treatment. Oh, it could happen, but usually the only thing that proves your screenwriting ability is a completed screenplay. Use a treatment as a tool to help you get that accomplished.

High Concepts and Mixed Ideas

If you mention the term "high concept" in Hollywood these days, it sounds dated. I first heard it while trying to sell a TV miniseries idea to Twentieth Century Fox. I didn't know what it was. Luckily, the TV executive was a friendly one who explained that she meant a couple sentences that described the story or at least the elements of the miniseries. Sometimes you get that with just the title, as with *Ghostbusters*.

People still use the high concept, but mostly in mixing a couple known movies to describe the script that they want to sell. If you wanted to make a movie about an innocent but not too bright black girl who was a love child in the 1970s and then became a successful businesswoman who finally found love, you might say it was "*Forrest Gump* (or *Forresta Gump*) meets *How Stella Got Her Groove Back*." I've heard people describe projects that oddly. Sometimes the combinations seem natural, but often they don't—and they can't help but sound derivative—so this practice is falling out of favor. You're better off just being able to describe it without comparisons to other films. Even then, the people you contact will mentally compare your description to films they know.

My "what if?" comes into play here. After *Die Hard* was such a huge success, it was probably easy to sell *Under Siege* as "*Die Hard* on a ship." Whether that's how it came about or not, that's how it was described in Hollywood. I can just imagine someone walking in and pitching, "What if *Die Hard* took place on a ship?" The box office bonanza figures would roll in the executive's eye a moment: "Okay, great. Tell me more!" Or you might say, "What if *Die Hard* took place on Air Force One, and the hero was the President?" That's *Air Force One*, with Harrison Ford in the lead role.

I try to be as nonderivative as possible in describing my projects, but if I have to, I'll do a high concept comparison. Because executives already know the hit movies, you don't have to worry about figuring out the high concept for them. They did that before you arrived.

It's Not for Us

Don't be ruled by fear. The first question I usually hear from writers is "What if they steal my idea?" Legally protect yourself as well as you can, but at some point you simply have to trust God or Providence or karma or whatever you call it, and simply tell people about your idea. Ideas are a dime a dozen, but not great ones.

As an exercise, do the following:

1. Write down a number of ideas for screenplays that you might write.

2. Give each of these ideas titles, if you can. Try to come up with titles that reveal what the movie is about, or are intriguing enough that you want to know what the movie is about.

3. Try to describe the high concept of each idea.

4. If applicable, come up with a couple movies that, mixed together, might match your idea.

5. Now see if you can apply the "what if?" principle to them.

6. See which idea(s) sound(s) most clear to you and (is) are the most easily described.

7. Pitch the winners to some friends you trust, and see what they think of the ideas.

Hollywood Heat

John Grisham is one of the most successful authors of our day, and most of his books have been made into films. I was once intrigued by an interview in which he said he would come up with a dozen or more fully fleshed-out ideas for novels, and present those to his New York agents to see which they thought were most commercial. I've known of screenwriters who do the same thing. They develop the rough story line of a dozen or so screenplays, meet with some trusted friends (working Hollywood professionals, usually), and see what they like most. Of course, the trick is in finding working pros! That's why I love the Internet.

The Log Line: The All-Important Twenty-Five Words or Less

These days, screenwriters are asked for the log line instead of the high concept. Where did the term originate? Imagine a busy production company. Even if they don't actively solicit them, they get dozens of screenplays every week. From agencies they get scripts, books, and writers to pitch ideas.

If they're active on the Internet (and most are these days), they also get e-mails. They might even have a Web site where they solicit properties, and they'll read your work after you've signed a *release* form posted on the site.

In addition to this, writers they know and have worked with are phoning, e-mailing, faxing, and mailing about new screenplays, books, and ideas. Those writers have friends whom they are introducing to the production company.

And when the boss comes in on Monday morning, he might be carrying a book or screenplays (or several) that people have recommended but that he hasn't had the time to read. And why should he read them, when he has a secretary or assistant to read them for him?

So here's where the log line comes in. Someone has to keep a record of everything received, for the production company or producer's own legal protection. What if the company makes a movie and someone says that it stole the idea or script? The production company keeps a log of properties received so that it can show what came in and what did not. It used to be a handwritten log, in a ledger or three-ring binder or whatever. These days, it's likely kept on a computer, in a Filemaker Pro database or some other software program. However it's kept, these companies have a log.

And in that log, each property is described in a sentence or two, usually with where it came from. For example, "True story about the first female mountain man in the West, perfect for Michelle Pfeiffer—CAA." I'm being facetious about this imaginary project sent over from Creative Artists Agency, but I'm sure that you get the idea. The "True story about the first female mountain man in the West" is the actual log line. The bit about Michelle Pfeiffer might be there simply to express a casting idea suggested by the agent at CAA, who knows that production company has a working relationship (or wants to) with Michelle Pfeiffer.

Think of the description of a movie that you see in the weekly magazine *TV Guide*. It's the old "25 words or less." It's easily written down in a log, or typed in. That's a log line.

When you've fully worked out your premise, you should be able to describe it to anyone in 50 words or less (25 words or less is hard to do for some beginning writers). If you find it difficult to explain your story in so few words, it's my guess (and the guess of many other experienced pros who agree with me) that you might not have your story fully worked out.

Script Notes

A **release** is a legal document that producers and production companies have unrepresented writers sign for protection. These can be very problematic. I've seen language that says, "We might have received a property that matches yours word for word," which asks you to hold them harmless if they buy that other supposed property. Before you sign any release, show it to an attorney.

Skip's Tips

Try pitching movie ideas in a mirror. You never know when you might get a chance to tell someone influential about your screenplay. Do it with as much emotion as possible, but don't fake it. (If you have to fake it, the passion isn't in the story.) Watch yourself as you tell the story—you might be surprised what you'll learn.

It's one thing to make an esoteric art film or write an experimental literary novel. If you want to write a Hollywood movie, you should be able to succinctly state the log line. That's what they'll use in formulating an advertising campaign, and it's what you'll see in a *TV Guide* listing, if you get lucky enough that your movie is seen in both theaters and on television.

The Least You Need to Know

➤ It's easy to formulate movie story ideas with the "what if?" approach—for example, "What if aliens invaded tomorrow?"

➤ A great premise immediately sets up the conflict to come.

➤ The theme of a movie is different from a premise; a theme describes the overall lesson that can be learned from the story.

➤ Don't send a message in a movie. Instead, pose situations that cause your viewers to ask themselves questions.

➤ The true definition of a "treatment" is a scene-by-scene description of the plot. It is a screenwriting tool, an outline expanded to serve as a guide while writing a screenplay.

➤ A high concept and a log line both describe the same thing, 50 words or less that say what your movie is about. The log line is the preferred term in Hollywood these days.

Chapter 10

What's Hot, What's Not, and What's in Your Heart

In This Chapter

➤ Changing tastes

➤ What goes around

➤ Different strokes for different blokes

➤ Predicting Hollywood's future

➤ Write what you want to see

Eric Hoffer, philosopher and author of *The Passionate State of Mind* (1955), said, "Man staggers through life yapped at by his reason, pulled and shoved by his appetites, whispered to by fears, beckoned by hopes. Small wonder that what he craves most is self-forgetting." Sounds like a screenwriter, doesn't it?

People watch movies to escape their troubles, to travel to different worlds, to vicariously live great adventures, and to forget themselves. Nevertheless, the movies they like most are about characters to whom they can relate. Perhaps that's why we see so many films about underdogs, people who suffer in everyday life but find a way to overcome their circumstances and triumph.

You can generally count on a great screenplay about an underdog to be popular, in almost any country. Sylvester Stallone scored a worldwide success with the *Rocky* movies, as George Lucas did with the *Star Wars* films. The heroes of those films were always the underdog, even when Rocky was the heavyweight champion.

Underdogs may always be popular. They have been since the beginning of film. Remember Charlie Chaplin's great Tramp character? But a screenwriter picking a genre can't simply write about an underdog and count on an audience. What other themes can a screenwriter trust? Let's take a look.

Tastes Change with Generations

When Walt Disney was alive, he did something very interesting. He recycled his films. As every new generation of children arrived, Disney features made their way back to the theater. And why not? Disney's first feature, *Snow White and the Seven Dwarfs* (1938), was just as fresh in 1958, 1968, 1978, or 1988 as it was when kids first sang along to "Whistle While You Work." When videocassette players came into vogue, however, the company Walt left behind was in a quandary. Should it issue the movies to video like every other studio and risk killing its generational golden goose? Eventually, the company compromised by releasing some films for a short period of time and then cutting off production, making them more valuable in the public mind. Some films Disney hesitated to put on video at all. *Song of the South,* based on "Uncle Remus" stories by Joel Chandler Harris (a nineteenth-century writer), was considered racist by some audiences. Disney execs knew something most consumers don't: That videotape (or any tape) deteriorates after a time. So that meant they could have repeat customers for videos.

Then digital video came along, and there went the repeat video sales idea. DVDs are virtually eternal, compared to videos. And in case you are not of the generation now in college, these folks have always known VCRs and CDs. They probably have no idea what an "album" or an 8mm "home movie" is. As a writer, you can drive yourself crazy trying to write for the largest moviegoing audience if you're not a part of that audience. You can get desperate if you don't have teenage kids or know people who do. You might hang around a video store, trying to chat up the clerks. That could get the cops called on you. Or you could take a clipboard down to the local mall to interview moviegoers about their likes and dislikes. They'll instantly know you're old if you do that. Take a Palm Pilot. (And if you don't know what that is, you'd better find out.)

Skip's Tips

Teenagers today know so little about history that you could assume that a historical movie might not be popular. Here's the catch. If you have Ben Affleck in *Shakespeare in Love* or Drew Barrymore in *Ever After,* teen audiences don't care that it's Elizabethan England or a fairy tale world. Not knowing their tastes is one thing; not knowing their favorite actors is inexcusable.

You've seen generational taste changes dramatized on TV season after season. Recent shows that play on the generations are very popular. *Dharma and Greg* is about Dharma, a child of hippie parents, who marries a straight-laced lawyer from an upper-crust background. *That '70s Show* is about teenagers in the 1970s. Naturally, the people who create such shows know something about those time periods, and if a TV show becomes popular, old fashions come back into vogue, just because the new generation thinks they look so weird and cool (or "bad," I should say).

If you're not a Generation Y writer but want appeal to a younger generation, look for stories that play to (or on) the *clashing* of generations. If you know what baby boomers are like, you probably know or can easily find out what their kids are rebelling against. Anyone who knew the 1950s parents from shows such as *Leave It to Beaver* knew exactly what Baby Boomers as teenagers were rebelling against. And when Michael J. Fox as Alex Keaton was a straight-laced Reagan Republican teenage son of former hippie parents in *Family Ties,* that was hilarious.

So why am I discussing TV when this is about screenwriting? Because that's what demographics experts study. Television has immediate impact and a broader reach than film. Plus, TV is so much less expensive than moviegoing, so it's easier to figure out what audiences like by simply watching television ratings.

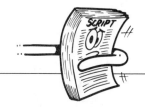

It's Not for Us

In Hollywood, a town obsessed with youth, it's better not to reveal your age, unless someone asks. If are not in your 20s but look like you are, let folks think it. Life experience makes better screenwriters, but people in neurotic Hollywood often don't think that idea through. They generally look for younger writers to speak to younger viewers.

If you, as a screenwriter, can successfully predict what movie audiences will see, based on generational tastes, you're way ahead of most screenwriters and, if you're right, on your way to being a highly successful producer or even running your own movie studio. The one thing you can count on is that tastes will change over the generations, usually toward the more outlandish. I can't really see my parents enjoying *Being John Malkovich* (1999). But then, the movie business always surprises me. I would never have predicted that a World War II submarine movie, *U-571* (2000), would be a hit, and I know one of the writers! Do your best to keep up with current generational tastes, but don't drive yourself crazy with it. A solid story works across generations and gets remade again and again.

What Goes Around Comes Back Around

In recent years, the 1960s and 1970s have been back in vogue. We can attribute part of that to the colorfulness of the times, but the biggest factor has been the coming of age of the children of Baby Boomers as moviemakers. It should come as no surprise to you that Michael Myers's parents were a very big influence on his very successful *Austin Powers* character.

The real reason that many movie trends come back around is a very simple one. It's somewhat like the Disney generational recycling mentioned previously. Savvy producers know that a new generation has never seen certain films because they weren't playing on TV as the generation grew up. Here's an example. You could walk into

Skip's Tips

When you spend millions to make a movie, you hedge your bets. That is why agents and producers package a project. They assemble a complete package of the most important elements: the script, the lead actor or actress, and a suitable director. Based on past revenues from the stars, director, or writers, the studio or financier can get some idea of expected revenues.

most high schools today and ask them who Frank Sinatra was and draw blank stares. When the new *Ocean's Eleven* "caper" movie comes out, with George Clooney in the lead role of Danny Oceans, you can bet that they'll see the film because Clooney turned his role on television series *E.R.* into movie stardom. The current generation of high schoolers might never see the original *Ocean's Eleven* (1960) starring Sinatra. It took a smart producer—Jerry Weintraub at Warner Brothers—to put two and two together and realize that this remake made sense. When director Steven Soderbergh came onboard, it became the hottest project in town.

If you study Hollywood film history, you'll find lots of examples of types of films that might be revived. It simply takes a smart person to realize what hasn't been around in a while and develop a project. If you read the chapter that covered genres, you might have developed some ideas there. Just as people in Hollywood love to say, "Wow, no one's ever done *that* before!" they also love to say, "Hey, nobody's done anything like *that* in a while!"

Just be prepared. If you didn't live through it and have to educate yourself on past film favorites that might work anew, expect that with at least one under-30 executive, you'll have to recite the biographical information of the superstar in the original film, no matter how legendary.

Different Strokes for Different Blokes: What They Like, Around the World

Unless you want to be a film distributor, you should concentrate on the North American audience and let the rest of the world take care of itself when you are considering what screenplay to write. There are, however, some basic things you should know.

Action plays well around the world, which probably comes as no surprise. Mel Gibson was a worldwide star in *Mad Max* before Hollywood paid much attention to him. The film did okay at the box office in the United States, but it made more than $100 million foreign. An action film usually works no matter what language it is originally written in, as *Runaway Train* (1985) proved. The writing credits are a United Nations of screenwriting: the script by Edward Bunkerm, Djordje Milicevic, and Paul Zindel; and the story by Ryuzo Kikushima, Akira Kurosawa, and Hideo Oguni.

Even if you write comedy, think action. Jerry Lewis's slapstick comedy movies of the 1950s and 1960s have made him a virtual cinema god in France. This was not lost on director Tom Shadyac and the other writers on the remake of *The Nutty Professor* (1996). This Eddie Murphy comedy comeback vehicle was so successful that it led to a sequel, *Nutty Professor II: The Klumps* (2000).

English-language remakes of foreign comedies, particularly French comedies, translate well for North American audiences. A successful example was *Three Men and a Cradle* (*Trois hommes et un couffin*) (1985), which became the very popular *Three Men and a Baby* (1987) and a sequel as well. If you never saw Tom Selleck, Ted Danson, and Steve Guttenberg in the American movies, they had to deal with the consequences of a trio of swinging bachelors who become the unwitting custodians of an infant. The secret of foreign remakes, at least with comedies, is that the situations play just as well to American audiences as they do to European ones.

Not so popular with North American audiences was the English-dubbed version of 1997's *La Vita è Bella* (*Life Is Beautiful*), the Best Foreign Language Film Oscar-winner starring and directed by Roberto Benigni, who wrote the screenplay with Vincenzo Cerami. Audiences seemed to prefer the Italian version with English subtitles. Why? This is a personal preference guess, but the movie was not a comedy. It was a serious film about a father who saves his wife and son even though they are all in a World War II concentration camp, by constructing an outrageous fable that his son believes. Given Begnini's comic genius, there were plenty of laughs, but the premise of the film itself was not, in contrast to *Trois hommes et un couffin*, comic by nature.

If you consider yourself to be a serious screenwriter not given to writing action of the dramatic or comic nature, you probably won't care about the possibilities of your film being seen by audiences around the world. You'll simply go for the artistic merit of what you write, and let the popcorn boxes fall where they may.

Hollywood Heat

Written and directed by Guy Ritchie, the low-budget but multi-award-winning number-one English film *Lock, Stock and Two Smoking Barrels* (1998) was shot on 16mm to give it a grainy look. The movie did respectable box office in England and abroad. The American remake rights to this comedy thriller shoot-'em-up about four young men who get into serious debt (£500,000) after a crooked card game reportedly sold to American superstar Tom Cruise's production company for $1.7 million (or, probably more than the original production cost). Action sells, big time.

Action plays everywhere. Comedic human situations play everywhere, but only situations that could take place anywhere. A comedy about a man with a hot dog stand might not work well in a country where few people have ever seen a hot dog. And comedy translates most easily around the world when a lot of funny physical things happen, such as three men trying to change a baby's dirty diaper.

When they begin filming a scene in Hollywood, they start with "Action!" It's a word the whole world understands.

Predicting the Future by Demographics

In Chapter 8, "What Your Audience Really Wants to See," my analysis was that movie popularity has a lot more to do with the age of the main characters than anything else. So let's now discuss the Baby Boomers, who are the most influential filmmakers today and the fastest-growing movie audience. What's a "Baby Boomer"? It's anyone born between the years 1946 and 1964, folks between 36 and 54 years old—in short, 29 percent of the U.S. population and 78 million U.S. citizens. Why "Boomer"? Because, after World War II and the Korean War, although the Cold War was in progress, the world was relatively at peace, and people got married and had babies. Those babies are the Boomers, the first generation to grow up watching television. Elvis Presley and the music of the 1960s are important to them.

A large number of them never plan to retire, and many of them are now experiencing or will soon experience a midlife crisis, that mental malady of people between 35 and 50 (males mostly) in which they get very neurotic as they feel the last of their youth evaporating. Does that give you any ideas for movies? *Middle Age Crazy* (1980) has already been done. What you should know about is the *interests* of Baby Boomers. After all, they're almost a third of the U.S. population, and as more of their children move out, leaving approximately 30 percent of them with an empty nest in 2000, they have free time on their hands. They also like to go to movies. If they don't go out, they have an expensive home theater on which they watch movies. As innovations such as the Phillips Flat TV and high-definition TV proliferate, home theater will only increase.

Lawrence K. Grossman, a former president of NBC News and PBS, wrote in the *Columbia Journalism Review* January/February 1998 issue that "TV time buyers pay $23.54 per thousand to reach 18-to-35-year-olds and only $9.57 per thousand for those over 35, according to industry sources." That tells me that a sizable, well-to-do market has been somewhat neglected.

Skip's Tips

Whether you're a Baby Boomer or not, check out the Web site www.bbhq.com. It's a chatty, witty site full of interesting tidbits and opinions (like Baby Boomers are). Another great site covering all the generations is www. demographics.com.

If you've been paying attention to the world around you, I'm sure you know that Generation Xers are the offspring of the Boomers, those born between (roughly) 1961 and 1979 (an 18-year gap, with age 18 being adulthood). That's about 50 million in the United States. The generations are quite a contrast. Whereas the Baby Boomers admired Marilyn Monroe, a lot of Gen-Xers admired Marilyn Manson. But, more of them graduated college and are into their careers now, even if they're a more pessimistic crowd than their parents. While Boomers in the 1960s might have complained about getting a bad "rap" (treatment) from police whom they called pigs, Xers can be absolutely piggish about rap music. Xers are more tolerant racially and are concerned about the environment, but they've also been called the "Baby Gloomers" because of their attitudes.

How tolerant are they? I remember seeing Bill Clinton playing the saxophone on TV when he was first running for President. I told a friend that a lot of young people were going to vote for him because of that. My older friend was active in politics and said that traditionally people barely legal to vote generally did not. I told him that it was going to change with the Gen-Xers, and I was proven right. When the Clinton scandals were in full swing, it seemed impossible to sell any screenplay or TV show of a political nature. I sensed that would change, but I didn't know why. Now *West Wing* is a hit show on NBC, and a number of political movies are about to be made. You can attribute some of that to the tastes of Generation X.

By the time you read this, *The First Gentleman,* a project inspired by the 1964 film *Kisses for My President,* about a female President of the United States and the first "First Husband" may be in the theaters. A number of other political films are in the works, including one with Jack Nicholson attached to star as an American general.

Does this mean that you should write a political film? No. I'm simply trying to point out two things: (First, you should trust your instinct, not prevailing "wisdom"; and second, moviemakers' tastes change with the social atmosphere and by generations.)

Like the Baby Boomers, Gen-Xers seem to marry later in life. What does that mean, moviewise? More "guy movies" for the males, perhaps? And more "date movies" to suit the females? If that notion doesn't seem very different, just remember that the Baby Boomers grew up enjoying a lot more movies that were about social issues (such as *To Kill a Mockingbird*), world figures (such as *Lawrence of Arabia*), or their generation (such as *The Graduate*). Movies about "social issues" today are usually about issues between sexes.

It's Not for Us

If by chance you study demographics and use your findings as a guidepost to pick which screenplay you choose to write, if you expect to use that as a bargaining tool to sell your script, don't expect to simply say it and have it accepted. You'd better be prepared to present charts and graphs and visual evidence. Otherwise, you'd better not mention it.

Have you ever heard of the CD *Frogstomp* by the group Silverchair? Well then, you're probably out of touch with Generation Y (also called the Echo Boom), the kids born from 1978 or so to around 1999. There are about 70 million of them. (Silverchair's album of teenage angst went double platinum in sales.) Older journalists thought they had Generation Y figured out, until the Ys started getting married. Suddenly, people noticed that they were more serious about relationships than the previous generation. They'd grown up in broken homes and seen too many divorced parents or even grandparents. They wanted more stable relationships. If you want a Hollywood example of this, try Macaulay Culkin, the *Home Alone* star who grew up and married at age 17. Another example (at least in appealing to Gen-Yers) is Drew Barrymore, who loves to do romantic movies that have fairy tale-like plots. Both of these successful actors grew up with parents who had 1960s values.

Hollywood Heat

Ken Kesey, famous for books that became movies—*One Flew Over the Cuckoo's Nest* and *Sometimes a Great Notion*—engineered a 1964 LSD-inspired bus trip across America that was immortalized in Tom Wolfe's *The Electric Kool-Aid Acid Test*. Kesey shot film on the trip but could never get the audio in sync—until, that is, Simon Babbs, the son of Kesey's old friend Ken Babbs, transferred the film and audiotape to a digital editing system. If you ever wondered what the hippiest hippies were all about, look for *Intrepid Traveler and His Merry Band of Pranksters Look for a Kool Place* soon at a theater near you. Groovy desktop, man.

There's another big difference between Generation X and Generation Y. A whole lot of the Gen-Yers grew up around computers. They're a big reason that viewing short films on the Internet has taken hold. They're big into downloaded MP-3 music cuts and don't hesitate about finding friends via e-mail and chat rooms. The current trend toward desktop moviemaking (wisely supported by Steve Jobs and Apple) fits perfectly with Generation Y, many of whom are starting their careers right now. And Gen-Yers as a whole seems to have a more positive attitude than Gen-Xers, while sharing the Gen-Xers' tolerance for others.

This brings us to the younger kids in the theater, which we've covered pretty well in an earlier chapter. There might be something else worth mentioning with regard to kids and movies, though. Did you ever know a kid who saw *Titanic* several times? Do you think it was only because they loved the movie that much? In case it has been a while since you were a kid, here's another reason: *popularity*. Kids like to be respected by their peers, and by seeing a popular movie the most times of anyone in their peer group, they feel that they've accomplished something. Not good for parents, great for Hollywood—something to consider. If you write a screenplay that a kid will like, chances are good that they'll see that film not just once, but several times. And if you don't believe me, ask James Cameron, of *Titanic* fame, or George Lucas, of *Star Wars,* for their opinions on the subject.

Does it seem like we've left someone out? Ah, that's right, the parents of the Baby Boomers, known in demographic parlance as "Matures." Of course, a lot of Boomers are becoming Matures these days, so the line blurs. Matures are a big segment of the population, and it's a bit of Hollywood's fault that they don't see more movies at the theater. Here's an example. Bobby Vinton, a singer you've probably never heard of, had a big hit song in the 1960s called "Blue Velvet." It was a lush, romantic, feel-good ballad. When David Lynch's *Blue Velvet* movie came out in 1986, many seniors paid the price of admission, thinking that they would see a romantic "song title" movie that followed at least to some degree the lyrics of the song. Brother, were they surprised when they saw a scene in which a man finds a severed human ear in a field and another about the perverse sexual habits of an evil man played by Dennis Hopper.

A more recent example of "what you think you're gonna see ain't what you get" is *American Beauty* (1999). A lot of older moviegoers weren't terribly happy about a middle-aged married man's sexual lust for a teenage girl. It's not that they were opposed to the story; they just didn't like being fooled by the advertising. From conversations I've had with them, experiences like that can dissuade seniors from returning to the movies, period. As a screenwriter, you might not care about such things and will have no control over the advertising anyway, but I thought I'd throw it in just in case.

If you want to go really wild trying to figure out long-term moviegoing trends by generations, you might delve even deeper and look into the Foundation for the Study of Cycles:

Foundation for the Study of Cycles
214 Carnegie Center, Suite 204
Princeton, NJ 08540
Phone: 610-995-2120
Fax: 610-995-2130
E-mail: fsc@cycles.org
Web site: www.cycles.org

Skip's Tips

According to the Foundation for the Study of Cycles, a cycle is "a rhythmic fluctuation that repeats over time with reasonable regularity. When it is sufficiently regular and persists over a long enough span of time, it cannot reasonably be the result of chance." Take a look sometime at the movie release patterns over the decades. You'll find definite recurring trends.

Skip's Tips

If you communicate with Hollywood executives but are not younger than 35, spend some time at younger people's hangouts. You can correspond and even transmit scripts via e-mail, or talk on the phone from all over, but you need to speak the generally younger "language" of Hollywood. By that, I mean the types of things on their minds, not yours.

This international research and educational institution was established in 1941 as a nonprofit corporation by Edward R. Dewey, who compiled huge charts of observed recurring cycles throughout history. Because I've personally seen them and studied them, I can simply tell you that they are fascinating. Dewey believed that when a cycle recurs, it is not a chance rhythm, and the longer that pattern continues, the more predictable it becomes. According to his Foundation, the timing of cycles suggests a geographical pattern, and cycles of the same period tend to synchronize, or crest, at the same calendar time. Most of this organization's publications center on economic factors, but its research encompasses all fields. The *Foundation Chart Book* shows in graphic form the economic history of western man. It's a fascinating volume, as is *Cycles in Humans and Nature,* by John T. Burns, a former executive director of the Foundation. It covers cycles in everything from astrophysics to economics to zoology.

Perhaps demographics and cycles are subjects too esoteric for someone studying screenwriting, but I've always believed that the better you understand your fellow human beings and the forces with which they deal, the more likely you are to write something notable that will stand the test of time and generations.

Write What You Want to See on the Screen

If you've never heard of *Being John Malkovich* (1999), *Buffalo 66* (1998), or *Happiness* (1998), or their directors—Spike Jonze, Vincent Gallo, and Todd Solondz, respectively—chances are really good that you shouldn't be writing for Generation X or Y (until you get an "education," that is).

If you think that you can simply write a teen movie and strike gold, think again. For every "teen heartthrob from TV now doing a feature" success such as *Scream* or *Varsity Blues,* there are flops in which producers miscalculate what teens want to see, such as the 1970s TV show remake of *The Mod Squad*. Remember that chapter on Shakespeare? The Bard even works with teen films. *Ten Things I Hate About You* was *The Taming of the Shrew* in high school. If you write a teen movie that's cheap to shoot (less than $15 million, a low budget for a studio) and has some new angle on a proven genre, you might be okay. You'd just better have a great story. The TV writing on teen series faves such as *Buffy, The Vampire Slayer* (which came from a feature film) is pretty good these days, and you have to better it.

You can get a degree in demographics. You can study cycles and sunspots, or graduate summa cum laude in psychology. All these things might help in determining what the public will respond to in a screenplay. The best answer to that question, though, is always this: *a great story*.

That will depend on how well you learn the craft of screenwriting, to supplement any natural writing talent that you may have. In determining what to write, you're best off simply writing something that you would really like to see on the screen.

If you want producers, directors, and stars to commit life years to something you've written, you need to be very passionate about it. When writers ask me what they should write next, I always advise them to complete that thing they would write if they had only six months to live and wanted to leave as their legacy. They usually have only one of those.

Script Notes

As soon as you make a script deal, you'll probably hear the term "development hell." The person controlling your script has to "get it in shape" to attract the financing to get the film made. You might earn money in development hell like I have, only to get kicked off the project or eventually get it back in "turn-around." Why? Because "that's Hollywood."

If you're lacking in a plot or simply can't decide on the right one, no matter what you do, you might follow the example of the late English novelist Barbara Cartland. She held the *Guinness Book* world record for "Top-selling living author of all time," with her 723 books exceeding one billion copies worldwide in 36 languages. Asked how she could turn out so many books, Cartland told the Associated Press: "I say a prayer. I really do. I say, 'Please God, get me a plot.' It's absolutely extraordinary: then a plot comes."

Whether by prayer, persistence, or perspicacious foresight, I hope you come up with something that you love and that a producer loves enough to get it made, allowing us all to love it just as much as you do.

The Least You Need to Know

➤ With Hollywood movies, what goes around comes back around. The only question is, "When?"

➤ No matter what generation you're from, if you write about the clashing of generations, you're probably on the right track.

➤ Action plays well around the world, whether in drama or comedy, for obvious reasons—language barriers.

➤ There are more Baby Boomers (79 million) in the United States than Generation Xers (50 million) or Generation Yers (70 million).

➤ Understanding demographics and the cycles of nature can put you ahead in the screenwriting game.

➤ Ultimately, the best screenplay for you to write is the one that you most want to see onscreen.

Chapter 11

Your Screenwriting Schedule and Why It Is Essential

In This Chapter

➤ Three pages at a time

➤ A workable schedule

➤ Living your schedule

➤ Graduation day

I had a major epiphany when I read a story about writer/director John Milius. Milius claimed to write two screenplay pages per day and only two pages per day. Thus, at the end of two months he had a completed 120-page screenplay. Of course, he probably had to rewrite it, but a four-pages-per-day rewrite would mean that he would have a polished second draft in roughly three months.

At the time, I was working as a word processor for law firms to make a living, so the idea of writing at night after typing all day was not something that I relished. Two pages, however, were manageable. I could even get a good night's sleep. That was the first time I ever realized how much mental impact a writing schedule can have, positive or negative. I've keep a regular schedule ever since, and it has made all the difference.

Getting It Done by Three-Page Scenes

The general length of a Hollywood screenplay is 120 pages. Why? Generally, a page of single-spaced script with 1-inch margins on 8½ × 11-inch paper works out to one page of onscreen time. That means that a movie from a 120-page script will run approximately two hours. These days scripts tend toward the shorter side, 90 to 110 pages, but if you write a 120-page script, you're in the ballpark of "standard" length.

Generally (there's that word again), a movie scene runs around three minutes, with some much less, as you've probably noticed. Some movie stars who like longer scenes (Paul Newman comes to mind) complain about this "three-minute rule" but writers follow it, more or less. The more talented and successful they are, the more likely they are to be able to break the rule, which goes for any artist in any profession. For now, though, let's go with the three-minute scene.

Skip's Tips

Here's something I use daily. When I was a kid, I drew pictures to entertain my younger brothers. Later in life, I realized that I had mentally "seen" those pictures on the paper and then traced around them. When writing these days, I keep the wall in front of my computer bare so that I can more easily "see" the scenes I envision.

You'll find goofy definitions of "scene" in some books. The word comes from the Greek *skene,* which is a temporary building or stage where a play took place or where the action occurs. The key words are *temporary* and *action*. In a screenplay, a scene is *a transitory sequence, usually in a single location, where something takes place that advances the story.*

This means that in a two-hour movie, you will have 40 scenes, give or take a longer or shorter scene here and there. If you wrote one scene per day, you could finish your first draft in the length of time that it took God to flood the world in Noah's time. Does that sound manageable? (The scenes, not the flood.)

Now, what's in each of those three-minute (or less) scenes? Choose from the following:

(A) Two people screaming about something on their minds

(B) A car being chased by a tractor-trailer down a mountain road

(C) A young woman holding a man around the waist, crying as she tells him how she loves him and never wants to lose him

(D) Torrents of rain, high winds, and giant bolts of lightning ripping an environment to pieces as people scurry to safety

The one you picked might say something about your film preferences. Choice A could be a scene from *Who's Afraid of Virginia Woolf?* (1966). Choice B might be taken from the TV movie *Duel* (1971). Choice C could have come from any number of films or soap operas, and choice D might be a scene out of *Twister* (1996). Or, they could all be one scene, cutting back and forth from the exterior of and into the interior of a car driving pell-mell in a tremendous thunderstorm down a mountain road, followed by other cars also fleeing to shelter. Just behind the car in which our heroes ride is a tractor-trailer in which the driver is riding the brakes, so heavy sparks are flying everywhere and the brakes are almost burned out. The driver of the car yells at his passenger to get back and give him some room; he can't drive with her crowded so close. She pushes back angrily, then screams at him that it was his idea to come on this camping trip in spite of heavy storm warnings. She wishes they had never gotten engaged!

This prompts him to return a sharp remark that stuns her. She looks around just in time to scream at something ahead—he's about to miss a turn and drive off the side of the mountain! Her fiancé re-acts, jerking the wheel to the left. They slide into a rest stop on the left, against the mountain—safe! The tractor-trailer, however, can't make the turn. It crashes through the metal barrier and plummets off the mountain. Watching, horrified, the woman breaks down in tears. She holds the man around the waist, blubbering that she's sorry for what she said. She loves him and never wants to lose him.

He hesitates and then pushes her away. She looks stunned until she sees what he's staring at out his window. Up the mountain, a muddy rivulet is about to turn into an flooding avalanche as boul-ders are being dislodged by the awful storm.

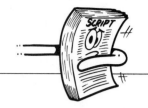

It's Not for Us

Don't take *any* scene for granted. Layer it: Rough it out; then rewrite; then polish it. Make a scene surprise you, with little regard for your outline. Write a scene like a small movie. When outlining, I rarely feel im-mersed in a scene as though I'm living it. When fleshing out a scene, I see directions I did not see from the outside.

"I hope I never lose you, either," he says, stepping on the gas. "So let's get out of here!"

And her eyes well up with a new kind of tears, those of admiration for a man saving their love from disaster.

Then a new scene begins as they escape the watery avalanche just in time and barely miss getting hit by another car as they roar back on the mountain highway.

This scene, like a screenplay, has a beginning, a middle, and an end. There's a twist at the end. You think that the characters have seen death and realized the folly of their argument, and then suddenly it seems like he has turned cold toward her. Only he's merely getting some physical maneuvering room so that he can pilot the car away from more impending danger. There is an emotional arc in the scene, and we learn something about the characters' relationship. We might not get a full idea of what the movie is about from this one scene, but the scene certainly moves the plot forward—whatever it takes, they have to get out of danger.

This scene, written by a pro, could be done in a page, or two, or three. It's all one scene because it takes place roughly in the same location, the mountain road. As the scene begins, the characters are in danger. As it ends, it seems they have escaped dan-ger. Then a new scene begins, placing them once again in harm's way.

Hollywood Heat

Diane Thomas was an unknown waitress in Malibu when Michael Douglas bought her script *Romancing the Stone* (1984). Unfortunately, she was tragically killed in an automobile accident just as her career was getting started. Now UCLA Extension Writers Program, where Thomas was a screenwriting student, holds a screenwriting competition in her name for people who study at its program. They offer "land" courses as well as over the Web. See www.unex.ucla.edu/writers/, or call 310-206-1542.

> UCLA Extension Writers' Program
> 10995 Le Conte Avenue, #440
> Los Angeles, CA 90024-2883
> 310-825-9415
> Outside California in the United States: 1–800–388–UCLA
> E-mail: writers@unex.ucla.edu

The continuous driving heartbeat of a story that is kept alive when strong scenes flow together is what keeps us going back to the movies. Two of the films that I mentioned previously, *Duel* and *Twister,* had Steven Spielberg involved, directing and executive producing, respectively. Whether you like his films or not, one thing is certain: He knows what makes a scene work and will often move you breathlessly into the next scene.

Whatever your daily schedule, you should be able to get your screenplay done if you approach it one little movie at a time. We'll delve into screenplay architecture later. When you start your first draft, only worry about it a scene at a time.

Great movies are composed of great scenes, and great scenes always have some element of the unexpected. Go on, surprise yourself. Write a great scene. Do it 40 times, and you have your movie.

Setting Up a Schedule That Works

Hollywood doesn't have room for excuses. It's a high-stakes game, and the script is crucial. "If it ain't on the page, it ain't on the stage" is an old theater maxim that you'll hear repeated among movie folk. They don't really care about how you had to take your kids to soccer practice and couldn't finish the script, or how those finals took precedence, or how many deaths there were in your family this week. All that matters is the script that you turn in.

Similarly, to most people the idea of writing a screenplay and having it turned into a "real Hollywood movie" is such a far-fetched notion that you're an extremely lucky soul if you have someone in your life who supports you, either financially or mentally, while you crank out your magnum opus. Your friends and family have their needs, and if you turn down a trip to the local amusements with them often enough, they'll get edgy.

The way around that is to establish a writing schedule. You have to set a regular time during the day or even once a week in which you write your script and do nothing but write your script (with due regard to bodily functions and emergencies). You'll find that when you start respecting your own schedule and maintaining it, the cynical jokes will fade away and people will start taking this notion of yours more seriously. You don't have to be nasty about it, just firm. After a while, you'll find people coming around with little things that help—a back rub, a hot cup of coffee or tea, a pillow, or a brighter light for your lamp.

Provided you know people who like you, of course.

To set up a schedule that works, you need to do an assessment of your life. The following ideas might help:

1. What do you do after you get home from work? Time it. If you're spending an hour with your friends, cut that in half and gain writing time. Or, drop this until the script is done.

2. Do you have everyday chores, such as feeding a pet? Do it first, instead of before bed. Get all your chores out of the way.

3. Turn off the phone ringer or turn on the answering machine.

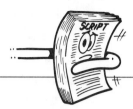

It's Not for Us

Don't be a schedule slave-driver. If you're a stubborn sort, you might have a tendency to overdo it in one sitting. Just as you can overwrite a scene, you can overdo a writing period. Stick to your schedule, even if it means stopping a scene in the middle. Ernest Hemingway used to do that on purpose, and he did all right.

Skip's Tips

If you're writing along and everything's going great—you're keeping to your schedule and people are actually taking you seriously about it—don't be surprised if some days you just don't have it in you. Don't hire a psychiatrist. Sometimes the mind just needs time to work things through subconsciously. Write a letter, take a walk, and don't worry about it.

4. Hide the remote control for the TV.

5. Eat what you need to before writing.

6. Find another time to check your e-mail and regular mail.

7. Lock the door and set yourself up with some kind of alarm clock, timed to help you take a break from writing at least every 45 minutes (or whatever works for you).

The best writing—at least for myself and every other writer I know—takes place when there are few or no interruptions. If you find that next to impossible due to your own living conditions, I suggest that you find a way to fix that, or get yourself some comfortable earplugs. With kids in the house who are old enough to not burn down the place (I hope!), I put on earphones and listen to music as I write. I have a piece of software on the computer that I can set to remind me to take a break. I know other writers who do things like this, but you might need complete peace and quiet to write. Whatever it takes to set up the right atmosphere for yourself, spare no effort in putting it in place. I think you'll find that your screenplay will thank you.

There is no set schedule when you are a freelancer or a someone writing a screenplay on the speculation that you'll sell it. A spec screenplay writer is the master or mistress of his own universe, or needs to be. Because you need to develop a certain frame of mind to be a professional writer, it's something that you'll have to work out on your own. You'll find that some pros work late at night, when the rest of the world is sleeping. Others have a set schedule that begins early in the morning and finishes at noon or so. Others like the afternoon and evening. It's your call.

When you're writing on a grueling deadline, as in TV staff writing, or like I'm doing while writing this book, you might write around the clock to get the job done. If you don't find a set time to write, though, it's my guess that you'll take a very long time getting your screenplay done. You might even abandon it. At times it seems as if we can control very little in our lives, but in our spare hours we can at least control how we use our time. If you can't find a way to do that, you might be in a situation that you need to handle before you try to tackle something as serious as writing.

I grew up in Texas, where the temperature gets very hot in the summer. I did a lot of hard work growing up, everything from chopping weeds in cotton patches to laying sewer lines and building streets and highways. No hard work I ever did was as draining as a hard week of writing. Why? When writing, you use your body, your mind, and at least a little bit of your soul. After all, you're not just working in a world— you're working as you build a world! Putting a schedule in place that works, one that you can keep in place, is the foundation upon which that world is built.

Taking Your Schedule Seriously

If you're like 99 percent of all other humans, you're at least a little disorganized. You'll find it hard to get going on your screenplay every time you're supposed to be writing copiously. So what do you do?

Hollywood Heat

Lew Hunter, Emmy-winning writer, former television and studio executive, long-time co-chairman of the UCLA Screenwriting Program, and author of Screenwriting 434 (the title of his master screenwriting class), lived in Burbank, California, until he retired to his hometown in Nebraska. Every month, Lew and his wife, Pamela, hosted an open party for writers called "Writer's Block." You could count on it. And in his ivy-covered writing shack behind his house he resisted getting a computer for years, preferring to write each day on an old typewriter that had belonged to TV legend Ernie Kovacs. Lew was a master of schedule and habit.

If you're a lawyer, you already know this trick. It's called "billable hours." You keep a running record of the time you're actually working for money: when you start, when you stop. If anyone questions the bill you send, you show them the log.

Of course, that might seem a bit over the top, or even ridiculous, to keep a log of the times you spend on the script, but after you've done it a while, you'll be surprised at the time you spend actually writing.

By the time you forget about your screenwriter's log, I'll bet you'll have established a schedule pattern that will get you through your first screenplay and your next one. And when someone hires you to write a screenplay, if you're so inclined, you'll be able to figure out your hourly rate.

Writing every day feels good, particularly when you can do it full-time. Living in Los Angeles, or in any filmmaking center, might help you get lucky. When I first started writing screenplays, it was because I could afford the luxury of doing it full-time. This was before widespread lotteries. I wasn't born rich, I never inherited much, and I know very little about playing the stock market. But I went on a game show and won more than $14,000 in cash and prizes. That allowed me to take off from work and write full-time. If there is any way you can do that, even for a month or two, I suggest that you make the arrangements. There is absolutely no substitute for a concentrated, full-time writing schedule, particularly while learning.

If you can take a vacation or a sabbatical to get your screenplay done but find that you have trouble disciplining yourself to maintain a writing schedule, it might be time for outside help. Don't get down-hearted about it; writing is a lonely discipline and a hard one. One company that is good at helping writers get disciplined is

Writers Boot Camp, which helps screenwriters take movie and TV sitcom ideas all the way from a concept to a finished draft in six weeks. This group's motto is, "The Secret to Writing is Writing." The catch is, classes are held only in Los Angeles, Chicago, and New York. For information, e-mail mbrennan@writersbootcamp.com, or call 1-800-800-1733.

Hey, if you're serious about movies, you gotta come to Los Angeles some time, right? Yes, you do.

Let's say that you manage to put in a screenwriting schedule, maintain it, crank out pages that you think are very good, and get a screenplay completed within the time period that you originally projected for yourself.

You must be God. Or a liar.

Just kidding, but would you mind working for the airlines to get their plane schedules coordinated? Seriously, it pays well.

When your script is done, the immediate gleeful instinct is to snatch it up, running screaming out the door with it, and show it to your best friend. Or, if your best friend happens to live with you, to yell "Yahoo! Look at this!" Your friends will instantly know what "this" is, but they might think of the Internet when you yell "Yahoo!"

Don't show off a first draft. Put it aside. Stick it in a drawer or somewhere safe. Forget about it for at least a couple days. Don't show it to anyone or admit that it even exists.

Hollywood Heat

Because it seems that he could write a grocery list and get it published and made into a movie, I don't mind telling stories about author Stephen King. Hey, he's even directed movies, if you count *Maximum Overdrive* (1986). He does something you might try: When a piece is done, he gives it to a number of trusted friends. If they all have different comments, he might ignore them. If they all offer the same comment(s), then he'll take the comments seriously and consider changes. It's a bit like the old adage that if enough people tell you that you're drunk, you'd better sit down.

This is an important part of your screenwriting schedule. Just as you may have worked out a system of penalties (two pieces of cheesecake tonight while struggling with a scene means no cheesecake tomorrow, only a cookie), you have to reward yourself for accomplishments. If you've reached your "pages target" at the end of a week, do something nice for yourself. When Act One is done, do something nicer.

Most screenplay problems come in Act Two, and you'll probably be pulling your hair out over that act sooner or later, so when it's finished, don't go crazy. Reward second acts cautiously.

When Act Three is finished, when you've typed "FADE OUT" on the right side and "THE END," centered, put that script away. Let it sit, like a fine wine needing to mature. Take at least a couple days before you look at it again.

If you work like me, and read the thing you wrote the day before (a chapter or a scene) and correct it before going on, you'll probably have an inclination to come back the next day and read through the whole screenplay and make corrections to everything. If you do that, you'll probably feel like chucking the entire thing because you've been too immersed in it for too long.

What if you swam the English Channel? It's a momentous accomplishment that few people can accomplish. But how soon do you think swimmers who achieve that mark want to get back in the water? Similarly, few people can accomplish writing a really good screenplay on their first attempt, but beginning screenwriters all too typically dive right back into that world they've been living in for X number of months. They don't give themselves time to gain perspective on the writing so that they can approach it with an exterior, less emotionally involved set of eyes.

Do yourself another favor. If you've written your screenplay on a computer or word processor, do *not* read it afresh on a screen. Print it out, grab a red pen or pencil, find a quiet place, and go through the script methodically. Take your time. Hollywood won't go bankrupt waiting for you to deliver your superstar screenplay. Your script needs to be as perfect as possible before you present it, and the rewrite will go much better if you create that last little bit of scheduling that allows you an unhurried time to page through your script with fresh, nonblurry eyes.

If you're happy with your first draft, and if have a friend whom you trust to read it over and give you an opinion, that's up to you. Just make sure that you schedule your own uncluttered time—after a break of at least a couple days—to read your script through from start to finish. Trust me on this one. I've made the mistake of not doing it more than once, and my scripts suffered accordingly.

It's Not for Us

These days, you almost can't log onto the Internet without running into a script consultant. I know, or know of, just about all of them. Forget them when all you have is a first draft. The two- to three-page synopsis they'll give you may have insight, but you're wasting your money. Beginners learn to write by rewriting, not by reading paid opinions.

The Day You Become a Screenwriter

If you want to stir up some heat, just go to a party and, when asked what you do, say, "I'm a screenwriter." Initially, most people will be very interested, but when you've answered all the other questions that will inevitably follow and they have determined that you're merely an *aspiring* screenwriter, expect some fallen faces and quick moves to the other side of the room, unless the person you're talking to is also an aspiring screenwriter or a working writer who understands what you're going through. *Just Write* (1997), written by Stan Williamson and starring Sherilyn Fenn as movie star Amanda Clark, and Jeremy Piven as tour bus driver-turned-screenwriter Harold McMurphy, is a great romantic comedy about the social intrigues that go on with aspiring screenwriters in Los Angeles. It's well worth a watch if you want to understand the social nuances of when someone is considered a screenwriter in Hollywood—and when someone is not.

Call me a hard liner, but I don't consider people to "be" their profession until they have received recognition from working professionals in their chosen activity. Usually, that comes in the form of money. When you have been paid for screenwriting, then you are a screenwriter, at least in my opinion. Others may have an even harsher definition, believing that you are not a screenwriter until something you have written has been seen on more than just a computer screen in a word-processing program. Purists think that you're not *really* a screenwriter until a feature film—not a Movie of the Week or a cable movie—that you wrote has been seen in a movie theater.

It's really not worth debating. If you want to call yourself a screenwriter as soon as you start writing your first script, that's your business. You may look like a fool to others, but if it helps you assume the right attitude to get the script done, good for you.

If you're not bothered by cynics or the sour comments of others who wanted to achieve something like selling a screenplay but failed, you could even insist that you're a screenwriter at a social gathering, with supreme confidence in your new craft.

I just wonder how you'll handle the question: "So what have you written that I've seen?"

Skip's Tips

A "page one" is what happens when a screenwriter rewrites someone's script so completely that it's like starting at the first page and creating a new screenplay. It's the kind of rewrite that you hope never happens to your own script, but it probably will. Hang in there—you might get to return the favor someday.

Skip's Tips

Only the most cynical (those you don't want to associate with, anyway) will fault you for identifying yourself as an "aspiring screenwriter." What are you saying about yourself? First, that you have goals. Second, that you're honest and open. In a screenwriter—or in anyone, frankly—those qualities are admirable. Don't say that you're "only" aspiring, just "aspiring."

That question always amazes me, just like the book question, "So what have you written that I've read?"

As if I can climb into their minds, take inventory, and report!

Sometimes it's qualified, as in: "So what have you written that I *might* have seen?" (That's a polite cynic speaking.)

If the preceding questions don't bother you, or you don't care what other people think and say to others, call yourself a screenwriter whenever you want. As for me, I didn't consider myself a screenwriter until I sold a co-written feature screenplay to a company that had just made a movie and I had the check in my hand. I'd had plenty of scripts "optioned." A one-hour video I'd written had won a national award, and I'd written some television.

To me, though, a sold feature script meant that I was a screenwriter.

You'll know you're a screenwriter the day you meet your own criteria of the definition of "screenwriter." Whatever that may be, I assure you that it's a very good feeling when it arrives.

The Least You Need to Know

➤ The standard length of a feature screenplay has long been 120 pages of approximately 40 three-page scenes.

➤ If you can't establish and keep a regular writing schedule that works, it might not be the right time for you to write.

➤ Few people will take your writing aspirations seriously until you do so yourself; keeping a schedule can help with that.

➤ A good three-minute scene has all the elements of a complete screenplay: a beginning, a middle, and an end with a tag.

➤ A system of rewards and penalties built around your writing helps; so does keeping a log of your time spent working.

➤ Don't expect everyone to consider you to be a screenwriter until you are recognized by working professionals.

Part 3

How to Write Your Screenplay

Want the nuts-and-bolts explanation of putting together a screen story, from premise to outline to completed script, with a complete step-by-step description of the best structure for your movie? You got it! We won't give you an office at a Hollywood studio when you're done, but you'll be convinced you deserve one! (Or at least a nice rest.) And then, just when you think you're driving the smartest new vehicle on the block, you learn the secrets of rewriting. Buckle your seat belt!

Chapter 12

Preparing Your Outline and Reordering Scenes

In This Chapter

➤ Getting your premise right

➤ How does your log line read?

➤ "Master minding" your screenplay

➤ 3 × 5 cards make it easy

➤ Three minutes at a time

➤ Anything less than a script

➤ Blueprinting for perfection

For some time now I've been noticing an electronic backlash. People accustomed to working in front of computer screens and watching television at night say "Enough!" and evaporate from the electronic stream. Writers pick up pens, pencils, and paper and retreat to a quiet place under a shady tree where they feel less assaulted by the world. I know of a number of successful writers who eschew computers, preferring to write out their work on yellow legal pads, which someone else transcribes.

There are software programs to help you formulate your premise, but that's just it—most of them are built around some formula. There are programs that let you type out your scenes on the electronic equivalent of a 3 × 5-inch card, which you can then electronically shuffle onscreen as you wish.

I prefer to reshuffle real cards. Call me antiquated, but there's something magical to me about a pen, paper, a cup of coffee, and a seat outdoors. I'm convinced that it helps my work.

Hollywood Heat

In 1990, I directed a 48-hour marathon screenwriting fund-raiser for the Independent Writers of Southern California. It got TV coverage on Showtime and (by a stroke of luck on a slow news day) appeared on West German TV. Using a story outline formulated by others and myself, people donated money, sat at a keyboard at the Century City Shopping Center near Beverly Hills, and wrote a scene based on the next available scene. In all, we ended up with around 100 writers. The result? Too many screenwriters = garbage.

Sorting Out Your Premise

I'd like you to think of a mountain lake. The water is clear and still that day, and you can see, at the bottom of that lake, a chest full of treasure. The chest is open, and you're amazed by gold coins and red rubies sparkling in the sunlight that illuminates the lakebed. And there you are, in a small rowboat, looking down at the treasure, wondering how you will retrieve it. It seems like this vision of treasure was meant for you and you alone, but the water looks deep and cold, so you're not sure.

Skip's Tips

When you're writing out a premise or outlining a screenplay, try to get into the mind-set of the genre. It helps you stay on track. If you were writing *Dumb and Dumber,* you could say, "Two dumb brothers go to Aspen with money they don't know they have." Or you could say, "Two reaaaalllly dumb brothers, almost too stoo-pid to know they're alive ...."

There might be so much treasure that it would sink your small boat. If you left it there and came back, could you find it again? What if someone else in a large boat came along and got it? What if someone was netting fish and pulled it up, or raked a bunch of debris on top of it? You'd need expensive equipment to locate it again. Where would you get that? As you continue worrying, you begin to wonder if it's really treasure down there at all.

Of course, there is one way you could forgo all subsequent problems. You could prepare yourself so that you would have absolute certainty about your treasure. You could have a global positioning device that would lock in the coordinates via orbiting satellite. No matter what conditions were in the future, you could locate the treasure again. That's how certain you need to be about the premise of your film. I hope that you never suffer from uncertainty, but if you do, there are ways to build certainty about your premise.

Comparing Your Log Line to Other Movies

A musician friend of mine went to bed one night convinced that, in noodling around on the piano, he had come up with a hit song that would make him a million dollars. Then the next morning when he woke up and started tinkering with it, he realized that he had written "Yesterday," Paul McCartney's great Beatles tune. I laughed and reminded him that McCartney at first just had the essence of the song, not the completed vision. He originally called it "Ham and Eggs." (Ham and eggs, oh, I really love my ham and eggs. If I cook them right, they never beg. Oh, I remember, ham and eggs.) Okay, so I'm not Paul McCartney. The point is, if my friend had taken the time to compare the song he had "written" to all the other songs he knew, he might have realized the truth.

To succeed at writing movies, you need to know movies. You need to watch a lot of movies, from all eras and as many countries as possible. The greatest movie education comes from the movies, period. If you haven't grown up watching a lot of film, a number of books offer capsulized descriptions of movie plots, probably the best being *Leonard Maltin's Movie and Video Guide 2000*, by Leonard Maltin (editor), Rob Edelman (editor), and Pete Hammond (contributor). This 1,641-page paperback, published in November 1999, is cheap; the one I saw on Amazon.com cost only $6.39. On the Internet Movie Database (imdb.com), which is now owned by Amazon.com, you'll find two types of plot summaries—the regular one, and Maltin's, which is always more complete.

Keep a book like this by your side, and don't rely on being able to check a plot on the Internet. Sure, you can search by keywords at imdb.com, but you'll find that it can become a laborious process to figure out if someone has matched or approximated your log line. A look through a book is usually much quicker.

It's Not for Us

Just as there are copycat killers, there are copycat moviemakers. When a movie is as successful as *Titanic*, someone will make a similar movie, and there also will probably be a porno "version." Do yourself a favor and don't write a copycat unless you truly have a new twist. Experienced filmmakers, who can shoot something as soon as it's written, will foil your efforts.

Still, there's nothing like seeing a lot of movies. I can't imagine how I would have been able to search Web pages to determine where I had seen the "Odessa Steps" sequence that I recognized in *The Untouchables*. I suppose that I might have located a paragraph stating it came from *Battleship Potemkin*, by Sergei Eisenstein, but because I'd seen the original, I realized fairly quickly what the "inspiration" of the scene had been. If I had only had an idea that I couldn't pin down, I might have logged onto the Internet newsgroup misc.writing.screenplays and posted a query. Or, I could have engaged in a chat at one of the many Web sites devoted to screenwriting.

Skip's Tips

"What if they steal my idea?" I hear that from neophyte screenwriters time after time. I reply, "They might." It's the "one-baby syndrome." If you only have one child, you worry over it endlessly. If you have a large family, bloody noses are not national emergencies. Take precautions, but at some point, you simply have to send your baby out into the world.

If you want to protect your idea, it's foolish to chat with unknown quantities about what you think is an original premise. You simply need to see a lot of movies so that you can compare your movie ideas against those that have already been made. The only ways around that are to consult with a very knowledgeable person or to participate in a group of writers whom you can trust. But not just any group ….

The "Master Mind" Method

In his *Keys to Success* (Plume, 1994), the great Napoleon Hill advises the reader to "form a mastermind alliance with yourself." He tells a story of a woman he convinced to stop dwelling on her problems so that she could concentrate on the "other" her, a positive, successful person. What you dwell upon, you get more of, Hill believed. In the book, this author of *Think and Grow Rich* describes how, after you have a definite purpose about what you're doing, if you maintain a positive attitude toward attaining your goal, you can attract other like-minded people. He also stressed the importance of maintaining harmony in your home and environment, to more easily achieve your aims.

In describing how to build an alliance of "masterminds" (people who think like you do), he cautions against teaming up with people just because you like them and they like you. Hill suggests teaming with people only if they have the ability to do the job in question and can get along with others. I highly recommend both of his books, as well as anything else he has written. Napoleon Hill was the original positive thinking guru, so if any of his suggestions sound old now, just know that he wrote them first.

I've seen this method work over and over in Hollywood. People who succeed rapidly in show business actively seek out and ally themselves with like-minded people of similar or higher ability. They are firm in what they are trying to accomplish. This is most often true with producers I've known, who are bound and determined to get a certain screenplay made. It's like they have blinders on, like a horse in a harness. They see only what is in front of them and don't get distracted by diversions.

If you are happy with the premise of your screenplay, you will be similarly focused. You will listen only to suggestions that move you toward your goal. Other things won't distract you, and the only people you will see are those of like mind.

It may surprise you to know that professional screenwriters are often eager to pass on their knowledge. Hollywood people are big on the idea of "giving back." It's an old tradition that I hope never dies. You can see some evidence of it with the free mentoring program of the Writers Guild of America (see www.wga.org for more information). Highly successful screenwriters, directors, and producers may not have the time or inclination to write a book, but they're often happy to talk with an aspiring writer.

Hollywood Heat

Although he knew aspiring screenwriters before he began writing screenplays, no one had as much early influence on David Ayer (*U–571* and the forthcoming *Training Day* and *Squids*) as Wesley Strick (*Arachnophobia, Cape Fear, Final Analysis*). While doing electrical work at Strick's Hollywood Hills home, Ayer showed Strick some stories about his naval experience. Strick liked them and kept after Ayer to write a screenplay. Ayer told me that he was at a crossroads; if a writer that successful took him seriously, he felt that he should do something about it. Did he ever. These days, Ayer is an "A-list" screenwriter in Hollywood, working with top producers and directors.

These days, I've had some success in a number of areas of writing, and I'm happy to pass on information to anyone—but then, I've always been that way. Some writers have to face mortality before they realize that they won't be around forever. That's when they start thinking about their legacy and passing on wisdom.

The criterion that I recommend in selecting other writers with whom to commune about movies and movie ideas is Hill's: *Do they have the ability to do the job in question?* If they do not, I'm not sure why you would be talking to them about your screenplay premise, unless you simply want to test it out on "common folk." I've seen more than one competent writer (including myself) chopped to pieces in a writing workshop by angry, cynical people. You may not be able to pick your enemies as a screenwriter, but you should be very careful about picking your friends.

The Beauty of the 3 × 5 Card

Before you piece together your plot, you need to decide which 3 × 5 card you plan to use—electronic, card stock, or Post-It sticker. It really depends on your mentality. If you like working at a computer, you can find a number of software programs that have this facility. Apple computers come with a program called "Stickies" that you can customize to default to that size. Some screenwriting format programs feature the ability to switch from 3 × 5 format to screenplay format, and back.

It's Not for Us

If you have a pitch card, a main card that expresses the premise of the script that you're working on, don't show it to anyone, no matter how clever you think it might be. I'm not paranoid, but I've learned the hard way that sharing your central idea before it's written and legally protected is a bad idea.

If you use Post-It notes on a big blank wall, you can arrange your scenes, moving them around as you want so that you can read your entire movie at eye level, hands-free. I suppose you could do the same thing with index cards, but it would take a lot of tape or pushpins to hold them on the wall.

My favorite is a stack of index cards held together by a rubber band. It's pocket-portable, and you can hike to the top of a mountain and outline your script, if you want. You could do that with a stack of Post-Its, but they're harder to move back and forth, with that sticky stuff on the back.

Try it sometime. Grab some index cards and go find a quiet place outdoors. Close your eyes, and start visualizing your movie. Let it unfold before you; when you see a full scene, write it down on an index card and then repeat the process. It's an intuitive way of putting together scenes that works for a lot of people I know.

Before you embark on that journey, fill out another card, the one that expresses the premise of your movie, your "what if?" I suggest using a different color card, or one with some colored tape on it, to make it stand out in a stack. Take your time on that card, which I call a *pitch card,* because it would be the one I'd have in my hand if I went in to pitch the story to a producer. Try to make it a clean, clear statement of what you want to say. Then, while you're outlining, if you hit a snag, you can check your progress against your pitch card. If you've gotten off-track, you can thumb back through the cards, and I'll bet you'll find a card/scene that shouldn't be there, one that doesn't forward the story. When I find one of those, I usually set it aside—it might work later. Even when I'm done with a script, I'll keep those cards if they look like good scene ideas—they might be useful later.

Last but not least, don't limit yourself to 40 cards. If you think of good scenes, write them all down on a card. It's much easier to throw away excess than it is to add scenes to flesh out a script.

Outlining by Three-Minute Scenes

Usually, when I conceive of an idea for a book or movie, I try to encapsulate the entire premise into the title. Sometimes the title tells you what the story is about, and sometimes it only alludes to it. I've found that this process works differently for everyone. Some people (like me) often get the beginning and ending of the story in a flash, along with the idea, leaving them to explore the details, the process of getting from A to Z. If you have trouble plotting out a movie scene by scene, plot it backward. That's easier than it sounds.

I think that if you start off trying to do one three-minute scene after another, you might handicap yourself because that's hard to do. Rather, it might be better to outline the overall highs and lows of the story—the peaks and that which the main characters race up and down on the way to their destination.

Let's take the premise of a screenplay of mine that started out as a stage play. I originally called it *Parts of a Hole* because a girl in a restaurant/bar one night said that the place where we hung out was a real "hole" (dive, lackluster establishment) and we were all parts of it. But, being me, I had to layer in something more esoteric, so the play evolved into something called *Fourth World,* which is the Native American Hopi tribe's description of the Paradise to come, with the present being the Third World. By the time it had reached a second draft with that title, the play was in good enough shape to become a finalist in two national competitions and a semifinalist in two others. If not for *Starman* (1984), starring Jeff Bridges, which came out just as my play was making the rounds, or the TV series derived from it (1986–1987), my play might have been staged in Los Angeles.

Or maybe not. Ten years after I wrote the play, I figured out what it was all about. That's right, I finally came up with a workable premise. (At least, I'm telling you the right way to do it.) I rewrote the play and titled it *Walking After Midnight,* using the title of an old hit country classic by Patsy Cline. My "what if?" went like this—*What if your Prince Charming finally arrives, only he's an alien?*

Then I did a staged reading of the new play, and two people in one week told me that it should be a screenplay, so I wrote the script. Because I had added a "time clock" of sorts to the script, of a girl turning 30 and worrying about her biological clock and the fact that she'd never been married, the story had more tension and started getting more notice. But, because of paying projects that got in the way, it would be another 10 years before I picked up the script again.

Skip's Tips

Unless you've set some silly time limit on your screenplay career, such as "Sell a script before I'm 30 or die!" take as long as it takes to get your premise and outline in shape. If you try to rush or gloss over that process, you'll pay for it later, fixing what you should have envisioned in the first place.

Skip's Tips

Someone might ask you to tell the story of your screenplay, but he or she doesn't have time for a long description. This person might ask you to just "hit the beats." A "beat" has two meanings in Hollywood. One is a pause that an actor takes while delivering dialogue. The other (the one that a producer wants) *is a high or important point of a story.*

When I had the premise in shape, the rest of the "world" of the script became more clear. I saw "beats" I would need—a birthday party planned for the heroine, a plan to build an amusement park called "Spaceland" in the UFO-friendly New Mexico setting of the piece, and a clash between the "maybe alien" boyfriend and the local deputy sheriff boyfriend. After working out the major beats of the story—about a dozen, or one every 10 minutes or less—it was easier to fill in the scenes between the beats. When I had all the cards filled out (35 as I recall), I could sit down and write out a treatment to follow, scene by scene, or I could simply write the screenplay from the 3 × 5s.

One-Sheets, Synopses, and Treatments

Here's a "one-sheet" of my script *Walking After Midnight,* which was optioned in 1999 for $5,000 for a one-year period. I'm revealing how much I made so that you'll understand that someone took this script quite seriously.

> WALKING AFTER MIDNIGHT
> © 1999 by Skip Press

How long would you look for a lost love? Would you travel across a galaxy? Would you search through a dozen lifetimes? What if you found your lost love, only to discover that you were not remembered?

Mirabelle Flowers isn't concerned with such far-flung ideas. The owner of an all-night diner in Gallup, New Mexico, she busies herself with her Midnight Poetry Society. Her odd collection of local poets includes: Jake, a drunken church deacon; Rob, a gruff old rancher; Joseph, a Hopi chieftain; and anyone else who shows up. Tonight, however, only Jake has come around, which is doubly perplexing because this is Mira's 30th birthday. She is openly anxious about the course of the rest of her life. This is not a night she wants to feel lonely.

Lloyd Buxtrum, a deputy sheriff who covers the night shift, drops by to flirt. He's had a relationship with Mira but blew it. Before they get much of a chance to talk, Lloyd is recruited by his current lover, Muriel, and her cousin Ramona to investigate what they say is a flying saucer crash on a nearby mesa.

Busying herself with sobering up Jake, Mira is startled by the arrival of a stranger who introduces himself as Kett Dakota. The man is handsome, charming, and eloquent, with an air of mystery. As the night unfolds and the regulars arrive, Kett changes each person's life in remarkable ways. When Jake is struck by a car outside the diner, Kett revives him by a laying-on of hands. When Lloyd returns to the diner almost naked, the victim of a revengeful trick by Muriel and Ramona, Kett helps avert a violent confrontation. When pressed to tell the group a story, Kett spins an entrancing yarn about lost love across eons and galaxies. Listening breathlessly, Mira has the oddest feeling that Kett is telling the story about her.

Finally, we learn of a plot between Lloyd and Japanese businessman Jakuro Ohito to use the body of an alien being as the centerpiece for a new amusement park called Spaceland. We also meet the loneliest lady ostrich in the world, who threatens to ruin their plans entirely.

Through a night of poetry, drunkenness, and outrageous behavior, Mira grows more enamored of Kett, only to see him suddenly disappear when her interest in him reaches a crescendo. Everyone around her has made a major change in their life on this night, but Mira has been abandoned to contemplate her future all alone. Or has she? As the movie closes, Mira learns that, despite all her fears, things work out for the best, as soon as you discover what the best really is.

If you were looking for the premise in the first line, you didn't see it. I'm not saying that's a perfect one-sheet, but it's the one I sent to the lady who ended up writing me a sizable check—and after reading it, she was sold, even before reading the script.

One-sheets are single-spaced. Usually writers cram as much on that one page as possible. You might also have deduced without much difficulty that a one-sheet made double-spaced would pretty much match the one-and-a-half- to two-and-a-half-page synopsis that most people expect in Hollywood when they ask for a synopsis.

Hollywood Heat

Joe Eszterhas, a native of Hungary, is famous for violent and sexy screenplays. His *Basic Instinct* sale caused the spec screenplay market to go nuts when it sold for $3 million. Eszterhas once sold a four-page outline called *Trapped* for up to $5 million (with the amount depending on whether the movie was produced with A-list talent). After a number of his scripts (such as *Showgirls*) became flop movies, however, Eszterhas backed off from Hollywood. Now his nonfiction book *American Rhapsody* from Knopf is a tell-all about Tinseltown. Something tells me he may not sell another $5 million synopsis ....

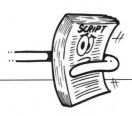

It's Not for Us

You might be told to never share a one-sheet or a synopsis with a producer. However, it could be a mistake to *not* share this selling tool. If you fax it to someone, you have a record of the transmission, as you do with e-mail "headers." You're protected, so go for it.

I might share a one-sheet or a synopsis, but I try not to show anyone a treatment. I use a treatment only as a guide for myself, a typed-out elaboration of my 3 × 5 cards, or to show to another writer with whom I might want to collaborate on the script. Other writers sell treatments and synopses, but they're usually very well-known screenwriters. And every time someone sells a treatment for a lot of money, the whole town watches to see if the screenplay that follows will be any good, and if the movie from the script will make money. Lots of producers have lost by spending money on nonscreenplays from proven writers, so why should they trust a neophyte?

Building the Perfect Blueprint

Okay, class of one, let's review. First, if anything I've explained to you here doesn't resonate with you, that doesn't surprise me, and I would never argue with you about it. Screenplays have definite, accepted formats that you can't deviate from as a beginner, and not even as a veteran unless you also plan to direct. In contrast, premises, log lines, outlines, one-sheets, synopses, and treatments are things that you have to work out for yourself. My suggestions are merely intended to give you some ideas of ways that I have been able to better work out screenplay stories. You will find, though, that "coverage" throughout the film industry is fairly standard—correspondingly, so are the way people write out log lines.

I must re-emphasize, however, the importance of working from a clear premise that you can easily describe in a log line, in 50 words or less—preferably, 25 words or less. When you've worked out your premise/log line, I would advise you to keep a primary "pitch card" around as a reminder of what you're trying to say with your screenplay.

Is there a perfect blueprint that works for everyone? I don't think so. I've known of successful writers who simply start off with an idea and see where the page takes them. Not just poets—authors, playwrights, and screenwriters, too. Some of them are very successful working that way. My friend Michael Dare, former movie critic of the *L.A. Weekly,* and writer and co-producer of the TV movie *The Bachelor's Baby* (1996), was once hired by Tom Robbins to script Robbins's novel *Still Life with Woodpecker* as Robbins wrote it. Dare was stunned to learn that Robbins never outlined. He just got a great opening line and then started writing the story. All Robbins's books were done that way. Of course, the screenplay arrangement was doomed to failure under those parameters, but Dare gave it a valiant effort. Dare still has hopes for Robbins's *Another Roadside Attraction* because he owns the movie rights. He tells me that he outlined the screenplay thoroughly.

Would you build a house without a perfect blueprint? I wouldn't, but then I grew up around the construction business. A great palace starts with a vision, which someone describes to an architect, who makes some sketches, revises them to suit himself, and then presents them to his client. The client makes a decision, the architect finalizes the plans, and the construction process gets under way. No one truly knows what the final product will be until it is nearly done.

It's pretty much the same with a movie, and a screenplay is a blueprint. When the movie is being filmed, the director might change that blueprint. The editor might even suggest changes that are implemented in the cutting room.

Some writers who know the business well write one script to sell. Then, after they have the deal, they do a rewrite that reflects the vision of the movie that they would *really* like to see. Maybe you'll be there some day. Meanwhile, I hope what I've shared helps you put together a blueprint that gets you your palace.

The Least You Need to Know

➤ The more clearly you can state your premise or log line, the more likely you are to write a coherent screenplay.

➤ There are resources to help you compare your movie idea to existing films, but none as good as personal knowledge of movies.

➤ In forming a "mastermind" peer group of screenwriters, choose only those who also have the ability to write a good script.

➤ A pitch card on which you've written your log line *is* a tool that you can use to keep yourself focused on your writing mission.

➤ It's okay to share a "one-sheet" synopsis of your screenplay with a potential buyer; unless that person specifically asks to read a synopsis or treatment, make him or her read the screenplay.

➤ In the end, the only correct method of getting your screenplay figured out and on paper is the one that works for you.

Chapter 13

The All-Important First Ten Pages

In This Chapter

➤ Back story is for the writer

➤ The life of a script reader

➤ Unforgettable opening scenes

➤ The digital age and screenplay openings

➤ Beat the best

Fair Game, a script that I wrote with Michael Sean Conley, impressed a prominent director at Columbia in 1984. At the time, the director had just come off the success of a cop movie and was one of the hottest directors in town. Our script was about modern-day piracy in the Caribbean. As it worked out, an article in the trades had reported that the director's next movie would be about that subject. Producers Ron Hamady and George Braunstein, who had optioned out the script and knew the director from days when he made commercials, called him up and asked if he had a script. He didn't, so he read ours.

Don't check your Internet Movie Database. The different versions of *Fair Game* listed there have nothing to do with our project. The first 10 pages of our script (and the whole script) impressed the director, but he chose to do a sports movie instead, which bombed. We later sold our script, after the setting had been changed to the South China Sea. It still hasn't been made.

The point is this: If you can hook the reader long enough to get them to read the first five pages, or the first 10, that reader is much more likely to read the rest of the script. The reader knows that the movie might hook the viewer with a quality opening. If the rest of the script maintains that quality, it's a hit movie.

Back Story Is for the Writer, Not the Viewer

Steve Allen, a multitalented funnyman who has written scores of songs and books, said to start a story where it begins. Allen pointed out that it often takes some writers 20 pages to get to the place where the story really starts. The best movies are not constructed in a way that you have to use multiple flashbacks to show the psychological evolution of a character's life so that you understand their current motivation. You learn that as we follow them along, and it's a much more effective way of writing. How much "back story" was there in the original *Star Wars*? As it turns out, three movies' worth, but we didn't know that or care to know that with the original film.

Skip's Tips

Can't figure out the beginning of your script? Divide your story into two worlds—the world in which your character starts and the one your character is in at the end. Even in the same environment, the character's outlook on it and place in it will have changed. What would it take to get this person started and keep from turning back?

Beginners seem to love to "flash back" from the present time of the story to some place in the past. Not only is it hard to follow onscreen, but it often disrupts the flow. I find that they usually do this only because they haven't figured out their plot and are trying to "think on paper." Only master screenwriters such as Richard Matheson can pull off the use of the flashback, as in *Somewhere in Time* (1980). Ryunosuke Akutagawa (from the stories *Rashomon* and *In a Grove*) and Shinobu Hashimoto and Akira Kurosawa also did it excellently with *Rashomon* (1950). When filmmakers make flashbacks work, the essence of the movie usually has to do with time itself, or some very troubling incident that needs psychological resolution, such as the rape of Sondra Locke's character in Clint Eastwood's *Sudden Impact* (1983, screenplay by Charles B. Pierce [also story], Earl E. Smith [also story], and Joseph Stinson).

Every great story has an *inciting incident,* the event that irrevocably propels the main character into the flow of the main story. Think of it as the character stepping into a whole new world. This incident is not always the first one we see in the film. Sometimes it takes place after the movie starts, and other times it takes place before. In *Star Wars,* the inciting incident is when Luke Skywalker's aunt and uncle get massacred by the overwhelming force of the Galactic Empire. Luke is forced to make his way in the world alone (albeit with robot R2-D2).

In *The Wizard of Oz* (1939), the incident is when Dorothy Gale (who, not so coincidentally, lives with her aunt and uncle) is threatened by Miss Gulch, who wants to take away Dorothy's dog, Toto. Some might argue that the inciting incident is the tornado that sweeps Dorothy off to Oz, but the key word is *inciting,* something that puts the main character on an irrevocable course of action that will lead to a new maturity and a true place in the world.

In *Mad Max* (1979, the movie that made Mel Gibson a star), Gibson is a cop in a post-apocalyptic world who loses his family. Like Luke and Dorothy, he has no choice, and his life has changed.

All these movies follow the Joseph Campbell "myth" structure. Two of them—*Star Wars* and *Mad Max*—were made by devotees of Campbell. Campbell had not even formulated his theory, however, when *The Wizard of Oz* was made. Myth structure or not, every movie worth anything has an inciting incident that gets the ball rolling. Sometimes it is an action scene, sometimes not. Are you thinking of Indiana Jones being literally chased by the giant rolling ball of rock in *Raiders of the Lost Ark* (1981)? That is not the inciting incident. It's merely an exciting opening that establishes his character. The real inciting incident takes place back at his university, where government officials inform "Indy" that the Nazis are about to grab the lost Ark of the Covenant, the all-powerful instrument of God mentioned in the Old Testament. It's a dialogue scene in an academic setting, yet it is clear to Indiana that he has no choice but to accept the mission. Truly, the fate of the entire world hangs in the balance.

Other times, the inciting incident is subtle, even sexy. For Tippi Hedren's Melanie Daniels in Alfred Hitchcock's *The Birds* (1963), the inciting incident comes when she flirts with Rod Taylor's Mitch Brenner in a pet shop in San Francisco. She pretends to be a shopgirl, to help him pick out a pair of lovebirds for his sister. Then he reveals that he knows who she is and knows some of her past. He's seen her operate in court. Doing what, we don't know; it doesn't matter—she's hooked. When he leaves, she tracks him down via his license plate, buys a pair of lovebirds to give him, and drives an hour north of the city to deliver them.

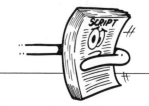

It's Not for Us

Don't make the mistake of not figuring out a back story for your main characters. The more you know about them, the better. That includes the villain. The more you fully understand the physiognomy, psychology, spiritual composition, and environmental influences of all characters, the better your script will be. Know their back-story inside and out—just don't show it to us up-front!

With none of these great movies did the writers or directors see any need to do a long, slow pictorial build that paints a picture of the setting, the characters, or the story. People just don't take the time for things like that. In the days of the big bands, there would often be a minute or more of instrumental lead-in to a big hit song. People took time to savor the appetizing melody while preparing for the main course to come. Not anymore. This is a culture with an expectance of instantaneous fulfillment. The ride must start now. If that doesn't suit you, you should probably be writing in Europe. Not that I agree with the way it is—I'm just telling you how it is. Personally, I dig a big band.

Hollywood Heat

Harry Cohn ran Columbia Pictures in the days of the studio system, when studio bosses were akin to gods (or wanted you to think they were). As the story goes, Cohn would use the "butt twitch" method while watching movies. That is, when he squirmed in his seat, something about the movie bothered him. And that's what the filmmakers would fix. You might guess that when Cohn's butt twitched too much, he fired someone or fixed his hemorrhoids. See how often you react nervously to something in your script. That's probably what you need to fix.

The Life of a Script Reader and What It Means to You

As I write this, I'm about to start working with a Web site called Filmtracker.com, a site where script readers, development executives, and producers at top Hollywood companies engage in online discussions about articles, stories, books, screenplays, and any other possible sources of hit movies. Hundreds of the very top production companies in the business stay on all day, conferring with each other about what might be hot. When a reader or development person finds something good, that person tells the boss (the producer) about it, and the ball starts rolling. A writer or agent is contacted, a meeting is set up, and a project might be on its way to being made.

Skip's Tips

Because of the masses of material on the market these days, development executives who like a log line will often agree to read a treatment, which they will generally consider to be a 15- to 20-page document, at most. That doesn't mean that you'll sell them that treatment. If they like it, *then* they will request the script. You still need a great screenplay.

If the subscribers on Filmtracker.com find something that they know is right for another company but not for them, they might pass it on. This type of community-mindedness is a relatively new thing in Hollywood, which I credit in large part to the instantaneous nature of the Internet. What this should tell you is that, these days, word on a good screenplay or a hot new writer gets around *very* fast. Similarly, if a writer is troublesome, that can also get around quickly.

Let's be conservative. Let's say, with all these inlets of material, that the average successful production

150

company gets 25 potential submissions per day. (Fifty would be a better estimate, but I don't want to scare you too much.) Twenty-five per day equals 125 per workweek. Let's say that they actually agree to read around half of those, or 65. That's more than a dozen scripts per business day. How many people do you know who could read 12 scripts in a day and report on them intelligently? If you were a kind soul (and most readers are, no matter what you've been led to believe), wouldn't you at least give the writer the benefit of the doubt and read the first 10 pages? But if you weren't hooked on those pages, or if you were put off by bad spelling, typos, coffee-stained pages, and other evidence of a sloppy mind, what would you do? I know exactly which round file I would put it in. And if the office policy was to not return any script that had no self-addressed, stamped envelope (SASE), I wouldn't think twice about filing that script in the trash. Sounds cold, I know, particularly because you might have spent a year of your life on that script, but them's the facts, Jack.

Can that office get through a dozen scripts a day? Maybe the company utilizes three readers who can cover three scripts a day, each being paid $50 a script for "coverage." That leaves 15 scripts not read at the end of the week. And that's what the development executive might take home to read on the weekend. Or, that stack might be split up with a producer in the office.

With that kind of reading burden, do you see how important it is that you follow acceptable etiquette in contacting a company, present your script in the proper format, and have a very impressive first 10 pages? And that comes only after you've impressed someone with a log line, and then perhaps a treatment, to even get them to read your screenplay.

With almost any successful production company I know, this scenario is average. Imagine what it's like with those that currently have a hit movie in the theaters, or a company such as Steven Spielberg's DreamWorks SKG? I hope that this helps you understand why some people do not accept unsolicited material.

Skip's Tips

You find the phone number of a production company, or their e-mail address. You've researched their history. You just know that you have the perfect thing for the company, something the execs will love. You get in touch and learn that they "don't accept unsolicited material." That means this: They don't know you, they didn't ask to hear from you, and they don't care what you have.

Now let's examine the opening scenes of some top movies, to see just how amply the writers of these screenplays delivered the goods that got their movies made.

Opening Scenes We Don't Forget

The scripts of great movies keep you reading even today, even if you've seen them repeatedly, because they're so well constructed. Let's start with a movie that almost all children see, *The Wizard of Oz* (1939, screenplay by Noel Langley, Frances Ryerson, and Edgar Allen Woolf). In the script, we find references to camera moves such as MS (medium shot), LS (long shot), and CU (close up), which screenwriters don't use anymore because that is considered the domain of the director and the director of photography.

As the film takes off, we learn that someone tried to hurt Dorothy's dog, Toto. She is running from the camera, to the farm where she lives. She finds Aunt Em, who is not her mother. Em is taking care of chicks, carefully counting them and bothered by Dorothy's interruption, even when Dorothy complains that mean Miss Gulch hit Toto with a rake. When Uncle Henry confers with Aunt Em, we learn that Dorothy is an orphan. Then Em responds: "We all got to work out our own problems, Henry."

And with that line, we have the theme of the movie.

Next we meet Zeke, Hunk, and Hickory, farm workers who will become the Cowardly Lion, the Scarecrow, and the Tin Woodsman, respectively. We learn that Dorothy doesn't have anyone to play with. When she asks Zeke (Bert Lahr) about Miss Gulch, he chickens out of offering any advice. He says he's gotta get those hogs in. Hunk (Ray Bolger) tells Dorothy that she isn't using her head, has no brains at all. "Well," he says, "your head ain't made of straw, you know." And in the barn, oil spurts in the face of Hickory (Jack Haley) as he works on his wind machine contraption, which is supposed to break up winds so that they won't have any more dust storms that ruin the crops. He says he feels like his joints are rusted and suggests that Dorothy try to have a little more heart.

Hollywood Heat

In the seventh minute of *The Wizard of Oz*, Judy Garland sings "Over the Rainbow." Maybe that minute was lucky—the song almost wasn't in the movie! I had dinner one night with Hy Kantor, who was in charge of music at MGM when the film was made. When they were debating whether to leave the sequence in the film, Kantor put his job on the line, saying that the song would make as much money as the film, which was almost as expensive to make as *Gone with the Wind*. He insisted that they leave it in. His bosses were glad they took that bet, and so are we.

All the advice from the farm workers, of course, is a projection of their own problems. When Dorothy talks with Zeke at the pigpen, he says that she should have more courage. When Dorothy falls in, he rescues her, only to reveal his own terror.

Seamlessly, all these things happen by page 5, setting up so much that we'll see later in the movie. The fretting, childlike Dorothy at the beginning rises to maturity by the end by being repeatedly forced to conquer attempts to keep her locked in childhood. Unlike the book, the film is a deep psychological study. For example, she wears red slippers. They were silver in Baum's book, in which Dorothy was half the age of the 12-year-old depicted in the film. Red is equivalent with blood, menstruation, and the ascent to womanhood.

When Aunt Em brings crullers for everyone, she advises Dorothy to find some place where she won't get into any trouble, which sets up Dorothy singing "Over the Rainbow," the signature song of the film. The lyrics are featured in the script, another thing that you never see today. And as soon as that wonderful sequence is over on page 8, Miss Gulch shows up to take Toto away. At the top of page 10, when Gulch grabs Toto, Dorothy calls her a wicked old witch, and everything in the movie that follows has been established. Despite the inclusion of what would be considered "clutter" today (the dedication, mention of shots, and song lyrics) this is an amazing but subtle first 10 pages.

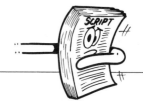

It's Not for Us

Don't get so bound by current form that you're afraid to stretch the boundaries. When Judy Garland's Dorothy Gale interacts with Professor Marvel (Frank Morgan) in the beginning of *The Wizard of Oz*, the four-and-a-half-minute sequence is crucial to the film. If it takes five minutes to get the scene done right, do it.

Now let's look at a sexually charged mystery/thriller, *Chinatown* (1974), with a screenplay by Robert Towne that has long been considered to be one of the very best, if not *the* best, ever written. Although it starts with an office scene, we instantly know that it's about behind-the-scenes dirty stuff as a fisherman named Curly looks over surveillance pictures of his wife having sex with another man, accompanied by an audio recording of the lovemaking. Private detective Jake Gittes (Jack Nicholson) is not happy showing this to Curly, who cries knowing that his wife is having an affair. When Curly inadvertently knocks movie stars' pictures on the wall askew, we know that Gittes has an influential (if immoral) clientele.

We learn that Gittes pinches pennies because he gives Curly the cheap whiskey out of a desk drawer, when he could have chosen a more expensive brand. We then see his cohorts, Duffy and Walsh, in an outer office, with a woman who is ostensibly married to Hollis Mulwray, the powerful head of the Water and Power Department in Los Angeles. When she hears the audiotape, she thinks that Gittes is having sex with a woman. Gittes is a clean freak: He wipes Curly's sweat off his desk with a handkerchief.

Curly wants to kill his wife, but Gittes angrily admonishes him, saying that you gotta be rich to kill somebody and get away with it. And when we learn that Curly hasn't paid Gittes off, and Gittes lets it slide, we're only four pages in. As Curly departs, we see lettering on Gittes' outer door that reads "Discreet Investigation." This, we now know for sure, is the only kind of detective work that Gittes and company does.

Hollywood Heat

Jack Nicholson has been nominated for 11 Academy Awards and won the following Oscars: in 1976 as Best Actor for *One Flew Over the Cuckoo's Nest* (1975); in 1984 as Best Supporting Actor for *Terms of Endearment* (1983); and in 1998 as Best Actor for *As Good as It Gets* (1997). He was once kicked out of the legendary Schwab's Drugstore for lounging around all day with his friend, writer/director Robert Towne, without buying more than a cup of coffee. He told the waitress that it was the last place he would ever get kicked out of. Shortly thereafter, he was cast in *Easy Rider* (1970), for which he received his first Best Supporting Actor nomination.

Within 10 pages, we've learned that Gittes thinks it's best for most women to forget their husband's indiscretions if they love them because that's simply the way men are. But money doesn't matter to "Mrs. Mulwray" (whom we later learn isn't who she claims to be), so Gittes takes the job. He goes to a City Hall meeting, where the former mayor, Sam Bagby, is pitching a dam project to bring badly needed water to the desert community of Los Angeles, but Mr. Mulwray (whom we learn is 60 years old) says that the Van Der Lip dam gave way and that this one will, too. Mulwray refuses to build the project. When a farmer brings in a flock of sheep, disrupting the meeting with a claim that Mulwray is stealing water from the Valley, we have all the elements in the movie (including an implication of kinky sex that will play out later). Once again, the first 10 pages establish everything in the film.

At first, you think that the first 10 pages of the *Witness* (1985) screenplay by Earl W. Wallace, William Kelley, and Pamela Wallace, is not a thriller, but a family drama. An Amish woman named Rachel (Kelly McGillis) has lost her husband. An Amish man, Daniel Hochstetler (Alexander Godunov), reveals that he likes her as she leaves with her son, Samuel (Lukas Haas), to visit relatives in the outside world, which the boy has never seen. Then, while in a train station bathroom stall, Samuel witnesses a murder and barely escapes being killed himself, right at the end of page 10.

On the first page of the romantic comedy *Shakespeare in Love* (1998), by Marc Norman and Tom Stoppard, we learn that two theaters, Richard Burbage's Curtain and Philiip Henslowe's Rose, are battling for dramatic supremacy in London of 1593. When we first see Henslowe (Geoffrey Ruse), he is being tortured because he owes a lot of money, but he talks his way out of it by offering a new play that he has commissioned from Will Shakespeare, entitled *Romeo and Ethel, the Pirate's Daughter*. Fennyman (Tom Wilkinson), the abusive financier, takes the bait. He intends to produce the play, dupe the actors and author out of money by offering profits but showing none, and get even with Henslowe. And when the theater owner goes to tell the obviously not quite successful Bard the news, we find Will Shakespeare (Joseph Fiennes) practicing his signature. He hasn't written a word of the play. He has writer's block, and who wouldn't when turning out plays such as *One Gentleman of Verona?* But he will get it done— as soon as he finds his muse (Gwyneth Paltrow's Viola). The premise is set up by the top of page five, and we're laughing all the way.

Skip's Tips

In preparing the opening of your screenplay, think of one perfect picture, which is the essence of the film contained in one scene. We find that in *Raiders of the Lost Ark,* and it is reflected in the movie poster. It's the same with *Jaws.* You needn't make up a poster, but every little bit helps. Set the scene, and they might keep it.

Let's switch gears to the amazing and refreshing *The Sixth Sense* (1999), by M. Night Shyamalan, who also directed the movie. In the first few pages, we learn that something weird is going on in the basement of Anna Crowe (Olivia Williams) as "dripping black" devours the room when she leaves. Her husband, Malcolm, (Bruce Willis) has been recognized with the Mayor's Citation of Professional Excellence from the City of Philadelphia for his work in child psychology. We know where we are and who they are, and by end of page five, their celebration has taken them to bed. But there is an intruder in the house, hiding in the bathroom off the master bedroom. He's 19, with a patch of white in his hair, a drugged-out psychotic whom Malcolm worked with when the man, Vincent Gray (Donnie Wahlberg), was a child of 10. Vincent says that Malcolm has failed him, and he's still terrified. He shoots Malcolm and then blows his own brains out on page nine. Fade to black, then a title card of "Two Years Later," and we find Malcolm sitting on an outside bench, looking over Vincent's file. The "Two Years Later" is a classic misdirectional touch that isn't revealed until the end of the film, and we have all this by page eight.

Last but not least is another film about a girl needing to mature. (Just kidding, Jack.) Actually, it's a middle-aged writer, Melvin Udall (played wonderfully by Jack Nicholson). *As Good as It Gets* (1997), by Mark Andrus (also story) and James L. Brooks, is one of my all-time favorite scripts. In the first *six* pages, we learn that Melvin is an ass, starting with his dumping a small dog named Verdell (who looks like Toto's cousin) down an apartment building garbage chute. We know that Melvin is a homophobe because he goes out of his way to insult the owner of the dog, across-the-hall neighbor Simon Bishop (Greg Kinnear). And, not surprisingly, Melvin is also a racist, as we learn when he insults the man who sells Simon's paintings, Frank Sachs (Cuba Gooding Jr.) As Melvin retreats into his apartment, we find out that he is incredibly superstitious as he locks and unlocks his door several times. Then we see that he's a germophobe as he washes his hands (but only with the third bar of soap that he unwraps). Then, and all within six pages, we learn that this inhuman insult machine writes romance novels! I can't imagine any reader not stamping "Recommend!" on this script, based on the first few marvelous pages.

The movies discussed here have won Academy Awards, have been box office successes, and are loved by audiences around the world. They are different types of films, from different time periods. What they have in common is stellar writing that, in 10 pages or less, sets up the entire movie in excellent fashion. As you might have noticed from these examples, more gets done in fewer pages these days than in the past, but things haven't changed that much. We can still tell a great script early, and readers (and audiences) are suckers for great openings.

How the Digital Age Affects Screenplay Openings

At one time when B-movie producers who had a track record for delivering movies that made money would think of an idea for a film, have a poster made up, and present the poster at film markets as product in their pipeline. Foreign distributors who responded would spend money to pre-buy the "movie" and the producers would then have the cash to commission the writing of the script and make the picture.

As computer graphics have proliferated and made the production of artwork much cheaper, I'm sure that this type of practice still goes on, just as a producer might use a "one-sheet" of text that you supply to try to generate interest before committing to buying the project from you. If any of this sounds unethical, welcome to Hollywood at the independent level.

Writers can combat this by becoming digital filmmakers. At this writing, for an investment of around $10,000, you can buy a high-end Apple computer, editing software, *and* a high-quality digital camera that would allow you to make a movie. Rather than simply trying to get your script read, you might think of shooting a key scene, or the opening scene, or several scenes of your script. If I were you, I would try to pick a scene that might be a small movie all its own, or rewrite a portion of your script as a small film that, expanded, would be your screenplay. Hollywood filmmakers do this type of thing all the time. The evolution of Billy Bob Thornton's *Sling Blade* (1996) is an example.

Do a Web search for a couple movies around eight minutes in length, such as *Sunday's Game* (about some old ladies who get together to play cards and Russian roulette) and *George Lucas in Love* (about the "real"

Script Notes

"Foreign pre-sales" are how many movies have been made, using advances from foreign distributors. That means that only the North American market is left to produce a profit. It's yet another reason why screenwriters very rarely make any money on the "back end" (post-expense profits). Actor Eddie Murphy calls net profit participation "monkey points" because only a monkey would expect to be paid.

156

inspiration for *Star Wars* that came when young Lucas was trying to graduate from film school at USC). Both films garnered high-visibility deals for the people who made them, partially due to exposure on the Web. Check out sites such as Webatomfilms.com. You'll probably find a hundred like it.

Another thing to keep in mind with regard to digital changes in Hollywood is music videos. Whether you like them or not, you'd better watch because directors of music videos often get first feature deals. The styles that you see on MTV today will turn up in the theaters tomorrow, so try to keep up. If you write the way they shoot, your script might sell more quickly.

Hollywood Heat

Supposedly, director John Huston asked reclusive novelist B. Traven to script his own novel, *The Treasure of the Sierra Madre* (1948). Traven turned him down, as he did when asked if he wanted to visit the set. Huston suspected that Traven did show up, posing as "Howe Crows—Translator, Acapulco," who served as technical adviser on the film. Now here's the Hollywood legend. Perhaps frustrated with Traven, the story goes that Huston told his secretary to turn the book into a script, and that's what he shot. Because Huston won the Oscar for Best Writing, Screenplay, on that film, the story is probably just gold dust in the wind.

See If You Can Beat the Best

There isn't room in this book to present the first 10 pages of the script that Columbia director said was the best first 10 pages he had ever read. Besides, I don't want to spoil the story or compete with the scripts mentioned previously. But I do suggest that you do yourself a favor: Get some of the scripts mentioned, or some others that you admire, and rewrite the first 5 or 10 pages. See if you can beat the best. If you like the results, share those pages with some friends. If they agree that yours are better, send them to the persons who produced and directed the original (if they're still alive, of course) and see what happens.

Who knows? They might be impressed and offer that Hollywood catchphrase that means you have their interest—*What else you got?* Believe me, stranger things have happened.

The Least You Need to Know

➤ Using flashbacks to show your character's back story is usually the mark of an amateur.

➤ Every decent movie has an inciting incident that irrevocably propels the main character into the flow of the main story.

➤ The average successful production company learns of 25 to 50 potential submissions per day, so yours had better be special.

➤ With many great films, the entire framework of the movie is set up within the first 10 pages—these days, usually less.

➤ A short film, shot digitally, might get you a major deal quicker than a screenplay alone.

➤ You become the best by studying and competing with the best, and you must keep track of what other upcoming talent is doing.

Chapter 14

The Structure of Hollywood Movies

In This Chapter

➤ Three acts and 2,500 years

➤ The myth structure

➤ Syd Field's influence

➤ New ideas

➤ The ultimate screenplay

Some people are natural storytellers. They have a gift of gab that they are able to translate to the written page, or they are quiet observers who can comment on the human condition in writing in a way that gives us all pause.

At least, that's what I've been told. I've never met a single one of those people in 20 years in Hollywood. I've been an entertainment journalist, a novelist, a magazine editor, and an actor. I helped get the Hollywood Film Festival started, but never once have I met a natural storyteller who just ventured into screenwriting and sold a screenplay without learning basic film structure. If you have, let me know. I love to be amazed.

Skip's Tips

If you're good at conversation, you might use a technique that some screenwriters use to test their story ideas. It's called "I knew this guy ...." Here's an example: "I knew this guy whose grandfather found the real Ark of the Covenant." And they say with enthusiastic interest, "Really?" (the reaction you want). And you tell them your Indiana Jones story.

Script Notes

Here's Aristotle on how comedy got it's name: "[C]ertain Dorians of the Peloponnese ... appeal to the evidence of language. The outlying villages, they say, are by them called Komai, by the Athenians demoi: and they assume that comedians were so named not from komazein, 'to revel,' but because they wandered from village to village (kata komas), being excluded contemptuously from the city."

Three Acts and Thousands of Years Later

At some point in your writing career, you absolutely *must* read Aristotle's *Poetics*. These days, you can even download it from the Internet. It's a very short work, although you'd better have your poetry dictionary by your side, to look up terms such as *anapaest* (a metrical foot composed of two short syllables followed by one long one, as in the word *seventeen*). Although it is a treatise on the elements of poetry—the method of dramatic presentation in Aristotle's time—it is filled with principles that rule dramatic structure even today.

The three-act structure comes from an Aristotelian observation. In speaking of drama, Aristotle says: "It should have for its subject a single action, whole and complete, with a beginning, a middle, and an end. It will thus resemble a living organism in all its unity, and produce the pleasure proper to it."

Ever wonder why movie stars are generally much better-looking than normal people and character actors are often very odd-looking? Perhaps this quote from Aristotle explains it: "Since the objects of imitation are men in action, and these men must be either of a higher or a lower type (for moral character mainly answers to these divisions, goodness and badness being the distinguishing marks of moral differences), it follows that we must represent men either as better than in real life, or as worse, or as they are."

Reading *Poetics*, you realize that the basics of entertainment haven't really changed that much in the past few thousand years. Reading it, I realized that the ongoing popularity of "road-trip" movies relates back to traveling comedians in ancient Greece. Here's Aristotle's definition of comedy, which seems the same to me: "Comedy is, as we have said, an imitation of characters of a lower type—not, however, in the full sense of the word *bad*, the ludicrous being merely a subdivision of the ugly. It consists in some defect or ugliness which is not painful or destructive."

Does the following seem applicable, in comparing filmmakers who want to ennoble culture to those who simply want a reaction? "Poetry now diverged in two directions, according to the individual character of the writers. The graver spirits imitated noble actions and the actions of good men. The more trivial sort imitated the actions of meaner persons, at first composing satires, as the former did hymns to the gods and the praises of famous men."

Would you say this definition of the elements of drama apply to movies? Says Aristotle: "Every Tragedy, therefore, must have six parts, which parts determine its quality—namely, Plot, Character, Diction, Thought, Spectacle, Song." He defines these at length in a few short pages. For example, diction is "the expression of the meaning in words." Movie stars who do that best, such as Jack Nicholson, inevitably become legends.

If you think there is too much emphasis on structuring a screenplay before you begin writing, consider this: "But most important of all is the structure of the incidents .... For Tragedy is an imitation, not of men, but of an action and of life, and life consists in action, and its end is a mode of action, not a quality. Tragedy is an imitation of an action that is complete, and whole, and of a certain magnitude; for there may be a whole that is wanting in magnitude." How many movies have you seen that don't seem to be about anything?

Hollywood Heat

Brilliantly written by Barry Levinson in his directorial debut, *Diner* (1982), about a group of friends who hang out in a Baltimore diner in the 1950s, marked the film debut of Ellen Barkin and Paul Reiser. Many more "unknowns" who starred in the film went on to great success: Steve Guttenberg, Daniel Stern, Mickey Rourke, Kevin Bacon, and Tim Daly. One of the funnier bits was provided by Tait Ruppert as Methan, who, as a one-man Greek chorus, floated through scenes reciting lines from *Sweet Smell of Success* (1957). Ruppert did not appear in another film for 17 years, which might go to show how hard it is to graduate from the chorus.

If no one has ever defined "beginning, middle, and end" for you, here it is, in Aristotle's words:

> A whole is that which has a beginning, a middle, and an end. A beginning is that which does not itself follow anything by causal necessity, but after which something naturally is or comes to be. An end, on the contrary, is that which

itself naturally follows some other thing, either by necessity, or as a rule, but has nothing following it. A middle is that which follows something as some other thing follows it. A well constructed plot, therefore, must neither begin nor end at haphazard, but conform to these principles.

Don't take my word for it. Get out your dictionary and read *Poetics,* if you have not. There is a reason this essay continues to be so influential long after the glories of Greece are dust.

The Influence of the Myth Structure

In the first chapter, we discussed briefly how Hollywood storytelling was influenced by the works of Joseph Campbell. I could list a number of movies that have followed the Campbell "myth structure," which he derived from stories and legends that he studied from around the world. Even though George Lucas is the most well-known proponent of Campbell and *Star Wars* is a very well-known movie, I'd rather use *The Wizard of Oz* to outline the basic Campbell "Hero's Journey" steps. Note that Campbell mostly wrote about male heroes.

Dividing a story into Aristotle's three acts, the following steps fit into Act One. Like all great myth structure stories, it starts in an everyday world, Dorothy Gale's farm home in Kansas:

It's Not for Us

Founded in 1990, The Joseph Campbell Foundation is a non-profit organization to "preserve, protect, and perpetuate Campbell's pioneering work by collecting and cataloging his books, papers, and recorded lectures." Unfortunately, this organization's hard-to-navigate Web site, at www.jcf.org, is filled with unexplained icons. It's as confusing as Campbell was informative. Read his books before you bother with the site.

The Call to Adventure. Miss Gulch is coming to take Toto.

Refusal of the Call. Dorothy runs away from home with Toto.

Supernatural Aid. The tornado transports them to Oz, and Glenda the Good Witch comes in.

The Crossing the First Threshold. Dorothy and Toto discover Munchkinland.

The Belly of the Whale. Dorothy and Toto travel to Oz on the Yellow Brick Road.

Here are the steps that fit into Act Two:

The Road of Trials. Dorothy accumulates allies on the way to Oz.

The Meeting with the Goddess. Dorothy and friends meet the Wizard.

Woman as the Temptress. Surrender, Dorothy!

Atonement with the Father. Dorothy destroys the Wicked Witch.

Apotheosis. Dorothy is immediately celebrated and elevated.

The Ultimate Boon. Dorothy has captured the Wicked Witch's broom.

Act Three would break down this way:

Refusal of the Return. Dorothy has second thoughts on leaving Oz.

The Magic Flight. The Wizard's balloon leaves without her.

Rescue from Without. Glenda arrives to explain the way.

Crossing the Return Threshold. Dorothy uses the ruby red slippers.

Master of the Two Worlds. She's no longer worried in Kansas.

Freedom to Live. There's no place like home!

I suspect that you might be wondering about some of the steps mentioned. In "The Meeting with the Goddess," remember that "the Goddess" symbolizes the world in which the story takes place. When Dorothy and friends meet the Wizard, they are conferring with the person whom they think is the spokesperson and ruler of the world of Oz. In the "Woman as the Temptress" step, as the Wicked Witch of the East skywrites "Surrender, Dorothy!" in black smoke over the Emerald City, we literally have a woman who is tempting Dorothy to stop on her adventure, to give up her quest.

Nevertheless, the "Atonement with the Father" is when Dorothy destroys the Wicked Witch. Why? Consider that "the Father," in this story, is the thing that gets the story started. In this case, it would be the dual Miss Gulch/Wicked Witch of the East character, played by Margaret Hamilton. To *atone* means "to make amends, as for a sin or fault." What's Dorothy's sin or fault? Basically, she's facing growing up and is assuming the responsibilities of adulthood, but she keeps running away from that. In the opening, she wants her Aunt Em and Uncle Henry to handle a situation

Skip's Tips

Reading Joseph Campbell is a storyteller must. Read *The Hero with a Thousand Faces* (Princeton University Press, 1972), but also study *An Open Life: Joseph Campbell in Conservation with Michael Toms* (Perennial Library, 1989); *The Hero's Journey: Joseph Campbell on His Life and Work* (Harper and Row, 1990); and *Joseph Campbell and the Power of Myth*, the interview series done by Bill Moyers for PBS (Mystic Fire Video, 1991).

that she got herself into (Toto chasing Miss Gulch's cat). By the time she kills the Wicked Witch (while defending her friend the Scarecrow, the one who wants to have a brain to think), she has grown up and will stand up to Miss Gulch/Wicked Witch of the East, with no concern for the consequences. After all, she has no idea that water

It's Not for Us

While screenwriting gurus may be in vogue in Hollywood, other types of gurus have fallen out of favor. For example, the first edition of Syd Field's *Screenplay* was dedicated to est founder Werner Erhard. The current expanded edition of the book is "To the students, writers, and readers of the screenplay everywhere." Leave your religion or quasi-religion out of your screenplay, please.

will kill the witch. Thus, Dorothy has made amends for not handling her own problems in the beginning, and we know that she'll be able to do so from there onward.

As you've probably noticed, there are many steps in Act Three, but they take place over relatively few minutes, compared to the other acts. That's because, in most films—particularly films built on the myth structure—Act Two is generally twice as long as either of the other acts. In Hero's Journey storytelling, Act One has to do with the mental and spiritual preparation that the hero or heroine goes through to get started on the journey. Act Two is concerned with all the obstacles that must be overcome to reach the elevated state of being that rescues these characters from the problems they had in the beginning. In Act Three, they undergo an assessment of their new situation and the new knowledge or ability that they possess that allows them to function in the world in which they began, as well as the one to which they traveled.

Every great story tells a tale of mental and spiritual growth, and that is precisely what makes it great.

Joseph Campbell managed to outline and elaborate on the exact steps of this process, and we're all the better for it. To miss studying his work is a true "Refusal of the Call."

Syd Field's Paradigm

Hollywood screenwriting has two time periods: B.S. (before *Screenplay*) and A.S. (after *Screenplay*). *Screenplay*, of course, is Syd Field's *Screenplay: The Foundations of Screenwriting, A Step-by-Step Guide from Concept to Finished Script* (Dell, 1994). When the first slim edition appeared in 1979, it took the industry by storm because no one had codified the basic structure of a screenplay in such a simple manner. His "paradigm," the skeletal structure of scripts, was photocopied and hung on walls of readers and development executives. Some critics (there are always critics in Hollywood) wondered, however, what Field's own writing credits were. Why was he qualified to comment on how to write a screenplay, much less define *the* method for writing one?

Subsequently, Field cleared that up, revealing that he had been a writer/producer for David L. Wolper, a well-known producer. He explained that he had been the head of the story department for Cinemobile Systems for around two years, during which time he read more than 2,000 scripts but recommended only 40.

Field, when asked to teach a class on screenwriting at Sherwood Oaks Experimental College, a school remembered fondly by anyone who started in Hollywood in the 1980s, Field examined what made the recommended scripts work and came up with the standard things: a clear beginning, middle, and end, and a great first few pages. Field used the word *paradigm*—an example that serves as pattern or model—to describe the structure that he saw at work in screenplays that sold. Act One was the beginning, the setup for the action that followed, and ended on page 30. Act Two was the middle, the major conflict of the film (he calls it "confrontation"), and ran to page 90. Act Three, the end, was where all the major conflicts were resolved, and this act ended on page 120.

Hollywood Heat

In the last couple years, consolidation has been in vogue in Hollywood, much as in the rest of corporate America. Perhaps that's why Syd Field affiliated himself with the Final Draft company, which makes the screenwriting formatting software in broadest use in the industry. Through Final Draft, he offers *Syd Field's Screenwriting Workshop Video Learning Series: Writing a Screenplay That Sells to Hollywood*, a two-tape screenwriting course. For details, see www.finaldraft.com, e-mail sales@finaldraft.com, or contact the company at Final Draft, Inc., 16000 Ventura Blvd., Suite 800, Encino, CA 91436, phone 1-800-231-4055 or 818-994-8995, fax 818-995-4422.

Field might have been revelatory for students of Aristotle, Lajos Egri, or Joseph Campbell, perhaps, but none of them had written specifically about the schematic structure of a successful screenplay (although Egri wrote about TV plays). Field, though, added something new—the plot point. One is in the first act, between pages 25 and 27, and another toward the end of the second act, between pages 85 and 90. And what might a plot point be? It's an event that anchors the story line and spins it around in another direction. He gives the example of *Chinatown*, in which Jack Nicholson's Jake Gittes meets Faye Dunaway and discovers that she is the real Evelyn Mulwray. The one who came to Gittes' office to have her husband investigated was an impostor.

The plot point in Act Two (I hope you've seen the movie) comes when detective Gittes discovers the glasses of the murdered Hollis Mulwray in a saltwater garden pool behind Mulwray's house. Suddenly he realizes why Mulwray was found to have salt water in his lungs. He was not murdered where it was thought he was murdered. All the unanswered questions that Gittes has start to unravel. Because of the new direction in which the movie has been spun—while remaining true to the premise of the film, "People with enough money and power can get away with murder or anything else"—Gittes is able to uncover the incest and murder at the root of the mystery.

It's Not for Us

Although being "true to your school" can be a noble thing, it's not always a good idea in Hollywood. You can always find an argument about the "best" screenwriting teacher. In my experience (and I've studied most of them), the truth is, they all have something to offer. Never settle for any one guru; the next teacher might solve the problem that no one else could.

Skip's Tips

The secret to learning Hollywood secrets is to accumulate knowledge over time, from as many sources as possible. One of the best places for that is the Sherwood Oaks Experimental College. Working pros such as James Cameron started there and come back to do seminars. Contact director (and founder) Gary Shusett at Sherwood Oaks Experimental College, 7095 Hollywood Blvd. #876, Los Angeles, CA 90028, or see www.sherwoodoakscollege.com.

There is great beauty in simple things, and Field's philosophy of plot points was somewhat of a revelation for aspiring screenwriters. Great writers had done it instinctively, but no one had really codified the technique before Field came along.

Field seems to be of the opinion that any film that gets made has plot points at the end of the first and second acts. It's likely that he's right, but then I've seen some films that seemed to have no point at all, much less a plot. When the first edition of *Screenplay* came out, however, it was adopted so broadly across Hollywood that writers adjusted their screenplays so that the plot points—which screenwriters had been calling "twists" for years—landed on exactly the same pages that Field said they would land.

Why? Because readers looked for them, and if the scripts did *not* fit Field's paradigm, particularly Plot Point I, scripts would be rejected right there. Writers learned quickly what the new rules in town were, those outlined in *Screenplay*. For some writers, though, Field's paradigm seemed like a cookie-cutter approach, and it drove them crazy.

Over the years, Field has gotten smarter about screenplay structure. The latest edition of *Screenplay* is excellent, as is *The Screenwriter's Problem Solver: How to Recognize, Identify, and Define Screenwriting Problems* (Dell, 1998). Whatever you do, study what he says about plot points. He's right.

New Approaches and Other Ideas

A couple years ago, a Web designer in San Francisco tried to convince me that his new 12-act screenplay structure was the ultimate authority on screenplays that work. He was convinced that there was a hidden, heretofore undiscovered method for constructing films that only a lucky few had subconsciously woven together. He even convinced me to read a screenplay that he'd written, which was constructed around his principles. Curious, I agreed. I found the script interesting, but not all that different. I certainly did not consider it extraordinary. Still, always willing to help new screenwriters, I offered to get it to someone whom I thought might like it.

He flippantly revealed that he had someone at Disney reading it (it could loosely be classified as a family film). I asked why he had sent it to me, given that I'd told him how busy I was. "Oh," he casually replied, "I just wanted another opinion."

A number of gurus and wannabes in recent years have decided that, for whatever reasons, all or part of existing story structure is antiquated and somewhat irrelevant.

One of them is John Truby (see www.truby.com). I like him better than some because he emphasizes studying the masters to gain an understanding of the craft of screenwriting. Truby offers books, software, and seminars to support his theories, and he has a theory and a book or software module for just about everything.

Putting the emphasis almost solely on software are Chris Huntley and Melanie Phillips, whose Dramatica Pro software program (see www.dramatica. com) was put together after the creators failed in their filmmaking aspirations. The software has been criticized heavily for trying to completely reinvent the storytelling wheel, but it keeps surviving, so maybe there's something to it. It seems to be most popular with young people totally new to screenwriting who may not have studied more classical methods.

Skip's Tips

A slug line is not the place where an exchange of dialogue starts a fight. It's the ALL CAPITALS line at the top of a scene that establishes place and time of day. "EXT." means "Exterior" or outside, and "INT." represents "Interior" or inside. "EXT. THE WHITE HOUSE—DAY" tells us we're outside 1600 Pennsylvania Avenue in the daytime.

Perhaps the most influential recent guru is Robert McKee (see www.mckeestory.com), the author of *Story* (ReganBooks, 1997). McKee's main pitch is the "Classic Five-Part Narrative Structure," consisting of: (1) inciting incident; (2) progressive complications; (3) crisis; (4) climax; and (5) resolution. Studying McKee, it is obvious that he was influenced by Campbell and classical sources. He is highly effective at getting his material across and is the most well-known of screenwriting gurus.

If you're the type of writer who not only wants to learn the rules but who also wants to find ways to bend and reshape them (which is most writers I know), you might take a look at *Alternative Scriptwriting: Writing Beyond the Rules* (Focal Press, 1991), by Ken Dancyger and Jeff Rush. Both men were academics when they wrote the book, with Dancyger the Head of Undergraduate Studies for the Department of Film and Television at New York University. They review existing theories and go to elaborate lengths to describe almost everything within the purview of screenwriting in their own terms. For example, they call a plot point a "turning point," which is a minor or major reversal.

Hollywood Heat

A friend of mine knew David E. Kelley, the megasuccessful creator of the TV series *Ally McBeal* and *The Practice*, before he became one of the heavy-hitter writer/producers of network television. At a party at his house, Kelley told several friends about his new script *White Picket Fences*, about an odd little town that looked normal on the surface but was weird underneath. None of them were terribly impressed, but network executives were. *Picket Fences* went on the air in 1992, garnered numerous awards before finishing its run, and established Kelley's reputation as a hitmaker.

It's all a matter of semantics, isn't it? To Aristotle and Dancyger and Rush, a twist is a reversal. To Field, it's a change in direction. Nevertheless, Dancyger and Rush discuss things that others don't, such as their examination of the Multiple Main-Character movie, *Mystic Pizza* (1988), the film that launched Julia Roberts. Although the book may seem a bit too intellectual for some, I recommend it as a must-read for other possible directions that you might take a script.

I cover (or try to cover) all the main gurus of Hollywood and screenwriting in my book *The Writer's Guide to Hollywood Producers, Directors, and Screenwriter's Agents* (Prima, 2000). The book is in its second edition as I write, with a new and expanded edition arriving in late 2000 or early 2001.

The Ultimate Screenplay Design

As I've said before and will likely say several times again, you're better off reading as many books and taking as many classes on the subject of screenwriting as you can. Film is a constantly evolving medium, and if you're not actively in the heart of film-making, making movies regularly, you need to keep up as best you can, at least until you break into the business.

Then you have to do better than keep up—you have to forge new trails to stay noticed.

Now here's something that I've observed and discussed with other screenwriters, but that I've not seen anyone else put in print. Perhaps I've simply not read enough or attended enough seminars. I've noticed that in almost all films, there is a distinct *midpoint change*, roughly in the middle of Act Two, where the main character, who has been the effect of events that he or she is battling against, becomes more positively causative over the opposing force. This usually coincides with Joseph Campbell's

"Woman as the Temptress" Hero's Journey step. By "woman," Campbell means life, with the hero "its knower and master." It is the moment when the hero becomes determined or empowered to do what it takes to achieve the goal. You see this in any number of James Bond movies, where he is captured by the villain and then escapes, knowing what he has to do to win.

Hopefully by now you have a screenplay idea in mind. I hope that you've tried it out on friends or professionals, that you have winnowed this idea out from at least a dozen other ideas, and that you're convinced that you have the right one for you to write. If you have done this, move to the head of the class. For everyone else, provided that you've done your homework, the following steps should put you well on the path to a professional screenplay. I'll use *The Wizard of Oz* and other movies to illustrate as we go.

It's Not for Us

Do yourself a big favor. Don't get cute with your first screenplay, or even your third. Pick an established genre and come up with an original story that fits the parameters of that genre. If you experiment before you master the basics, it might blow up in your face.

1. Develop a premise whose "what if?" question personally excites you. For example, what if a girl on the edge of adulthood were transported to a magical land where, through fantastic adventures, she reaches the level of mature adult responsibility? Write your premise down on a "pitch card" and keep it posted nearby.

2. Determine whether you have a theme for your movie. If you do, write it down. In the case of *The Wizard of Oz,* it would be Aunt Em's line to Uncle Henry: "We all got to work out our own problems." If you don't have a theme, don't worry about it. It will emerge on its own, or not.

3. Try to give your movie a title that provides the reader/viewer with a good idea of what the movie is about, as in *Witness,* or alludes to the subtext and theme, as in *As Good as It Gets.*

4. Figure out where your story begins. You're looking for the inciting incident from which the main character will not be able to turn back. If your movie is an ensemble piece, you will still have an inciting incident that will propel the group into some irreversible course of events. In *The Big Chill,* that event was the suicide of everyone's mutual friend, played by Kevin Costner, whose face we never see onscreen. If you have "back story" beginning scenes, set them aside for reference.

5. If it has not already occurred to you, try to establish an ending to your film, the logical progression from the beginning point of your movie. In *The Wizard of Oz,* Dorothy must learn to work out her own problems, and she must overcome tremendous obstacles to reach that point of maturity.

Skip's Tips

Don't leave out the denouement, the icing on the cake of a great screenplay that provides a final clarification of what the hero has accomplished. Think of the wonderful ironic twist at the end of *Raiders of the Lost Ark*, as the Ark of the Covenant is filed away to be forgotten in a U.S. government warehouse. Audiences expect it, so give it to them.

6. Lay out a rough description of the scenes in your movie, with each one *roughly* three minutes or less in length.

7. Divide your scenes into acts, with Act Two being roughly twice as long as either Act One or Act Three. It might help if you use actual index cards, which you can sort into stacks.

8. Try to locate where your plot or turning points are located, usually a scene or two before the end of Acts One and Two. These are events that accelerate the story by sending it in a new direction, which may even be a full reversal of events up to that time.

9. Find the scene roughly in the middle of Act Two that is your *midpoint change,* where the hero makes a shift, however subtle, from being more effect of the opposing force to being more causative than effect. If you don't have this scene, devise it.

10. Flesh out your scenes on index cards, if the scenes are not already fully described. Do your best to add a denouement, or tag, at the end of Act Three.

11. Write out a treatment of your screenplay, using your cards to describe your movie scene by scene as they flow.

12. Set aside your treatment for at least a couple days, and then read it in a quiet place to see how the movie plays in your mind.

If we take the three-act structure, assume that there is a turning point before the end of Act One, a midpoint change in the middle of Act Two, a turning point before the end of Act Two, and a denouement or "tag" at the end of Act Three (such as Dorothy's speech at the end of *The Wizard of Oz*)—then we actually have five distinct parts of a movie, don't we? (Act One to first turning point, first turning point to midpoint change, midpoint change to second turning point, second turning point to end of Act Three, denouement.)

Hmmm. Sounds like Shakespeare, doesn't it? As I hope you've noticed so far, storytelling and screenwriting are evolving disciplines. And that's one of the reasons they keep coming back for more, isn't it?

The Least You Need to Know

➤ The beginning, middle, and end dramatic structure described in Aristotle's *Poetics* remains the predominant storytelling framework today.

➤ The myth structure outlined by Joseph Campbell in *Hero with a Thousand Faces* is crucial to understanding epic stories.

➤ The "paradigm" story schematic in Syd Field's *Screenplay*, with its change of direction plot points before the end of Acts One and Two, should be studied by all screenwriters.

➤ With many story gurus proposing new storytelling methods, some of the more interesting ideas come from *Alternative Scriptwriting: Writing Beyond the Rules* (Focal Press, 1991), by Ken Dancyger and Jeff Rush.

➤ In almost all films, a midpoint change occurs in which the main character transitions from being mostly the effect of the opposing force to a causatively positive state.

➤ In 12 short steps, you can create all the necessary elements for writing a professional screenplay.

Chapter 15

Writing the Feature Film

In This Chapter

➤ Beginning, middle, and end

➤ First acts

➤ The second act *is it*

➤ The second act needs fixing

➤ Spielberg's second acts

➤ The midpoint

➤ The crucial third act

➤ Denouement

After you've outlined your scenes, pick a couple that you think are crucial and outline them again. This time, though, see if you can determine where the scene really should begin. Then find the middle of the scene, where it turns in another direction. When the scene ends, you should want to know what happens next. If you aren't feeling compelled to read on, there could be something wrong with the ending. That's right, every scene has a three-part structure, just like you find in a good screenplay.

Scenes in a well-constructed screenplay are like the many layers of an onion, organically connected one to the other at a base that we might compare to the premise of the story. If one scene is removed, it collapses those above it, and the overall look is a hollow one. With no base, the layers go everywhere. Each scene must have an integrity equal to that of the script itself, a microcosm inside a macrocosm. If you think that example smells, think of the painted Russian dolls that are one inside another, with halves that come apart until you get down to the inner doll.

Script Notes

Writer/director/producer James Cameron's *Titanic* script was maligned by some critics, but he does something at the end of many scenes that propels you into the next one. Read the script sometime, and you'll see what I mean. You'll find little scene-ending "tags" that move the story. The movie was not a blockbuster merely because people liked watching a ship sink.

Skip's Tips

Script lengths vary by genre. The epic *Star Wars: The Phantom Menace,* ran 133 minutes. Like Spielberg films, the second act was extended because of so much action. Kids' animated movies, such as *Toy Story* and *The Lion King,* however, run between 80 and 90 minutes.

Making the Beginning, Middle, and End Work

At the end of the last chapter was a 12-step program (no jokes, please) prescribing a path to a full treatment (expanded outline) from which to write your screenplay. Assuming that you wrote that, are you happy with it? Whether you're happy or uncertain about it, let's go over the overall structure of your screenplay. Do you have your *inciting incident?* In action films, these are easy to point out, but they're obvious in other films, too. Some examples are included here:

➤ A beautiful young female swimmer is eaten by the great white shark in *Jaws.* This danger to the community must be dealt with so that the bay is safe and the tourist season is not harmed.

➤ In *Chinatown,* a woman posing as Evelyn Mulwray hires detective Jake Gittes to spy on her husband. Gittes is committed to the case because he is being paid and because his office needs the money.

➤ In *The Sixth Sense,* an intruder kills child psychologist Malcolm Crowe. Although we don't know it until the end, Crowe must (like all ghosts) attempt to finish the cut-short efforts of his life.

➤ In *As Good as It Gets,* ultimate grouch Melvin Udall tries to hurt an innocent little dog. When he is challenged by the dog's owner, it is karma's first demand that Melvin faces his own flawed character.

➤ Jim Carrey plays a divorced father who always makes excuses in *Liar, Liar.* When he misses his son's birthday party and lies about it, that incites his son to wish that his father can never lie.

If you're not sure whether you have your inciting incident, think about the ending that you have in mind for your screenplay. If you know where you're going, ask yourself this question:

> *Will this event put my main character on a path to his ultimate goal from which there is no turning back?*

Lajos Egri believed in the "unity of opposites." He thought that the villain had to be the equal of the hero, the yin to the hero's yang. They oppose each other in a life-and-death struggle that one must lose. Like an electric motor, their opposite poles drive the engine of the story, based on the premise. Does your inciting incident place your hero and villain in irreversible conflict?

Here's a very easily seen example. In *Armageddon*, Bruce Willis and his crew must destroy the approaching asteroid, or life on Earth will end. Earth governments learning about the asteroid is the inciting incident. There is absolutely no turning back.

When you have your inciting incident (which may occur before the movie begins, as in *The Wizard of Oz*) you should be able to begin writing your script. The first big break will be the end of Act One, which comes when your main character has undergone all the steps necessary to *set up* the major conflict that is the extended Act Two. Remember, Act Two is at least twice as long as the other acts, roughly a 1:2:1 ratio. If your script is 120 pages, the acts will be 30:60:30 minutes long. If your script is 110 pages long, as many are these days, the acts will be 27.5:55:27.5. Because comedy scripts are generally shorter, let's say that you have a 90-minute comedy, so the acts will be 22.5:45:22.5. (Remember, these are simply suggestions, not absolutes.)

For easy math purposes, let's say that your script will end up 120 pages long, and your Act One is roughly 10 3-minute scenes. What happens in Scene 9? Is it a turning point that will reverse what your main character knows up to then? When the next scene finishes, is the hero fully prepared for the main confrontation?

It's Not for Us

I would never recommend that anyone tailor scenes to fit some rigid skeletal structure. That takes away the intuitive nature of great storytelling. When you've fixed your story in your mind, by whatever method works for you, just write. Let it flow. Use the scenes that you've outlined as guideposts on your journey. If a more appealing path appears, don't be afraid to take it.

Script Notes

If you think audiences these days are intellectual and thus demand mind-challenging plot points, consider this. Aristotle used the term "perepetia" to refer to a moment of reversal in the plot. In the magic of writing from a good premise, perepetia will often arise naturally. To my mind, those ancient Greeks were the intellectuals.

On to Act Two, which is roughly 20 three-minute scenes. When 10 of those are completed (the *midpoint change*), has your main character undergone some change that will shift his focus slightly so that he becomes more the attacker than the attacked? Is it clear that the hero, while not being in control, is more in control than not?

Now, nine more scenes along, is there a scene that will again send your main character in a new direction and prepare him for the resolution of the conflict? That's your second turning point. I hope you have it, because you're on the brink of the place where, in rapid succession, the hero defeats the villain and reaches the goal that began with your inciting incident. In certain films, particularly those by Steven Spielberg and James Bond movies, this sequence will be more extended, providing more room for exciting action.

By now you're probably wondering what to do with 10 3-minute scenes that make up a 30-minute Act Three. Chances are, you won't have that many because your third act will be shorter. That has been the trend of movies for some time now. If you had seven scenes in Act Three, with your other acts roughly the "normal" length of 30 minutes and 60 minutes, you'd end up with about 110 minutes, which is very normal for a Hollywood drama these days.

And then the tag at the end of Act Three, the denouement. How long should it be? Well, how long was the scene in which Dorothy woke up in her home in Kansas? How long was Tom Hanks' scene at the end of *Forrest Gump*? After that story was told, the white feather of life that we saw in the beginning floated off to touch another soul. Denouements in uplifting films are short and to the point, and inevitably provoke a smile. In other dramas, they provoke irony.

First Acts Don't Last Forever

Syd Field puts the end of Act One at page 30 and puts his first plot point between pages 25 and 27. Former UCLA screenwriting department co-chairman Lew Hunter feels that Act One, which he calls "The Situation," usually ends around page 17. I asked Lew about that one day over lunch, and he replied that he simply noticed that with most good scripts, you know what's going on by page 17. I've observed roughly the same thing, which means that you have to get going fast, on the first page. Here's an example from a thriller that I wrote and sold with Peter Flynn. The premise of *Allure* is this: *What if models in lingerie commercials started getting killed in real life?*

FADE IN:

EXT. DOWNTOWN LOS ANGELES STREET—NIGHT

SEXY SAXOPHONE MUSIC COMES UP as LOIS CHAMBERS, a beautiful model, drives a white Pontiac Fiero through downtown Los Angeles streets toward the Static Club, the hottest spot in the downtown L.A. scene.

Lois slows and starts to turn into the parking lot, but the ATTEN-DANT flashes a sign that says "Lot Full!"

Lois looks around, but the streets are packed with cars.

And lots of young, hip people are going into the club, laughing, having a good time. It's the place to be.

Lois GUNS the Fiero down the street. Gotta find some parking.

EXT. ANOTHER DOWNTOWN LOS ANGELES STREET—NIGHT

Lois finally finds a place to park, only it's in a very shabby, downright frightening neighborhood.

INT. LOIS'S FIERO—NIGHT

She checks the rear-view mirror and sees nothing. These streets are more or less deserted this late at night. She checks her lipstick and then, satisfied, grabs her purse and gets out.

SAXOPHONE FADES IN as she walks along slowly, sensually, all business and in no hurry. Suddenly, she hears a MOTORCYCLE ROAR and turns to face it.

As it comes her way, her pace quickens, but it's only a PIZZA DELIVERY BOY on his way somewhere in a hurry. She LAUGHS to herself at her alarm, then slows down.

But on the night streets there is something else, and she hears it and turns again. It is a black car, with darkened glass windows, going very slowly, as if following her. It is between her and her car—there's no going back there. Lois turns and tries to ignore it, her pace quickening. Behind her, she hears the black car speed up.

She gauges the distance to the brightly lit main street up ahead. There are no police, not even other people headed to the club. She starts trotting, her breath coming hard. She looks back, and the car is closer and closer, edging close to the curb, definitely following. She begins to run, SCREAMING at the black car.

We sold that script before anyone aired lingerie commercials on television. I saw that day coming, so I incorporated it into the script. The screenplay was shelved and then resold. It might get made someday—who knows? I would write some of the description differently now, to suggest (but not describe) more shots. I would rewrite the last two paragraphs of page one like this:

Something else. She hears it, turns. A jet-black car, darkened glass windows. Moving slowly. Stalking. Between her and the Fiero, there's no going back. Lois turns, speeds up, tries to ignore it. The black car speeds up.

The brightly lit main street. She gauges the distance. No police. No one. Her feet quicken, then trot. Her breath, coming hard. She looks back. The black car closes. It's edging the curb. She's running, **SCREAMING**. Dying.

Some people would advise you to be less specific than "SAXOPHONE FADES IN" and say only "MUSIC UP"—if you say more, you're attempting to do the job of the composer or soundtrack supervisor. A saxophone usually evokes a sexy vibe, though, so I put it in.

If you've never seen a screenplay before, I should clue you in that the first time we see a character's NAME it is ALL CAPS. Similarly, SOUNDS are capitalized only if important to the action or to denote sounds from a character, such as Lois's nervous LAUGH.

Hollywood Heat

In Hollywood, synchronicity happens often. It's a Jungian term popularized by The Police that refers to a state in which things happen, exist, or arise at precisely the same time. When I was first writing the script *Allure*, set in the modeling business, my future wife, Debbie, was a Ford model in New York who was being courted as a spokesperson for a new line of perfume named Allure. The female lead in the screenplay, a policewoman named Ruby Stephens, goes undercover as a reporter for the fictitious *Interplay* magazine. When I met my wife, she was studying acting at a theater in Chelsea run by a comedy group named Interplay.

As you might imagine, Lois isn't the only model for the "Allure" line who gets killed. Who is doing it and why is the plot of the movie. On page two, Lois is hit by the car and killed, and the pizza delivery boy returns and finds her. In the next scene, we are introduced to the male lead, JOHN PALMER, as he drives from downtown Los Angeles toward Hollywood. This was done to establish for the audience what city we are in (they don't see the EXT. LOS ANGELES STREET on the script, so how could they know?). I wouldn't do that today.

Instead, I would go directly to the next scene, which features another beautiful model in a fancy, high-rise, West Side apartment building. She is alone in the apartment, wearing an emerald green lingerie ensemble. She finds a handsome cat burglar in her apartment and starts to fight him, then they discover an instant animal attraction. As she pulls off his mask and the wind blows her sheer robe around her body, we hear a sultry, female narrator say: "Allure. There's danger in the night."

And then APPLAUSE as we see that this has been a commercial on a TV monitor in a television studio where the director of the commercials, John Palmer, is the guest on a morning talk show. The commercials are controversial (maybe because they're a bit corny?), and people are protesting them, you see. But not half as much as they will after they learn that Lois has been murdered.

This is exactly why I would have a real murder lead directly into the "dangerous" commercial, to make the audience keep guessing about what is real and what isn't in this movie. Remember, Act One is all about setting up the conflict battled out in Act Two.

It's Not for Us

Don't get in a hurry to finish Act One. Dwelling on this act in your first draft will serve you well. It sets up all the action in Act Two, which is the bulk of the story. In rewrites, Act Two will often need the most work, but rewrites go much easier when Act One is in good shape.

By page five of *Allure,* we've met CYNTHIA NIELSEN, the creator of the Allure lingerie line and the one who hired John to direct when no one else would hire him to do film. You see, John has a bit of a past. We know that because CAPTAIN CONLEY and his partner, LIEUTENANT FROMER, show up at the TV studio to ask some questions about Lois. When John learns what happened to Lois, he is reminded of the death of LAUREN ASHLEY, a supermodel whom he was dating when they were both on top of the world, success-wise.

By page 10, it's clear that John is a suspect in Lois's murder, and then Cynthia lies, saying he was with her the night before, providing him an alibi for reasons that John doesn't understand. Then we see John's studio and watch him work a commercial photo shot. His assistant, BETTY, obviously has some issues with him, but we don't know if it's because his client has been waiting and is upset, or if it's some other issue. And we see John's assistant, BOBBY, a wisecracking Lothario who might be capable of anything.

By the top of page 17, we've met all the important characters in the screenplay, and John Palmer is propelled into a murder mystery in which he'll have to prove his own innocence and determine who the real killer is in time to save his own life and that of others. Our script is 102 pages long. There's a turning point on page 20, introducing the undercover policewoman who cracks the case, but the point wasn't written very well, frankly. It did send the story in another direction, but not as effectively as I could have done it today.

Hopefully this example gives you some idea of at least a decent first page and Act One. The people who bought *Allure* told me that they considered 250 feature scripts before picking ours.

Skip's Tips

Producer Joel Silver, with pictures to his credit such as *The Matrix* (1999), the *Die Hard* movies, and the *Lethal Weapon* series, has often said that in action films, some major shoot-'em-up or explosive event should occur onscreen about every 10 minutes. Watch one of his films some day and time it out. He's not kidding, and neither are his box-office figures.

The Second Act Is the Movie

In case you didn't know it, the biggest box office star of the last few years is Will Smith. Not Tom Cruise or Harrison Ford or anyone else—the former Fresh Prince of Bel Air has it nailed down. My favorite Smith film is *Men in Black,* a masterful script written by Ed Solomon (with some uncredited help from others) from a hit comic book by Lowell Cunningham.

Act One of the script ends when Smith's James Edwards goes with Tommy Lee Jones's Kay into a pawnshop owned by a fellow named Jeebs. When Kay blows off Jeebs' head with a "Cricket," a strange futuristic pistol, Edwards knows that they aren't in Kansas any more. Why? Because Jeebs, the alien, grows another head immediately. Everything in this 98-page script is set up by page 18. But guess what? It is not until the end of page 93 that Act Two ends. That comes when Edwards distracts the giant alien bug intent on destroying the galaxy long enough for Kay, who has tricked the bug into swallowing him, to blast his way out of the bug's belly with a gun that the bug ate.

Did you remember that general 1:2:1 pages-to-act ratio that I mentioned earlier? Try to apply it to *Men in Black*. Obviously, it would be way off. The ratio in *MIB* would be 18:75:5. Stunning, isn't it? That's because *Act Two is the movie*. That's particularly true in an all-out action movie like *MIB*. When the action is finished, the movie is basically over. Of course, that's true with most films, but in a pure drama, an Act Three usually lasts longer. There are issues to be handled, things to be worked out and wrapped up.

Hollywood Heat

Staying power equals success. Many early stars gained that by screenwriting. W. C. Fields was in his mid-30s when he starred in a short entitled *Pool Sharks* (1915). Because he was a star on Broadway, it was nine years before he starred in the feature *Sally of the Sawdust* directed by D. W. Griffith. Fields's last feature was in 1941, the classic *Never Give a Sucker an Even Break*. He wrote the story of that film as "Otis Cribblecoblis." He wrote a lot of his own material, with screenplay credit for his famous film, *The Bank Dick* (1940, writing as "Mahatma Kane Jeeves"). Fields's Hollywood career was a great second act.

When you're writing your second act, you're really writing the movie. The first 10 pages are essential in grabbing the readers/viewers and keeping them with you, and the act break that happens between pages 17 and 27 or so (depending on the length of your script and how you write) is crucial, as is any turning point(s) that you have in the first act. Act Two, though, is the movie, so you'd better have your schedule locked in and your outline or treatment in good shape before you embark on that writing journey.

Usually, the Second Act Most Needs Fixing

The late great Diane Thomas, who wrote *Romancing the Stone,* was loved by producers because she believed so much in making sure that the second act was top-notch. According to the producer I talked with, when they started talking story problems, she would immediately zero in on the second act and go fix it. Thomas was right. Think of all the things that happen in Act Two:

➤ The main character engages in the immediate conflict of the movie. If it's a comedy, some of the more outlandish things happen that truly establish the pickle that the main character is in, such as Jim Carrey in *Liar, Liar* losing his girlfriend over telling her the truth—that sex with her isn't the best.

➤ Act Two events lead to a midpoint change, such as when lawyer Carrey realizes that he's stuck with "telling the truth no matter what" and so he has to use that while trying to win a case in court for his ditzy client, played by Jennifer Tilly.

➤ With the new empowerment that came at the midpoint change, the struggle intensifies, crescendoing at the end of the act. In *Liar, Liar,* it looks like Jim Carrey will most certainly lose the divorce case he's fighting (turning point) but ...

➤ ... he wins the case for his client by proving that she was a minor when she married her husband, and thus didn't have parental consent. So, the marriage was invalid and the husband is in trouble. Thus, Carrey uses lying, the very thing the movie is about, to win. He has learned his lesson about lying and no longer lies himself, but he uses the lie of someone else to win.

The *Liar, Liar* example is a good one for pointing out how the hero can use personal weaknesses established at the beginning of the film to defeat the bad guy in Act Two. In this case, it's a dual bad

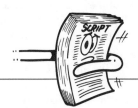

It's Not for Us

Don't just sit down and write your screenplay. Before you write, try to find some movies that are similar in theme and structure to what you plan to write. Sit down and see if you can spot all the key elements of those films—the act breaks, the turning points, and so on. Then see how they match against your own outline.

guy. Carrey is a villain to his son because he lies to him, resulting in the son's wish (which comes true) that his father can never lie. So, Carrey has to conquer himself.

Carrey's battle with himself that will allow him to reconcile with his family is the "A" story of the movie, with the court case the "B" plot line. The other villains that Carrey fights are the husband and the lawyer on the other side of the courtroom in the divorce case. It is very poignant how, having conquered his own character flaw, he uses it at the end of Act Two to defeat the "B" villain.

As another example, in *Casablanca,* Humphrey Bogart's Rick has a weakness for Ilsa, played by Ingrid Bergman. But Ilsa is married. Rick has a deeper weakness as well. He is running his club and staying neutral in the struggle of World War II, so he's somewhat of a coward. In contrast, Ilsa's husband, Victor Laszlo (played by Paul Henreid), is a freedom fighter. By making the decision in Act Two to help Ilsa and her husband escape, Rick conquers his weaknesses and sacrifices his own desires for a greater cause. In doing so, the local police chief swings over to his side.

Script Notes

You'll often hear the term "character arc" in Hollywood. I like to think of that as a golf shot to an uphill green. The hero's journey in the story rises to an apex and then descends to its final destination. The apex is the midpoint change, where the necessary (inner) "motion" has taken place. The ball (hero), now mid-action, completes the journey with accelerated force.

Steven Spielberg's Second Acts

Using the example of the original cut of *Close Encounters of the Third Kind* (1977) as an example, Syd Field feels that Spielberg created a new storytelling form, with acts of that screenplay of roughly the same length—a 1:1:1 ratio. While this could be debated, the fact remains that the film (as with many Spielberg films) is longer than the "normal" two hours. If you're a fan of Spielberg, as I am, you probably already know that he dwells long on the action of a movie and doesn't spend much time wrapping things up once the story is done. To me, he does that with an extended Act Two. *Saving Private Ryan* is an example, as are the *Jurassic Park* movies and the *Indiana Jones* films. What do you think? Sit down with a stopwatch and some videos sometime, and see if you can figure out where Spielberg's Act Twos end.

The Midpoint and the Hero's Orientation

Rather than provide you with further examples, it's best that you do your own homework. Do the following with at least a dozen films, and see if the midpoint change happens, ratio-wise, at roughly the same time in all movies. I believe you'll find it does in James Bond movies, which generally follow the same formula, but 007 might not be to your taste. Whatever you review, do this:

1. In the first act, try to spot what you think is the main weakness of the hero, at the very least with regard to dealing with the main villain of the film.

2. Locate as many examples as you can of how this hero weakness is exploited by the villain, keeping the hero at effect.

3. Spot the point in the movie where a change comes over the hero in which he or she becomes more determined to defeat the villain, no matter what might happen to him or her personally.

Great films are really about personal transformation, and understanding what personal transformation your hero undergoes is crucial to telling your story effectively. While you don't have to preach, the more movies audiences relate to your hero's struggle, the better off you are at the box office. If you hear audience members say that they imagine themselves in that role, you're doing your job.

The Short but Crucial Third Act

At the end of *Men in Black,* there are five pages for the last five steps of the Joseph Campbell myth structure to work out—only five pages to conclude the entire screenplay and add a tag at the end. How was this done? Assuming that you've read the screenplay or seen the movie, let's take a look:

➤ **Refusal of the Return.** Kay (Tommy Lee Jones) won't reveal to Jay (Will Smith) whether getting eaten by the bug was part of his plan; he merely shrugs and says "Worked."

➤ **The Magic Flight.** Zed (Rip Torn), their boss back at headquarters, tells them that the aliens who live on Earth are returning, now that it's safe again.

➤ **Rescue from Without.** Laurel (Linda Fiorentino), a coroner whom they rescued from the giant alien bug, saves Kay and Jay (Will Smith's new identity) as they argue by blasting the menacing front half of the still-menacing alien into oblivion with an "atomizer."

➤ **Crossing the Return Threshold.** Back at the MIB building, Kay reveals to Jay that he hasn't been training a new partner. He's been training a replacement. K wants to quit and go home.

➤ **Master of the Two Worlds.** Jay is reading a tabloid that includes a picture of Kay with the woman he left to join the Men in Black.

Hollywood Heat

Daniel Petrie Jr. (*Beverly Hills Cop*) once had an office in Beverly Hills in the same building with Billy Wilder. Petrie told me that Wilder was always concerned that the third act be just right. The endings of his films always wrap up nicely. My favorite Wilder movie is *Some Like It Hot* (1959). Get your third acts right, and you might become a legend.

The headline reads "MAN AWAKENS FROM 30-YEAR COMA: Returns to Girl He Left Behind." Jay now understands fully how some of the outlandish stories in the tabloids are actually real.

➤ **Freedom to Live.** At the curb in the LTD is Elle (formerly known as Laurel). She is now a Woman in Black, Jay's new partner. When Jay returns, she tells him that Zed has called, wanting tickets to a New York Knicks vs. Chicago Bulls basketball game. Jay can get them because Dennis Rodman is an alien from that planet. Jay is now truly the master of two worlds.

Although third acts are shorter these days, they are not dispensable. No matter how much action has taken place, audiences need to have things tied up for them neatly so that they feel all is right within this new world they've been experiencing, at least for now. We rarely see anything as corny as "There's no place like home!" in films these days, unless they're satires. Nevertheless, for the foreseeable future, third acts will still be with us because they wrap up the psychological package that the audience has spent the last hour or two of their lives purchasing.

You'll find your own way to write a satisfying third act. Meanwhile, you can do a lot worse than using the Joseph Campbell myth structure steps outlined as a guideline.

Skip's Tips

Think of your audience as you write your denouement. Don't give them a cliché "boy and girl get married" scene, unless you can do it in a new and memorable way. People often remember best what they read last. When you release your viewer from the seat, if they walk out of the theater with a little smile, you've probably "tagged" them just right.

Tag, You're a Denouement

The dictionary definition of a *denouement* is "the final outcome of the main dramatic complications in a literary work." That's a bit misleading with regard to movies. The root of the word literally means "to untie." The tag at the end of a film is that bit which, if a thriller or horror movie, gives us one additional hesitated beat of the heart. If it's a comedy, it's yet another chuckle. With other films, it's another bit of good feeling, as when James Bond and the lady Chinese agent ignore their rescuers while they "get to know each other better."

What the denouement actually does is allow us to let go of the movie, to mentally return to our own world. Remember when Jody Foster's Clarice Starling gets the phone call from the escaped Hannibal Lecter (Anthony Hopkins) at the end of *Silence of the Lambs?* When Hannibal the Cannibal then loses himself on the street, it's a thrilling little scene that would go well with a glass of Chianti. Pour that wine like a practiced maître d'.

The Least You Need to Know

➤ Like the overall movie, every scene has a three-part structure.

➤ Every good movie begins with an inciting incident that places the hero and villain in irreversible conflict.

➤ Generally, the acts of a screenplay have a 1:2:1 length ratio, but that can vary greatly.

➤ Good screenplays have a midpoint change, an event where the hero shifts to being more causative than effect of the villain.

➤ The second act is so important that you can say it *is* the movie.

➤ Third acts and the denouement, or "tag" at the end of the act, wrap up the movie for the audience and allow them to mentally return to the real world.

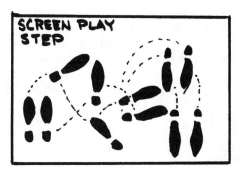

Chapter 16

SCREEN PLAY STEP

The Screenplay, Step by Step

In This Chapter

➤ The initial concept

➤ The proper treatment

➤ Drafting mastery

➤ Importance of format

➤ The Hemingway trick

If you have a personal computer, I strongly suggest that you invest in a screenplay-formatting program before you begin writing your screenplay. If you want a full description of all the available programs and add-ons to existing software programs, buy my *Writer's Guide to Hollywood Producers, Directors, and Screenwriter's Agents,* or spend some time on the Internet newsgroup misc.writing.screenplays. You will also find reviews at the Writer's Guild of America (WGA) site at www.wga.org.

The All-Important Initial Concept

In his intriguing book *Blue Highways,* Native American author William Least Heat Moon describes a process that the Hopi Indians use called "sitting in pictures." The Hopi are perhaps the most peaceful of all indigenous American tribes and have inhabited their land for as long as they have legends. They are one of the very few Native American groups (if not the only such group) never displaced from their homeland. That speaks of some kind of power.

When they sit in pictures, they engage in an ancient form of creative visualization. They close their eyes and evoke the help of their departed ancestors when, for example, they "see" in their minds thunder clouds forming on the horizon to bring needed rain. Although I've never seen the practice in person, the mental pictures that Least Heat Moon painted in my mind were so vivid that the idea stuck with me. I wrote a scene into a published novel featuring my character Alexander Cloud, who is half-Hopi, sitting with his grandmother to bring rain before he asks for her advice on a mystery he is solving. I also incorporated the scene into an earlier screenplay featuring an older Alex that I wrote for a producer and director who optioned a short story. Picture that.

Hollywood Heat

The amazing documentary *Koyaanisqatsi* (1983) sprang from Hopi words meaning "life out of balance." Directed by Godfrey Reggio, four writing credits are listed, to Ron Fricke, Michael Hoenig, Alton Walpole, and Reggio (who also produced with Francis Ford Coppola). Featuring an original score by composer Philip Glass, the movie was made without a script. Producer Lawrence Taub of the Institute for Regional Education in Santa Fe, New Mexico (see www.koyaanisqatsi.org), told me that all the credited writers were "dramaturgical contributors" who helped piece together a treatment as the film was made. Unfortunately, the home video version of this beautiful film is hung up in litigation. Talk about life out of balance!

I hope that when you receive or conceive of your initial concept, it is like a flash of invigorated life that causes scenes to unfold before you, as though you are sitting in pictures watching the movie that you will soon be writing. Other screenwriters tell me that the process happens for them much the same way.

I generally am not satisfied until I have an idea whose logical conclusion appears almost simultaneously with the beginning. If you find it hard to visualize scenes based on your concept, I have a suggestion. *Throw the idea away.* Accept nothing but the most brilliant, shining concepts, those that will keep you excited through the long, hard process of writing a screenplay. Just keep throwing ideas away until you get one like that. Believe me, it's like driving a luxury car for the first time—you don't know what you're missing until you get the real thing in your hands.

Giving Yourself the Proper Treatment

Some writers I know don't write a treatment. They would rather just write the script from a brief outline or from cards. The truth about treatments is that they will change while you write the screenplay. That's normal—don't worry about it. When you breathe life into your characters, they will, like children gaining powers of independence, start saying things and doing things that you did not think about when you slaved over your rough outline (which some call a "beat" or "step" outline). Whether treatment, index cards, or Post-its, only do what works for you.

I find it helpful to work from a treatment because I can follow the flow of the story more easily. I know what a treatment is for me, but, unfortunately, there is no clear consensus in Hollywood about what a treatment is. Some will tell you that it's 10 pages or less. Others will insist that it's the script minus all or almost all the dialogue. Still others will say that 20 to 30 pages should do it. That's the size I tend to favor. It is double-spaced, written in prose style, in present tense, and maintains as much dramatic tension in the narrative as possible.

Why does the subject of treatments keep coming up in Hollywood? Because busy or lazy executives will ask for them. Rather than having to digest an entire script, not trusting a judgment based on page-and-a-half "coverage," they'll read a treatment and think they understand the movie. Rarely is that possible, of course. Some writers are good at writing treatments that match a screenplay; others are not. I've written lots of them, so they're second nature to me.

Skip's Tips

One of the very best sites for beginning screenwriters on the Internet is Wordplay from Terry Rossio and Ted Elliott, the duo who wrote Disney's *Aladdin, The Mask of Zorro,* and many other films. At www.wordplayer.com/columns/wp37.Proper.Treatment.html you'll find a great article on various treatments they have used. You can find a sample treatment of their *Sinbad* comedy script at www.wordplayer.com/columns/wp37-xtras/wp37x.SINBAD.html.

Let's hope that you get into the position where you're doing business with a production company and the company asks for a treatment. Because you don't know what that particular company expects to see, say, "Great. What format do you prefer?" Your contacts might tell you 5 pages, or 20. They'll probably expect you to simply tell the story as I've outlined already. They may ask for headings such as Setting or Main Character. If they are that specific, however, they'll probably have a treatment in the office from someone else that they've adopted as their preferred style.

Don't use treatments as a selling tool unless specifically asked for them, until you are a "known" writer whose scripts have proven your writing ability. Even then, sharing treatments with others can make you crazy. With a script, they take it or leave it.

It's Not for Us

Never assume that just because one production company does things a certain way, others will, even if they are on the same studio lot. Production companies move all the time, change personnel a lot, and are largely personality-driven. If the Director of Development today loves to read treatments, the one next week may think you're an amateur if you even mention submitting one.

Script Notes

"CUT TO:" means to abruptly switch from one scene to another. **"DISSOLVE TO:"** means that one scene fades as another scene comes into focus. These are essentially camera and editing decisions (and a director or cinematographer's job), so scene changes are increasingly left out of professional scripts.

Drafting Beats Dreaming

Screenwriting seems like a sexy occupation. In reality, it's hard work and, in some ways, an abused part of Hollywood. Studio executive Irving Thalberg reportedly said, "The screenwriter is the only absolutely essential element in this town, and he must never find out." You might write something that nets you a million dollars one day, but the star of the movie will likely make $20 million. So get used to the grind.

Set up a schedule that you can live with, and stop waiting for your "muse." The muse is busy—there are a lot of aspiring screenwriters these days. Even if you don't feel like it, there comes a day when you simply have to sit down and start typing out the scenes. No matter how bad they look, you must write them. But first, a commercial announcement from your guardian angel, who really does want your script to be read all the way through.

The Importance of Being Formatted

It's different keystrokes for different key folks with regard to treatments, but script formats are much more standardized. Even so, you'll still find some disagreements. (We'll assume here that you are *not* using a screenplay-formatting program.)

Some people advise a margin of 1 inch on both the top and the bottom of your 8½ × 11-inch page, but the default setting for Final Draft software, the industry leader, is a text margin of 1.12 inch at the top and 0.75 inch at the bottom, with .5 inch from the top of the paper to the page number, and .5 inch from the bottom of the paper to footers such as (CONTINUED). Such a footer indicates that a scene is continued on the next page. Because (CONTINUED) is falling out of favor (it's an option in all formatting software), however, you're best counting on a .75-inch margin on the bottom of the page.

The left margin should be 1.5 inches because scripts are copied onto or printed on three-hole paper. If you use a lesser margin, it might be hard to read the left side of your script after it is bound. Many people advise that the right margin should be .5 inch from the edge of the paper, but in the Final Draft program, the default margins are set at 12 and 72, which is a wider right margin.

Use a 12-point Courier font, not Courier New or some other font.

Why Courier 12? Because it is a fixed-pitch font with 10 characters per horizontal inch and 6 lines per vertical inch. That means that what you see is what you get, and a page will roughly add up to one-minute screen time. Do *not* use a proportional font or a justified right margin. The first line of text on the first page, which has *no* number, should begin 0.75 inch from the top. Starting on the *second page,* the distance from the top to your page number should be three carriage returns, or .5 inch. Then a single blank line separates the page number and the body of the script, which begins at .75 inch. Numbers should align aesthetically past the right margin (they're set at 79 in Courier font in Final Draft). (Note: there is a period after the number and no "Page Number.") The bottom page margin should be at least .5 inch (three carriage returns) or the end of a scene. If you leave a 1-inch margin (six carriage returns) at the bottom, no one will complain.

There are three other format spacing concerns for a script. Again, let's go with the defaults for Final Draft because it leads the industry. A character's first name is in all capitals, as in "SKIP." We usually do not use both names, unless the person has a title in front, such as "COL. PRESS." A character's name appears four tabs, or 20 spaces, over from the left margin. With the Final Draft left margin set at 12, the character's name is at 32.

Dialogue appears two tabs, or 10 spaces, over from the left margin. With Final Draft, this is at 22. The right margin for dialogue is two tabs, or 10 spaces, in from the right margin (62 in Final Draft). *Parentheticals* (dialogue directions) appear one extra tab over from the left, as in the following example:

```
                    SKIP
                 (quietly)
        How does it look so far?
```

Scene transitions, such as …

```
                                              CUT TO:
```

… should be aligned against the right margin. (Note the colon that follows any indication of scene change.) These are generally left out these days because it is considered obvious that the scene has changed when we see a new location listed below a scene.

When someone speaks offscreen but is in the scene, write this:

```
            SKIP (O.S.)
```

When someone speaks off-camera but is not in the scene, write this:

```
                        SKIP
                       (V.O.)
```

V.O. is an abbreviation for "voice over."

It is a time-honored tradition to begin each script with:

```
    FADE IN:
```

I don't expect a change of that norm anytime soon, but some writers leave it off. The title of the script is generally left off the first page, as is the byline. If you add it, it's likely that no one will complain. If it's added, center it with this format:

```
              MY SCREENPLAY
            by Joe Screenwriter
```

However, you must still put the title and byline on a separate title page preceding the script. In Hollywood, simplicity is the best policy. If there's a doubt, leave it out. That's why, when you break dialogue at the bottom of a page, you should break it only at the end of a complete sentence. Do *not* add "(MORE)" centered beneath the line to indicate that more dialogue follows on the next page. That has fallen out of favor. Instead, on the following page, type "(CONT'D)" directly after the character name. Example:

```
                       SKIP
          You must get your format right.
----------------------page break----------------------
                   SKIP (CONT'D)
      If you don't, you'll just look foolish,
          and your script may be rejected.
```

Do not break dialogue with hyphens. Use whole words only, and keep the parts of hyphenated words together on the same line, if at all possible. Again, it's an aesthetic consideration, but it's important.

When breaking the narrative, the convention is generally to break it only at the end of a complete sentence or even a paragraph, because action description is best done in short paragraphs of only a few lines. The convention of breaking only at the end of a complete sentence is wavering somewhat, but you're better off adhering to it. Just don't leave a one-line "widow" hanging at the end of a page or on the beginning of the next page.

Don't worry about a "CONTINUED" to show that an action description has been broken up. Just let the lines flow, as in this example:

```
Tarzan chases Jane across the floor of the valley, grinning
as he watches her dart in and out of the long grass. She's
stunning.
-----------------------page break---------------------
CRACK! Too late, he stops. He's stepped onto a thatched lion
trap. Only this one is meant for a man. Down he plunges,
YELLING.
```

Shot headings, also known as "slug lines," show where the scene is located, the time of day or night, and if it is an inside shot or an outside shot. Use two blank lines between the end of one scene and a new slug line. Some authorities will tell you to use three lines, but two is still broadly preferred.

"EXT." is for "EXTERIOR" shots, and "INT." is for "INTERIOR" shots. If you have any "trick" locations, such as in the ocean or out in space, simply state where you are and don't worry about it. Only differentiate the time of day if it is absolutely essential (example follows).

Note the spacing and punctuation in these examples:

```
EXT. PARAMOUNT STUDIOS—DAY

INT. PARAMOUNT STUDIOS—NIGHT

100 FEET BELOW OCEAN SURFACE—DAY

EXT. SPACE STATION
```

Hollywood Heat

In 1982, Chuck Ross wrote an article for *American Film* magazine, the official organ of the American Film Institute. He described how he retyped the screenplay of the immortal *Casablanca* and titled it *Everybody Comes to Rick's.* He submitted the script to 217 agencies, but only 85 of them read it. 38 agencies rejected it completely, 33 thought that it seemed familiar, but only 8 recognized it as *Casablanca.* All told, only three agencies thought that it was saleable, and one suggested that it be turned into a novel!

With the slug line denoting that we are under the ocean, I wrote "DAY" assuming that the next scene will be on the surface during the day, or that we can see at the top of the water that it is daylight.

Because day or night is not a consideration in space, I left off the time of day. The previous slug line indicates that the point of view is outside a space station. If we were inside, it would be this:

```
INT. SPACE STATION
```

The first time we see a location, it is necessary to establish it with an "EXT." description. Preferably, at least one line of description follows. Then we can venture inside with an "INT." shot and delineate the location further by adding to that. Take a look at these examples:

```
EXT. PARAMOUNT STUDIOS—EARLY MORNING

On Melrose Avenue, the last major studio actually located in
Hollywood is open, but even the gate guard looks sleepy.
```

```
INT. PARAMOUNT STUDIOS, SKIP PRESS'S OFFICE—EARLY MORNING

SKIP PRESS, so-called writer, flops in his chair, feet on
desk, head tilted back, SNORING. He's a wreck. Takeout remains
are scattered on the floor. The coffee pot on a hot plate is
smoking. He's been here all night. The computer SHRIEKS out an
alarm.
```

(*Note the two line breaks between these scenes.*)

Unless it is necessary for dramatic purposes of the screenplay, stay away from writing a camera point of view (POV), like this:

```
SKIP'S POV
```

Also leave out "we see" descriptions such as this:

```
We see DEBBIE enter the ballroom, looking beautiful.
```

Leave out all "we sees" and anything that reminds the reader they are reading a screenplay.

Because Debbie is my wife's name and I find her impressive, you might write in a POV for me, allowing the camera to dwell on her entrance, followed by a simple reaction shot on me:

```
DEBBIE enters the ballroom, more dazzling than ever.

Skip REACTS.
```

Let the director and actor decide *how* the actor reacts.

Do *not* concern yourself with defining individual shots unless you have a very specific reason for doing so, such as someone looking at an object closely. That would be described this way:

```
INSERT

The diamond. It sparkles like a
captive sun.
```

Followed by:

```
RETURN TO SCENE
```

(If you return to the scene you were in before the INSERT.)

Never let a shot heading be widowed at the bottom of a page. Move it to the next page, please.

As mentioned previously regarding the page from my script *Allure,* major sound effects are CAPITALIZED.

As also mentioned, the Cole-Haag book on screenplay formats is generally considered the standard reference. Again, I highly recommend that you get a screenwriting program to make your life easier. It will pay for itself by saving you extra work.

Skip's Tips

A master scene script is the only one that you want to worry about writing. You simply describe the action as cleanly as possible, define each character with minimal superlatives, and write what each character says with few comments on how they say it. That way, the director and the actors remain your friends.

Hollywood Heat

When a concept is good enough, it never dies. The second script that I wrote struck the interest of Rona Edwards when she was working in development. It wasn't even properly formatted. She couldn't convince her boss of the script's worth, but years later, when I interviewed Edwards for a book, she remembered the script, asked about it, and optioned it. While producing movies such as *Out of Sync* (2000) on VH-1, Edwards is still waiting for me to rewrite my script so that we can get the movie financed.

On the following page is a title page properly formatted. (Note that although some people to prefer **bold the title**, the more prevailing standard is an <u>underlined title</u>.)

If you are you are a writing team, use an ampersand (and):

<pre>
                        by

        Joe Screenwriter & Jane Screenwriter
</pre>

If you worked on the script separately, do it this way:

<pre>
                        By
                Joe Screenwriter
                       and
                Jane Screenwriter
</pre>

Therefore, a writing team and another writer would read:

<pre>
                        By
        Joe Screenwriter & Jane Screenwriter
                       and
                Nancy Goodfriend
</pre>

Following the title page is a sample page from *South China Sea* (a.k.a. *Fair Game*) by Michael Sean Conley and myself. The inciting incident is presented, but the hero is not in this scene.

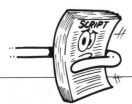

It's Not for Us

Although minimal is in, some times you have to use a "CUT TO:"—specifically a "SMASH CUT TO:"—in a horror movie such as Scream. This signifies an especially sharp and rapid transition, usually to something terrifying, such as a guy coming after you with a knife.

SAMPLE TITLE PAGE

My Screenplay
by
Jane Screenwriter

(Based on, if applicable)

Name
Address
Phone
E-mail
(Don't list a Web site unless it's about you or this script only.)

The powerboat approaches from out of the sun.

INT. GALLEY AREA IN SALON—DAY

Sandi starts the blender. It makes a horrible RACKET. A BEAT, then she frowns, hearing the RUMBLE of twin diesel engines. She looks out the open porthole toward the bow.

EXT. OFF THE YACHT'S BOW—DAY

SANDI'S POV OUT PORTHOLE as the W.W. II-vintage PT boat cuts engines to an IDLE and slides closer. Its torpedo launchers and .50-caliber guns have been removed. The Thai government's marine police <u>insignia</u> is on the bow.

There are four UNIFORMED MEN on board. On the foredeck. One at the helm. A third beside him. A forth in a side turret aft of the bridge and forward of the day cabin.

INT. SALON—DAY

Sandi crosses to the ladder, passing an array of expensive underwater camera gear laid out on the dining bench.

EXT. YACHT AND PT BOAT—DAY

The PT boat has drawn alongside. Sandi frowns, studying the man on the bow, a muscle-bound blond Dutchman armed with a submachine gun. The other three men don't look Thai, either.

       SANDI
   Who are you?

The man GUNS HER DOWN in a fatal burst!

Jimmy turns at the staccato gunfire to finally see the PT boat goons. And his sister. Jimmy DROPS HIS BEER and rips the headset off in panic.

       JIMMY
    SANDI!!

Sandy falls slowly onto the cockpit decking, dead.

You may be wondering why we say "DAY" or "NIGHT" with each new scene. When the film is shot, the scenes will likely be lifted out and filmed separate of each other, not in sequence. The underlined insignia is to draw attention to it. The BEAT mentioned with Sandy denotes that she pauses and then continues.

One more item that will also rarely fade from use. At the end of your script, you type, justified against the right margin:

FADE OUT.

(Note the period.) And then ...

THE END

"THE END" is in bold. You'll be feeling bold when you finally wrap up the first draft of your script!

Winning the Daily Battle with the Hemingway Trick

When you're drafting out your first screenplay, even if you are using a software program that makes formatting as easy as tabbing and returning, you'll still find yourself hassling with format and technical details. Try to avoid too many technical concerns. Just write. Don't worry too much about how many pages are in which act. Just write. Get the screenplay written. Try to set up a regular rhythm. If you can't write every day for the same amount of time, try to write on the same day each week for the same amount of time. Remember that each scene should have a beginning, middle, and end, just like the screenplay.

Don't be surprised if the movie in your mind that you think will turn into a 120-page screenplay ends up being 135 pages by the time you complete your first draft. Don't worry about it. Just write, and fix it later.

Ernest Hemingway had a little trick when writing novels. To make sure that he would be engaged with his work when he returned to it the next day, he would end his daily writing in the middle of a scene, even in the middle of a sentence. That way, he was forced to become re-enmeshed in the scene upon his return. He would have to start reading from the beginning of the scene to get back into it and finish it.

I'll often reread yesterday's chapter when writing a book, or read the last two scenes when writing a script, much the way Hemingway did, but I find that I'm usually still excited without having to end mid-scene. Whatever works for you, do that. Just don't wear yourself out so much that you can't bear to write the next time.

And, remember, it's only a first draft. It won't really be a screenplay until you're done with at least one rewrite.

The Least You Need to Know

➤ A good screenplay-formatting program can save you time, headaches, and the need to learn the proper format settings.

➤ Sometimes the only way to develop a marketable concept is to throw a few away.

➤ Screenplay treatments are roughly 7 to 30 pages, or even longer, double-spaced, written in prose style and in present tense, and maintaining as much dramatic tension as possible.

➤ Although there are many opinions about what constitutes a treatment, the format for screenplays is well established.

➤ Screenplay text fits within the following margins: .75 inch on the top and bottom, 1.5 inches on the left, and .5 inch on the right.

➤ A "master scene script" without camera angles or dialogue directions for actors is the only one that you should try to write.

➤ Just write. Your first draft isn't really a screenplay until you are done with at least one rewrite.

Chapter 17

The Rewrite Is the Secret

In This Chapter

➤ First drafts

➤ Scene length

➤ Collaborators

➤ Who should read your script

➤ Rewrites and polishes

➤ Rewrite it better

Think of a life. Your life. Or a life of someone you admire. Do you believe that it's "once around life" and that's the only chance we get? Everything about life tells me that everything in the universe is recycled. I believe that a benevolent Creator gives us more than one chance to get it right. What if you could edit life and take out the bad parts?

Whatever your philosophy, with your screenplay (at least, until you sell it), you are God. You create the characters and tell them what to say, until you reach that point (and you will) when they start speaking for themselves, coming up with things that you never imagined. We rarely get a chance to redo life, to perfect what we have created on a day-by-day basis. That might be just as well, because some of the things we do on impulse are hard to face later. You might find it to be the same with first-draft screenplays.

When you begin the rewrite of your screenplay, treat it like a benevolent God, respecting the essence of the life before you, with an eye toward making it stronger and more capable of shining its own special light to the world. When the process is done right, it shines with a brilliant light indeed. Work as if the whole world is watching and, someday, it may be.

Skip's Tips

There's an old adage called Keep It Simple, Stupid (KISS). If you can't easily describe your screenplay, you may be in trouble. It's the same with novels. In his *How to Grow a Novel* (St. Martin's Press, 1999), Sol Stein says, "All of the most successful novels I have edited over the years have had stories that could by synopsized in a single paragraph."

Why First Drafts Are Drafty

I've found that beginning screenwriters inevitably "think on paper." In the heat of writing scenes, getting lost in them, being fascinated by the leading man or lady, or relishing in the stunningly clever viciousness of their villain, they write things in scenes that they have not yet thought through thoroughly. It's the old "What was I thinking?" principle. While you're in the midst of doing it, it makes perfect sense. Or, swept along in the creative flow, you might not even be thinking of sense or nonsense. You're just watching it appear before you onscreen.

One of the biggest hurdles for beginning writers to get over is what I call the "one-baby" syndrome. When you have only one child, the entire world revolves around its welfare. The more children you have, the less important a bloody nose is—you just doctor it and go on with the other urgencies of life. I'm reminded of the scene in Monty Python's *The Meaning of Life* (1983) in which John Cleese, dressed in drag as a Welsh woman who has one child after another, is surrounded by whining kids. A new "baby" (a doll) drops from between his legs, and he trills to one of the other children: "Get that, will you, dear?" while talking on the phone. You don't have to get that callous, but I hope you get the point.

Beginning writers are so protective of their first work that their inevitable first question is: "I'd like to tell someone about my screenplay, but how do I know that they won't steal my idea?"

To which I always reply: "You don't." I might tell them how I'm convinced that at least one of my screenplays (one I co-wrote with Linda Blair, of *The Exorcist*) was stolen and made into a movie that flopped, that I'm convinced would not have flopped if the story we presented had not been changed. Or I might not tell them about that story, because it doesn't matter. What really matters is that, if you write a screenplay that's good enough, it gets treated like a rare treasure. Everyone wants to see it, to get hold of it, and to be involved in the hoopla. The way you get screenplays that good is by writing a lot of them, and rewriting all of them to make them meet a high standard.

When drafting out screenplays, I've seen writers (including myself) usually end up with one or more of the following problems:

➤ **No pearl in this oyster.** You write a screenplay that isn't that marketable in the first place. No amount of hot sauce will make it taste any better. You're left with a hollow shell.

➤ **Surfing in shallow water.** Incomplete research is done before writing the screenplay, resulting in shallow scenes and speeches that won't play well with audiences.

➤ **Rudderless ship.** The screenplay wanders away from the strong main current of the story and drifts along, lost.

➤ **Horse latitudes.** Like shipmates adrift on a windless sea, characters drone on endlessly but never advance the story.

➤ **Sinking leaky boats.** Scenes are repeatedly launched before they are ready, sinking the entire enterprise.

➤ **Titanic indifference.** Ignoring a major problem, the script churns onward blindly, resulting in a massive loss of life.

➤ **A drunken captain.** You're writing a screenplay about an unlikable hero or heroine that no one trusts or wants to emulate.

Skip's Tips

A hole in a screenplay denotes something dangerous, as though the very life of the script might drain out of it if not fixed. It could be a small hole that the viewer barely notices, or one so big that you could drive a Mack truck through, that will result in a collective groan from a theater audience if filmed as written.

You might be that rare prescient person who comes up with story lines and subjects that the rest of the world just doesn't quite "get" yet. John Lennon said that if he wrote a song his friends liked immediately, he thought something was wrong with it. It was the songs that people had to take a while to assimilate that he wanted. When someone is as successful in his or her field as Lennon, I pay attention. I know that I've come up with story ideas that weren't popular until years later, but I was not, like the founder of The Beatles, in a position to put them before the public based on my name alone. I had to deal with the current marketplace and prevailing "common wisdom"— and so, most likely, do you.

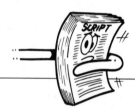

It's Not for Us

"I'll fix it later" is okay when doing a first draft, but when rewriting you have no excuse. You can't ignore nagging major problems. Are you too deep in your story to be objective? If you can't solve a script problem, get some professional mentoring. A pro might see something that you don't because he or she is not immersed in the story as you are.

When you're a practiced screenwriter, you'll have far fewer holes in first drafts. Due to the collaborative nature of the business, however, you'll simply have to get used to rewriting because (rightly or wrongly) every person influential in getting your script on film will have ideas that you will have to at least consider while defending your own ideas.

I used oceanic references previously because I often feel at sea while engaged in the rewrite process. I try to look at constructing a screenplay the way I would building a beautiful, sleek yacht to sell for a great deal of money, one that I would have to deliver to a buyer across potentially rough seas. I try to build it strong and beautiful, going over it until I'm convinced that there are no holes or places it can spring a leak. When you set sail with your own screenplay, you should be completely confident of getting that vessel to its final harbor—a sale! (Punny, huh?)

Good screenwriters are like good sailors. They master their craft. They learn the tides and currents but know that such things are changeable and tricky. When they have survived enough voyages, they feel confident of weathering just about anything. And sometimes, they know it's better to stay in port and let the bad weather pass, or to abandon some voyages altogether.

Scene Length and Readability

I have a built-in Harry Cohn "butt twitch" mechanism in my brain to tell me when scenes are too long, but poetry is my weakness. The first major poem I wrote was a 12-page epic in the fifth grade about the fatal charge of the Confederate General Pickett at the Battle of Gettysburg. The teacher wouldn't let me turn it in because she said that it would "embarrass the other children." (Hey, my fourth grade teacher told me that the difference between an A and an A+ was doing what's required and something extra, so I was just following the rules.) In one screenplay, I wrote a cowboy poem for one character that was a story in itself and that would have run up to three minutes onscreen. I expect that the audience would have been exiting in droves, had it been filmed. I was reminded of William Faulkner's admonition to kill your darlings when you are rewriting. I cut out the speech.

Think now for a moment about the reader, the first person who might see your script. Even if you get a producer or director to read your script directly, busy people read a lot of screenplays, take a lot of phone calls, and cover all types of material. If you have long speeches and scenes longer than three minutes, they'd better be so fascinating that they'll capture the attention of super-busy executives. Although you might do research on the background of people who might read your script, synchronicity with their own prejudices and fascinations isn't something that you can generally arrange. The material has to move quickly and succinctly from one scene to the next. Long passages of text rarely help.

Maybe you have a fervor for chili peppers and write that into a speech from your main character. Let's say that he's a hard-boiled detective who operates in the underbelly of Phoenix and frequents a certain Mexican restaurant. If he runs through a litany of chilies and engages in a minute-long epiphany on why a habanero earns its reputation as "the bullet from hell," your reader might be reaching for a glass of water as they round-file your script.

Hollywood Heat

One of the first influential people I met in Hollywood was director/producer Richard Donner. He told me that the first draft of *Superman* (1978) that he received from Mario Puzo was more than 500 pages long. The author and screenwriter of *The Godfather* (1972) received story credit and shared screenplay credit with David Newman, Leslie Newman, and Robert Benton. Puzo might have felt he that had leeway because of winning two Oscars for screenplays based on his *Godfather* novel. How they got the "super-script" down to manageable length, Donner didn't say.

On the other hand, if there's a real reason for the placement of such a speech, it could be a highlight of the film, like the endless "shrimp" conversation in Forrest Gump that ultimately led to the Bubba Gump Shrimp Company, which made the fortune of the lead character. Any time a main character is involved in a long conversation or delivers a long speech, it's usually a turning point in the film or a summation, like Jimmy Stewart delivers in *Mr. Smith Goes to Washington* or Gary Cooper delivers in *Meet John Doe* (both by Frank Capra, who loved long speeches). You usually don't see long sequences in movies unless the director loves the idea or designs it, as in Robert Altman's opening in *The Player*.

The first thing to look for as you mark up your script with red ink is length—length of scenes first, and length of speeches second. You might also use a checklist like this one:

- ❏ Is this scene necessary at all?
- ❏ What is the essence of this scene?
- ❏ Do all parts of this scene contribute to its essence?
- ❏ Does every character in this scene contribute to its essence?
- ❏ Do the beginning, middle, and end of this scene follow a 1:2:1 ratio?

Skip's Tips

Successful pitchmen in Hollywood don't wait around when someone buys their idea. They stand up, shake hands, and leave before the buyer can change his or her mind. Use the same technique in writing scenes. Don't try to get cute and add extra unnecessary touches. At the point where the scene peaks, instantly move on to the next scene.

❏ Can this scene be written with less dialogue, or none at all?

❏ Does the end of the scene propel the reader into the next?

The more scenes you write, and the more ways you try to rewrite scenes, the more likely you are to develop an integrity about what works and what does not, with a complete loss of ego about utterly destroying something that you might have spent hours creating. When you reach that point, your chances of becoming professional are much more likely than they have ever been.

Collaborators and Craft

When you begin your screenwriting career, you might feel uneasy about your own ability. That's normal. That's one reason why we see so many screenwriting teams. Another reason is that, in television, scripts are often worked on by a staff of writers. Most TV writers live in Los Angeles, and the Writers Guild of America west's working writers are predominated by television writers. It's unlikely that you can collaborate with them as a neophyte writer, though. Why should any writer working on a deadline get involved with an unproven neophyte? If you want to write for television, you'll have to prove your writing ability first, and if you're not young and willing to relocate to southern California, your chances are slim. So, when I discuss collaboration, know that I'm talking about only screenplays for feature films, even if the movie gets made as a movie for television or cable television.

When you prove your writing ability with an excellent feature screenplay of your own, you may be able to engender the interest of a proven screenwriter. They'll likely want to meet or work with you in person, but in our electronic age, you can work with a collaborator no matter where you live.

Hollywood Heat

Long before the Internet and e-mail became broadly popular, one of the most successful writing teams in Hollywood was separated by thousands of miles. Jim Cash and Jack Epps Jr. wrote movies such as *Top Gun* (1986) and worked on many others before Cash's untimely death in March 2000 from an intestinal ailment. While Epps maintained a Hollywood studio office, Cash mostly worked from home in Michigan. Other teams have had similar arrangements, but few with the excellent results of Cash and Epps.

My best advice is that you find a writer or writers who are of equal or better ability than your own. Equal experience is important, but not crucial. I know of an Oscar winner who collaborated with a barely proven writer of ability.

I've had two long-distance collaborations, both with writers in the United Kingdom. Despite having never met each other in person and barely having spoken on the phone, in both instances we managed to come up with marketable material.

The first screenplay that I collaborated on was with two nonwriters who assured me that they could get the low-budget film financed. I had reason to believe them, but it was faulty reason. They were full of hot air, and I never fell for that trap again. My more recent collaborative experience, with U.K. friends, was pleasant partially because they were thrilled to "know" someone working in Hollywood, and if I must say, the stories that I submitted to them that got the collaborations going weren't half-bad.

Skip's Tips

According to the Writers Guild of America Minimum Basic Agreement (MBA), article 1.B.7/1.C.2, a rewrite is defined as follows: "the writing of significant changes in plot, story line, or interrelationship of characters in a screenplay/ teleplay." A polish is this: "the writing of changes in dialogue, narration, or action, but not including a rewrite." If any producer tells you either is anything different, that person is wrong.

An old theatrical adage says, "If it ain't on the page, it ain't on the stage." That applies to screenplays as well. If the script doesn't put it there, the director probably won't. Conversely, if there's too much on the page, the audience might not stay in their seats. Working with collaborators is like testing scenes on mini-audiences. Just check your ego at the door.

Who Should Read Your Script and Why

The only people whom I let read my screenplays are my wife, who has a keen eye and is a successful writer herself; and other professionals whom I know will give me their honest opinion, whether I agree with them or not.

When you finish your first screenplay, you'll be as proud of it as a grade schooler with a gold star on a report card. Chances are, you'll be equally naive. No matter how giant an emotional rush you feel when you type "The End" on the final page, I hope that you'll take my advice and set the script aside for at least a couple days before you start marking it up for a rewrite. I also hope that you will not show anyone a first draft—at least, not when you are beginning your career. You'll fully understand this after you've completed a few scripts. I still cringe when looking at the first drafts of my old scripts, even though my very first screenplay got optioned.

When you wrap up a rewrite, you want it to be the very best that you can deliver at that moment in time. The great thing about screenwriting is that you will continue to improve the more you write and the more you read great screenplays and watch great movies with a screenwriter's eye. Movies are the most collaborative of all the arts, but they are made by collaborating professionals. That's whom you should try to associate with.

It's Not for Us

Please do the writing world a favor and don't open your criticism of other people's work with "Let me play the devil's advocate here." After you've heard that cliché enough times, your immediate reaction is an urge to strangle someone. I've never heard it from seasoned writers—instead, they ask why you took a certain approach, or they offer an alternate "what if?"

I try to follow Clint Eastwood's example. When he first began his Hollywood career, he took pains to learn how everything worked on a movie set, to find out what every job was about. It helped him grow as an actor and to learn what producing and directing was all about. He was working with professionals, Hollywood veterans eager to share what they knew. The trick is getting yourself into regular association with such pros.

I almost gave up writing because once of a playwriting workshop in Los Angeles. The woman who hosted the workshop was the wife of a prominent entertainment manager, and I thought that she knew her business. After we did a reading of a play of mine, however, the workshop leader's best friend (who had not sold any writing in years) shredded it. I announced that I thought I was ready to give up writing. Less than a month later, a stage director called me about wanting to do a professional reading of the play, and I reconsidered the opinions of "the group."

Wherever you live, if you get involved in writing workshops, make sure that they aren't just social clubs in which the organizer is trying to "rule the roost." Find out what the professional credits are of the people involved. Sit in on a couple meetings before you join, particularly one in which a critique is taking place.

Normally, the following people are not good candidates to read and comment on your screenplay: your mom, your roommate, your significant other, and your teacher or professor. Unless you live in a major metropolitan area, rarely are college professors successful screenwriters themselves. If they were, why would they be teaching full-time? If you think that your professor is particularly insightful based on your class experience, you might still ask about his or her own background before you ask that person to take a look at nonclass work.

When you've made your screenplay as good as you can, the only people who should read it are people who are in a position to buy it or get it sold. Isn't that what it's really all about?

The Difference Between a Rewrite and a Polish

When you first try to sell a script, you're eager to get any acceptance from a working producer. However, Hollywood has many layers, which is a word for a state of mind that I use to describe moviemaking worldwide. The Writers Guild of America Minimum Basic Agreement (MBA) has a very specific definition of a rewrite and the key phrase is this: "significant changes in plot, story line, or interrelationship of characters." This means that if a producer meets with you after reading your rewrite (the only screenplay that I hope you submit) and wants significant changes made, he or she is asking you to do a rewrite, work that the Writers Guild says you should be paid to do.

Of course, by WGA rules, you also should be paid a minimum of 10 percent of the final purchase price of the script before you're asked to write anything. If someone wants changes "in dialogue, narration or action" that do not significantly change the plot, story line, or similar element, this is a polish, not a rewrite.

Hollywood Heat

Being rewritten by others is a source of endless discussion among members of the Writers Guild of America. It can be so touchy that some screenwriters refuse to do it. Do a search with "rewrite" at the WGA site, and read all about it. If you are offered the chance to do a rewrite and are willing to do it, but you don't know how much to charge, find out about WGA minimums at www.wga.org, or call the Guild at 323-782-4520. More information can be obtained from the WGA Contracts Department at 323-782-4501. There are rules about the original writer being given chances to do rewrites. Find out if that took place—this could apply to you.

What changes are "significant"? Here's an example. The *Fair Game* script that I wrote with Mike Conley had a great number of scenes set on the ocean or near the ocean. One group of potential financiers asked if it could take place in the desert. We didn't rewrite. It was later optioned by the producers of *Red Scorpion* (1989), who asked us to change it from a Caribbean setting to the South China Sea because they thought that the Prime Minister of Malaysia was going to finance it. They paid for the rewrite, and we did it.

Unfortunately, the major trend these days among independent producers is to get writers to work for nothing. They offer to try to "set up" your script (meaning, to get

It's Not for Us

In Hollywood, ego kills projects. As I wrote this book, I was helping put together a TV project featuring a household name. Unfortunately, the conduit to that name had some bad ideas about what would work on television. When I tried to explain, he went into an unfounded rant about why he was right. Both myself and the other experienced professional immediately pulled out.

it financed) if you will sign an option agreement in which you give them the right to shop it for up to 18 months, all for the princely sum of $1. Because I've done this before (but won't do it now), I can tell you that sometimes you don't even get the dollar. If that arrangement wasn't bad enough, some producers will also ask you to do a rewrite—a rewrite, not a polish—for nothing, based on their "notes." They will do their best to convince you that their experience and time is valuable, and that if you are merely willing to write these changes, you'll end up with a better script that they can sell.

There is also a trend of manager/producers who work on scripts like this and then take a 15 percent commission when it sells. When/if the movie actually goes into production, some of these people will pay you back the 15 percent out of their producing fee; some will not. Needless to say, such practices are frowned on by the Writers Guild of America, but the rules matter as much when you're trying to sell your first script so that you can join the WGA.

It's entirely up to you how you want to handle a situation like those I've described. I tell writers that they might learn something, if the producers have a decent track record. On the other hand, I say, doesn't it make you wonder why they don't have any money with which to option your screenplay?

Resources for Better Rewriting

There's an old Hollywood saying: "Great scripts aren't written; they're rewritten." These days, there is a veritable industry in place to help you rewrite, for a fee.

Lew Hunter, while still working as co-chairman of the UCLA Screenwriting Program, did evaluations of screenplays for around $1,000. He used the money for his grand-children's college fund. I told him that some of his peers were charging as much as five times as much, and he was stunned. I hope that he raised his rate.

If you pay anyone for helping you with a rewrite, I advise you to do that only after you've rewritten it yourself. If you use people based in Hollywood, ask point-blank who they can help you get your script to—and insist that they be very specific—once you've followed their rewrite advice. There is enough competition out there these days that almost all these type of mentors offer some follow-up contacts.

A number of books on the market offer advice on rewriting, but the leader is Linda Seger's *Making a Good Script Great, Revised and Expanded 2nd Edition* (Samuel French,

1997). Seger is a script consultant who is very perceptive about the subject that she teaches, even though she has little or no screenwriting experience of her own. Chapter 13 of her book, a case study of how the movie *Witness* was born and evolved through many rewrites, including changes made while filming and during editing, is as good an education on the screenplay to film evolution as you can get, barring experiencing the actual process.

And last but not least, the Writers Guild of America offers a free online Mentor program administered by its members. Check it out at www.wga.org.

Skip's Tips

If you can't decide who to go with in getting help on a rewrite, pick the one who can most easily take it or leave it, or whom you simply like. They're likely the most reasonable and professional.

I once wrote and co-produced a safety video called *A Woman's Guide to Firearms*. I was not a shooting enthusiast when I started. In fact, I didn't own a gun. I researched the video by taking a firearms safety course from the two top marksmen in the United States, Mickey Fowler and Mike Dalton. I did some other research and then wrote the script. When it was done, the producer and originator of the video called me and said: "We've got a problem."

I cringed because I'd just gone through that with the executive producer of another video, Jan Stephenson's *How to Golf*. Although I had put together that video, bringing in the director and Jan Stephenson, the exec had asked me to rewrite the script in a way that I thought was unethical, so I took some money and profit points and walked away from the production.

When the first draft of the firearms video was perceived to be problematic, I listened to the "notes" from the producer, all of which were technical details and not nearly as serious as he believed they were. He was testy when he first called me, expecting, I think, a voracious defense on my part of my work. Instead, I convinced him that if it didn't work for him, it surely wouldn't work for our ultimate audience. In presenting a documentary on a complex subject, we had to be clear.

If I'd let my ego or past bad experience get in the way, I might never have kept working on the show all the way through production and editing. The video won a Silver Medal at the New York International Film Festival.

The best way to learn how to rewrite is to work on a script all the way through production. If you don't have that luxury, I hope that some of the notes I've given you here help. If you don't think they do, let me know how you think I should rewrite them.

The Least You Need to Know

➤ Writers of only one screenplay are like overly protective parents with only one child. The "one-baby" syndrome is easily cured by more "children."

➤ You'd better get used to rewriting; if you start working as a screenwriter, you'll be doing a lot of it.

➤ Screenwriter and author William Faulkner's advice about rewriting was to "kill your darlings." These days, you might have to vaporize them.

➤ If you keep a long speech in a screenplay, you'd better have a short and reasonable explanation for doing so.

➤ Try to collaborate only with a writer or writers who are of equal or better ability than your own.

➤ Ultimately, the only people who read your screenplay that matter are those who are in a position to buy it or get it sold.

➤ For the best advice on rewrites and polishes of your screenplay, check in with the Writers Guild of America.

➤ In Hollywood, ego kills projects. Check yours at the door.

Chapter 18

Polish Makes Perfect

In This Chapter

➤ Studio movies with many writers

➤ How screen credits are determined

➤ Tools to perfection

➤ The completed product

So you write a first draft, and you do a rewrite. Then you find a producer who likes your script, and you work together and do another rewrite. Maybe the producer is a Writers Guild signatory and will treat you according to the rules. Then the producer has a meeting at the studio and is told, "We need to find a writer." Huh!? Who wrote the original? This happens all the time because of various needs or perceived needs once a picture is seriously being considered for financing. I hope that you never get rewritten, but you probably will.

When a movie might actually get made, particularly at a major studio, rules get bent and rumors abound. It's impossible to find out the truth unless you are a part of the process or know someone who is involved. When you are polishing up your screenplay, you need to seriously think of who might be right to star in the lead roles, and you also should have some idea of who these people have worked with in the past and would want to work with again. You will be asked about your preferences, you know.

Why Studio Movies Have So Many Writers

Many writers work on scripts but are uncredited, due to Writers Guild rules. When you get a chance, buy a bound movie script—not a script in a book, or those you download from the Internet (which are often illegal transcripts that violate copyright laws). Spend some time browsing through legitimate scripts, and before long you'll find one that lists all the writers who received Writers Guild credits on the movie.

Skip's Tips

If you're not online, this tip won't help you. Let's say that you want Mel Gibson to star in your film. Want to see if he has worked with a certain director? Look up Gibson's name at the Internet Movie Database (www. imdb.com), and then scroll to the bottom of the page and type in the director's name at the "Mel Gibson and _____" box.

Skip's Tips

If you want to know the full story of how onscreen writing credits are determined, read the Writers Guild of America Screen Credits Manual. You can do a search for it and download it at www.wga.org, or call the Writers Guild at 323-951-4000 (West Coast) or 212-767-7800 (East Coast).

A store I like is Book City in Burbank, California (308 N. San Fernando Blvd., 91502, 818-848-4417). It sells accurate, final-draft scripts from real studios. Some of them have a page in the front that lists a number of colored script pages in order of the revision number. In order, after white comes blue, pink, yellow, green, gold, and then back to white (and who knows what shades after that). That is how production companies keep track of script changes. The changed pages are a code that tells people which draft of the script they are working from. You don't need to worry about using any color but white at this point, so I won't bore you with the code details. But you may be wondering, why are there so many writers on studio movies?

I once befriended a producer named James Nelson (*Borderline*, 1980) and worked with him on trying to get a property of mine sold. One day he told me that he had the rights to the Bob Wills story. Being from Texas, where the King of Western Swing music hailed from, I grinned. Nelson said Jack Nicholson wanted to play Bob Wills. I wondered out loud what was stopping the movie from being made. Nelson informed me that Nicholson insisted that the screenplay be written by Thomas McGuane, who had been a writer on *The Missouri Breaks* (1976), a Western starring Nicholson. I only knew that McGuane was married to Margot Kidder, so again I asked what was the problem. "McGuane won't start on the script for less than $250,000," Nelson said, "which I don't have."

Thus began my education into the vagaries of Hollywood. I knew that, at one point, Bob Wills had been so popular that he sold more records than Bing "White Christmas" Crosby and appeared in a number of Hollywood movies. He was a notorious Lothario; reportedly, 300 crying women appeared at his funeral. But with no McGuane script, no Jack Nicholson, so no movie. And that's how it often goes with A-list actors and producers.

Let's say that you write a script that everyone wants to make. I hope you do. What if you write one good enough to be purchased, but it's your first script, and directors (many of whom write) and stars who get involved want some mental reassurance that they will be working from the best script possible? If they don't write themselves, they will hire writers whom they trust and will insist that those writers be hired to take a pass at the script.

The studio executive, eager to accommodate their stars and cover every base in every ballpark on every lot, also have lists of writers they work with or want to work with. They will have a certain amount of development funds to "get the script right." And so it goes, sometimes on and on and on for years.

David Saperstein, whose unpublished manuscript became the movie *Cocoon* (1985), told me that five writers were hired at various times to adapt his novel. The fifth one, Tom Benedek, called Saperstein and said he didn't like any of the previous drafts; he simply planned to adapt the story the way it was laid out. And Benedek got the sole screenplay credit.

If you've done a rewrite on your script and are satisfied with it, set it aside again for a couple weeks or a month. Watch a number of movies that you think might be similar to your movie. Then come back to your script and read it again. If you see things that you would like to tune up, that's where the polish comes in.

It's Not for Us

Don't get cheated out of the screenplay credits you are due. Read *The Writer Got Screwed (But Didn't Have To): A Guide to the Legal and Business Practices of Writing for the Entertainment Industry*, by Brooke A. Wharton (HarperCollins, 1996). You'll save yourself a lot of heartache and worry by reading about every legal angle in the business.

How Screen Credits Are Determined by the Writers Guild of America

Many beginning screenwriters ignore the Writers Guild of America until they earn the number of credits necessary to join. Only when they sell a screenplay to a producer who is signatory to the WGA, meaning that the producer cooperates with the stipulations of the WGA's Theatrical and Television Agreement, do writers contact the Guild.

And that's too bad. The Guild is more easily joined by getting involved, and the best way to start is by availing yourself of the many publications from the WGA, both in print and online. One of the best places to start reading is the Credits Manual for film (another exists for television).

The WGA Theatrical and Television Basic Agreement is more commonly called the Writers Guild Minimum Basic Agreement, or MBA. If you are a Guild member, the Working Rules prohibit you from working for a company that is not signatory to the MBA. The companies have to sign an application to become signatory, so check to see that they did that; call the Guild's Signatories Department to find out. To join the WGA, you must sell material to a signatory company. You'll have to prove that you made the sale to join, so keep copies of all e-mails, letters, phone logs, and checks.

Skip's Tips

When you are writing a master scene script, the scenes are not numbered, and shots such as "ANGLE ON GEORGE" are mostly left out. When a script is prepared for production, a "shooting script" is prepared that has all these things. Credits on a film are determined according to content of the shooting script.

Let's say that you sell your script and qualify for membership in the WGA, but other writers are hired to rewrite your script. Will you still receive a screenplay credit or a "story by" credit (not as good, but your name is still on the screen)? That's why you need to read the Credits Manual, so that you'll know the rules. Most writers don't and then are dumbfounded when they learn that the script they sold doesn't have their name on it in the theater.

If you work with a producer who is nonsignatory to the WGA's MBA, then you're on your own (or with your lawyer or agent) in getting the credits you want. If you do work with a nonsignatory and disagree with its assessment of credits, try convincing the company to use WGA arbitration procedures to work things out.

When a project is completed, the company that made the movie submits materials to the Guild so that a Notice of Tentative Writing Credits can be issued. They determine who gets writing credits and who does not. If the writers who worked on the project do not agree with the NTWC, they can protest. For a theatrical motion picture, they have 12 business days to register a protest. For television programs, they have only seven business days to register a protest.

If a protest is lodged, an arbitration can be held. When an arbitration of credits is called for, the company in question must submit three copies of the literary materials of each writer involved to the Guild. All source materials—book, play, whatever—must also be submitted. Every possible aspect of contributory material is covered; it's quite a task.

Each participating writer is then responsible for seeing that submitted materials are accurate and complete, even if they have to visit the Guild office to review the materials. If you don't agree with all the materials submitted for consideration, you can request a prearbitration hearing. When the materials are verified, they are looked at by the Arbitration Committee (consisting of three WGA members), who only know each writer in question by a letter of the alphabet. Each committee also has a consultant available to answer questions; the consultant is a WGA member with substantial experience as an arbiter. None of the arbiters know who the other two arbiters are, which keeps the whole affair as collusion-free as possible.

Every writer involved can also submit a statement to the Arbitration Committee about his or her contributions. This must be submitted within 24 hours of the time you are notified about the arbitration. You are told whether you are Writer A, B, or whatever. Then the Arbitration Committee reads through all the material and makes a decision based on what it feels is each writer's contribution to the final shooting script. Basically, nothing else matters.

Hollywood Heat

Rumors about what writers work on which scripts fly fast and furious around Hollywood. For example, it was wildly rumored that Robert Towne "really" wrote *Good Will Hunting* (1997), despite the fact that Matt Damon and Ben Affleck won an Oscar for their script! All Towne did, apparently, was offer them advice over lunch. One thing is certain, however. Experienced and trusted screenwriters can make great amounts of money to "fix" certain aspects of a screenplay. For example, I was told that a certain "princess" got $100,000 for a weekend's work doctoring the female dialogue in a 1993 film about a Secret Service agent.

Because this method of determining credits evolved over time and was developed by professional writers, they've thought of everything. Let's say that you have enemies and don't want them judging you wrongly (gee, another writer with an axe to grind?), you get a chance to look over the "Arbiters List," which shows who all the eligible arbiters are. You get a chance to delete names of people whom you think might not treat you fairly or who would be prejudiced toward you. The Guild doesn't ask for a reason why you make a deletion—that's your business.

When each member of the Committee has studied all the available material, they all report their decisions to both the Guild and the consultant assigned to the committee. A Guild credits employee then notifies each writer involved.

So how do members of a committee determine who gets credit? Says the Credits Manual: "Any writer whose work represents a contribution of more than 33 percent of a screenplay shall be entitled to screenplay credit, except where the screenplay is an original screenplay. In the case of an original screenplay, any subsequent writer or writing team must contribute 50 percent to the final screenplay."

The Credits Manual defines original screenplays as those "which are not based on source material and on which the first writer writes a screenplay without there being any other intervening literary material by another writer pertaining to the project." Got that? If you write your script without basing it on any other existing literary material (something someone else created), then you're in good shape toward getting screenplay credit.

You might be wondering why I would tell you about screenplay credits when you're waiting to hear about polishing your screenplay. The reason is simple: Beginning screenwriters are stunningly naive about show business. If you get your script in good

Skip's Tips

If you do your homework and learn some of the rules, you'll impress producers with your acumen about the business. Most beginners don't even know the Minimum Basic Agreement exists, much less what the details are. If you can speak to it, a producer might think twice about trying to get around the rules, whether they are WGA signatory or not.

enough shape, you might never have to be involved in an arbitration. It might resonate so well with everyone who reads it that they want to shoot what you have written and not bother with thoughts of other writers. Believe me, it can happen, but only with the very best scripts. When you polish up your work, that's the kind you want to end up with.

Dialogue Specialists, Purchased Scripts, and Other Tools

As you may have noticed throughout this book, I mention the Internet Movie Database a lot. If you've tried it by now, you may have noticed that almost every popular movie has a section of Memorable Quotes from the film. That could be because Amazon.com bought IMDB.com some time back and sells videos of the films as well as books that correspond to the movie on the site (via a click to Amazon). The main reason the quotes are there, I believe, is because people remember and quote lines of dialogue more often than any other element of film. How many variations of "We don't need no steenkin' badges" from *The Treasure of the Sierra Madre* have you heard in your life? This despite the fact that the film is more than 50 years old! How many times have you heard "They're here!" trilled out as someone arrived at your door, emulating little Heather O'Rourke as Carol Anne Freeling in *Poltergeist* (1982)?

Great lines of dialogue are what we repeat while socializing, and, as writers, wish we'd written. Unfortunately, most writers don't know where to start in creating memorable dialogue or improving existing dialogue during a rewrite or a polish.

I used to argue with fellow writers that the great playwrights had not written normal, everyday dialogue at all. Rather, I insisted, they had written elevated dialogue that might have sounded like normal speech but was actually a higher level of thought than that of people in the street. Nevertheless, their dialogue was not so sophisticated that it could not be understood by common people; even Shakespeare had to make sure the "groundling" commoners in his audiences understood what was going on, I said. When the Bard wrote a double entendre in a play that only French-speaking people would understand, he was simply writing in layers.

Most of the time, when I began my "elevated" rap, I would get argued down. Then David Mamet came along with his plays and screenplays, and suddenly I didn't look like such an idiot after all.

Hollywood Heat

The great Gary Cooper was a handsome leading man who appeared in some of the most heroic films of all time, including *Sergeant York* (1942, for which he won the Best Actor Oscar) and *High Noon* (1952, for which he earned another Oscar). Cooper's frequent hesitations in delivering his lines were a source of comment and envy among fellow actors, some of whom imitated his easy-going delivery. Once, a reporter asked Cooper about his style. The trademark wry smile spread across his mouth, and "Coop" revealed his secret: "Well," he said slowly, "I'm just trying to ... remember my lines."

I grew up being fascinated by film dialogue, whether it was Jimmy Stewart speeches in Frank Capra movies that I saw on television, or even the comic blusterings of John Travolta's Tony Manero in *Saturday Night Fever* (1977).

What dialogue do you quote? Matt Damon's Will Hunting talking about why he shouldn't work for the N.S.A. in *Good Will Hunting* (1997)? (Whew, talk about a long speech. If he could get away with that and win the Academy Award, maybe he could be elected president, after all.) Or is it "Show me the money!"?

The best authority on dialogue I ever met is Sol Stein, former publisher of Stein and Day; author of many books, including the million-selling *The Magician;* and a founding member of the Playwright's Wing of the Actor's Studio. Stein was the editor of fellow Actor's Studio playwright Elia Kazan, a writer/director who had a major impact on Hollywood with films such as *On the Waterfront* (1954). He was a playwright for 15 years before he became a novelist, both of which helped prepare him for teaching the first university dialogue course in the nation, in 1990 at the University of California at Irvine.

The course was popular and expanded into larger quarters in years that followed. Stein taught his students something simple but profound, that "dialogue is a new language and not recorded speech." To illustrate this principle, he would take an interchange of four boring lines and make them sparkle by changing one line at a time. He later detailed these methods in "The Secrets of Good Dialogue" chapter in his book *Stein on Writing,* and then he expanded upon it in the recently published *How to Grow a Novel* (St. Martin's Press, 1999). The essence of the 12-week course that he taught at UCI became a "Dialogue for Writers" audiotape that is free to anyone who tries any of his software WritePro programs (WritePro, FirstAid for Writers, FictionMaster). For details, call 1-800-755-1124 during East Coast business hours, or read about it at the WritePro Web site, www.writepro.com.

Skip's Tips

You'll be told to write dialogue "the way people really talk." I have no idea where that started, or why. The way people really talk is with stops and starts and mumbles and "uh" and "um" and long pauses. You're better off writing dialogue that, while refraining from clichéd speech, reflects the essence of the character speaking.

It's Not for Us

When you write something "too on the nose," that means you've written unimaginatively. Viewers like to be surprised, not bored by clichés. Think less in terms of authenticity and more in terms of surprise. Which is more interesting, a lumberjack drinking himself to sleep, or one who stays up late reading *The Theory of Relativity*?

"What counts in dialogue," Stein told me, "is not what is said, but what is meant. Whenever possible, it should be adversarial. Characters reveal themselves best in dialogue. Dialogue helps to show rather than tell a story."

As you look through your script, you might well remember Stein's admonitions that "characters reveal themselves best in dialogue" and that good dialogue is "not what is said, but what is meant." These sentiments are shared by many successful screenwriters and playwrights. By "not what is said, but what is meant," Stein is talking about a concept known as subtext. You know what the character really means, despite what is being said. How do you achieve subtext? Playwright Jeffrey Sweet, author of *The Dramatist's Toolkit* (Heinemann, 1993), under the billing "creative consultant," wrote the screenplay for the TV movie version of Hugh Whitemore's play *Pack of Lies* (1987). Sweet says that he looks for the most important word in a passage and then tries to take it out. When the audience fills it in anyway, the result is subtext. The first chapter of his next book, *Solving Your Script* (Heinemann, 2001), is about the power of the unspoken word. (For more information, see his Web site at www.jeffreysweet.com.)

My favorite example of not-so-subtle subtext is when a teenaged Lauren Bacall in *To Have and Have Not* (1944) tells Humphrey Bogart's Steve how to whistle. When she says that he should just put his lips together and blow, we know what she's talking about, and it sure ain't whistling. Scenes with sexual tension are the easiest ones in which to insert subtext that might have nothing to do with dialogue. Sexual tension can be telegraphed with a look, but what is the character saying?

Here's a different bit of subtext. When Claude Rains as Captain Louis Renault in *Casablanca* (1942) exclaims in Rick's club that he is "shocked, shocked!" at the gambling taking place, we know that he isn't really. The subtext is that he is putting on a show for the German occupation forces. It tells us a lot about the dynamics of the tough situation that the good guys are in.

During a rewrite, you work on the structure of your script. By the time your rewrite is done, you should be relatively satisfied with the basic story line, the turning points, the act breaks, and so on. Think of it this way—you've built the skeleton, laid on the muscles, rigged up the nerves and blood vessels, and engaged the brain. With the polish, you're making the skin perfect, painting the eyes, and getting the hair and smile just right.

Rather than launching from page one and attempting to polish up your dialogue and the overall context of each scene in succession, pick a couple of your favorite scenes, hopefully crucial ones, and work on polishing them. When you've cut your teeth on those and improved your best scenes, the lesser ones will benefit. You'll be force to bring them up to the quality level of your best, now improved scenes.

While I don't follow a checklist in polishing scenes, if I did it would read something like this:

1. What does this scene say?

2. How does this scene serve the dynamics of the story?

3. What are the characters in this scene saying?

4. What's really on their minds?

5. What is the beginning, middle, and end of this scene?

6. How does the end of this scene propel us into the next one?

7. Is this scene memorable apart from the overall movie?

Hollywood Heat

Robert E. Thompson was nominated for a WGA Screen Award, Best Comedy Written Directly for the Screen, for *Hearts of the West* (1975). It's a hilarious look at an aspiring writer getting skewered in Hollywood. The film stars Jeff Bridges as Lewis Tater, a Midwestern farm boy dying to be a "real Western writer" who stumbles into the chance to star in 1930s Westerns. Andy Griffith as Howard Pike rewrites Bridges' script, *Hearts of the West*, by changing only the name of the writer. The film pays homage to Republic Pictures Westerns and paints a perfect portrait of naive writers in Hollywood. And guess what? There was another *Hearts of the West*, in 1925.

That last item might seem egotistical, but when you've written enough screenplays (or maybe even your first), you'll find yourself admiring a scene as if it exists all alone in the universe, created by someone other than yourself. You've plugged into the magnificent aesthetic flow of the world and diverted for a moment into your screenplay.

Sometimes great scenes turn on a line that epitomizes the essence of the interaction of the main characters.

In one script I worked on, when the apprehended femme fatale is facing a gun wielded by the male hero she thinks she's fooled, she exclaims in shock, "But I thought you fell in love with me!" He replies wryly, "I didn't fall for you, Laura. I just looked over the edge."

How You Know When It's Ready

What you want to end up with is an unchallengeable script. You want a screenplay that people will remark upon years later by saying something like, "That script? Wow. We just shot it."

Skip's Tips

I've mentioned playwriting a lot in this chapter because dialogue is the primary story tool in a play. In screenplays, the primary tool is the moving picture. Therefore, the adage of "less is more" is usually best with regard to dialogue. Read through your screenplay without reading any dialogue, and see if the pictures tell your story. If they don't, it probably needs work.

The problem is, that's almost an impossible task. If you can write a script like that with your first screenplay (or your next), you're a better man than I, Gunga Din. I still chew my fingernails over rewrites and polishes. I flinch when the phone rings and I sense that it could be someone ready to comment on my new script. Every time I've felt puffed up about the bulletproof nature of a new script, my ego has been carpet-bombed shortly thereafter by some agent or producer. And when I've thought that a script is as good as I can do at the moment and don't have a clue whether someone will like it or not, I've mostly received positive responses. Seriously. I know it sounds weird, but it has mostly worked that way for me.

When you've gotten comments from people you trust and have rewritten your script, you might want to make a list and decide who provided you with the most positive or helpful comments. Don't ask these people to reread the screenplay after you've done the rewrite. Wait until you've tinkered with it some more and put a polish on it.

And when you've done that polish, other than doing a spell and format check on it, don't read it again yourself. If you're a perfectionist like some, you could run the risk of "grinding." You'll start nagging at the edges of scenes, messing with them when they don't need to be messed with. Just print out that polished script and set it aside.

When you feel that the time is right, pick it up and read a scene or two. If you like it, then ask your selected readers to give it another read.

If they're professionals and you've done the right work, you'll get superlative comments. You may even get a "Wow, I'd really like to see this movie." Or, you might get something better, the response you really want.

"Who have you shown this to?" they'll ask.

And you'll mention whoever you feel like mentioning.

Then they'll say something like, "Well, if you wouldn't mind, I know somebody at [insert production company or agency name here] that I'd like to take a look at this."

That's when you know it's ready—when a professional is willing to put his or her reputation on the line to get your work read.

So polish it up and make it shine, and hopefully you'll get there.

The Least You Need to Know

➤ Studio movies often have too many writers because producers and executives want to please all the major players involved and cover all possible weaknesses in the script before filming.

➤ Everything you could ever need to know about how screenplay credits are determined is available in the Credits Manual from the Writers Guild of America, both in print and online.

➤ You have nothing to fear if your screenplay is subjected to credit arbitration by the Writers Guild; it's a fair process.

➤ Great dialogue and great scenes are often marked by the subtext (hidden meaning) of the words and actions onscreen.

➤ Many great scenes turn on a line that epitomizes the essence of the interaction of the main characters.

➤ Don't ask someone to reread your screenplay after you've done the rewrite. Wait until you've put a polish on it.

Part 4

Post-Script Possibilities

Come behind-the-scenes to learn what that wrecking crew known as a "production company" does with your screenplay after it's rewritten. Learn up front what happens once a script is purchased, so you won't need a shoulder to cry on, then. We'll explain how the film industry works and dive into the subtle and not so subtle nuances of writing both TV movies and short films for the Internet.

Chapter 19

What a Reading Can Show You

In This Chapter

➤ Hollywood's theatre tradition

➤ How to find actors

➤ Organizing a reading

➤ Writers' gatherings

Writers get the wrong idea about how to get their scripts made. I hear from them all the time asking about how to get a certain actor to read their screenplays. They've done enough reading or watched enough talk shows to know that actors love to chat about how important they were to getting a project done. The truth is that actors usually help only people they know from their struggling days, or people close to them. That's how *Dances with Wolves* (1990) got to the screen, and it's also how *The Big Kahuna* (1999) made it. *Dances with Wolves* came about because writer Michael Blake (who also wrote the novel) was a houseguest of Costner. With *The Big Kahuna*, directed by John Swanbeck and written by Roger Rueff, who also wrote the stage play, Kevin Spacey liked the material and wanted to help a friend.

Every actor starts somewhere. Even if you don't live in Los Angeles (as Costner and Blake did) or in New York (where Spacey and friends live), there may be a professional theater company near you. With digital movies being made cheaply, material that could be shot in one room, such as *The Big Kahuna,* or even something with minimal locations gives you a better chance than ever of getting your movie made. One way to get that process started is a reading, just the way they do it in the theater.

The Theatrical Tradition in Hollywood

I first began to realize how things really work when I was casting a one-act play I'd written. I was at a Super Bowl party and was introduced to an actress who was a star of a soap opera. Because I didn't watch soaps, I had no idea who she was, but she asked if she could read my play. I got a copy to her, and she called and said she'd be happy to do it. I asked our mutual friend about her, who assured me that the actress would draw a lot of publicity for the play, perhaps even get it reviewed in the *Los Angeles Times*.

We staged two of my one-acts, and we did get a review in the *Times*, but that was due to a personal contact of the star of the other play, who persuaded the *Times* reviewer to stop by. Sure enough, though, the actress in the first play was the one whose picture was featured in the review.

The actor with the *Times* connection, Michael Savage, reaped high rewards for his performance and efforts to promote the play. He was cast in the West Coast premiere of Tennessee Williams' *Le Vieux Carre* at the Beverly Hills Playhouse, which lead to an ongoing role on TV's *General Hospital*.

Actors in Los Angeles love to do nonpaying roles in equity-waiver theater for several reasons:

➤ They get to work with up-and-coming writing talent, and they know that writers often become directors, or writer/producers in television.

➤ If they are known as situation comedy performers, they can do a drama and show off another side of their abilities.

➤ When they are not working, they can generate some publicity for themselves and drum up some paying work.

➤ It can be a whole lot of fun.

Skip's Tips

When you organize a reading of your script, make the actors as comfortable as possible, mentally and physically. A feel-good atmosphere creates a lot more energy for everyone.

Skip's Tips

Actors who perform in large theaters normally belong to the Actors Equity union. When they perform in a venue of 99 seats or less, they are allowed to do so by the union without pay so that they can showcase their talent. This is known as "equity waiver."

I know. You're thinking that if you don't live in southern California or write plays, you're out of the loop on this angle. What matters is that the same principle works anywhere. Hollywood holds a fascination all over the world, so if you live in Keokuk, Iowa, and write a screenplay, you might find that actors will flock to you for the chance to participate in a reading. They know that there's a chance you might actually sell your screenplay, just as they might someday be cast in a Hollywood movie, and getting to know you and helping you now might pay off in the long run.

How to Find Actors for a Reading

If you're located in a very small town, this could be difficult. You could get yourself in trouble by using locals for a reading, if you've patterned some of your characters after people that some or all of the readers will know.

But guess what? Hollywood is a small town. It really is. In a city of millions of people, the relevancy of the John Guare play that became a movie, *Six Degrees of Separation* (1993), continues to amaze me. I tell people that if they do some research, they might be amazed to discover who their friends and relatives know or can reach. In fact, when I taught at the UCLA Extension Writers Program, the largest program of its kind in the world, researching extended contacts was an exercise that I gave budding writers.

It's Not for Us

Don't make any promises, and don't lead anyone on. If you have a reading of your script, no one who participates should believe that by being a part of the process, they will be promised anything down the line. As a beginning writer, you simply won't have the power to make that commitment. Lasting friendships begin with honesty. Make friends and keep in touch.

Now, you might think that it was easy for them, living in Los Angeles, but many of them had never met a movie star or producer and didn't know anyone who worked in "the business." When they did the prescribed homework and began explaining that they had written a story and wanted a professional to read it and comment—did their friend/relative know anyone?—they were stunned with the positive results. At least, most of them were.

Let's assume for a moment that you live in an area where a troupe of actors can be found. They're probably doing equity waiver theater, which means that they look high and low for plays that they can afford to license for a production, that they think the public will be happy to pay to see. And so, they are not terribly likely to want to do original material from unknown playwrights.

All those actors, it would be safe to say, have some Hollywood dream, whether it's a realistic dream or not. So, if you contact the group to arrange a reading of your *screenplay,* they may be more interested than they would be if you had a stage play.

If there isn't a theater near you, how about a college with a theater department? It doesn't matter if the students are all young and you've written older characters. Remember, most movie stars are relatively young, and so are the majority of moviegoers, so having young actors read your work might make you rethink some roles in a way that will make your screenplay more commercial.

If you contact a theater group, the normal person to contact is the *dramaturge*. This is the person who initially reviews all material for performance. If there is no dramaturge, there will be a theater director, but don't just blurt out what you would like to do over the phone. Tell this person that you have a project you need help with and that you would like to buy him or her lunch to explain. A free lunch is almost always appealing for a struggling actor, which most people in theater are, sadly enough. You don't have to be coy about your intent—it's simply better to explain something in person. The worst thing that could happen is that the person will say no or, after reading your script, turn you down.

Hollywood Heat

Actors can be forgotten quickly in Hollywood, even when they are legends. When she was older and had not worked in more than a year, superstar Bette Davis actually put a full-page ad in *Variety* to alert casting directors, directors, and producers that she was available for work. Such ads are looked upon as desperate measures among most Hollywood folk, which is precisely why they do plays and readings in equity-waiver theaters in Los Angeles.

If there's no theater company nearby, or no local college, unless you have a reason for having a high school drama club read your screenplay, your next best bet is a commercial venue such as a Barnes and Noble or Borders bookstore. I'd advise you to find any place that has a built-in, regular "audience," as well as refreshment facilities such as a coffee or snack bar. Although you might rather support a local bookstore rather than a chain, I mention Barnes and Noble because they all have a Community Relations Coordinator whose job it is to promote events. Also, if you're having a screenplay reading, that gives the bookstore a chance to sell the many books that it has about Hollywood and screenwriting, including this one. (See? I'm not a complete idiot.) Plus, if aspiring actors know that they can be seen "performing" in a public place, they're much more likely to get involved.

If you have a circle of friends whose reading and speaking abilities you trust, whether they are actors or not, you might be able to pull together a reading that works. I also suggest, if appropriate in your community, that you place an ad in a local newspaper to broaden your chances for better actors.

Keep this in mind—ultimately, this reading is for you. You want people who will contribute to the process and read the screenplay without injecting their own peculiar personality quirks. You want people who will be there to support making your screenplay better, not to get all the attention focused on themselves.

Here's an important part of your reading. You need a *narrator*. Whether or not you actually have a narrator featured in your screenplay (which most screenplays don't), you need someone who will read the set directions with some life in their voice. You might choose to take on this role yourself, but I would advise against it because it may conflict with your objective view of the reading process.

Try to find a narrator who is insightful and has a voice that is easily heard. The last person you want is a droning, monotonic Ben Stein type of actor who will sound bored while reading the description. You need someone who might sound just a little excited when Indiana Jones runs ahead of the gigantic rock. But not too excited—sort of like Steven Spielberg.

Skip's Tips

Don't just blindly call a theater and ask about arranging a reading. Go to one of the plays the theater puts on, and ask around at intermission. Try to get an idea about the personality of the dramaturge before you bring up your project. "How do you find your plays, anyway?" you might ask. People met in person are much more friendly.

Although I've found that it's much better to watch a reading of your script without also participating as a reader, I would suggest that at some point you get some acting experience of your own, in a formal setting. You might want to look into helping with a production at the local theater, or auditioning for a role. Take an acting class locally. People are much more willing to trust and help folks with whom they've shared substantive experience. If you've ever been on a sports team or struggled through a traumatic experience with a group of people, you understand my meaning here. Writers some times complain that actors don't understand what they have written, but when they do complain, I often find that the writers don't understand acting.

Lastly, you might want to consider arranging for someone to direct or produce the reading with you. If that sounds like a bit much for the reading of a little old screenplay, you probably haven't had much experience in theater, where the writer has final casting approval and complete script approval. A stage director runs readings of plays, while the writer sits by quietly, watching. An arrangement like that will give you something called "altitude," and you might find that your script gets treated with more respect.

Organizing a Reading That Works

As you are lining up your actors, make sure that you set a date that will give you enough leeway to make all the necessary arrangements that I'm about to suggest. As you might have suspected, I don't advise simply sitting around in chairs over pizza and Pepsi. The more quality you put into the reading, the more quality you'll get out of it.

First, I suggest that you find a way to videotape the reading. If aspiring actors don't have any footage on themselves at all, they might appreciate a short snippet from the reading to use in promoting their acting. You will also see things in reviewing the videotape that you probably won't see while the reading is taking place. And who knows? What if one of the actors at the reading goes on to superstardom? Wouldn't you like to have a video of a young Ben Affleck reading from your screenplay? I'm guessing that it would be good blackmail material!

At the very least, audiotape the reading for your own benefit. Playing back someone delivering the lines as you rewrite later might help in making the dialogue more fluid.

Hollywood Heat

Whether they came from the theater or not, with top Hollywood writers, screenplay readings are common practice and a major social event. Equally a success on Broadway and in Hollywood, Neil Simon began writing in the early days of television, working on programs such as *Your Show of Shows* (with Sid Ceasar) as a staff writer. In television, shows are always read around a table before they are rehearsed so that adjustments can be made. The same thing happens in the theater. Thus, when Simon comes up with an original screenplay, or an adaptation of one of his plays, he always stages a reading of the script.

Next, if you have more than one actor in mind for certain parts, you might have to audition. If you've never done it, don't worry about it—just do it. Trust me, actors run into much worse characters than yourself in their careers. Select a pertinent scene from the script, and print out or photocopy plenty of copies. Meet the candidates in a clean, well-lit place if you don't want them in your living room, and be professional and courteous without making any commitment until you're convinced. The more professionally you treat the process, the better the results you will get.

Third, make sure that everyone selected to be involved in the reading has a character description, some background notes from which to formulate a mind-set before the reading. Unless you know and trust the actors, *do not* give them a copy of the screenplay before the reading. Here's why. When actors audition for a part, they do what is called a "cold reading." They are expected to perform from a script on the fly, without studying it beforehand. That way, the casting director can watch for glimpses of the craft that the actor brings to the work, or doesn't. Actors will be given a scene to study for a few minutes before the reading at most. When you're doing a reading of your screenplay, you want it to be a process of discovery for everyone involved. As actors read the lines, injecting their own unique look and personality, everyone forms mental pictures of the movie, in an organic fashion quite different from someone silently reading a script.

It's probably best if you give your narrator a copy of the script beforehand, as long as you can trust that person to confidentiality. Should you ask the narrator or anyone else to sign a confidentiality agreement? That's up to you and your legal adviser or agent. However, it might make you look too rigid and formal, which is something that actors generally disdain.

After you've finalized your cast, make sure that you have a few extra people on the list who can both serve as an audience and fill in on some parts if an actor or two doesn't make it to the reading. There's nothing more disheartening than an important actor not showing up on the day of a reading. Even if other actors can double up on key roles and do different voices as necessary, it's a distracting bit of business that you don't want to have as a part of your reading. (This is the voice of experience speaking here, with one voice.) You'll also find that the actors will feel better if they're a bit pampered, so if someone is around to bring them little snacks and drinks and such, it's a more congenial atmosphere, and the reading will not be broken up by people getting up to help themselves.

Skip's Tips

Sides are pages from a screenplay that are given to actors when they audition for a part. Often while filming a movie, actors who are not leads do not receive the entire screenplay. They merely get pages containing their performance, perhaps with some background information. This helps maintain confidentiality about the project.

A couple days before the reading is set to take place, phone everyone to make sure that they have the event marked on their calendars. This gives you an opportunity to make any last-minute adjustments necessary or to answer any questions that may be lingering. If you call a week before the reading, your participants might forget. If you call the day before and they don't feel prepared, they might panic. You need to do everything you can to maintain an atmosphere of calm preparation.

Of course, if you've written a screenplay about a serial killer from hell, you might be dealing with a slightly different crowd, who might not care about mental equilibrium. I'm simply making suggestions for people with a normal screenplay.

When all the arrangements have been made for the reading, if you feel that it is applicable, you might consider getting in touch with local media about it. If you live in a metropolitan area, TV, radio, and newspapers probably won't care about the reading unless famous names are involved, and maybe not even then. In areas where few movies are made, however, on a "slow news day" with no explosions, murders, or calamitous weather about, you might actually get the reading covered.

Hollywood Heat

If you live in Los Angeles or go there for any extended period of time and want a reading of your screenplay done, here's a group that might help:

Dennis Safren, Literary Manager
FirstStage
P.O. Box 38280
Los Angeles, CA 90038
Phone: 323-850-6271
Fax: 323-850-6295
E-mail: Safstar@aol.com

FirstStage is a development organization, not a production company. Send the organization your complete script, along with a bio and a cover letter, and, it might stage a reading. There is no fee, but you can become a FirstStage member, if you want. The organization accepts scripts throughout the year, with no restriction on style or content, but it must not have been previously produced. The group also does not accept TV pilots, children's theater, or musicals, unless a musical director is involved.

If you get lucky enough to have a TV news crew at the reading, let your actors loose and give them the opportunity to really act out their parts. Even if they go "over the top" with it, no more than a minute or so will be shown on the news, and you can use that tape to promote your screenplay. No one in Hollywood is likely to care about a screenplay reading in Princeton/Bluefield, West Virginia, but if you have local resident Bob Denver (Gilligan from the *Gilligan's Island* TV series) participating, they'll pay attention. Even if no recognizable actor is on the tape, if you get your local TV news, or even the local newspaper (make sure that someone's picture gets in the article), to cover the event, a producer may deduce that you're an inventive writer who might have a decent script.

The day or night that the reading takes place, give everyone ample time to get loosened up and grow familiar with each other, if the actors are unfamiliar with each other. Make sure that everyone is comfortable and has everything they might want to snack on or drink (check with them beforehand for diet peculiarities).

When you begin the reading, introduce the narrator, if the actors don't already know him or her. Explain that the narrator will read the slug lines (locations) as well as the descriptions of the action. Make sure that everyone knows where the restrooms are, and ask that they take care of business before the beginning of the reading. Make sure that it's okay with everyone to read the script straight through without a break. After all, they sit through most movies in one sitting. If you're videotaping or audiotaping, you'll have to change tapes at certain times, so a short break then wouldn't hurt the flow of the reading.

Just before you start, explain that although you would like the script to be read without interruption, you're willing to provide short clarifications if someone has a question during the reading. When you're ready to start, turn it over to the narrator. Let the fun begin, fade into the background, and pay attention. Just make sure that the narrator starts by reading the title and your name. That will set the right tone and promote respect for the work. And everyone will smile at you—for now.

You might want to have comment sheets that people can fill out to help you sort out all the opinions. Even if you're taping the reading, people have things on their minds that they might not reveal except on paper. If you use this follow-up, give them the opportunity to deliver, mail, fax, or e-mail the answers to you later. That way, if they think it's a pain in the butt to fill out a questionnaire, they can conveniently forget.

Make sure that you leave plenty of writing space on a questionnaire and have plenty of pens and pencils available. Pencils with erasers are better so that people can change their minds neatly. You might want to know something like the following:

➤ How did you like the screenplay overall?

➤ Did you find the story compelling?

➤ Did any particular character appeal to you? If so, why?

➤ Would you pay to see this movie in the theater? (Be honest!)

➤ If you would not pay to see this movie, what could be done to improve it so that you would feel good about paying to see it?

➤ How does this movie compare to other films you've seen lately?

➤ Any other comments?

It's Not for Us

Don't take it personally. If people don't like your script at a reading, don't get upset or explain what you were trying to say. If they didn't get it, that's the way it is. Your rebuff will be countered with, "If it ain't on the page, it ain't on the stage." Just write down their comments and thank them for sharing them.

Skip's Tips

I knew a genial English lady who was the secretary to a superstar for many years. Unfortunately, this star was ill educated, so he would have scripts and books covered, with synopses recorded on audiotape. Under certain circumstances, having your reading taped could have interesting uses later, particularly if you say in a query letter that you have them available.

When the reading is wrapped up, thank everyone and tell them that you'd be happy to discuss your screenplay with them privately, particularly if they liked it and know someone who might help bring it to the screen. This last is an old sales technique called "prospecting at the close." When it's delivered with self-deprecating humor and sincerity, it can work wonders.

If you run a reading well and your script is of at least passable quality, you'll probably find that you've made some new friends. If the script has really impressed people—particularly if they're aspiring actors—you could make some good friends.

If you've read this section this far, you're probably of a mind to do a formal reading. For those not so inclined, I hope you and your buddies ordered enough really tasty pizza and didn't drink too much beer.

Writers Conferences and Other Irregularities

I've spoken at a number of writers conferences around California and across the country, and I can tell you that they all operate in much the same way. The people who speak there (including myself) are generally doing one or more of the following:

➤ Selling a book or books

➤ Looking for consultation clients

➤ Getting paid to appear

➤ Enjoying a new venue as they (hopefully) build their reputation as a guru

We'll have a section on mentors and gurus later. I don't like being considered a guru, even though people all over the world ask me questions on daily basis, via e-mail, phone, or the occasional letter. I'd rather be writing something original, but when I see a need that isn't being completely filled, I'll get involved, as I did with this book and my *Writer's Guide to Hollywood Producers, Directors, and Screenwiter's Agents*.

Here's where you'll wish that you had a computer, or at least Internet access, if you don't have them. The very best one-stop shop to finding a writers conference near you is on the Internet, at the ShawGuides, Inc., site www.shawguides.com/writing/. In coordination with *Writer's Digest*, this compilation of writers conferences from across the United States and throughout the world on the site allows you to search through hundreds of events. You can search by your area of focus, such as "screen-writing."

The data isn't perfect. For example, I've spoken for three years now at the Aspen Summer Words festival, but I'm not listed. ShawGuides also still lists the head of the Aspen Writers Foundation as Jeanne Small, although the new executive director is my former UCLA Extension Writers Program student, Julie Comins. But what the heck, it's free information! (If you want information on the Aspen event, contact Aspen Writers' Foundation, P.O. Box 7726, Aspen, CO 81612, phone: 1-800-925-2526, 970-925-3122, fax: 970-920-5700, or e-mail: Aspenwrite@aol.com.)

Hollywood Heat

Hollywood is too small of a town. In early 2000, I had lunch with a producer and her friend to talk over a possible project. The friend and I kept telling each other that we looked familiar, and then she mentioned the WGA event "Word into Pictures," which she produced. Suddenly (and don't ask me why), I remembered dating her once and told her all the details. This is one example of why—despite all stories to the contrary—people in Hollywood generally try to be nice to each other and not burn bridges. You never know when you'll run into them again.

For pure advice on screenwriting, the annual Writers Guild of America's "Words into Pictures" event is probably your best bet. See the WGA Web site for information on last year's event or this year's conference. They also have audiotapes and videotapes available from a company called Sound Images— call 303-649-1811, or go to www.soundimages.net/ wgf.html for more information. With seminars such as "Chick Flick vs. Dick Flick," which explored the comparative dearth of female-focused films, and "TV's Top Guns: Writer/Producers of Comedy and Drama Swap Tales from the Trenches," the "Words into Pictures" event is the most comprehensive screenwriting conference in the world, with all the seminars involving people currently working in Hollywood.

Skip's Tips

If you don't live in southern California but would like to go there for a conference, your best bets for week-long affairs are the "Words into Pictures" WGA event, the Hollywood Film Festival (the only one in Hollywood, www.hollywoodfilmfestival.com), and "Selling to Hollywood" (www.sellingtohollywood.com).

If you're Internet-impaired, you can also contact the WGA for information at this address:

Writers Guild of America, West
7000 West Third St.
Los Angeles, CA 90048
Main: 323-951-4000
Public Affairs: 323-782-4574
Outside Southern California: 1-800-548-4532

Or, of course, you could read all about it and all the seminar descriptions online at www.wga.org/thewga_index.html.

If you're of a mind to enter a screenplay contest after you've had a reading and fixed up your script even more, there are lots of them out there. Thankfully, there is another one-stop shop to find the details for all contests:

Movie Bytes
254 S. Greenwood Ave.
Palatine, IL 60067
847-776-0747

You also can visit the Movie Bytes Web site, at www.moviebytes.com. If you write or e-mail the owner, Frederick Mensch (fmensch@moviebytes.com), he'll probably just say, "Why are you bothering me? It's all on the Web site."

Whether you're looking for a conference or a contest, I hope that you find the information that you need to make your script saleable, whether it comes from a mentor or from the feedback that you get from a reading. Just remember, whatever anyone tells you, it has to make sense to you, or it isn't helpful.

The Least You Need to Know

➤ Actors will often do nonpaying roles, even a screenplay reading, if there's potentially something in it for them.

➤ Hollywood is a small town; you may be closer to a helpful contact there than you think.

➤ A screenplay reading should be well organized and planned well in advance. After all, it's for *you.*

➤ Local theater groups are good sources for actors for readings, but don't be afraid to hold auditions.

➤ Before a reading, share your full screenplay only with the people reading the lead roles.

➤ The more professionally you conduct a reading, the more likely you'll get the results that you want.

➤ Although you can research all writing conferences at writing.shawguides.com, the best one for screenwriters is the "Words into Pictures" event, by the Writers Guild of America.

Chapter 20

Why the Screenplay Is Merely a Blueprint

In This Chapter

➤ About movie budgets

➤ How scripts get changed

➤ Star power

➤ After the purchase

➤ Script resources

I wish I had an example for you of a master scene screenplay by a screenwriter who did not direct but that was filmed identically as written. I imagine that there might be one out there, but I don't know about it. The fact is, no matter how good you think your script is, after it's sold, the collaboration starts. Actually, it will probably start before you sell it, if your agent gives you rewrite suggestions. Film is the most collaborative of all the arts. You might as well tattoo that 13-letter word, *collaboration*, on the inside of your eyelids right now because you'll likely see a lot of it when you sell a script.

After a script is purchased, it's all business until the day the movie starts filming. It is a serious commitment to set aside even a few hundred thousand dollars, much less many millions. The average homeowner spends decades paying for a house that costs as much as a very low-budget film. And that's not a bad analogy, to think of a screenplay as the blueprint for a house. Someone has to line up all the contractors—that's the producer. You need a construction supervisor, or contractor—that's the director. There will be an inspector—that's the representative of the guaranty bond company that ensures the movie will be made and that investors' monies won't be lost. Then there are the various workers and vendors who do specific jobs. For example, you might think of the art director like the interior decorator of the home.

It's Not for Us

Numbered scenes—as in "1. EXT. SPORTS BAR—NIGHT"—are what you see in a shooting script. Software programs put them in automatically, and some older books tell you to write them that way. Don't do it. A script isn't formatted that way until preproduction of the movie begins.

Skip's Tips

Preproduction is the process that occurs when the money is in the bank to make a movie and the project is moving forward. The script is set and casting is in progress. If someone tells you they are in preproduction and the money isn't in the bank, then they're not in preproduction.

Would the architect be necessary after the blueprint is in hand? Not really. And that explains why the writer often gets shoved aside when the film or tape starts rolling. To help prevent that from happening, you need to learn as much about the filmmaking process as you possibly can.

What You Should Know About Movie Budgets

The Blair Witch Project (1999) was made for only $1,800, right? Or was it the official $22,000 figure? I don't know exactly how much the original footage cost. A lot of rumors were floating around when the film made such a splash. I do know that the filmmakers had the help of Louise Levinson in drawing up a business plan that raised the money needed to get the film in shape to be picked up for distribution. (Levinson is the author of *Filmmakers and Financing: Business Plans for Independents, 2nd edition* (Focal Press, 1998) and has a Web page with her e-mail address at indienetwork.com/levison/index.html.

I also know that the original *El Mariachi* (1992), written and directed by Robert Rodriguez, was made on a budget of $7,000, with a final cost of $220,000 after post-production. Rodriguez chronicled the process excellently in his book, *Rebel Without a Crew: Or How a 23-Year-Old Filmmaker With $7,000 Became a Hollywood Player* (Plume, 1996).

The Blair Witch Project grossed in the neighborhood of $150 million, and *El Mariachi* made more than $2 million, and those are the U.S. figures only. Both of these inexpensive films in their own way changed how Hollywood looked at filmmaking, at least for the up-and-coming generation. *Blair Witch* was made from an outline, while *El Mariachi* was scripted during and largely funded by Robert Rodriguez's stay in a hospital as one of the subjects of a cholesterol-reducing drug test. What matters is that both projects were done by the people who conceived them. If you're writing a screenplay only to sell, a budget might not be a major consideration for you, but you should at least have some idea of how much it costs to make movies.

I remember reading a friend's outlandish science-fiction fantasy script years before computerized special effects were common. I told him that the script was okay but that it would be difficult to make because it would cost so much for the special effects. He was insulted and said that they would find a way to make it.

Maybe today they would (if the script had been better). Generally, I tell writers today to write the script with little consideration for budget because anything a writer can conceive can be filmed, thanks to computers. But there's a catch.

Hollywood Heat

Producer Laurence Perreira was meeting with Barry Diller at 20th Century Fox to tell him about a project. Diller wasn't interested; he said that he really needed to find something for Arnold Schwarzenegger, right now. Perreira remembered *Predator*, a script by Jim Thomas and John Thomas, a first script by two brothers from a farm community north of Los Angeles. A military man leads a team against an invisible alien hunter in a jungle— perfect for Schwarzenegger. Diller liked it. The script was read, and the movie was made in 1987. Unlike the alien facing the wrath of Schwarzenegger, this producer was in the right place at the right time.

The caveat to the advice of "Just write!" is this: If you have written a thoughtful character piece, set in a small town, but at the end you have a giant UFO landing like something out of *Independence Day,* forget it. You've mixed genres badly. That scene will be the first thing cut from the film, for budgetary reasons. Computer-generated images are expensive. The equipment is expensive. The artists who operate the equipment are expensive. You'll be left with your characters staring in awe at the night sky as blinding rainbow lights are bathed across their faces, simulating a UFO.

The real truth for screenwriters with regard to being concerned about budgets is simple: Just write, but keep the type of action consistent throughout the script.

If you write an action film, many of the scenes will be equally expensive. If you write a self-contained film such as *Clerks* (1994), which covers one eventful day on the job of some guys working at a convenience store and a video store, the cost per scene will be about roughly consistent. Oh, I know. You're thinking that there are quiet indoor scenes in movies such as *The Mummy* (1999). Go through a film like that sometime, and time the placement of scenes. You'll find that action films and horror films have quiet scenes and comedic scenes as rhythmic devices, to give the audience time to catch its collective breath or to relieve tension.

Skip's Tips

If someone wants to make your film but asks you to take less for the script due to budgetary considerations, you might want to agree, but only if you can get "gross points" (a percentage of the profits before expenses are deducted). If you can't get that, you're dealing with someone who's greedy. Take your script elsewhere.

It's important that you understand at least rudimentary elements of budgeting. For example, if you are certain that you have a great TV movie script, it's doubtful that a TV network will spend much more than $3 million making your film. If you have elements in the script that will throw the film overbudget, they have two choices if they want to make your movie:

1. Spend more because it's worth it (not likely).
2. Cut that part out of the script, or substitute something less expensive (highly likely).

The next time you watch a video of a movie that you think is somewhat like your film, look for consistency of content. Are there a lot of computer-generated effects? (If a man turns into a donkey before your eyes, that's probably done by a computer.) Do some scenes clearly take place beneath the Eiffel Tower? Does the film star Tom Cruise? (That's a $20-million ticket right there, not counting how much he makes when gross profits are realized.)

Although there is much, much more to learn about what goes into movie budgets, you should at the very least be prepared when you are told that certain things must change in your script because they can't do it within the budget. No amount of fervent artistic arguing on your part will change financial facts. If you write a feature film script that's spectacular enough, though, the budget will be one of the least considerations.

How Your Cowboy Villain Became an English Terrorist

So you've written a Western. It's a different Western, and it has to be, because not many Westerns get made anymore. But you have something really different—a gunslinger who can't be killed because he's a vampire. He rules a town with an evil hand. We'll call it Darkness Gulch (it used to be Happy Valley). Then the girl arrives in town, and she's packing a pistol. We'll call her Mean Matilda. She doesn't like men. She's been traveling the West, gunning down famous gunslingers such as Biter Bill, and now she's come for him. Only Matilda doesn't know that he's a vampire, you see; she just knows his evil reputation.

Now, Bill might just sneer and shoot her right between the eyes, but she's very beautiful and, well, he's kind of taken with her, partner. He decides to put off his evil ways for a few days as he tries to cover up reality and woo her. And, dang if ole Matilda don't fall for it, shucks—until that is, she finds out that he's not only a vampire, but the varmint that shot down her father, the very creep she's been gunning for all this time.

Hollywood Heat

Behind-the-scenes Hollywood information can lead to screenwriting sales. *Lust in the Dust* (1985) was written by Philip John Taylor, an acquaintance of mine in the late 1980s. This spoof Western with the tagline "He Rode The West ... The Girls Rode The Rest! Together They Ravaged The Land!" featured Tab Hunter as Abel Wood. Taylor told me that his script had been inspired by an earlier Hunter film called *The Burning Hills* (1956), a serious Western written by Irving Wallace from a Louis L'Amour novel. With Natalie Wood as the female lead, it seems that there was so much hanky-panky going on around the set that the crew nickname for the production was "Lust in the Dust."

Your script—we'll call it *Dark Lust in the Dust*—is well written and just quirky enough that a producer buys it from you. But all the Western sets are being used. For some reason, suddenly there's a renewed interest in Westerns. Then he learns that a rundown urban area in his city, thanks to funding from the federal government, is offering concessions to filmmakers who will film there and put economically disadvantaged people to work. About the same time, the producer learns that an English actor who once was riding high on a hit TV series, who left the series early but flopped as a movie star, is looking hard for a comeback vehicle. The producer does some quick calculations and figures that your script can now be filmed for one third of the original projected budget.

Darkness Gulch becomes a beat-up neighborhood at Main and 230th called "Hell Hood." That's where a vampire runs the largest street gang in the state. And, on top of that, he's a disgraced member of the British Secret Service, a really nasty ex–James Bond type, who plans to take over the city. Bail Bond, that's his name. And Matilda becomes Juicy Jones, the best undercover detective on the force, the only woman with the cajones to venture into Hell Hood.

And when the producer explains this to you, you're absolutely dumbfounded. What happened to the great sweeping vistas of the Old West? They've been replaced by the city skyline. What happened to the beautiful black horse with red eyes? It has been replaced by a souped-up street bike. And so it goes, straight across your screenplay.

"Ludicrous!" you say. "I can't allow it!"

"Happens all the time," I reply calmly. "Get used to it."

Skip's Tips

"The back end" is a term that refers to box office revenue. If you get lucky enough to get paid "on the back end," that means you will be a profit participant. But, most likely, this will happen only if you own a percentage of gross profits. Make sure you have a good lawyer.

Remember my story about the script set at sea that the financier wanted changed to the desert? If you want to work as a screenwriter, you have a couple choices: Write something so spectacular that no one would think of changing it, or be flexible about changes, particularly those that have to do with budget.

This doesn't mean that you have to sacrifice artistic integrity altogether. You merely need to be willing to bend; you don't have to break to get your screenplay made. Of course, if you feel that strongly about it, you might be better off making it yourself.

Star Power Changes Screenplays

Because his movie hasn't gone into production yet as I write, allow me to simply say that a friend of mine wrote a screenplay that got a lot of attention. He was being mentored by a very successful screenwriter, so that helped, but my friend has a lot of talent. He's always had great ideas, from the time I first knew him as a teenager. Now he knows how to put them in screenplay form.

Through his mentor, my friend met the husband of a well-known film actress—an Academy Award nominee, as a matter of fact. And, small town that Hollywood is, another friend of mine recently completed the novelization of the screenplay of an upcoming film that this actress happens to be starring in. But back to our story. The actress's husband was a television director looking to direct his first feature film. Naturally, he didn't expect it to be a high-budget film, and, relationships being relationships, the director didn't want to take advantage of his wife's star power. Besides, my screenwriter friend's script did not feature a strong female lead.

But it was a fine action screenplay with a simple but great "what if?" premise.

To make a long story short, because of the script circulating in relatively high-level circles in Hollywood, it came to the attention of a very well-known male actor, and a notice appeared in "the trades" stating that this actor was scheduled to star in my friend's script.

Suddenly, a pretty good script set to be directed by a television director as his first feature film became important. My friend became very important. While word of his talent was already circulating, announcements in *Daily Variety* and *The Hollywood Reporter* about the project made him suddenly very hot as a writer. The reason was simple: star power.

Hollywood Heat

In recent years, some superstar-headed production companies have aggressively sought to cultivate writers on their own, whether the screenwriters are agented or not. One reason for this is the Internet, and another is worldwide interest in working with stars. One of the more open companies is Saturn Films, founded by actor Nicolas Cage and producer Jeff Levine. At their Web site at www.saturnfilms.com you'll find their address, along with information about projects such as *Shadow of the Vampire,* starring John Malkovich, which was financed by the Lewis Horwitz Organization and co-produced by London-based BBC Films.

It's difficult to get a true star to read a script. Here's why. If you don't know them, they don't want to waste their time. They know that Hollywood stardom can be fleeting and that "You're only as good as your last picture." This means that they're often neurotic about what their next movie will be, particularly if box office results on the last one were disappointing. They want money, not promises. Then there's the Hollywood benchmark called "pay or play." Some stars insist that the money to make the movie is in the bank before they will even read the script. They take down payments on their services, just as writers "option" their scripts for 10 percent down against the full 100 percent when the movie is financed. Only stars get treated better. If the production of the film falls through, they keep all the money. Why? Because they've marked out a place on their schedule during which the "pay or play" movie is supposed to be filmed. And some stars want money put into an escrow account before they'll read the script.

Does that sound harsh? Well, actors often struggle for years before their breakthrough film. They are made promises that are broken, suffering like writers. So, when they make it to the top, they don't want their time wasted. How can you blame them? When they put their name on a project, suddenly it can become very hot, and all the financing may fall into place quickly.

If you can somehow manage to get a top actor interested in your screenplay, you might become an A-list Hollywood screenwriter, like my friend. Just know this—with few exceptions, you will have to get to them through channels that they trust, whether it be official business friends, Hollywood professional friends, or long-standing family or college friends. Remember, they could be "bankable," meaning that a studio or financier knows that if that particular actor stars in a film, it is virtually guaranteed a certain return at the box office and so they will finance the film with much more ease.

It's Not for Us

Concentrating on "If I can just get my script to a star" will not help you much. Stars read scripts all the time, with offers attached. Yours, with nothing attached but a card stock cover, had better be something truly spectacular to get them interested.

Don't bother trying to get movie stars to read your script if you don't have a personal conduit to them. A mutual friend is best. You might get lucky, but usually the only stars interested in seeing scripts from unknown screenwriters are those who have established their own production companies. If serendipity strikes and you happen to make the acquaintance of a popular actor, great. Just don't walk up and introduce yourself and hand him your script while he's eating.

Even if you manage to get a star to not only read your script but also like it, if that star does not have production experience or does not own a production company, he or she still must convince an agent to like it, which could be difficult. The agent would rather field offers, and actors with pet projects are notorious for failing badly, as John Travolta did with *Battlefield Earth* (2000).

How a Purchased Script Gets Read

When producers read a script with an eye to buying it, the first thing they think of is casting. They know what stars are available to work and when. Next, they think of their own markets, the studio(s) where they do business, the cable networks looking for original material, and on down the line. If they know that certain stars are available and they've worked with them in the past, they might call the stars and tell them about the project, or even have a meal with them.

Hollywood is built on relationships, probably no more than any other billion-dollar business. Because of its nature, these relationships are broadly interesting to the general public. When Joe Roth left his executive position at Disney in 2000 and started a company that he later named Revolution Studios, the first star he made a deal with was Julia Roberts, the most popular actress in the world. That made news in nonentertainment media.

No producer should be discussing a screenplay before securing the rights by optioning the material, but producers are human, and so they do. When they start promoting a screenplay to secure financing, however, they must have it optioned, or the person they promote it to might option it out from under them.

So, the third thing producers think about when reading a screenplay (or in some cases, maybe the first thing) is who will direct the movie. They know the work of many directors and have worked with some. They know what actors the directors have relationships with and what studios like those directors.

Next comes the budget. Just as a producer will ask a writer who should star in the screenplay, a studio executive will want to know who might star and whether this person knows about the project; what director is interested, if any; and what the proposed budget is. If the producer has any qualms about the script, the executive (if interested in the project) will also discuss who can rewrite it, and whether that writer is available.

All of these factors are the basic things that producers think about when they read a script. Other things come into play, such as money-saving possibilities. If a country such as Ireland or a state like Indiana wants productions shot in the area, it might make it very attractive for producers to film, giving them tax concessions, lowered or nonexistent filming fees, and a film commission that acts like government-level "go-fers" to ensure that the producer gets whatever the producer wants. Many television shows and films are made in Canada, for a number of reasons. The American dollar is stronger than the Canadian dollar, so that represents cost savings. The technical personnel are qualified, which helps. But best of all, American producers shooting there get a 15 percent of the budget kickback when the production is completed. That can be a lot of change.

In return, the Canadians get a certain amount of "Canadian content" in addition to the benefits to the local economies where the productions take place. Canadian content means that a certain number of main characters, writers, and others must be of Canadian heritage or residency. Other countries do similar things.

Like other countries, states in the United States want movies to showcase the beautiful geography of the region so that tourists and other filmmakers will want to come there. It's a win-win situation.

So, there you are as a screenwriter, wondering why in the world you are being told that your carefully crafted tale about the first Native American family to discover fire in California has suddenly become a story about the French family in early Quebec that built the first waterwheel-driven wheat mill in Canada so that they could make flour to make into bread. I know, it sounds ridiculous, but that's how things can get turned around.

Skip's Tips

If you wonder whether or not a certain actor or director has a lot of clout among the money powers that be in Hollywood, look them up on the "Star Power" area of www.HollywoodReporter.com. It will cost you a few bucks to do so, but the education is worth it.

Skip's Tips

As soon as you make some money screenwriting, set aside some of it in a savings account labeled "Forget You Money." Hopefully, you'll reach a point where you have enough money saved up to say, "Forget you," to a producer or development executive who offends you with suggested changes. You might have another word for it.

It's Not for Us

Being flexible is one thing; being a doormat is another. Writer's reputations are built up easily and hard to live down. If you do not maintain your artistic integrity, no one will. Don't let anyone ruin your hard-written script under the guise of collaboration and flexibility.

The script of *The Big Easy* (1987), written by Daniel Petrie Jr. and named after the nickname for New Orleans, Louisiana, was originally titled *Windy City* and set in Chicago. And another Petrie script, *Beverly Hills Cop,* was originally set to star Mickey Rourke and then, when that wasn't feasible, Sylvester Stallone. Isn't it amazing that they settled for that "nobody," Eddie Murphy?

This is why the core of your story—your premise—and your plot needs to be so strong. The vast majority of good movies do not have to be location-specific, and changing characters to suit available stars may often actually add to the film's flavor. If you as a screenwriter are inflexible about such things, you might be looked upon as being "hard to work with," which will not help your career. It's a fine line, trying to maintain your standards and the integrity of your story, while still doing what you can to contribute to the collaborative nature of getting your movie made.

Experience helps, and you'll get that experience if you're as flexible as possible. Just don't be a pushover. There are so many insecure people in show business that if you maintain an air of composure and certainty, it might rub off. Even on you.

Script Resources That You Should Explore

It would greatly behoove you to do all you can to read as many versions of successful scripts as possible. Try to read the script that sold and all other versions of the screenplay, right on through the "shooting script" and versions published in books.

On the Internet, you can find all sorts of scripts to download. Many books with screenplays comment on the process that the script took from creation to screen. I won't attempt to list them; do your own research in your local bookstore. (Your local library might not help; the publishing of screenplays in book form is a relatively new phenomenon.)

You can buy screenplays over the Internet at sites such as www.scriptshop.com and www.scriptshack.com. Because these are merchants and, therefore, will have to answer to their customers, you're more likely to get the kind of scripts that you need to study. Still, the scripts available at free sites such as www.script-o-rama.com are pretty good. In fact, one site might be as good as the commercial sites. *Writer's Digest* in April 2000 wrote, "Whether you want to get tips from the pros or simply read top-notch scripts, ScreenTalk is the best site ever!" The publication was referring to www.screentalk.org, which also was selected as one of the top 101 Web sites for writers, only one of three screenwriting Web sites mentioned. (The other two sites,

Moviebytes.com and TheWritersStore.com, serve very different functions for writers.) ScreenTalk also publishes both an online and a print magazine, based in—are you ready for this?—Give, Denmark. These days, that's Hollywood!

The Least You Need to Know

➤ Movies such as *The Blair Witch Project* and *El Mariachi* were made cheaply but grossed millions. The catch is, the writers were also the directors.

➤ A screenwriter's only budget consideration should be in keeping the type of action consistent throughout the script.

➤ If you're unwilling to cut or amend your script to suit the budget, you may get cut yourself.

➤ If you want your screenplay filmed the way you wrote it, write something so spectacular that no one would think of changing it.

➤ Don't bother trying to get movie stars to read your script if you don't have a personal conduit to them, unless they have their own production company actively looking for material.

➤ When reading screenplays that they might produce, producers will consider factors that may never occur to the screenwriter.

➤ To understand how screenplays are changed between sale and production, screenwriters need to read as many versions of successful scripts as possible.

Chapter 21

The Real Role of the Screenwriter

In This Chapter

➤ The cineplex patron

➤ Are auteurs dying?

➤ After a script is bought

➤ How Hollywood is changing

Flash from Hollywood! Breaking news! The screenwriter is God, at least to the movies. Just like authors of novels, and just like the playwright in the theater, the screenwriter is the one on whom everyone else depends, without whom there would be no movie. I'm sure I'll get chastised for that statement. Who knows? I might get tarred and feathered and hung from the Hollywood sign. I don't care, because it's true.

Think about it. How many people actually see God? Not many. How many people outside of Hollywood actually see the screenwriter? Not many. Who does the work that gets everything started? In the world, most would say—God. In Hollywood, that would be the screenwriter. Like God, the screenwriter often goes unappreciated, until the producer who thinks that he's God needs a rewrite done. God help the screen-writer.

We're in transition in Hollywood at the moment, with the old gods of producing and directing and distribution hanging fitfully by carefully manicured fingernails from a trembling, crumbling Mount Movie. As more members of that polytheistic pantheon fall to Earth, they are replaced by simple scribes holding a screenplay in one hand and a digital camera in the other. The latter legions have one mantra: "It all depends on the script." No one will fool them about where that screenplay came from—the writer.

In television, writer/producers rule. Networks want people whom they can depend on, to create hit shows, write them, and get them made. Perhaps because most screenwriters who make a living writing scripts (most don't) get their checks from television, that general attitude has bled over into the film arena. Writers are increasingly also directing, and some of them are making huge splashes, as M. Night Shamalayan did with *The Sixth Sense*. With the advent of digital filmmaking and the ability to edit on a desktop computer, expect the trend to grow. This chapter suggests ways to make this new wave of moviemaking work for you, but it's mostly about attitudes: those of moviegoers, those of other people in "the industry" toward screenwriters, and the changing attitudes that have resulted due to new technologies.

Writing for the Cineplex Patron

Every time things change in Hollywood, the patron saints of the establishment bemoan the passing grievously. I remember the hue and cry that went up years ago when a major Hollywood movie palace on Hollywood Boulevard was renovated, splitting it into two theaters. This was when cineplexes were first coming into vogue. It was done purely for financial reasons because audiences simply weren't filling the big theater. With the ability to show two films, revenues went way up. Down the Boulevard, the classic Mann's Chinese Theatre added an annex, and some people complained, but the additional dollars allowed the main theater to stay profitable. It all comes down to the bottom line: bucks.

Hollywood Heat

There are two billion-dollar film businesses in Southern California. One is Hollywood, and the other is Encino—or more specifically, the pornographic film business. More than 10,000 porn films were made in Southern California in 1999 in an industry employing tens of thousands of people, including the "actors." When mainstream film production suffers because of migration to Canada and states offering incentives for production, many mainstream production personnel quietly take work making porn movies. It's even generally considered that the superior-quality Betamax videotape format lost to VHS because pornographers chose the cheaper format. (Betamax is still around. Because of its more compact nature, it's used on U.S. Navy ships and submarines.)

Now, more than a decade later, with the Academy of Motion Picture Arts and Sciences putting up its new building on Hollywood Boulevard and a billion dollars being spent (yes, you read that right) to spruce up the old town, some movie theaters in recent years have been restored to their former glory. Meanwhile, in downtown Los Angeles, grand old theaters are rented out for special performances of old films, sometimes with full orchestras. And large-format Imax theaters keep springing up all over the world. There's room for everything, but right now, most people see films in Cineplexes. That's an important thing to keep in mind, if you aspire to screenwriting success.

Why? Some people think that they have to write down to the normal moviegoer, and that's where they err. The fact is, the average person in the cineplex is more story-savvy than ever before. They want something that challenges their intellectual acumen, thrills them with improved images, and makes them think about their lives and relationships.

Skip's Tips

When you're planning your script, see what's playing at your local cineplex, and determine the premise of each film. Check back each week for a month, and see which ones remain; then analyze the premises again. It's likely that the ones with staying power, superstars or not, came from the most well written screenplays.

If you don't think that moviegoers are generally smart, if you believe that you can simply write some variation of old tired themes and succeed, I'm afraid you're in the wrong business. Successful films of recent vintage scream otherwise. *Gladiator* (2000) showed that, by creating the massive spectacle that was the Roman Colosseum in a new, expanded way, audiences would flock to see the, well, spectacle. If the director had assumed that it had already been done in *Ben Hur* (1959), he would have been ignoring what the cineplex audience wants. *Titan A.E.* (2000), from Don Bluth, added tremendous dimension to animation, as did Disney's *Dinosaur* (2000). Similarly, *The Sixth Sense* (1999) offered a new look at the spiritual nature of life. While promoted as a horror film, it was not, and it became one of the top 10 successes of all time because of its innovative storytelling.

So here's the point: Although you may think that you are writing for sophisticated Hollywood executives who want the same old thing with some new twist to pack 'em into the theaters, the opposite is true. To achieve outstanding success, you're actually writing for sophisticated movie audiences in the cineplexes, which means that the first script you sell might have to be stunningly good. If your script doesn't sell, don't complain, "Well, it was better than so and so." To make a breakthrough, you have to be superior to everything else out there. Screenwriting is the same as any other business. To get your foot in the door, you must exhibit a lot more effort than you do once established.

Are Auteurs Dying in a Screenwriter Uprising?

As I write this book, the war of words between the Writers Guild of America and the Directors Guild of America over creative rights is escalating. It has been percolating for a long time over a simple phrase: "A Film By …." I never did agree with that credit, but then, I'm a writer at heart. I know that directors work hard making a movie. They're in charge of the set and usually the post-production process as well, but "A Film By …" is a denigration of the writer in my mind. In October 1999, in the WGA West's in-house magazine *Written By,* an article stated that "A Film By …" credit was a "moral crime." The next month, the editor of the DGA magazine accused the WGA of demeaning film directors. When the WGA wrote a letter in response, the editor refused to print it in the DGA magazine (or so said the WGA).

Hollywood Heat

Hollywood can be notorious for mistreating screenwriters and other people who own net profit participation in a film. Writer and columnist Art Buchwald won a plagiarism case against Paramount Pictures over *Coming to America* yet still was not paid because Paramount claimed that the movie had not turned a profit, despite grossing more than $300 million. Buchwald wryly told the press that he finally understood when he realized Paramount was a nonprofit corporation.

The fact is, the "auteur theory" that the director is the author of a film has never helped anyone in Hollywood except directors. It has created bad blood between people who contribute to getting a film on the screen. And it has served to demean screenwriters and lessen their contributions to the filmmaking process. When press kits are compiled to use in promoting a film, they usually contain biographies of the main actors and the producer(s) and director, but rarely the screenwriter.

In recent years, the WGA has tried to counter that by arranging "Meet the Screenwriters" public relations junkets featuring writers such as Callie Khouri, who wrote the wildly popular "chick flick" *Thelma and Louise.* Coupled with the boom in interest in screenwriting and the continuing expansion of the publication of screenplays, it appears that screenwriting is coming into its own as a respected art form, and the "A Film By …" credit may die a not-so-quiet death before long.

Here's the truth about "A Film By …": After your first film is made, if it is a success, you might be able to convince someone to let you direct your next screenplay. If you have two script-to-feature successes, you definitely will. If you direct your first feature and it is a success, suddenly you will be much in demand. You truly will be the author of a film because you can both write and direct. Your career and fees will escalate skyward. I've known many writer/directors and seen this process work time after time. That's why I urge beginning screenwriters to think long-term by thinking like a filmmaker, not just a screenwriter.

In most cases, being both a writer and director (and/or producer) is by far the best of both worlds. It takes longer to achieve, but the rewards are geometrically greater.

Skip's Tips

A movie in Hollywood that has staying power is said to "have legs." Those legs refer to the power of word-of-mouth, the people in the theaters who get up and go tell a friend about the show they just saw and enjoyed. (I hope your career has "legs.")

What Happens After a Script Is Bought

When a production company or studio takes on a script, the first thing that it must do is figure out which producer will helm the production. That's not a consideration if the company is a sole proprietorship. When the producer starts working the script, he'll list possible casting and directors, and figure out potential locations and studio needs. How much will be shot on location, and where? Will the film require a lot of computer work? How much takes place at night, and how much during the day? All these things and more go into figuring out a budget, which is probably compiled with the help of a program such as Movie Magic Budgeting from Screenplay Systems (www.screenplaysystems.com for more information). They might do two different budget estimates—one for a low-budget movie and another for a high-budget film with major stars. Naturally, the optimum scenario for the producer is the high-budget version because the production fees will be higher, and so might the long-term profits. Also, studios will put a lot more money into promoting high-budget films.

As a screenwriter, it helps you to have some idea of what the budget of your movie might be because it affects how much you could be paid for the script. If it's a low-budget film and your first sale, you might expect only WGA minimum or a little more.

If the film has major stars in it, the budget could go to $80 million or more. A rough general rule of how much a screenwriter is paid is from 2.5 percent to 5 percent of the production budget. This means that for a film of $40 million or more, you could expect a paycheck of more than $1 million. Even if you get only half that, that kind of money explains why so many people are writing screenplays.

When the producer has a budget and a rough schedule calculated, financing is secured and then he (or she) and the director select a casting director to work with.

Casting directors have become very important in Hollywood over the past decade and can be crucial in attracting A-level talent to a project, almost as much as a director. Hollywood depends a lot on word-of-mouth and reputation, and if a casting director hires onto a production, that can say a lot about the quality of the script.

Next comes a director of photography, usually the one the director prefers. Just as certain artists are known for a certain style, so are cinematographers. For example, the look you might get from Haskell Wexler, who has been working since the 1950s, might be very different from the stylings of Caleb Deschanel, who does high-profile studio films such as *The Patriot* (2000) but has also directed several features on his own.

Hollywood Heat

Some producers are role models for the fine way they treat writers and other behind-the-camera personnel. Although he was once sued by a screenwriter, Clint Eastwood nevertheless has a reputation for taking great pains to see that writers are well-paid. Even better is George Lucas. When he was running low on funds while making *Star Wars*, Lucas offered net point participation to some crewmembers. They took it, probably not expecting to ever see any money. Lucas not only proved "normal" expectations wrong, but many of the writers became millionaires.

Why isn't the producer considered the "author" of a film? After all, the producer finds the script, hires the director, works with the director and casting director, or even secures the lead stars. The producer gets the financing in place and makes the distribution deals. The producer has to see that the filming schedule is finalized, that wardrobe is taken care of, and that props and any special needs are provided for. More likely than not, it's the producer who brings the script supervisor onboard (that person who keeps track of the position of the script at the end of every shot and keeps the producer apprised of how many pages of the script are filmed each day).

And what about transportation, catering, and where the "dailies" of that day's filming are shown for the cast and crew? Ultimately, that's the producer's responsibility.

If certain scenes do not require on-camera appearances of the leads or other actors, they will be shot by a "second unit" director and crew. In some cases, a producer might also serve as second unit director. Doesn't that give him (or her) even more ammunition for claiming authorship of the film?

Last but not least, who sets up the publicity and advertising? Who selects the poster for the film and makes the arrangements for the shooting of the "electronic press kit" (video documentary with the stars and director talking about their movie, with the screenwriter almost never on-camera)? Wouldn't that person be the producer? Yes, it would.

Does that give them more credence as the author of the film? Well, let's examine it. The authors of books usually do the promotion as well. We know that the actors aren't the authors of a film, but then, characters from a book can't speak, can they? Directors can speak on-camera, and so can producers. Can screenwriters speak? Who knows? We rarely see them.

Okay, I know. I'm being more than a little sarcastic here, and hopefully facetious. I hope that I have illustrated, however, the enormous amount of work that a producer does to get a film made, compared to the director or even the screenwriter. I find it strange, though, that in the entire time I've been in and around Hollywood, no producer has ever claimed to author a film.

It's Not for Us

Don't sign away everything because you think you must. The Writers Guild stresses that writers maintain their "reserved rights," which includes merchandising rights, publication rights, and interactive rights (video games). They stress that to buy the writer's reserved rights, the acquisition must be covered in a separate document. Don't buy the "Oh, that's just boilerplate material" contract argument.

But, back to the other folks who get a film made. The "D of P" (director of photography) usually has his own crew, and so does the film's editor, who can often "save" a film that is in trouble after shooting or discover (via smart edits) a view of the film that has not been envisioned by the writer, producer, or director. For example, it was widely rumored that the innovative end of *Pulp Fiction* (1994), in which we return to the opening scene with Honey Bunny (Amanda Plummer) and Pumpkin (Tim Roth) holding up the restaurant, was an editing glitch and was not written into the original script. We return to the scene in the opening of the film despite the fact that we are seeing John Travolta again after seeing him get killed. If the rumor was true, was it the idea of editor Sally Menke, or did it come from writer/director/producer Quentin Tarantino? Maybe you know the answer; I'm still wondering.

Experienced producers (who are the real final word behind most films) can also have a major effect on the movie story line. For example, screenwriter Scott Michael Rosenberg wanted a warm, family ending to his *Con Air* (1997), but the reigning king of action movie producers, Jerry Bruckheimer, had another idea. Bruckheimer insisted that the movie close on Steve Buscemi's vicious convict character, Garland "The Marietta Mangler" Greene, now escaped, gambling inside a Las Vegas casino. The closing scene came on the heels of Nicolas Cage as Cameron Poe being happily

Skip's Tips

Even if your script isn't purchased, it might make a good "sample." That means that it illustrates the quality of your writing. A great sample can get you assignment work, which is by and large the most lucrative area of screenwriting.

It's Not for Us

Despite my horror stories and those of others, don't assume that Hollywood is largely a pit of vipers. You'll find that, once people know your work, you'll be accorded a generous amount of respect. Getting them to know your work is the trick.

reunited with his family. The producer convinced the screenwriter, leaving audiences with a chill reminiscent of the phone call to Jody Foster's Clarice Starling from Anthony Hopkins's "Hannibal the Cannibal" at the end of *Silence of the Lambs* (1991).

It's clear that Quentin Tarantino was the genius behind *Pulp Fiction,* with great performances from his actors. But then, he handpicked them with a little help from synchronicity. When he met with John Travolta about the movie, he happened to be living in an apartment that Travolta had lived in when starting out in Hollywood. Amanda Plummer and Tim Roth's roles were written with them specifically in mind.

So who made *Con Air* work? Was it Simon West's tremendous direction? Was it the compelling onscreen charisma of Nicolas Cage? Or was it Jerry Bruckheimer's amazing knack for picking hit material and knowing what works?

Maybe Steve Buscemi was the magic touch. After all, he was in both films. He's in a lot of films and is always interesting.

The facts? No one would have become involved in either film if not for a spectacular script. John Travolta had been a superstar who had fallen when *Pulp Fiction* came his way. His fine performance put him back on top, and the movie vaulted Quentin Tarantino into comparisons with other "do everything" Hollywood legends such as Orson Welles.

It all starts with the screenplay. Even though many, many people contribute to the awesome collaboration that goes into getting a film made, no activity would ever take place without the engine of the script pushing the project forward.

Steven Spielberg once announced publicly that he could make a film without much of a script, that it wasn't that important to him. Well, maybe so, but Spielberg himself turned to directing after being unhappy with the filmed result of a script that he co-wrote with Claudia Salte (writing as Chips Rosen), *Ace Eli and Rodger of the Skies* (1973). He told me that personally, and I have it on tape, so I have to believe him. It all starts with the writing.

As a beginning screenwriter, you will probably be in awe of "real Hollywood people" for some time. That's only natural, but remember that almost no one in Hollywood could build a notable career without great scripts. Whoever the author of a film may be, the script came from a writer.

Don't you dare forget that.

How Hollywood Is Changing and What You Can Do to Help

If you intend to make a serious attempt at a screenwriting career, I urge you to not attempt to launch it when you have written only one screenplay, no matter how good you think that screenplay may be. According to the Writers Guild of America, only slightly more than 50 percent of its members are "employed slightly" on a yearly basis—this out of a membership base of around 10,000. The good news is that working WGA screenwriters are at all-time high growth levels, due to the expansion of cable television outlets and, recently, the explosion in short films "ported" to the Internet. About one third of WGA members are employed by television, but the vast majority of those writers are living and working in southern California. If you do not live in Los Angeles, your chances are lessened. If you move there to make it, you'll probably need more than one screenplay to break in.

Over the past half-decade, screenwriting earnings have grown by more than 50 percent. It's safe to say that this could be the best time to be a screenwriter since the days of the old studio system, when writers of all disciplines flocked to Tinseltown from across the country to take advantage of high salaries.

This might prompt you to think that the competition must also be fierce, and that the word is out and your chances might be lessened once you or your script make it to Hollywood. You could adopt that attitude, and if you do, it might be true. The real deal is that great scripts will always be in demand. A successful producer once told me that great scripts are not worth their weight in gold, but in platinum. That is still true.

The most successful screenwriters are generally those who are the most well-educated about the business of Hollywood. They don't read one book and rely on it; they read a library. They study old films and new films until screenplay structure becomes second nature to them. They work hard at improving their craft while keeping up with new developments and dreaming up new innovations.

For some time now, the new game in town has been the empowerment offered by advances in digital video production. Apple Computer, under the direction of Steve Jobs, seized upon this trend when it developed its iMac, G3, and G4 computers and FinalCut Pro film editing software. Suddenly, it became feasible to acquire the equipment necessary to film and edit a movie for under $10,000. This figure was completely unheard of only a couple of years before. Given how the prices of electronics drop, this situation will only improve in coming years.

Apple's FinalCut Pro followed on the heels of another program, Adobe Premiere. A number of software solutions now are available to the aspiring filmmaker, all the way up to full editing studio suites such as Media100. If you're inclined to look into the idea of filming (or videoing, I might say) your own script, do some reading first. One good place to start is *Videomaker* magazine, which you can read all about at www. videomaker.com. Alternatively, you can contact the magazine at P.O. Box 4591, Chico, CA 95927, phone: 530-891-8410, fax: 530-891-8443. The company that produces this publication, York Publishing, also puts on conferences in various parts of the country at which vendors appear and persons knowledgeable about all aspects of filmmaking (not only video) speak on various subjects. Having attended one of these events in Burbank, California, I'll vouch for their tremendous worth.

Many organizations around the country offer membership and help to aspiring filmmakers. Some of them are geared toward "guerrilla" filmmakers, while others offer a more traditional approach. Because there are so many (largely thanks to the digital explosion), I'll simply advise you to do an Internet search and see what you come up with, or check with your local or state film commission for suggestions.

Although it is impossible to advise you here on which ones are legitimate and which are not (there isn't room in this book), I'll simply say that those based in Los Angeles, New York, Chicago, Dallas, and major cities in Florida—where most productions and commercial productions take place—are more likely to provide you with the information and guidance that you need.

It's Not for Us

Don't think that you could never produce or direct a film because you don't know the nuts and bolts of filmmaking. There are always people available to teach you, even on the set. "Line producers" get films made for producers, and first-time directors almost always have an experienced person to show them the ropes, usually a skillful director of photography.

Before launching into videomaking, you might want to do a career plan. Take your screenwriting seriously enough to think that you might be able to do it full-time. Even if you never direct a film, the more complete your education is about the filmmaking process, the more likely you are to write a marketable screenplay.

Here are some steps that might help transform you from screenwriter to writer/director or producer:

1. Make a list of all the script projects that you would like to write in the foreseeable future.

2. Divide them up into low-budget ideas and higher-budget ideas.

3. Pick the low-budget idea that you like the most. Low-budget ideas are generally scripts with only a few locations and a minimal cast of characters. For example, stage plays these days generally have a cast of six or fewer, to accommodate the usual skimpy budgets of regional and equity-waiver theaters across the country. Most low-budget films have no more than six main characters, and usually only two or three.

4. While you work on selling your first script or writing your second, when you feel a need to change pace, start working on your low-budget script. When you sell your first script, you'll most likely be asked what else you have available. If you just happen to have a low-budget script ready that would be inexpensive to film, you might be able to talk someone into giving you a chance. And if you make that film work, you'll move up to a whole new plateau of your Hollywood career.

Not every screenwriter should become a director or producer. It's hard work, and you need good people skills. Some people are simply better suited to working alone or as part of a writing team, taking an occasional meeting to sell projects or discuss writing assignments. All I know is that the directors I've admired the most also happened to be great writers, and the screenwriters I that admire most inevitably turn up directing films.

If you want to understand all the jobs in Hollywood, I suggest the book *Hollywood 101, the Film Industry: How to Succeed in Hollywood Without Connections,* by Frederick Levy (Renaissance Books, 2000). It provides as good a rudimentary understanding of the entire structure of "the business" as any other reference.

Meanwhile, help yourself and other screenwriters by getting involved in the process. Take my word for it, being involved in a production is a lot of fun, and you'll be amazed at what you'll learn. It's so much fun, in fact, that while you're doing it, you don't even think about who is authoring the film.

The Least You Need to Know

➤ The screenwriter is God in Hollywood, but it's hard to sell that religion to producers and directors.

➤ The cineplex patron, the ultimate recipient of screenwriting, is a lot more savvy than most people believe.

➤ Writing down to the normal moviegoer is a huge mistake.

➤ To break in as a screenwriter, you must exhibit a lot more effort than you do after you're established.

➤ The Hollywood battle over the simple phrase "A Film By ..." between writers and directors is not likely to end soon.

➤ Producers expend more effort in getting a film made than just about anyone, but they are never considered the "author" of a film.

➤ There are currently more opportunities for working as a screenwriter and also making your own movie than ever before.

➤ A great number of great directors began as screenwriters.

Chapter 22

Writing for Television

In This Chapter

➤ TV movie seven-act structure

➤ The TV queue

➤ Network preferences

➤ Miniseries and other forms

➤ Should it be a book?

Here's the long and short of writing for television. Until you are an established writer, to write for TV, you probably need to live where television shows are made. Shows are made in Canada, Florida, New York and other places, but the majority of the shows that air in the United States are made in Los Angeles. The studio facilities are here, the actors are here, and the beaches are here. What's good for writers is that this has been changing in the last decade, and it will continue to change as computers and the Web evolve. After all, if you prefer the Rocky Mountains outside your front door, why live in smoggy L.A. and fight the traffic, if you can create a show in your own home studio and port it to the network via high-speed modem?

If you want to write hit sitcoms, you definitely need to live in Los Angeles and be under the age of 30 (sorry, that's the way it is, kids). If you want to write TV movies or miniseries, that's almost impossible if you don't have an established career, but that is changing as well, thanks to cable television. It's possible to break in via sales of original screenplays, usually to "lesser" channels such as Lifetime or the Disney Channel. HBO and Showtime are still reserved for the "big guns" and will probably remain so for the near future. Still, there are opportunities to be exploited. When new cable channels crop up and do well, sooner or later they want to make their own movies, to distribute in theaters as well as on their own airspace. All this is good news for writers. Let's explore how to get there.

Hollywood Heat

Algo's Factory ("Algo" being short for "algorithm") was a kids' science show broadcast on UPN, a sort of latter-day "Mr. Wizard" (an early TV hit). I was a staff writer in the first season. Created by Perfectly Round Productions in Wichita, Kansas, and shot in Minneapolis, Minnesota, all the shows were written by writers in California who never had a joint staff meeting and never met the producer. All the shows were written and e-mailed in, with some discussions over the phone. As the Internet grows and computer technology becomes more spectacular, we'll see more shows done in this way.

The TV Movie and the Seven-Act Structure

A former agent asked me if I had any screenplays that would fit a certain star who had a TV movie "pay or play" deal with a network. First, she explained "pay or play" The star was paid to reserve her time and would get the money whether or not she did any of the three movies on her contract within a specific time. Then the agent told me that if I did have a script, I would get only $60,000 for it. "But hey," she said, "$60,000 is $60,000, and that's double WGA minimum." Better than doing word processing for a law firm, which is how I made my living at the time. I said I might have something. "Great," said the agent. "Just make sure that you use the seven-act structure, okay?"

I agreed, hung up, and then went scrambling around to find out what the hell she was talking about. Seven acts! Good lord, Shakespeare used only five! Then I sat down and thought about it. It didn't take a genius to divide a two-hour TV movie into 15-minute segments and calculate that an act might just end every time we saw a commercial. But I got my hands on some scripts so that I wasn't just guessing when I typed out "End Act One" on a certain page.

If you have a good screenplay that's suitable for a cable channel or even one of the major networks, no one will shoot you for not putting it in the format of a TV movie, but you might as well know what that format looks like. It probably won't take you long to convert your script, and if you submit it in seven-act format, you might just impress someone as a serious professional.

Let's use the pilot script of what became the most successful show in the world as an example. It was set in southern California and featured a lot of sunshine and water. That's right, *BayWatch*. TV shows often have some kind of black-and-white illustration on the cover page. If you're trying to sell an original screenplay as the lead-in to a series, that's the toughest sale in Hollywood because usually the only people who get a chance to do that are people who are established television writer/producers. If you have a really good illustration and logo to include on the cover page, it's probably okay. The *BayWatch* illustration was a lifeguard stand in the foreground, with lines that could be heat waves or ocean waves behind it. The *BayWatch* (two words) logo was to the right, superimposed on a setting sun. Nice work.

Skip's Tips

If you have a screenplay that fits a certain genre but isn't something that you could see as a major summer or winter theatrical release, you might determine what cable channel would like it and then find out what production companies have done movies for them. For example, Esperza-Katz, who did the *Selena* feature, has done a lot of work with Turner Network Television.

Hollywood Heat

Sabrina the Teenage Witch was a hit comedy on ABC before moving to the Warner Brothers Network. Originating from an *Archie* comic book character, *Sabrina* began as a 1996 movie on Showtime, a cable channel that is also part of Viacom, the company that produces the show. If you also saw the movie that inspired the show, you might have noticed that Salem Saberhagan, the animatronic robot black cat, is much less realistic that the computer-generated image (CGI) cat in the movie. Why didn't they use the CGI for the show? Very simple: They couldn't afford it on a weekly basis.

Like a stage play, the *BayWatch* script (revision 11/8/88) featured a CAST LIST (centered, middle of the page) with two sections: SERIES LEADS and RECURRING CHARACTERS (both flush left), listing character names IN ALL CAPS two tabs in from the left. Similarly, on the next page was an EPISODE CAST (centered, middle of the page) for the first episode (the two-hour movie), again listing their names IN ALL CAPS two tabs in from the left. On the next page was a SET LIST (centered, middle of the page). INTERIORS (centered, middle of the page) were listed on the first page, with EXTERIORS (centered, middle of the page) on the next. The LIFEGUARD HEADQUARTERS were divided into the eight sets there (MITCH'S OFFICE, and so on), indented two tabs over from the left. All other LOCATIONS including the exteriors (such as SANTA MONICA PIER) were listed line by line, flush left.

Skip's Tips

A "back-door pilot" is a term for a two-hour TV movie whose story stands on its own, yet establishes the main characters and the milieu that can be used later in a series, usually a one-hour episodic series such as *NYPD Blue*.

The first part of a TV movie is sort of a reverse denouement called a "teaser." It's a few-minute lead-in to the show that establishes the main character(s), perhaps the main location, and what's going on. The format on the title page begins: "Title" TEASER EXT. LOCATION—ANY MORE SPECIFIC PART OF LOCATION—DAY OR NIGHT. Then comes a space and the first line of the script. Like a normal screenplay, the first page is not numbered. (The scenes of this draft are numbered to the right, but don't worry about doing that with your script. Write unnumbered "master scenes.")

The *BayWatch* teaser starts with lifeguard Lieutenant MITCH TAYLOR tutoring a new lifeguard, EDDIE KRAMMER. We also learn about Mitch's mentor, AL DEMPSEY, who figures prominently later. This is followed by a crisis in a lifeguard tower as a PCP-crazed man sets it on fire, and other lifeguards rush to the rescue while Mitch and Eddie try to remedy the situation at the scene. They are barely able to get the man out of the burning tower in time to save him, and after other lifeguards (establishing their characters) arrive and help subdue the man with a choke hold, Eddie has learned graphically that there's a lot more to lifeguarding than being a good swimmer.

And then we go directly to the high-energy MAIN TITLE MONTAGE that we saw every week as each new episode of *BayWatch* appeared. The teaser ends in the middle of page eight. The rest of the page is blank space. Act One begins on the top of page nine this way: ACT ONE. Again, no title line. From there we simply add a blank line and then start the script again normally. Act One ends at the bottom of page 26 with a FADE OUT: END OF ACT ONE.

As with any feature-length screenplay, within Act One the story and characters have been set up. With TV shows and movies, however, there is always some sort of "cliffhanger" type of action that makes the viewer want to come back after the commercial to see what happens. In the *BayWatch* script, a girl named WENDY HARRIS has been saved by CPR and mouth-to-mouth resuscitation by lifeguard CRAIG POMEROY, but there's something going on with her psychologically, or at least there appears to be.

To compare a seven-act TV movie to a normal, three-act screenplay, you might consider that the teaser and Act One would comprise the normal first act, while Acts Two through Five would comprise the normal second act. Acts Six and Seven make up the normal third act. Each act ends the same way, format-wise—FADE OUT: END OF [NAME OF ACT].

The new act always begins on a new page. In the *BayWatch* script that I'm using as an example, Act Two begins on page 27 and ends on page 38. Act Three begins on page 39 and ends on page 57. Act Four begins on page 58 and ends on page 74. Act Five begins on page 75 and ends on page 88. Act Six begins on page 89 and ends on page 104. The script is 113 pages long, with Act Seven beginning on page 105. Both Act Seven and the opening Teaser are roughly of the same length. Other than what I've mentioned, a TV movie script page looks exactly like a regular screenplay, following the same rules. It's usually no more than 110 pages.

In contrast, a one-hour TV show (usually 52 to 56 pages) follows this format:

Teaser

Act One

Act Two

Act Three

Act Four, with commercials after each of the previous items, followed by the end credits

> **Skip's Tips**
>
> Try it before you knock it. It's easy to deride TV movies and series. For example, the slang term for the *BayWatch* series was "Babe Watch." The truth, however, is that most TV movies are written by experienced writers who have structure down cold. You'd do well to study some.

By the end of Act Five, we know what Wendy's problem was that was hinted at when Act One ended. She is suffering from sexual molestation by her stepfather, JACK HARRIS. The midpoint change (teenage Wendy's budding friendship with married lifeguard Craig) comes at the end of Act Three, when he finds her in his lifeguard tower with a picnic lunch. The normal screenplay turning point toward the end of Act One (that sends the story in another direction) comes at the end of Act Two in this seven-act script. The second turning point that would be toward the end of Act Two comes at the end of this script's Act Four, when Wendy's father locks her in her room. In Act Six, Wendy's stepfather is confronted by Craig about the sexual molestation.

Episodes of *BayWatch* almost always interwove A, B, and C story lines. By my estimation, the A story line in the pilot MOW is Craig learning what lifeguarding is about and our look into the lives of all the lifeguards. The B story line is the "episode" story

Skip's Tips

"Having TV-Q" means that the public will watch a program based on a certain actor's appearance alone. For screenwriters, it means that they're on a network's approved writer list. Whether based on the idea of people forming single-line queues outside a theater or someone taking a "cue" before doing something, this discriminatory practice exists, even though it's not supposed to, legally.

of molested and confused teenage beauty Wendy. The C story line is the passing of the mantle of lifeguard legends. As Act Seven of the movie opens, lifeguard mentor Al Dempsey goes fishing off Malibu with HOBIE TAYLOR on an excursion fishing boat. At the end of the act, however, a fire in the galley of the boat causes the boat to explode. Naturally, all the lifeguards must rescue the fishermen. When they arrive on the scene in their boat, Al, the legend, is trying to find his buddy, Hobie. When the lifeguards arrive, Al doesn't let them take over. Worn out, he hyperventilates before diving but manages to help Mitch get victims out of the capsized boat below, only to be trapped himself. Mitch gets Al to the surface, but too late. Al is dead.

The denouement of the film is Al's funeral. It lasts a page and a half, with a half-page eulogy to Al from Mitch that nicely summarizes a lifeguard's life. I remember being dumbfounded at a Los Angeles party of Australian film professionals when I learned that the show David Hasselhoff made famous was no. 1 not only in Australia, but also all over the world. Now, after reading the tight pilot teleplay by Michael Berk and Douglas Schwartz (writing team), with the story by Michael Berk and Douglas Schwartz, and Gregory J. Bonann, I'm not surprised that the show sold or that it became such a success.

The TV Queue That Supposedly Doesn't Exist

I knew a screenwriter who had his first feature made. I thought that he would quickly sell another feature (he had some good ideas) and then perhaps direct his third. He did direct his third script, but his second one was a writing assignment of a TV movie set in Texas. As it usually goes with things in TV, budget was a primary consideration. One of the reasons my friend got the job was because he still worked relatively cheap. Even then, however, he was not a writer known to the network on which the TV movie aired, so the producer had to fight to keep the writer on the project. It helped that, because of the budget, despite the fact that it was set in Texas, the movie was cheaper to make in the writer's native Australia, with Australian actors doing American accents! That was one of the first times I'd heard about "having TV-Q" as a writer or actor, but it makes sense. Just as studios will hedge their bets by hiring a number of screenwriters, and funding only films with proven or "bankable" actors in the cast, it's no puzzle that TV networks would be even more cost-conscious.

With a feature film, the sky could be the limit, profit-wise. TV movie or miniseries, however, have only a limited numbers of showings and sales of prepackaged videos. Execs know how much revenue (roughly) will come in from commercials, so they set prices for the script and other things, and that's that. Whereas I generally advise

writers not to try to get their scripts to actors without production companies, in television it can be a good idea.

You can't see a "TV-Q" list because they supposedly don't exist. Unless you know someone inside a top agency or a network, try selecting actors with hit TV shows, comedy or drama, or those who repeatedly show up in TV movies. Melissa Gilbert, for example, draws tremendous audiences within the female profile (ages 18 to 49). If she wanted to do a script of yours, you'd probably have a network deal. To find out how to reach an actor, contact the Screen Actors Guild (SAG) National office. You can find all their contact information on the Web at www.sag.org/whoswho.html, or you can contact: 5757 Wilshire Blvd., Los Angeles, CA 90036-3600; main: 323-954-1600; fax: 323-549-6603; TTY/TTD: 323-549-6648. The Actors to Locate number is the one that you want to use to find out a SAG member's representative, at 323-549-6737.

It's Not for Us

Full-length screenplays to debut a new TV series are not done that often today. "Back-door pilots" are not dead, but normally only a simple one-hour episode or a half-hour sitcom is shot. Networks may fund a sample show and no more until they see what kind of ratings it pulls.

Hollywood Heat

If you hear the term "CBSP" or "NBCP," it refers to the in-house production companies of the various networks, which increasingly make as many TV shows and TV movies as possible, cutting out the independent producer. (CBSP would be CBS Productions.) Many producers got rich in earlier years by supplying content to television, but when the "financial syndication" (a.k.a. "fin-syn") rules changed due to legislation, networks were able to get around what had formerly been in place to prevent monopoly abuse. The face of television (and the opportunities for TV moviemakers) dwindled until cable channels opened things up a little.

When you reach the agent, simply say that you have a script perfect for the actor, and ask if that actor has a production company. If not, your chances of getting your script read drastically lessen, but you won't know until you try. Remember, if you don't have an agent and that agent/agency represents writers, they might take you on and make commissions on: the actor, you, other people they put in the "package," and a 10 percent "packaging fee." (Please don't e-mail me about how to get in touch with Melissa Gilbert.)

Again, it's tough to sell a screenplay to television. You'll most likely either have to sell your script to a production company that does TV movies, or find an agent to do that for you.

Plotting by Network

If you're really serious about writing a movie for television, plot it by networks and the kind of films that they usually do. Even the main broadcast (free) networks have their own unique signatures. CBS, for example, has traditionally skewed to older audiences. Or, if you have a movie set in World War II, your agent might be able to sell it to the History Channel. You'll have to do some homework.

Check your *TV Guide* or favorite TV Web site to see what movies are coming up that you think might be cousins to your screenplay. Watch at least the beginning, but definitely the end. As you've probably noticed, in the United States, credits on TV movies are shown at the end. You'll probably see only the logo and the name of the production company, or maybe several companies. If you're not sure what you saw, you can most likely find a listing for the film on the Internet Movie Database (www.imdb.com). Then you'll have to search through a print directory or use an online subscription service such as ShowBizData.com or inhollywood.com to look up the contact information for the company or companies that made the movie.

You can learn about fall TV schedules in advance by subscribing to *Daily Variety* or *The Hollywood Reporter*. Both have extensive special issues that cover things like this. Each weekly print magazine has production charts as well, usually with contact information on relevant production companies, so that's another way to keep up on both what's being made and by whom.

The Hollywood Reporter, at www.hollywoodreporter.com, lists the entire fall schedule on its Web site under "Fall TV Sked" (on the left banner when this was written). You won't see TV movies listed, but you'll see what shows are on and can calculate from there, by stars of shows. *Daily Variety*, with its "Variety Extra" online function (subscription fee) offers both film and TV production charts and is searchable.

Even though MTV is making its own movies now, as are many other cable channels, it's still most likely that you'll need a credit or two before you'll be considered suitable for networks that aren't one of the top six (ABC, CBS, Fox, NBC, WB, and UPN). To illustrate, my producer/manager friend Rona Edwards told me about *Out of Sync* (2000), a film that she executive produced for VH-1. The script was by Eric Williams, who shared a story credit with Tom Matthews on *Mad City* (1997). Another caveat is that movies for cable channels usually fit very definite parameters. In the case of VH-1, the network's aim is to make movies with music, about music. The network titles its movie series "Movies That Rock."

Don't get completely discouraged. There are always exceptions. I know one writer on the East Coast who, via a manager in Santa Ynez, California (two hours north of Los Angeles), sold a feature to Disney and another to Showtime via actress Mimi Rogers's Millbrook Farms production company. The manager now has an agent's license, and the screenwriter is well on the way to a lucrative Hollywood career. So, as usual in Hollywood, anything can happen. TV movies sales usually occur via the normal channels and methods, and you generally must first prove yourself as a writer.

A Long Form Is Not What You Fill Out to Sell a Miniseries

Anything longer than a one-hour show on television is known around network circles as a "long form." Most people will never get a chance to write a miniseries in their lives, but I may have figured out a way you can do it. Try one of the following:

1. Become Peter Barnes. He wrote *Arabian Nights* (2000), *The Magical Legend of the Leprechauns* (1999), and *Merlin* (1998), working with Hallmark Entertainment.

2. Become Simon Moore. He wrote *Dinotopia* (2001), *The 10th Kingdom* (2000), and the miniseries of *Gulliver's Travels* (1996).

3. Buy Hallmark Entertainment from Robert Halmi Sr. The company produced the minis listed with Peter Barnes, as well as *The 10th Kingdom* (2000), *20,000 Leagues Under the Sea* (1997), *The Odyssey* (1997), and dozens more programs. Find a popular legend or great story of mankind that has not yet become a miniseries, and film it.

4. Take over Stephen King's body and "field offers."

5. Write a thick best-selling novel and field offers.

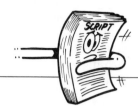

It's Not for Us

You can't do everything via free areas of the Internet. If you pinch pennies, you might kill your career. I tell writers repeatedly to subscribe to trade publications and online directories, or to buy print directories. I can't tell you how many times I've mentioned a certain production company and received an e-mail asking "Got a URL?" (uniform resource locator). I don't answer.

Skip's Tips

If you really want to write for television, read *A Friend in the Business: Honest Advice for Anyone Trying to Break into Television Writing,* by Robert Massello (Perigee, 2000) or *The TV Writer.Com Book of Television Writing,* an electronic book by veteran TV writer Larry Brody, available at his Web site, www. tvwriter.com.

You're not amused? I've insulted your original miniseries without even seeing it? Sorry. Maybe you've scripted a major historical event (a fave miniseries subject). The first miniseries was from a best-selling book, *QB VII,* in 1975. It seems like I've been hearing writers mention their original miniseries since that time. How many of them sold? As I recall, sadly, zero.

> **Script Notes**
>
> In England, "limited series" are made. The BBC or another channel will contract for a limited number of episodes (for example, 12) and then simply end the show. For U.S. networks, that's like killing the golden goose before it lays an egg that you can sell.

> **It's Not for Us**
>
> If you really want to write for television, don't sit around in Keokuk hoping that technology will bring Hollywood to you. Make arrangements and move there for at least a year. Otherwise, you will probably never know for sure if you could make it.

If the Idea's That Good, Write a Book

In my *Writer's Guide to Hollywood,* I surprised some people when one of the first chapters was titled "Maybe You Should Write a Book." That sentiment hasn't changed in the four years since I wrote the first edition of that guide to selling to Hollywood.

A long time ago, when I heard that New York publishers came out with around 50,000 books per year, with half of those fiction, I compared that to the roughly 500 movies made by Hollywood each year. That 500 compared to 25,000 means that you have roughly a 50 to 1 better chance of selling a story in book form than you do selling a screenplay.

In books, you get to write about things such as characters' thoughts, which you can almost never portray onscreen. You can take your time developing the background of an area or a person, using paragraphs of words that would get your screenplay round-filed in Hollywood.

You might think that you have to publish a book in hard cover to get it taken seriously in Hollywood, but that isn't so. My three "You Solve It Mystery" books for young adults appeared only as paperbacks, yet they were optioned by a billionaire's production company in Beverly Hills. Even electronic books (e-books) have a chance. When I received an e-mail stating that the electronic version of my *How To Write What You Want & Sell What You Write* was a finalist in the first annual "Eppie" Awards for electronic books, I began trading e-mails with the person who had notified me. Within weeks, she and her e-publisher were in negotiations about the film rights to one of her e-novels with a very high-profile Hollywood company.

If you become a successful screenwriter and a member of the Writers Guild of America and the WGA goes on strike, guess what? You can't work until the strike is settled, unless you are one of the producers of the movie or show. No one will complain about you writing and selling a novel. If your book's successful, you'll get the money from the book sale and the money for the film and TV rights, and you can probably talk them into letting you write at least the first draft of the screenplay. Hollywood respects authors. If you start off writing screenplays and then write books, you might have a book editor say to you: "You write so cinematically!" I still laugh at that one.

I personally prefer writing books, then movies, then TV. Given that, I'll probably end up a TV mogul. Maybe in my next life ....

The Least You Need to Know

➤ In most cases, only established writers write movies for television, but there are always exceptions.

➤ TV movies are rarely longer than 110 pages, with a seven-act structure that includes a "teaser" at the beginning.

➤ The seven-act structure of a TV movie roughly corresponds to the three-act turning points, midpoint, denouement of a feature film screenplay.

➤ TV movies and one-hour episodes often have an A, B, and C story line.

➤ Networks insist on stars with "TV-Q" (popularity) to star in their films.

➤ Writers of TV movies are also judged by TV-Q and are either on an approved list or not.

➤ Writing TV movies to cater to network preferences is smart marketing.

➤ You will probably never get to write a miniseries unless you write a book first, which isn't a bad idea, anyway, because it vastly increases your odds of selling a big story.

Chapter 23

Short Films and the Digital Age

> **In This Chapter**
>
> ➤ Blame it on MTV
>
> ➤ Download logic
>
> ➤ Short films
>
> ➤ Filming your own scripts

More than 100 years after the beginning of film, we return again to the short film. In these digital days, it is possible to create your own short animations with software such as Macromedia Flash and then post it on a Web page for the world to see. And if the world likes what you do, it can lead to major Hollywood deals and major money.

Just ask the fellows who created *South Park* on the Web. You know them, don't you? They wore dresses to the 2000 Oscars to see if their song "Blame Canada" won for Best Song. (Maybe they just felt happy.) In December 1999, Matt Stone and Trey Parker made a deal to create 39 original two- to five-minute animated shorts for Shockwave.com that they never could have made with a TV or film studio. They were given control and ownership that simply wouldn't have been allowed in traditional media. Just before starting this book, I signed a deal to create and write an original animated Web show for WireBreak.com. My show may be up if you surf there now, or it may not. Who knows? By the time you read this, it could be turned into a major television prime time hit. That's the way it is in the new Hollywood.

For less than $10,000, you now can buy both a digital video camera and a computer with editing software that will allow you to make films to port to the Web. The only additional cost in showing the world your writing and filmmaking skills is the cost of

Skip's Tips

Is your only access to the Internet America Online? Get a real Internet service provider (ISP), preferably with a DSL or cable modem connection. You really do need the higher-speed lines to view short Web films properly. A 56K modem is the bare minimum.

Script Notes

In case no one has ever explained this to you, a URL is a uniform resource locator. Web sites are so prevalent in Hollywood these days that serious young filmmakers are almost expected to have one. "What's your URL?" is a common question at parties.

videotape and production. If you use a PC, you have many options, but Apple Computers seemed to have a particular emphasis on selling the full setup. As I wrote this chapter, the Apple home page featured a Canon ZR10 camera and an iMac DV with editing software as part of the package. Never before have such opportunities abounded for a screenwriter willing to try making a film.

Blame It on MTV: How Short Films Affect Screenwriting

I'm old enough to remember the time in movie theaters when there was always an animated cartoon before the movie or double feature. The first movie experience that I can recall was a Woody Woodpecker cartoon in which Woody battled his nemesis, Buzz Buzzard, with some barrels of oil. Years later, when I first came to Hollywood, I got a hand-drawn portrait of Woody from the wacky woodpecker's creator, Walter Lantz. I still treasure it. Shortly after that, when I was making the rounds as a singer/songwriter in Los Angeles, I had an idea that I tried to talk some filmmaking friends into doing. I wanted to make short, funny musical films the length of an average song and convince movie theaters to play them. But no one was interested.

My problem was that, I was thinking in the wrong medium. A year later, Music Television (MTV) was launched on its own cable channel, and the era of the music video began. Instead of following the antic tradition of Beatles films like *A Hard Day's Night,* or TV show song bits like those on *The Monkees* or *The Partridge Family,* MTV offered something new and primal, with an emphasis on youth and sex. (A combination that generally always works.)

It changed filmmaking for young people forever. I don't have to tell you the history of MTV or VH-1. You probably grew up with them as constants in your life. The point is, it serves you well to study filmmaking styles on MTV, VH-1, and other, similar cable channels. The people who make top music videos today will be helming feature films tomorrow. The emphasis is on fewer words and slick shots, style and flash.

Although short films on the Web may ultimately change the way Hollywood discovers new film-makers, many now often break in via music videos on MTV. Remember the exercise of writing a silent film to learn movie structure? Try that sometime with music videos. Turn on the VCR and turn off the volume. Tape some videos that you think are particularly interesting, and then sit down at your computer and play the tapes back slowly, writing scripts for them as you watch. The good ones will tell a story in pictures and jam a lot of information into a relatively small space.

If you want to succeed at writing action films, you'll need to learn to create the kind of jam-packed visual style of MTV. Take a silent look at the explosive sequences in a film such as *Con Air* sometime, and imagine it set to music—you'll see what I mean.

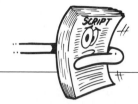

It's Not for Us

Even though you can learn a lot about putting together effective moving pictures by watching MTV, don't write specific song titles into a script unless you have a very good reason. The producer might not be able to secure a license to use that song, and your effect might be ruined.

Downloads and Debuts

Although short films on the Web have exploded lately, one Web company is the clear leader. Founded in 1998, Seattle-based AtomFilms.com offers animations and short films, and manages to get greater exposure than any other similar entertainment company. Every week the company offers a new collection of short videos, and the site is searchable.

As an example of the high profile that AtomFilms has achieved, one of the shorts featured on the site was the 1999 Academy Award nominee *Holiday Romance*. AtomFilms has secured distribution deals with @Home, Blockbuster, HBO, Infoseek, Reel.com, The Sundance Channel, and Warner Bros. Online, among others.

You can read about leading short filmmakers and buy video compilations from the site at a discount. The company must have impressed the USC School of Cinema-Television, because in February 2000, the school agreed to an exclusive online deal to stream 100 student titles during the following 18 months. Among USC's 75-year-old film collection are thousands of films made by students who later became famous. George Lucas's feature *THX 1138*, for example, started as a USC student film.

Last but not least, AtomFilms signed with U.K. animation house Aardman Animation to put its delightful clay animation films online. If you haven't seen any of Nick Park's Oscar-wining *Wallace and Gromit* shorts, you've truly missed something special. No more checking the *TV Guide* for the occasional TV broadcast.

A click away on the Web are some of the most inventive films of recent years. If you make your own short films now, you're coming in at an auspicious time. If your film gets accepted by AtomFilms.com, that might allow you to be showcased via Blockbuster Video stores (millions of viewers), whether viewers visit the AtomFilms site or not. Or, if you gain exposure via competitor iFilm.com, who has a deal with digital video recorder company TiVo, you can reach viewers that you simply never could have reached via previous media routes, except perhaps local public access cable channels.

Hollywood Heat

Established Hollywood filmmakers are happy to jump on the short films on the Web bandwagon. One of the big attractions at AtomFilms.com in June 2000 was an exclusive showing of George Lucas's groundbreaking USC student film *Electronic Labyrinth*. Another was *The Lift,* by Robert Zemeckis. Isn't it wild that the student films of now-famous filmmakers are now only a few mouse clicks away?

In the world of Web movies, iFilm.com may emerge as the winner. In early 2000, the San Francisco–based company secured $35 million in financing from heavyweight entertainment investors, which allowed it to broadcast even more shorts and full-length features and to begin making show business acquisitions in Los Angeles.

The stated goal of iFilm is "to provide tools, access, and opportunity to filmmakers and would-be filmmakers worldwide." To do that, iFilm acquired companies such as the Hollywood Creative Directory, long considered the most comprehensive publicly available source of industry contact information. This was after it acquired Lone Eagle Publishing, another Hollywood publisher of industry information. Next on the buy list was script coverage service ScriptShark.com, a Web site launched in 1999 by development executives Ed Kashiba and Roy Lee. The site offers writers the chance to have their scripts evaluated by professional showbiz readers for $100 per script. If (and only if) a reader likes a script, the writer gets introduced to agents and potential buyers.

So what do you think at this point? Would you rather write a 110-page script and run it through a service such as ScriptShark.com hoping that it will past muster, or make your own short film and give anyone with Web access the chance to see your finished product?

In the world of Hollywood on the net, the sites that get the most "buzz" lead to the most bucks. iFilm delivered that in 1999 when it aired *Sunday's Game,* a short about old ladies who get together to play cards and Russian roulette. While many people objected to the "humor" of old ladies blowing their brains out with a gun, David Garrett and Jason Ward, the writers and producers behind the film, inked a one-year development deal with Fox Television Studios after the short aired, agreeing to do at least two pilot scripts while pursuing other film deals that they already had in the works.

Skip's Tips

If you decide to make a short film, make sure that you have someone involved who knows lighting well, and use a good cameraman. If your script is good and you have an eye for talented actors, you could be on the road to Hollywood success.

Garrett and Ward subsequently became head writers of Fox Family's animated series *Da Mob,* with a 26-episode commitment. Garrett told reporters that within 48 hours of the airing of the approximately eight-minute short on October 11, 1999, the duo had set up meetings "with several studios and nearly 20 production companies." Even more interesting is the fact that a mere 700+ "industry only" people saw the short at iFilmPro.com, the professional version of iFilm.com. (You had to prove that you were working in the business to see the dark comedy.)

Just guessing that you didn't see it, let me describe it to you roughly. It starts in the kitchen of an old lady's house. The doorbell rings, and she scurries off to answer it. In comes another senior citizen, and they begin playing cards on a table set up in the living room. Only there's a loaded gun. When the quartet of grannies start playing cards, one of them picks up the pistol and smiles as she blows her brains out. And on it goes.

Hollywood Heat

Scour.net began as a brainchild of five computer science students at the University of California (UCLA). Its search engine, so named because of its ability to scour millions of online multimedia files, drew so much attention that major Hollywood player Michael Ovitz bought a majority stake, and the kids quit school (like Bill Gates, remember?). But within a relatively short time, the site looked like it might fail. That's Hollywood.

Although animation writers are not covered under the WGA rules, let's say for sake of argument that writer/producers Garrett and Ward get $5,000 for each script of the animated series *Da Mob*. A 26-episode commitment means $130,000 or so. The two pilot scripts that the studio put in the deal might go for a minimum of $20,000 each. So, that means the duo would make a rough minimum of nearly $200,000 because of putting a short "comedy" on a Web site that only 700 or so people could access. Now how do you feel about writing and producing a short film?

Short Film Format

When I began writing my series for WireBreak.com, I was faced with a dilemma. There was no pre-existing format for short films. No *storyboard,* no template, no book, no article posted on the Web. Should I write the script in the format of a 30-minute situation comedy for TV? Would an industrial (audiovisual) format, with dialogue on one side and action in the opposite column, be more appropriate?

I settled on standard feature film screenplay format, which I've presented in this book in a previous chapter. When I turned in the scripts, no one complained or even mentioned the format, so I suppose that what I did was suitable. I was writing for presentation in the limited-action Macromedia Flash format, however, and there were some pre-existing examples of that to learn from on the Web. Because my show (the name of which I can't mention here due to contractual limitations) was animated, I knew that the rules of screenplays changed slightly:

➤ In animation, you are God. You write every single thing that happens on the screen, including angles that you think are necessary.

➤ You also write the way your actors say their lines. An actor will go in the sound studio and record the lines, with (most likely) a director on hand to coax them into the best delivery.

➤ Although there is still a beginning, middle, and end, the longer the short film becomes, the harder it is for a "B" story.

Script Notes

A **storyboard** is a must if you make a short film. Think in terms of the panels in a cartoon strip, and you have the right idea. With even rudimentary sketches of the scenes that you want in your film, you can much more easily show people what you're trying to achieve. Computer software also is available to create a storyboard.

Next came the problem of length. Due to the prevalence of 56K modems when I started writing the scripts, the optimum length of each short to me was important. After watching other shorts on the Web, I decided on scripts of around two minutes in length.

Hollywood "players" can usually afford higher-speed Internet connections, and people working in large offices or attending colleges often have cable modems or even super-fast T1 connections. For the normal person logging onto the Web, though, it takes a long time to download a film of that length with a 56K modem. A couple minutes is manageable.

Longer shorts such as the live-action (with real actors) eight-minute *Sunday's Game,* mentioned previously, are generally made to be screened at film festivals in hopes of winning competitions. I took all these things into consideration when writing my scripts. WireBreak.com, founded by former Paramount Studios Digital Entertainment head David Wertheimer, was put together to cater to the young professional who "lives digital" at work. When these people take a break, they hit the Internet to check their personal e-mail or to watch some short bit of entertainment. With a high-speed connection, it's nothing for a person like that—on a "wire break"—to download and watch a short film. If you have a high-speed modem, you know that a download like that takes place in the blink of an eye.

Still, most people at the time I started writing the WireBreak.com scripts used 56K modems, so that was my target audience. I didn't worry about "streaming video," which allows you to download only a small guide file before beginning to watch the show. I simply wrote under the assumption that someone with a 56K modem would download the show and watch, so I tried to keep them short.

It's Not for Us

If anyone tells you that there exists a standard screenplay format for short films that will be ported to the Internet, it's probably only that person's opinion. The facts are, regular screenplay format works, as does dual-column audiovisual script format. What matters most is simply communicating your intent to the animator(s) and then to a Web-savvy audience with a short attention span.

My next consideration was sound. The download of a sound file on the Internet can be almost as harrowing an ordeal as waiting for a video to save to your hard drive. Plus, the more dialogue I wrote, the more actors would have to be hired. Although music was a part of the mix, that could be accomplished with stock music cuts from various sources and would remain relatively inexpensive. Still, the more music was included, the larger the sound file.

I decided to concentrate on the moving images. I was constrained by the limitations of Macromedia Flash, which is not full-motion animation like an animated feature. But, Flash is as entertaining as limited-motion animation, such as the "Sailor Moon" kids' TV series, so a lot could be done with moving pictures alone. This led me to the conclusion that the models for my show were the stars of the early days of Hollywood like Buster Keaton.

David Wertheimer, Matt Nesburn, Mike Berman, and animator Tony Peluce at WireBreak.com agreed. And so, with four main characters and a couple peripheral characters scheduled to appear in later shows, I began writing scripts under those parameters, with great old sight gag short silent films such as Keaton's *The General* as my model.

Hollywood Heat

In June 2000, the Board of the Academy of Motion Picture Arts & Sciences (AMPAS) modified its eligibility rules. It stipulated, "A film cannot appear on the Internet before its theatrical release and be eligible for an Oscar." The logic was that an Internet transmission was more like a television broadcast than a feature film. To get around this hurdle, iFilm.com teamed up with AMC Theaters to create the iFilm@AMC Cinema Series theatrical showcase for short films. The arrangement to show a short twice daily for three consecutive days to a paying theater audience satisfied the AMPAS requirements for Academy Award eligibility and allowed short films to then be broadcast on the Internet.

Now, here's the potentially confusing part. As you no doubt noted before, the use of SHOTS in the normal "master scene" screenplay format is now frowned upon. (You'd be doing the director's job, remember?) If you want the animator to understand what you envision, however, you might have to write "ANGLE ON SMITTY" (assuming that you have a character named Smitty). Or, you could simply write (I'll add some description) "SMITTY lowers his shoulder, ROARS at this affront to his manhood, and CHARGES screen left to bowl over ROGER as he walks in the door. SPLASHES OF DAY-GLO COLOR go flying all over the screen."

If you're writing live action, you would use standard formatting, but keep framing in mind. If you write a broad, sweeping scene that pans across the horizon, that might be hard to make out on a computer screen, particularly if the Web video is not viewed full-screen (most are not, in case you don't know).

Skip's Tips

If you plan to make a short film, do yourself a favor and attend a digital video convention before you commit to any computer platform, software, or digital video camera. Manufacturers bend over backward to get their latest and greatest products on display and will eagerly answer all your questions. Plus, you'll be offered substantial convention-only discounts.

Everything You Need to Film Your Own Scripts

By the time you read this, a book about digital filmmaking by Maxie Collier may be on the market, courtesy of iFilmPro.com. I expect any book from this experienced DV filmmaker to be good, and apparently this one will come with a CD full of surprises. Because I don't have a review copy to comment on (it wasn't finished), here are some tips that might help.

If you're a college student, you're in luck. Nibblebox.com, a company from Santa Monica, California, set up business with the intent of helping college students (not only film students, but any students) make movies. In June 2000, it was reported in Hollywood trade papers that Nibblebox was not a simple Web portal for short films. The company was willing to look at proposals from wannabe filmmakers. When an idea was approved, the originator would be loaned camera and computer equipment, given financing to make the film, and, as a bonus, paired up with an experienced filmmaker.

The company was founded by David Bartis, someone I shared a panel with at the first Screenwriters Festival in Providence, Rhode Island. Bartis said that the company wanted to keep as many as 50 projects in development at all times, with as many as 15 short films in production. Will the plan work? Maybe, maybe not.

The critically acclaimed *George Lucas in Love,* in contrast to net-only short films, was shown at regular film festivals and won awards. It was so popular on the Net (because it's a great, funny film) that it was packaged for sale with other shorts in regular video format and, in April 2000, was a number-one seller on Amazon.com. It just goes to show that quality prospers in any medium.

With all this in mind, what do you need to do to be able to put your short screenplay onto tape or the Web? Well, I've covered a number of ideas about the composition of short films. If you want to make animations, learn Macromedia Flash software. It's not that difficult. Read all about it at www.macromedia.com.

If you want to create live-action films, I highly suggest an Apple G4 for editing, simply because it's easier to use and faster than comparable PCs. Macs also tend to last a lot longer than PC systems, which makes up for their normal extra cost.

Although the iMac DV (around $1,500) comes with editing software, iMovie2 is rather rudimentary compared to Apple's major product, Final Cut Pro. Adobe Premiere (www.adobe.com) is another good product. Both of these software packages cost in the neighborhood of $1,000. An Apple G4 450 suitable for editing costs around $2,500 (although you're better off with a G4 500 for $3,500). A Cinema Display monitor is around $500.

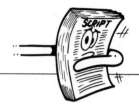

It's Not for Us

If you don't passionately want to see something that you write on-screen, don't waste your time looking into digital filmmaking. You'll just waste money and time. But then, I would wonder why you're writing screenplays if you're not passionate.

Script Notes

A film festival is where feature-length films, documentaries, and short films are showcased to potential buyers. The most famous is the Sundance Film Festival, founded by Robert Redford. Contact your local film commission, or have a look at filmfestivals.com to learn more about festivals.

I'll leave it to you to determine what kind of digital camera you use; get professional advice before buying. You can get a broadcast-quality camera for a few thousand. As anyone can quickly calculate, for less than $10,000 you can have the equipment necessary to become a filmmaker. If you buy computer equipment and rent a camera, it's $5,000 or less. What should you concentrate on in the story of a short video or film? Think of a chapter in a novel or a short story. There should be a beginning, middle, and end, and a character arc so that the main sympathetic character undergoes some kind of transformation (good or bad).

You need an inciting incident to put the main character in conflict. Then, just when it looks like your main character is doomed, he or she solves the crisis through some innovative action. In *George Lucas in Love,* the crisis was his looming final exam. If he didn't turn in a script, he didn't graduate. Lord knows what the crisis was in the lives of the old women who blew their brains out in *Sunday's Game,* but they certainly resolved their lives (though not in a very pleasant way).

If you have a denouement at the end, it might be only a single shot that closes the story. A short is a lot like a feature film. That's why someone who does well with a short film might be a lot closer to writing and directing a feature film or TV show than he or she would be merely by impressing someone with a screenplay. It's certainly worth a try.

The Least You Need to Know

➤ Hot new filmmakers often start on MTV; study their music videos and see the future.

➤ One good way to learn to write effective short films is by taping music videos and watching them with the sound off as you try to write a script that matches the video.

➤ Two Web sites, AtomFilms.com and iFilm.com, are the places to go to study the latest and greatest in short films.

➤ A great short film with enough exposure on the Web can quickly lead to a studio or network deal.

➤ In writing short animated films, you must write all the details, as if you are God creating a world.

➤ In writing short live-action films, the rules of regular screenplays apply.

➤ The structure of short films is a condensed feature film, usually with only one story line.

Part 5
It's All in the Details

There are some things that you learn only by working in Hollywood. We don't know what they are. Just kidding! Herein lies a map through the Movieland jungle, replete with descriptions of snakes, quicksand, and ridiculous Hollywood practices. For example, one must use two brads (not three) when binding one's script. You'll learn about (and, when appropriate, avoid) amateur technical mistakes, screenwriting gurus, and Tinseltown bozos. We'll give you the bona fide tour on selling scripts, and tell you how to plan a screenwriting career that goes forever once you get it successfully launched. All aboard!

Chapter 24

Sweating the Small Stuff

In This Chapter

➤ Two brads, please

➤ Elegant simplicity

➤ No funky fonts

➤ Quirky perqs

➤ How old are you?

➤ Persistence wins

On the Usenet newsgroup misc.writing.screenplays, a number of screenwriting veterans from around the world read and post messages on a daily basis. When they are avoiding writing (as writers are prone to do), they might post on an hourly basis. Invariably, each week, someone will turn up who is new to the group, who will ask about mundane aspects of Hollywood conventions. That often prompts jokes or even sarcastic comments or insults known on Usenet as "flames." (Of course, I would never do anything like that, would I? Heh heh.)

If the posters known as "newbies" are patient, sooner or later they'll get their questions answered or be referred to a FAQ (frequently asked questions) file that someone maintains. Someone will eventually answer the question because he'll remember when he was new to the business and asked all the same dumb questions. So don't be afraid, ask. We've all been idiots!

This chapter (I hope) will answer the dumb questions that you might not know to ask. The idea is to provide you with elements of screenwriting etiquette that will keep you from being branded an amateur when you submit your script. Read the whole thing. You won't believe some of the things I'm going to tell you, but you'll get a few laughs at Hollywood's expense.

Script Notes

A **brad** is a round-head solid brass fastener used to bind screenplays. I prefer the Acco No. 6R, which is 1½ inch (3.8 cm) in length and comes in a box of 100. Some people prefer the 5R, 1¼-inch brad or the 7R, 2-inch brad. I never use the companion brass washers to hold the brads in place on the other side.

It's Not for Us

Do not use the brass washers that are meant to accompany brass brads and hold them in place on the other side. Although it makes the binding more secure, the use of a washer is seen as the sign of an amateur. Ain't Hollywood grand?

Two Brads, Not Three

Here's the drill. Now that you have the drill, make three holes in your screenplay on the left side. Okay, I'm just kidding, but unless there is a sea change of major proportions in Hollywood screenplay protocol (not likely), print your screenplay only on three-hole 8½ × 11-inch paper, or use a three-hole punch to make three equally spaced holes along the left side of the script.

When you print out a completed screenplay on three-hole paper and you bind it with brads and start reading it, you'll see why you need to leave plenty of room on the left. If you don't, you'll find that reading along the left side is cramped. Pages read will not lay down easily. If you submit a script like that to a busy agent, development executive or producer, they might get tired of holding down pages they've turned and chuck your script in the trash, the round file, the waste bin, the deep six.

Got the picture? The idea is to do everything that you can to conform to the standards so that they think about only the content of your screenplay. You don't give them a chance to get distracted. Four companies that I know of make the brass fasteners known in the business as *brads*. Acco, Labelon/Noesting, and Stockwell all make solid brass brads. Brads from Oio are brass-plated but feel flimsy to me. The solid brass brads feel more solid and substantial, so those are the ones that I use. In North America, brads can generally be found at any major office supply store, such as Staples or Office Depot, both of which have Web sites. I mention this last because many European screenwriters these days want to present their work to American studios with the "proper" binding on 8½ × 11 paper, not the two-hole punched A4 standard (297mm × 210mm) used in Europe.

I'll tell you why to only use brads in a moment. Meanwhile, do not use any of the following to bind your screenplay:

➤ **Banker's clasps.** Long, thin stainless steel fasteners often used as money clips

➤ **Binder clips.** Black, hollow prism shape with two wire "handles"

➤ **Thick cardstock covers.** Particularly the kind with built-in prong fasteners

➤ **Bulldog clips.** Silver spring-loaded clips with circular, thumb-sized "handles"

➤ **Chicago screws.** Solid aluminum posts $\frac{3}{16}$ inch in diameter that screw into $\frac{3}{8}$-inch aluminum heads

➤ **Ideal paper clamps.** Looks a bit like three steel triangles formed from one piece of wire

➤ **Loose-leaf rings.** Metal rings that clasp together in the middle

➤ **Prong fasteners.** Flat, stainless steel strips with pointed ends that are held in place on the back with prong compressors

➤ **Regal clips.** Thick, steel wire paper holders that roughly resemble the face of an owl

➤ **Self-adhesive fasteners.** Identical to prong fasteners, with an adhesive strip on one side so that a compressor isn't needed

➤ **Spiral binding.** Usually done with a clear front cover

➤ **Solid-spine binding.** Favored by large offices with a plastic spine created by heat sealing

➤ **Anything else.** Use brass brads!

Skip's Tips

When you find a good source of brass brads, buy more than one box at a time. I know, it sounds stupid, no doubt, but there are so many people writing screen-plays these days, that brads are often in short supply, if you can find them at all.

You're probably thinking I'm nuts by now, but here's another rule for you: Although there are three holes in the paper, use brads only in the top and bottom holes. I'll explain. When people like a screenplay, they want to share it with others. Although you as the writer hold the copyright, meaning that they are supposed to ask your permission to photocopy your work, no one does.

They simply run it through the copy machine. To facilitate the ease of this practice, people in Hollywood like scripts with two brads and no fasteners. Use the no. 5 brads mentioned previously if your scripts are 110 pages or less. If your script is longer, you might want to use the no. 6 size brads. I always use no. 6 so that I never have prongs barely holding on. That's worse than having too long brads sliding all over the place to snag clothes.

You might assume that, to keep people from catching their fingers on the bent-over brads in the back, you should bend the pointed ends of the brads under. No. That makes the script lay funny on top of other scripts. You need the prongs to lie flat. I've found it useful to use a small rubber mallet, lay the script on a flat surface, and tap the brad prongs flat, hopefully without denting the round head on the front. Sounds goofy, I know, but most screenwriters I know use some variation of this method.

Hollywood Heat

I wrote a script named *Gold Bricks* that got optioned immediately by an actress who wanted an old boyfriend to produce it. He said that he would, but he didn't. Back to selling my script, I headed over to the main script copying place in Hollywood, Barbara's Place, on Santa Monica Boulevard. I found a shiny gold plastic cover and had the shop print the title on each cover. I sent producer David Permut a copy, and he called after reading the first 40 pages. He liked the writing a lot, he said, even though he almost didn't read it because the crazy gold cover was very amateurish.

Even though I've mentioned logos and artwork being printed on title pages of network movie scripts and TV shows, leave them off your covers. Leave them off your title page. Use card stock covers, one on the front and one on the back. I use white, but pale blue and light tan is also common. If you've been in a producer's office and seen the title handwritten with a felt-tipped pen on the spine of the script, don't do that for them—let them do that. A producer would think that a spine-marked script had already been read elsewhere and that you didn't even do him the courtesy of printing up a new script. And now your brad and cover education is complete. Are you excited?

Simple Is Elegant

Hopefully my little thesis has shown you something about tastes in Hollywood offices. Now let me elaborate further. The development executives that I know tend to dress casually but conservatively. The women wear chunky black dress shoes with low heels. The men wear conservative but hip shoes (I've never seen any wingtips). Offices may be piled high with scripts, but they're generally fairly neat and the furniture has simple lines. Producers' offices can be quite the opposite, very colorful and eccentric. It's not uncommon to see expensive jukeboxes or video parlor games against a wall.

With development executives, the overall impression that I'm generally left with is that they have so much going on in their lives—so many scripts to read and so much "coverage" to generate—that they disdain anything out of the ordinary. They want the scripts that come in to have a uniform look. Tricks and gimmicks generally don't go over too well. If you're thinking of putting on a grizzly suit to hand-deliver your script about a man chased by a grizzly bear, with a blood-red grizzly paw print on the cover, good luck. Your script probably won't get read, and you might get shot by a security guard. (Well, probably not, but you won't make friends.)

Here's something else to consider. Every time I've been in an office to pitch a script, I've seen books that are under consideration stacked on shelves off the floor. Scripts—even those from major agencies, which you might assume are the best—are piled all over, often against a wall on the floor. Scripts that have received great coverage, or scripts that the company has in production or is putting in production will be on the executive's desk. Their priorities, like anyone, are based on what they consider important. Books are generally more "important" than most scripts, even though a script would have to be written from a book. If you send in a script that is properly formatted, the right length, in a plain envelope, with the receiving person's name spelled correctly, you're more likely to be viewed as "could become important." If you try a bunch of tricks, importance probably won't happen.

Even though Hollywood puts wild and crazy images on the screen, and celebrity antics fill the tabloids, screenwriters breaking in generally must follow very conservative rules of production company etiquette when your work is presented for the first time. Even when companies are prosperous and the men can afford expensive suits, they're usually all Armani. And the simple black dresses that the women wear are made by expensive designers. Conformity and uniformity are constants in Hollywood. When you've seen enough of it, you realize just how much it is show business.

When you get your first chance to meet someone in person, don't worry about any of that expensive stuff. Just about anyone can afford to print a simple script on white paper and send it in a manila envelope. (No, they don't insist that it come in a manila envelope; just don't draw little doodles to get attention.) And it's generally assumed that beginning screenwriters fit the profile of the "starving writer."

It's a stereotype that isn't always true, but it's often assumed. So, if you get a chance to meet someone in person, just dress neatly and cleanly. Your grooming is your own business; if you're selling a script called *Megadeath Below Hell,* you might want to wear

Script Notes

A staple is a small piece of wire used to bind a synopsis or treatment in the upper-left corner. I'm sure you know what a staple is, but that's all you need to use. If you use brads, use a small one, ½ inch or so. School report binders with clear plastic covers are okay, too, for synopses and treatments.

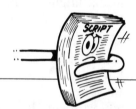

It's Not for Us

If you run into someone who doesn't seem to care whether your script is formatted in an industry-standard fashion, don't assume you've stumbled on some new hip style. That's probably just an anomaly and that person's preference. Stick with accepted standards.

appropriate clothing. Even then, most people I know prefer nonsmelly breath. If you're ever in question about which way to go in Hollywood, think simple. Scripts from very successful writers are very simply presented. Good writers show up for meetings on time, are usually soft-spoken (until they start passionately presenting a story), and don't do anything to make other people's lives more complicated. The "simple is elegant" approach has always worked, in my experience.

The Funky Font Don't Fly

These days, so many fonts are available for computers that we have complete software programs that do nothing but manage fonts. Just as I once used a shiny gold cover to try to make a script stand out, I've seen many beginning screenwriters use a special font on title pages or within a script, in an attempt to make something look prominent. Don't do it—you'll just look amateur.

Use Courier 12 pitch. I know, I know. You don't like it because Bookman looks cleaner, or New York looks more bold. You might prefer Times or Times New Roman. Some people have given me long dissertations about Courier being a dinosaur from the days of the typewriter. They'll tell me that they prefer reading pages that have a justified right margin, so why can't they do that with character description? Oh boy. I've heard it all.

Never, ever, though, have I heard a professional, working screenwriter question the use of Courier 12 pitch. I have rarely seen a sold script that was written in anything but Courier 12 pitch. I've very rarely seen a script not written in Courier 12 pitch, period. It's just the way it's done, as predictable as the sun coming up in the morning and setting in the evening. Why rock the boat and use something else?

Hollywood Heat

David E. Kelley was a Boston lawyer when he wrote *From the Hip* (1987). That experience brought him to Los Angeles, but he didn't expect to stay. That changed when producers Steven Bochco and Terry Louise Fisher hired him for *L.A. Law*. Kelley eventually took over as executive producer. He's a virtual writing machine these days, penning every episode in some years of *Chicago Hope*, *Picket Fences*, *Ally McBeal*, and *The Practice*. In 1999, the latter two shows won the Emmy for Best Comedy Series and Best Dramatic Series. And he's married to superstar Michelle Pfeiffer! But he's never worried about script format. All his scripts are handwritten on yellow legal pads and then are transcribed for him.

I've sold more books than screenplays and teleplays, and I prefer writing in Bookman some times. But guess what? The publishing industry also prefers the use of Courier 12 pitch. The publisher of this book, in fact, insisted on it in the author guidelines.

There's a reason for the madness. There isn't some Courier cabal that gets a kickback every time someone uses that font. Properly formatted screenplays in Courier 12 generally work out to a minute a page, in screen time. Properly formatted manuscript pages generally work out to a certain number of words per page, double-spaced (250 per page is my general rule). When all sorts of other fonts start getting used, that throws predictability out the window. So do yourself a favor and use Courier 12 pitch. Period.

Shane Black and Other Quirky Perqs

I once belonged to a writing workshop that met every month at some NBC offices in Burbank. The workshop wasn't officially sanctioned by the television network, but that didn't stop us from calling it the NBC Writers Workshop. Maybe that's why a lot of top names would show up to give us tips about breaking into Hollywood.

One night, Shane Black arrived to talk about screenwriting. I wondered what an actor was doing talking to us about writing scripts. I knew Black only from his appearance in *Predator* (1987). I loved that film, and I also knew the executive producer, Laurence Pereira. I didn't read the trades in those days, so I didn't know that Black had just sold two scripts that would be made into films in 1987, *The Monster Squad* and a little something call *Lethal Weapon,* which would make a superstar of Mel Gibson. With sales that followed, Black quickly became one of the highest-paid writers in Hollywood, receiving up to $4 million for a script.

I spoke to Black briefly that night about *Predator.* When he said he'd sold *Lethal Weapon* to a director I knew, Richard Donner, I was intrigued, so I began following his career. I wasn't the only screenwriter interested in what Black was writing. I began reading the trades after the NBC Workshop, and one day my eyes bugged when I saw that Black had sold a script for $1.75 million (the biggest sale in 1990). I got one of his scripts and read it. The same self-deprecating humor that I'd seen that night at NBC was all over some pages.

What Black did differently was throw in descriptive paragraphs that spoke directly to the reader. For example, he might describe a house lavishly and throw in a line such as, "The kind of house I'm going to run out and buy after you buy this script." Some of the descriptions of the character Riggs in *Lethal Weapon* were darkly amusing, given

Skip's Tips

A writer's "voice" comes about for two reasons: writing and rewriting enough words to learn the craft, and certainty gained due to other's appreciation of your work. Rather than attempt to emulate other's styles, keep writing and rewriting until your own uniqueness blooms. Have faith; it will.

It's Not for Us

If you just happen to be a wildly different character, don't tone down your personality just to try to blend into Hollywood. This is a town that loves larger-than-life personalities, but only if they are genuine.

the suicidal tendencies of that character, but when Black "spoke" to the reader, it made you empathize with the script and wonder about the screenwriter personally. The problem for screenwriters who tried to emulate this style was that Black originated it. It was truly his own unique voice, which was refreshing to readers who had never seen such a thing. Plus, Black is a fine screenwriter, so his quirkiness was not bothersome. His descriptive method didn't always work for others who didn't have his writing skills.

That's the way it is in Hollywood, or any other major industry, for that matter. If you're good enough, you get the perquisites, or "perqs." A hot screenwriter will be granted their eccentricity just like a movie star. I heard from a writer who sold a script that John Milius directed that Milius would go to meetings with gun belts draped across his chest, like some Mexican bandit. In a politically gun-shy town such as Hollywood, that's quite a perq. But, like Black, Milius is an excellent writer and could get away with things that normal writers could not. What I can guarantee you is that with less talent, their personal quirks might not have been as readily appreciated.

Every writer wants to do something to stand out, to make a mark, or even to get very rich. Just about anyone who arrives in Los Angeles can find a way to get in a door for a meeting, but quirky comments in a script or dressing up in a bandoleer won't guarantee success. You'll have to back it up with the writing—the plot, dialogue, and character development in your screenplay. Remember, every time you read about some eccentric Hollywood person or event, it's in print because it's news that sells newspapers and gets people to watch TV. For 99 percent of all screenwriters, only the script matters.

Hollywood and Ageism

If you're entering a screenwriting career later in life, meaning after the age of 30, you might hear rumors that older writers find it hard to get work or sell scripts. Unfortunately, in television (where most WGA writers work), that can be true, particularly in situation comedy land. In June 2000, *Variety* reported that a law firm probing age-discrimination allegations by Writers Guild of America West members had offered to represent members without cost. The investigation came about due to a 1998 report that revealed "sharply decreased opportunities" for writers over 40. If you're groaning right about now, let me share with you what I've observed. I'm over the age of 40, but I've never had anyone ask me my age except someone in the book business. It has just never come up.

I know of a writer who sold a screenplay to Will Smith's company, Overbrook, at age 58. He said that no one ever mentioned his age. And in May 2000, the *Los Angeles Times* ran a long feature about "Hollywood's Grays" that flew in the face of the "conventional wisdom" of Hollywood's youth fixation. The first person mentioned was Larry Abbott, 64-year-old makeup artist.

Next was 78-year-old actress Judy Woodbury, then Pete "Papa" Papanickolas, at 77, the oldest working crew person in Hollywood. My favorite story, though, was about 73-year-old Jack Mendelsohn, who was in his mid-60s when he wrote 181 half-hour episodes of the *Teenage Mutant Ninja Turtles* TV series. Mendelsohn, who has been writing for TV shows since 1964 (with credits that include The Beatles movie *Yellow Submarine*), is a real inspiration.

There was a catch about all the people mentioned in the article, however, including 85-year-old director Robert Wise. They had all been working in Hollywood for decades. They at least defied the "older people don't work" mantra, but I've seen people break into the business at an age much later than most people think possible. One of the people who contacted me after reading my *Writer's Guide to Hollywood* was a woman in her 50s living in Santa Fe, New Mexico. She was an excellent writer, and I tried to help open some doors for her. On her own, though, she got a job writing some episodes for a syndicated animation series. And that's why I love the Internet. In cyberspace, with e-mail, no one can tell how old you are. The essence of the ideas come across. You can send someone a script and let it stand on its own, with no consideration for your age on the other end. (That is, if your dialogue and description accurately reflect young people today, if that's who you write about.)

Even on the phone, it's sometimes hard to tell someone's age. And you know what? In the end, it really doesn't matter. If it's on the page, it'll make the stage. Will Smith bought a script from someone old enough to be his grandfather, and Smith has been more successful at the box office in recent years than any other actor. If you're an older screenwriter, don't worry about Hollywood ageism. A lot of older writers do not work because they are inflexible about their ideas. They refuse to grow with the culture.

As the Baby Boom generation gets older, they'll be much more less likely to judge by age. The Boomers' generation was the one that loved a Roger Corman movie called *Wild in the Streets,* whose big line was "Don't trust anyone over 30." Now, with most successful producers a part of the Baby Boom generation and gray all over their heads, something tells me that they don't feel that way anymore. Just write a great script, and people won't even look up to see the wrinkles in your face until they read "THE END."

Persistence Makes Perfect

I could write about Hollywood "rules" until the last film in the last theater on Earth runs the final credits, and there would still be successful exceptions, even to the Courier 12 pitch screenplay standard. You can read about rules, talk about rules, and

Skip's Tips

If you're a writer of grandparent age looking to break in, I'd advise you to write films or TV movies that kids love. It's one area of Hollywood that doesn't seem to care so much about age.

listen to rumors until your eyes are permanently bloodshot. It's better to spend your time perfecting your craft and learning how the film industry works when you're not writing.

The day before I wrote this chapter, I heard from a writer named Dwayne A. Smith who had just sold a script called *Joe's Last Chance*. I'd read about the sale in *Variety* and noticed that he popped up on the misc.writing.screenplays group the next day. I shared a story I'd heard about Burt Reynolds and Clint Eastwood. Supposedly, they'd both gotten fired from their contracts at the same studio on the same day. They began comparing notes after they both became superstars and figured out that it had taken each of them about 15 years to make it. Dwayne said that's how long it took him, too, and he added that he'd been reading my posts on the newsgroup for years. While I believe that cream rises to the top, that doesn't necessarily mean that someone always skims it off and consumes it. Keep writing and perfecting your voice, and someday you'll get noticed by the big cats.

The Least You Need to Know

➤ Use only solid brass brads to bind your three-hole punched script—one in the top hole, one in the bottom, none in the middle—and no washers to secure the brads.

➤ Use card stock covers for your scripts—one front, one back—in white, light blue, or tan. Don't get fancy.

➤ Screenwriters breaking in should generally know and follow very conservative rules of production company etiquette.

➤ Use only Courier 12 pitch type in your screenplay.

➤ Highly successful screenwriters such as Shane Black have unique voices in their screenplays, but they are allowed such "perqs" only because they are such good writers.

➤ Hollywood ageism exists, but talent, persistence, young thinking, and the use of the Internet all help overcome it.

➤ Often enough, it can take a decade or longer to make it in Hollywood, so for cream to rise to the top, it must be persistent.

Fixing Amateur Technical Mistakes

Now that we've gone over some of the ins and outs of dealing with Hollywood, let's talk about some of the amateur mistakes that will get your script rejected. I've read a lot of scripts in my time and seen the mistakes that I discuss here repeated over and over. I don't know why that is because I know that people aren't reading books that recommend these mistakes. Maybe it's simply because people have seen a lot of films on television that were made by people who simply didn't know any better.

I've taught writing at all levels, from grade schoolers in small towns to post-college courses at the UCLA Extension Writers Program (the largest of its kind in the world) and online at WritersWrite.com (the largest Web site for writers in the world). I don't mean to boast here; I simply mean to illustrate that I've seen it all, and writers seem to follow the same patterns over and over. If they don't want to write screenplays, they generally start off with children's books, poetry, or short stories. If they write screenplays, those are usually jammed with dialogue and are better suited for the stage, not a motion picture theater.

It's Not for Us

After you learn basic screenplay structure, don't assume that your education is over. The only way to earn a graduate degree in Hollywood is an obituary in *Variety* or *The Hollywood Reporter*.

Skip's Tips

Buy yourself a baby names book, whether you expect to be a parent or not. Or, get some software that displays the meaning of names. You'll come up with characters whose names suit them. For example, "Skip" is a Norwegian word for a leader on a ship.

There's a lot to learn about screenwriting. I'm still scrambling to catch up on everything that I want to know about the subject. After 15 years of writing and selling scripts and all sorts of other things, I'm only now beginning to feel like I can write a screenplay that I'll love. That's why I hope to help you avoid clichés and keep your script from being tossed in the trash.

Flashbacks and Fools

I hope that, when you outlined your script, you did at least a rudimentary background sketch of all your main characters. I hope that you worked out their "back story" well enough that you know how they will react in almost any given situation, often in ways that the audience does not expect. If you did not do this and you're still preparing your script, the following elements are things that you might consider:

➤ **Name.** Come up with a full name, and delve into the origin of those names. It's my feeling that a well-named character affects audiences on a primal level.

➤ **Nickname.** If your character is Southern and a big person, chances are good that someone called them "Tiny" at some point. A girl nicknamed "Darling Sugar" tells us that she's probably spoiled.

➤ **Position in family.** A middle child has a very different outlook on life than a firstborn or "baby" of a family.

➤ **Family stability.** If the character's family moved a lot in youth, it might make the character do anything for security.

➤ **Religion, or lack of it.** Don't always go with the standard religions. The superstitious Santeria-following slugger in *Major League* was a breath of comic fresh air.

➤ **Phobias.** Things that your character is deathly afraid of can be a tremendous source of both drama and comedy.

➤ **Hidden past.** This could be a hidden former identity, or simply some past embarrassment that your character doesn't want revealed.

➤ **Sexual preferences.** You should know this, whether we see them having sex or not.

➤ **Undisclosed agenda.** If you don't know what each main character wants most out of life during the time period of your screenplay, you've done yourself a disservice.

I'm sure you can think of many other items to list. What's important is that you have a storehouse of information on your characters that you do *not* put onscreen. Most beginning screenwriters, in their rush to grab Hollywood glory, don't take enough time to work things out before they write. Thus, when they start the script, they "think on paper," using flashbacks to reveal troubling elements of a character's past.

Well, guess what. The audience has usually seen it. In fact, they've seen too much of it. Expert handling of flashbacks is done with a very specific purpose, often to deal with a single important element of the story. When it's done right, as in *Rashomon* or *Somewhere in Time,* flashbacks build to an emotional crescendo that is resolved in the last act. When it is not done well, you simply confuse or even lose the audience. That's why experienced filmmakers use black-and-white or sepia tones in flashbacks, so the audience can easily follow.

Until someone takes a screenplay of yours seriously enough to option or buy it, or ask for more material, I'd advise you to stay away from flashbacks. I've rarely seen a beginning writer handle them well. Simply writing "FLASHBACK" as a script direction might make it clear for the reader what's going on, but the person in the movie theater doesn't have that luxury. Try to write without them so that the flow of your story is not broken up. After you're truly confident of your screenwriting ability, then try them.

Hollywood Heat

Even as a movie title, a flashback can be troublesome. *Flashback* (1990) seemed like a clever idea, telling the story of yuppie FBI agent John Buckner (Kiefer Sutherland) rousting 1960s hippie radical Huey Walker (Dennis Hopper) out of the underground to bring him to prison. Unfortunately, it came off like a watered-down version of *Midnight Run* (1988). When well-known critic Leonard Maltin reviewed it, he gave it a very low rating, a ½ star.

Don't You Just Love Watching People Talk on the Phone While They're Eating?

Here's an exercise for you. If you live with someone, sit down some time and watch them talk on the phone. See if you can stand it for at least 30 seconds. (If they're naked, it doesn't count.) I'll bet you won't make it 20 seconds, unless you're a part of the conversation they're having. Nevertheless, I see scenes in screenplays all the time with people having long conversations on the phone. I even see antiquated techniques like a split-screen, which allows you to show both sides of a conversation at once.

Like a flashback, unless you have a very good reason for having a phone conversation in your script, either:

A. Keep it very short.

B. Leave it out altogether.

C. Come up with some unique presentation that we haven't seen before.

The advent of portable phones and cell phones has helped revive this stagnant device, letting you do things like take your detective character throughout a crime scene while talking on the phone, but generally people use phone scenes only to convey information that could be better done with moving pictures. I've found, generally, that phone conversations tend to break up the flow of a story, so I try not to use them.

Skip's Tips

The word "villain" comes from the word *villa,* or "country estate." Maybe that's why so many movie villains are rich. Remember, all villains consider themselves to be the hero of their movie. Actors love to play bad guys because they're generally so much less restrained. Keep their "hero" viewpoint in mind as you write villains' lines, and you'll have a much better screenplay.

On the other hand, if you find an interesting way to use a phone call, it can be riveting. When the killer calls in the *Scream* movies and we hear his menacing voice, we share the terror of his victims. Other than in thrillers and horror movies, though, can you remember a single phone scene from a single movie that is all-time memorable? I can't think of any, except perhaps the happy one at the end of *It's a Wonderful Life.*

If you have phone scenes in your movie, try going over your script to see if you can have your character learn something or discover something *without* answering that phone. That includes using "I gotta take this phone call" to get a character out of a scene. I'll bet you can come up with richer ideas.

Now here's another staple of movies, particularly in ensemble films such as Barry Levinson's fabulous *Diner* (1982). Eating scenes. One screenwriting guru, UCLA Screenwriting Department co-chairman Richard Walter, hates watching people onscreen having conversations over dinner and advises against writing them. When I first read that bit of advice, I wanted to agree, but then I thought of a number of great eating scenes I'd enjoyed.

The stimulating *My Dinner with André* (1981), directed by Louis Malle, took place almost completely over dinner in a nice restaurant. And who could the forget the "Who do you and your girlfriend make out to, Mathis or Sinatra?" conversation in *Diner?* Or the food fight in the cafeteria in *Animal House* (1978). Or Bill Murray's repeated attempts to seduce Andie MacDowell in the restaurant in *Groundhog Day* (1993). Or the lack of a tip that leads to splitting a winning lottery ticket in *It Could Happen to You* (1994, a.k.a. *Cop Tips Waitress $2 Million*). Or the alien hatchling popping out of someone's stomach during a meal on the mining ship in *Alien* (1979).

And then there is possibly the greatest conversation over dinner of all time. It's certainly the funniest. Actually, it's more than a conversation. It's Meg Ryan showing Billy Crystal how women can easily fake a convincing orgasm in *When Harry Met Sally* (1989). I still laugh out loud when I think of how the director, Rob Reiner, cut to his mother, Estelle Reiner (playing "Older Woman Customer"), at the end of the scene so that she could say to the waiter, "I'll have what she's having!"

That's the way it is in writing screenplays. For every Hollywood "rule" that someone puts forth, people can come up with numerous examples of something opposite working onscreen. How does that happen? Just take a look at the scenes mentioned previously. There's a rule that applies across the board to every one of them. Allow me to play the "Jeopardy" quiz show theme here while you try to figure out what it is .... Time's up!

Memorable meal conversations in movies speak to the central issue of the film.

My Dinner with André was about having a deep, earnest conversation about the examination of life. Perfect to do over dinner.

Diner was about the coming of age of a group of friends in Baltimore, Maryland, in 1959. The singers used to put their girlfriends in the mood for love fits the theme of the film.

The food fight in *Animal House* is perfectly illustrative of a bizarre, out-of-control fraternity on a college campus.

As Bill Murray keeps repeating the same day in *Groundhog Day,* he is able to glean information from Andie MacDowell (who isn't in on the time loop) that makes her like him. What it takes for Murray's miserable character to become likable is the theme of the film.

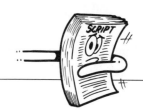

It's Not for Us

Don't settle for any meal scene in your movie until you have one that is memorable. In this day of inexpensive digital movies, it's easy to write in a dinner conversation, but if it isn't unique, you might feed your audience a sleeping pill.

It Could Happen to You, a.k.a. *Cop Tips Waitress $2 Million,* based on a true story, is about selfless giving and values being more important than money.

The plot of *Alien* revolves around a bizarre species who parasitically destroy human life, so a hatchling ripping out the man's stomach is a microcosm of the aliens' over-all plan.

When Harry Met Sally stems from the age-old question of whether an attractive man and an attractive woman can simply be friends without evolving into a sexual relationship. When Meg Ryan fakes her orgasm so convincingly, it invites Billy Crystal to think of her sexually, but it also adds to his confusion over what their long-term friendly relationship is really all about.

Let me say it again—I think that memorable meal conversations in movies work only when they speak directly to the central issue of the film. Maybe that's because the stomach is central to a human being's survival.

If you can come up with a better idea about how to make a dinner conversation scene work in a movie, I'll buy you dinner. Of course, you'll have to convince me first.

Voiceovers as Sleep Aids

Just like the ubiquitous phone conversation, I often see *voiceovers* abused in screen-plays from beginners. Why does this happen? They probably saw a lot of Disney nature films on the Disney Channel. It's sort of the movie equivalent of the children's stories that beginners serve up in some of my writing classes. When you think of what purpose a voiceover serves, isn't it usually as a narrator? That's the only time I use it.

The exception may be when you transition between scenes, and someone from the previous scene is still talking in *voiceover* (*V.O.*) as the new scene begins. That's an editing device that smoothly furthers the flow of the story. Use it if you can easily visualize the scene working onscreen, but I'd recommend not getting that fancy with your first script or two. Just cut cleanly between scenes if you can, with no carryovers.

If you feel compelled to use a narrator voiceover in your movie, you might consider opening the film with it and then coming back to it at the end, as was done in *To Kill a Mockingbird* (1962), *Sophie's Choice* (1982), *Stand by Me* (1986), and *The Shawshank Redemption* (1994). You might have recognized that all those films had something in common. They origi-nated in literature, with two of them from Stephen King, as a matter of fact.

Script Notes

A **voiceover** (**V.O.**) is when a character is speaking but is not physically present in the scene. The notation **offscreen** (**O.S.**) usually denotes that the person is present but cannot be seen within the framed shot. Either one should be typed just to the right of the character's capital-ized name, as in "SKIP (V.O.)" or "SKIP (O.S.)."

There's another element as well. They're all coming-of-age stories narrated by someone looking back at memorable, life-changing events in life. Novels are generally deeper and more thoughtful than screenplays, and using a voiceover to open and close a film helps convey that sense of thoughtfulness, particularly when the story is told in reflection. A full-circle loop of a tale that leaves us with the feeling that things work out all right after all and with voiceovers at each end are somewhat like the voice of an all-knowing God.

The other type of effective voiceover is in film noir, such as the Humphrey Bogart movies derived from Raymond Chandler novels. The hard-boiled detective's ironic commentary was used so much, however, that using it in a film now almost seems like satire. Nevertheless, *L.A. Confidential* opened with a great voiceover by Danny DeVito. If you can find a way to make it work, as in the original *Blade Runner,* go for it, but I'll bet that you'll run into people who want to take it out of the script.

Hollywood Heat

If you don't have a DVD player, you might not have seen the Ridley Scott Director's Cut of *Blade Runner* (1982). Unlike the theatrically released version, in the DVD the voiceovers of Harrison Ford as the detective Deckard are gone. The missing narration is compensated by more moving pictures. For example, when we see the advertising slogan on a passing blimp while Deckard waits for a seat at a noodle bar, it's longer than in the original. Of course, I enjoyed Ford's resonant voice narrating the denouement as he flew out of the city with the beautiful android played by Sean Young. How about you?

Some films by their very nature call for a narrator who will appear at appropriate points throughout the film—a movie with animals and kids, for example. When a voiceover is used in that context, it's pretty much an acceptable convention. You'll have to use your own judgment on how you go about using or not using voiceovers. I know this, though: If you use it too much, readers will think you're an amateur. How much is too much? I don't know; I haven't read your script.

Cute Is for Babies

I wrote a script once about a Swedish au pair coming to live with a professional Southern California couple who needed a caregiver for their small child. I wrote it after meeting some beautiful Swedish au pairs one Christmas at a party. They told me that there were thousands of young women from Sweden doing this kind of work in the Los Angeles area. I did some research and came up with a figure of around 10,000. Wow, I thought, what a setup for a movie, particularly with the male of the family working at home in his garage recording studio and his lawyer wife away at the office. Temptation, temptation.

Skip's Tips

When you finish your script, do something William Faulkner advised: *Kill your darlings.* Go through your script and see if you can find an element, even a character, that just doesn't add anything or that conflicts with the overall theme of the movie. Lose anything that takes away from the integrity of your script, no matter how much you like the little darling.

I had the script completed four days after I got the initial idea. *The Swedish Touch* was mostly set in one house, making it cheap to shoot, and the number of characters were minimal. So how to get it made? I'd just completed working on a how-to home video, and I told my partner on that project about the script. He read it and liked it, but had something else in mind. He took me to a meeting with actress Linda Blair, who wanted to do a how-to about horse care. It turned out that she was an accomplished equestrienne who had been riding since an early age.

We never made that video, but Linda did want to play the wife in *The Swedish Touch* and made some minimal attempts to help me set up the movie. For the husband, I had in mind Tony Dow, and he read the script and agreed to do it. That's right, Wally Cleaver of *Leave It to Beaver* meets the possessed girl in *The Exorcist*. That's low-budget filmmaking! Then I needed a director, so I called Ed Hunt, who wrote and directed movies such as *The Brain* (1988). Ed liked the script and wanted to direct it. We even drew up a detailed budget.

Still, the screenplay never got filmed, even with the basic elements in place. I never figured out why until several years later. Shortly after I wrote the *Writer's Guide to Hollywood,* I began contacting producers, after several years away from the business. I found a producing team who liked the script, but they wanted to change the punk rock band in the original script into rappers, which made their lust for the beautiful au pair even more controversial. I tried to revise the script, but paying work called, so I never got to it. Then one day as I was doodling around with the screenplay, I realized what was wrong.

The baby boy, BRYAN, was the culprit. Here I was writing a sex comedy about lust and temptation and cross-cultural sexual mores, and right in the middle of it was a small baby boy that the au pair looked after.

That just didn't work. Bryan was cute, with very minimal lines, but he didn't belong in the environment I'd placed him in. And without the kid—who managed to get moved to Grandma's house so that he was out of the way at certain times—who needs an au pair? So there went the movie. No one had ever brought up this point to me, but I'm sure that I'm right about it.

It's one thing to write a movie such as *Baby Boom* (1987) in which yuppie executive Diane Keaton has to change her lifestyle to accommodate an inherited baby. That movie was cute (even though it was a box office disappointment). Unlike my script, no elements of the movie clashed with the presence of the baby. When Keaton falls for a man from the country played by Sam Shepard, it's warm and fuzzy, like a Rock Hudson and Doris Day movie from the 1950s.

Not my script. The baby's gurgling up his pablum in one scene, and a few pages later the Swedish au pair is taking off her bikini top by the pool and being ogled by the husband and the musicians. The two things just didn't quite mix. Since then, I've realized that writing for a definite age range is the best way to go. If you're going to write a family movie, you need to keep certain elements (like naked au pairs) out of it. If you're writing about hot music and hot bodies, you're not writing for The Disney Channel.

Cute is for babies, not sex-charged young professionals. Just as you can get in trouble mixing genres, inappropriate elements can mess up your movie. I hope that you never get confused about keeping the elements of your scripts unified, like I did. But then, I'm never of the opinion that I've written a bad script. I'm always convinced that I've simply scripted a good idea badly.

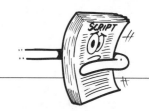

It's Not for Us

In an effort to be different, you might try mixing up genres and keeping your script as unpredictable as possible. Different is appreciated in Hollywood. Too different is not. If your screenplay could not be placed on an established category shelf in a video store, you're probably in trouble. It's best to learn to paint within the lines before you go wandering around outside them.

Who Needs Actors and Directors, Anyway?

When your script is taken seriously enough to go into production, if you remain the main writer on the project, you'll experience a reading of the screenplay. If it's the first time you've heard your screenplay read out loud, you'll be stunned at how they laugh at things that you didn't mean to be funny and don't get jokes that you think are a scream. Scene transitions that are perfectly logical to you will seem confusing to others. Actors will ask about their character's motivation in scenes, or maybe the entire screenplay.

Before that happens, though, the director will give you notes on your script and suggest changes. Some directors will even try to steal the project from you entirely and ask the producer to do a rewrite. (I had a production completely ruined like that not long ago, despite the fact that I introduced the director to the producer!)

Or, you might write such a good script that no one wants to mess with it. They'll defer to you, compliment you on your work, and ask what you're working on next. They'll see you as a long-term asset.

Skip's Tips

If you've never taken an improvisational acting class, you should. If you can't find an improv company in your town, read *Improvisation for the Theater: A Handbook of Teaching and Directing Techniques (Drama and Performance Studies), 3rd Edition,* by Viola Spolin, edited by Paul Sills (Northwestern University Press, 1999). Writers need to understand how actors think; this book will greatly help.

At some point in your screenwriting career, you'll probably hit a point at which you wonder what kind of crazy pill actors and directors take, where they get them, and why they swallow so many. Well, chill out. Get over it. Filmmaking is the most collaborative art on Earth, and unless you write, produce, direct, and star in your own films, like Woody Allen, it's unlikely that you'll be able to get around the reality of working with others. That's why I reassure writers who get peeved at some note from a reader or development executive trashing their script.

It's all part of the collaborative process. I'm constantly reminded of that old Indian saying: "Sometimes you eat the bear, sometimes the bear eats you." What you need to do as a screenwriter is map out as much of the dark, spooky woods of Hollywood as possible. The best light for that journey is the sunshine of a smile. If you let the process get to you and get angry about things you don't like, it dims your light.

There are 13 letters in the word *collaboration,* but that's unlucky only if you make it so. The best thing that a screenwriter can do is get inside the heads of the other people involved in making a movie. Actors' comments might seem ridiculous to you, but if you tell them that and they've already been cast by the director, they might try to sabotage your film. If you don't want to change an element in the script to fit a high-profile actor who has been cast, you're simply not cut out for filmmaking. Unless you have a very strong argument for making the actor bend to fit the role, you'll rarely win, particularly if it's a star.

The good news is, in most cases, the more successful you become, the nicer and more accommodating people are. No matter what you've read in the tabloids, the majority of people in Hollywood are consummate professionals with unique looks and skills. They still struggled for years to make it and will empathize with you.

Top film professionals will go out of their way to explain why they feel a certain way about a scene or a line of dialogue. Argument and bitterness generally arise only out of insecurity, and you get that more often from people who haven't made it than you do from people happy with their careers.

If you run into trouble, hang in there. Keep smiling and keep learning. There's an old saying in Hollywood that you see the same people on the way up as you do on the way down, so you might as well be nice to everyone. It's a hard thing to remember sometimes—I certainly haven't always done it—but it's as good an axiom as any in Screenland.

The Least You Need to Know

➤ Too often, writers who use flashbacks haven't developed their characters enough and are "thinking on paper."

➤ Beginning screenwriters should try to stay away from the use of flashbacks and should write linear stories instead.

➤ Phone conversations in scripts too often break up the action. Either come up with some unique presentation that we haven't seen before, or try to use something other than a phone call.

➤ Memorable meal conversations in movies speak to the central issue of the film.

➤ Narrator voiceovers in movies are best used in coming-of-age stories narrated by someone looking back at life-changing events.

➤ Inappropriate elements in a screenplay can cause as much script trouble as mixing genres.

➤ Film is the most collaborative of all arts, so it is important for a screenwriter to learn as much as possible about the way actors and directors exercise their craft.

Chapter 26

The Mentor Merry-Go-Round

In This Chapter

➤ Guru world

➤ Are they experienced?

➤ Legitimate resources

➤ The Writers Guild of America

➤ Festivals and pundits

➤ Online oracles

➤ Real schooling

According to the great Chinese historian Szuma Ch'ien, there was a meeting between the Chinese philosophers Confucius and Lao-tze (author of the *Tao-Te-Ching* [*Book of the Way and of Virtue*]). Lao-tze (also known as Lao-tzu) was 87 when the meeting took place. Confucius was 34. The elder philosopher told the young inquirer that a man of great achievement is simple in manners and appearance. He advised Confucius to get rid of his pride and his many ambitions, his affectation and extravagant aims, because his character gained nothing from any of them. Confucius later told his own pupils that meeting with Lao-tze was comparable to meeting a dragon, the most revered creature of all of Chinese philosophy.

There is another Lao-Tze story that I find more interesting. Lao-Tze was a librarian, a man of simple tastes who valued rural life. Impressing rulers or important officials was

Skip's Tips

The true test of a teacher is not his credentials, but his students. Some people are simply better at observing and teaching that anything else. Find out what a potential guru's students have accomplished, and you have a clue to the teacher's real worth.

never important to him, even though they were impressed by him. When he wrote poetry, he tested it by giving it to the flower lady on the corner. If she liked it, he thought that it was good.

In finding help to improve your screenplays, do not limit yourself to Hollywood. Look for sincerity. That is honest character, the thing we all want. I've gleaned story advice from novelists, publishers, and even my mother. Screenplay how-to books and services have become a cottage industry, and some people make a large living traveling the country to tell people how to write and sell screenplays. I show up at occasional conferences, but I would rather be at home with my family, writing my own stories. I do what I do for writers, writing books and giving mostly free advice, simply because I hope for better stories from others. If I help improve the culture, we'll have a better world.

The Galloping Gurus

When I consider experts in any field, I wonder if they could make a living doing anything other than giving seminars and doing consulting work. Without naming names, I've seen a few too many gurus jump on the advice bandwagon in recent years—enough, in fact, that I wonder how many people are left to watch the parade.

I get challenged about credits occasionally, but inevitably the person doing it has some hidden agenda, such as a stalker who tried to trash me all over the Internet until I found out that he had a book that competed with my *Writer's Guide to Hollywood*. When I discovered who he was and where he lived, I didn't call my lawyer, even though he was guilty of libel. I simply announced on a newsgroup that I knew who he was, and he shut up. Not so surprisingly, his credits weren't as substantial as mine. But then, as Lao-tze said, "Reversal is the nature of the Tao."

The next thing I look for in an expert is humility and humor. Truly knowledgeable people are too fascinated with the work they do and the wonder of life itself to be full of themselves. When I encounter arrogance or an inability to laugh, I know that I'm dealing with an insecure person who is covering up. Sincerity is one thing; a too-serious person who doesn't laugh much generally won't enlighten your life with wisdom.

My next criteria in the worth of a screenwriting guru is whether that person seems to always have a show on the road. If so, he or she is in the seminar business, not the writing business. If someone comes to your city with a seminar and then returns within six months, wouldn't you have to assume that this person makes a living running seminars?

Hollywood Heat

A great many Hollywood screenwriting successes have friends or co-writers who, if not actually writing or ghostwriting with them, act as professional sounding boards for their material. A woman whose name is on a substantial prize in filmdom had a co-writer, and so did a man who had a weather vane in the shape of the Oscar that he won on the top of his house in Malibu. How do I know? I've met them.

This isn't to imply that there isn't worth in what these people have to say. I listen to them all, but which is more important—hearing from people who are actively working in a business every day, or hearing from someone who made his biggest mark years ago and now spends more time in hotels than in Hollywood? I'll leave it to your discerning wisdom to sort out who and what is best for you.

Book Writers and Real-Life Experience

I've seen two types of writers of advice books (and not only in the screenwriting field). The first and worst type is persons looking to aggrandize themselves, make a name, get noticed in the media, and gain followers hungry for direction in life.

Unfortunately, there are a lot of lost souls out there, and too many people are ready to keep them lost while professing to do just the opposite. You meet them all if you stick around Los Angeles long enough, and I've been taken in by the best. Once I knew a telemarketer wanted for tax evasion in Canada. Supposedly he was an actor, but he never seemed to work much at that. I knew him only because he married a friend of mine. After their daughter was a couple years old, he abandoned my friend, her son from another marriage, and his daughter to take up with a lady who wrote love advice books and did seminars all over the country. The lady's ex-husband also dished love advice (and still does).

Skip's Tips

Watch out for repackaged terms. Sometimes a guru definition is really only another way of saying something that has been around for a long time. For example, a plot point was known for a long time as a turning point, "the point at which a very significant change occurs; a decisive moment." If someone adds some new perspective to the idea, that's different.

Not only did I wonder why she couldn't make their own marriage work, but I also wondered why the lady dedicated several subsequent books to the irresponsible actor/telemarketer. I suppose that her followers never realized what she was really like. I was clued in by the ex-wife, who had to deal with repeated loony statements and actions because of the daughter. Of course, she was probably no worse than a radio love adviser who has a degree in exercising, acts like she knows everything about life, and ignores the fact that her naked pictures are on the Internet.

I met Tony Robbins once when he was living in a tiny apartment near the beach. He told me that his mission was to interview all types of successful people, find out what they do that works, and then write a book about it. It sounded logical, but it never occurred to me that someone would turn other's people advice into an advice-dispensing empire. Later, I found out that he'd simply copied the methods of Napoleon Hill, of *Think & Grow Rich*.

This brings us around to screenwriting advisers. I have one criterion in judging the worth of what they offer:

Do I put into use and remember what they teach me?

I've read a lot of pop psychology books, as well as books of wisdom that have survived the ages. Even when a book is all the rage, if I read it and don't find a use for the advice contained inside, I consider it worthless. Maybe it's worthwhile to someone else, but not for me. Whether or not the writer has racked up big screenplay sales doesn't matter to me. Christopher Vogler, author of *The Writer's Journey,* to my knowledge had never sold a screenplay before he developed his assessment of the Joseph Campbell myth structure that so ably speaks to screenwriters. But then, Campbell had never authored a great novel or even a short story, as far as I know. Nevertheless, I use, remember, and refer back to their material repeatedly. The same holds true for Syd Fields' "paradigm" screenplay schematic, Robert McKee's "expectation gap" for characters in scenes, and Lew Hunter's idea that with most good scripts, you know what's happening by page 17.

If you can't use it, lose it, and that goes for anything in this book. Some people will provide vague promises of access, and others will tell you the rules. The best ones give you tools that you use to make screenplays that sell.

Sherwood Oaks Experimental College and Other Legitimate Resources

A friend of mine told me a story about how he supported his wife's decision to get into the filmmaking program at the American Film Institute (AFI). The program cost $15,000 a year for two years, and she had always wanted to do it. "Sure," he said, "if you can get accepted." He knew that it was very difficult to get into the program and thought that she would probably be turned down. To his amazement, she was accepted. Still, his assessment had been correct; his wife had simply heavily impressed the faculty. With most top film programs in Los Angeles, it's difficult to make the cut.

The good thing is, if you live in southern California, there are many easier opportunities to gain a working knowledge of the film and television business. I cover a lot of them in my *Writer's Guide to Hollywood,* but I have a couple favorites that are accessible to the general public.

The first organization that I like a lot is one founded and directed by Gary Shusett:

> Sherwood Oaks Experimental College
> 7095 Hollywood Blvd. #876
> Los Angeles, CA 90028
> Phone: 323-851-1769
> Fax: 323-850-5302
> E-mail: jason@sherwoodoakscollege.com
> Web site: www.sherwoodoakscollege.com

This organization offers regular weekend seminars and week-long seminars such as "Becoming a Working Writer" at various locations in Hollywood and Beverly Hills.

Hollywood Heat

The first class that I took at the old Sherwood Oaks Experimental College was taught by a lady who had written a number of "Classics Illustrated" comic books. I treasured these illustrated Cliff Notes-like comics when I was a kid. To me at the time, anyone who had written for them was akin to a legend. As it turned out, her adroitness at distilling the most important elements of thick classic novels made her perfect for adapting books into screenplays. As a result, she worked a lot, and when she began teaching, she had a lot of useful information to pass on.

I first came across Sherwood Oaks in the 1980s, as did a lot of other people who are much more successful than myself. For example, James Cameron studied screenwriting at Sherwood Oaks, which is why he and people like him are quite willing to come back and speak to aspiring Hollywoodians on occasion.

Gary Shusett was a former schoolteacher who simply saw a need for a part-time school to help people break into Hollywood. Here's a sample of the types of companies that participated in one of its programs I attended, "Pitching One on One to the Industry." Representatives who met with aspiring screenwriters came from Nicolas Cage's Saturn Films, DreamWorks (*American Beauty*), Miramax (*Cider House Rules*),

Imagine (*The Nutty Professor*), Lobel Films and Regent Films (*Gods and Monsters*), Rheme Productions (*Patriot Games*), Scott Rudin (*Wonder Boys*), Joel Silver Pictures (*Matrix*), Suite A Literary Management, Warden White and Associates, Wardlow Agency, and 25 other companies.

Although Sherwood Oaks is always careful to note that "Guests are subject to availability," having participated in some of their panels and events in recent years, I can assure you that you get the real thing—a chance to meet real Hollywood players that you might not gain access to on your own.

My other favorite is the UCLA Extension Writers Program, which offers 450 individual courses annually as well as certificate programs. I spent a year teaching at Extension, the nation's largest university-related writing program. Extension is affiliated with the university but supports itself, allowing it to bring in teachers who are working professionals who may or may not have university degrees or teaching credentials. Admissions are open, so all you have to do is pay the price of admission and show up for class.

Any time I've read through the catalog I've seen a lot of familiar names (familiar to anyone working in Hollywood). If you think you might spend some time in Los Angeles and try the program, contact:

> UCLA Extension Writers' Program
> 10995 Le Conte Avenue, #440
> Los Angeles, CA 90024-2883
> E-mail: writers@uclaextension.org
> Web site: www.unex.ucla.edu/writers/

To receive a copy of the latest quarter's classes, call the general information number at 310-825-9415. For screenwriting and online screenwriting classes, call Kathy Pomerantz or Brandon Gannon at 310-206-1542, or e-mail the organization. If you're outside California in the United States, call 1-800-388-8252.

"Words into Pictures" and the Writers Guild of America

Not to be outdone by the plethora of screenwriting seminars, traveling gurus, and film festival panels, in 1998 the Writers Guild of America created an event called "Words into Pictures." The 1999 program was billed as "the best three days of informative discussion and lively networking you'll ever spend." Unlike similar events, people from production companies don't show up to tell you what they know, answer your questions, and possibly meet you. "Words into Pictures" is simply a discussion forum that cover issues affecting writers. The tickets are a bit pricey, with discounts for WGA members, full-time academic faculty, and full-time students, but the social events that take place during the conference might be worth the money.

Here's a sampling of some of the people who spoke at the 1999 event: Ron Bass, Shane Black, Albert Brooks, James L. Brooks, Julia Cameron, Wes Craven, Scott Frank, Janeane Garofolo, Bo Goldman, Matt Groening, Brian Helgeland, Jonathan Hensleigh, Amy Holden Jones, Gale Anne Hurd, Callie Khouri, David Koepp, Kasi Lemmons, Norm MacDonald, Marc Norman, Jim Sheridan, Ed Solomon, Aaron Sorkin, Chris Vogler, and Alan Wertheimer. (If you don't recognize the names, get an education on them at www.imdb.com.)

Hot topics of discussion included the "Sony Deal," which at the time gave 34 top screenwriters a percentage of gross profits of scripts that they wrote for that studio, potentially changing respect for screenwriters across the industry. Only the top writers in the industry qualified for the deal, but many of them were there to comment upon it at the event. Interested in "Words into Pictures"? Details are available at www.wga.org.

Skip's Tips

There are two types of screen-writing seminars: how-to-do seminars and how-to-sell seminars. The how-to-sell events that are worthwhile have people present who can buy your work, usually on the panel. If those people aren't from companies that have made films in the last year, the event might not be worth it.

Film Festivals and Panels of Pundits

Because I helped put together the Hollywood Film Festival, in its fourth year as I write this book, I'm a bit prejudiced. (See www.hollywoodfilmfestival.com.) Author and entrepreneur Carlos de Abreu had a simple idea. There were film festivals all over the world, with Cannes being most notable for major motion pictures and Sundance being the mecca of the independent filmmaker. Why wasn't there a festival in Hollywood so that Hollywood executives would not have to travel to meet filmmakers?

It made a lot of sense to me. When he asked me whether he should hold the festival in Beverly Hills or Hollywood, I advised de Abreu to set up shop in the Hollywood Roosevelt, a classic hotel named after President Theodore Roosevelt, just across from the Mann Chinese Theater on Hollywood Boulevard. It was simply the only venue on Hollywood Boulevard that made sense. Also, the first Academy Awards had been held in the Blossom Room of the Roosevelt, so having the first Hollywood Film Festival there was a nice way to honor a fine tradition.

That first year, I put together and chaired two panels at the week-long festival, one on film and another on television. I invited recognizable Hollywood players that I knew personally, including Robert Katz, producer of *Gettysburg, Selena,* and other impressive films. I held my breath as each event began, not knowing whether anyone would show up, despite my publicity efforts and those of de Abreu's organization. To my relief, several dozen attendees came to each event, and I didn't embarrass my guests, who gave freely and willingly of their time to offer advice.

Script Notes

A **film festival** is organized to showcase films and provide film-makers with the possible prestige of winning a prize. For screen-writers, these are good to attend because you meet people currently involved in the filmmaking process.

Skip's Tips

You can keep track of film festivals around the world by logging onto www.filmfestivals.com. If that Web site isn't working, contact your state film commission. You likely have a film festival closer to you than you think.

Robert Katz was asked by one member of the film panel audience why he, a busy producer, would take the time to show up at a new event such as the Hollywood Film Festival and speak to a room of only a few dozen people. Katz's reply was frank. He informed the questioner that it had not been that long since he himself had been a member of the audience, script in hand, trying to get someone interested in his project. He remembered well the passion he had felt and the frustration he had experienced in trying to break in. Katz simply wanted to make it easier for others than it had been for him.

"Giving back," I heard several panelists murmur in concurrence, nodding their heads in affirmation.

"Besides," Katz continued, "we need you." He explained that all the top agents in the world submitting scripts were no guarantee that producers would find the stellar screenplays and top properties that they needed to keep their careers in high gear. That's why most successful producers he knew attended events such as the Festival, hoping to meet that special writer who has a story that audiences will pay to see.

There are *film festivals* all over the world. I've never been to Cannes or Sundance, simply because I've never had a film to sell. That's the main focus of all festivals, even Hollywood. Filmmakers show up with finished product, hoping to get it noticed and strike a distribution deal. I learned that when I began attending the annual American Film Market in Santa Monica, California, where buyers and distributors from all over the world arrive to make deals with filmmakers. For this reason, at most festivals writers are, as usual, secondary. One other festival seems to have as much interest in writers as the Hollywood Film Festival.

That's the annual Heart of Film contest at the Austin Film Festival in my home state of Texas. See www.austinfilmfestival.org for details; it's a great fest in a great city.

I've appeared on panels as far away as Providence, Rhode Island, but I still like the Hollywood Film Festival best. What's important is that you get to a good festival and meet someone who can help you make the transition from hopeful screenwriter to *sold* screenwriter. It's a people business, and you have to go where the people are.

Online Oracles and Internet Interpreters

Because I'm a well-known provider of "inside" information on Hollywood (which really means only that I'm working in the business and paying attention), and because I hear from hopeful screenwriters around the world constantly, and because I'm not full of myself (I hope), I've had various entreaties in the past few years from people setting up Web sites to sell access to Hollywood.

(Sheesh, was that a sentence or a book? I'd better stick to screenplays.)

These folks, all of whom I've liked well enough, wanted my "blessing" on the services they offered, which generally consisted of the following:

➤ Potential access to industry movers and shakers, due to their personal experience with the same

➤ Script coverage, which, if positive, would be passed on to said movers and shakers for possible consideration

➤ Advice (for a price) on improving submitted screenplays

Thankfully, I didn't encounter anyone who seemed to be running a scam. Sometimes I got evasive answers about who the contacts were and what interaction they'd had. Always, the price for the services was more than the normal $50 or so paid to a freelance script reader by producers. And in some cases, people who had been agents or producers made me wonder why they weren't making money doing *that* instead of a Web site.

Then, in 2000, big-time acquisitions and mergers began taking place in Hollywood, and several of the online coverage services that had contacted me were acquired by companies such as iFilm.com and CreativePlanet.com, which had major financial backing. A rush was on to create a battle of the titans over Hollywood contacts and inside information.

Script Notes

Coverage is what a producer has done to tell him whether he wants to read a script for possible purchase. If your script coverage will not go before a producer, it's worthless, and you shouldn't pay anyone to have it done.

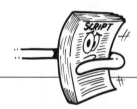

It's Not for Us

Coverage done at studios and networks does not go away. If your property is read on a studio lot, the coverage is kept on file seemingly forever. If you submit your script to another production company on a lot after being rejected, you should probably change the title to ensure a fresh read. Ethical? Hey, this is Hollywood!

I never affiliated with anyone until I joined FilmTracker.com, which provides access to a site where hundreds of top production companies and agencies can contact writers directly if they see a log line that looks interesting.

And (big and), the writer can opt to know who looks at their material. It's the only way of online showcasing that makes sense to me.

Schools and Other Institutions

There are film schools all over the world, and no matter who I mention here, someone is certain to give me grief over not mentioning some alma mater. Let me just say this. The main universities important to screenwriters in Los Angeles are the University of Southern California (USC, a private school) and the University of California at Los Angeles (UCLA, a state school). Naturally, tuition at UCLA is less expensive for anyone who is a California resident. I won't speak to the relative worth of either; they both have graduates with remarkable track records. See usc.edu and ucla.edu for more information.

The other Los Angeles school that's a definite "must see" is the aforementioned American Film Institute, which also has occasional programs in other parts of the country. For details, have a look at www.afionline.org/home.html.

But, just so my East Coast friends don't yell too loudly at me, I should mention that in 1998, two screenwriting program graduates from Columbia University in New York were nominated for screenwriting Oscars—Bill Condon for *Gods and Monsters,* and Scott B. Smith for *A Simple Plan.* So, have a look at www.columbia.edu if you think that New York City is a more likely bet for you.

However you learn about screenwriting, I hope that you remember that old line from Mark Twain, and don't let your schooling get in the way of your education. In Hollywood, the latter never ends.

The Least You Need to Know

➤ With gurus, first ask whether they can make a living doing what they're telling you how to do.

➤ Experts without humility and humor are probably hiding something.

➤ Gurus who always have their show on the road are in the seminar business, not the screenwriting business.

➤ My primary criterion in judging the worth of what any guru offers is this: *Do I put into use and remember what they teach me?*

➤ If you come to southern California long enough to attend events at industry-centric schools such as Sherwood Oaks Experimental College, you can easily meet and interact with industry pros.

➤ The annual "Words into Pictures" screenwriting event put on by The Writers Guild of America West is the best of its kind.

➤ While most film festivals are great places to meet filmmakers, the Hollywood Film Festival offers better access to top Hollywood professionals.

➤ For my money, FilmTracker.com is the best online service in the business, with regard to contacting top production companies and Hollywood agencies.

➤ The main three university-based programs for screenwriting in southern California are USC, UCLA, and AFI.

➤ No matter where you study, the business of screenwriting is a continuing education.

Chapter 27

The Truth About Selling Scripts

In This Chapter

➤ Making a query letter work

➤ Use the telephone

➤ Effective e-mails

➤ All about gatekeepers

➤ Internet impact

➤ Do it in person

It's a jungle out there. These days, it seems like there are more people available to tell you how to sell your script than there are people around to *buy* your script. But don't despair. There's a very simple way to sell a script.

Write a great one. If you do, and you get it to anyone at all who can do something with it, you have a very good chance. If you show any kind of talent at all in Holly-wood, you'll get noticed. The rest depends on making friends, persistence, timing, and luck, in that order. As long as you know your own strengths and write commercially interesting screenplays (the kind people will pay to see), you're in the running.

Hollywood Heat

Sometimes a script floats around Hollywood for a long time. People know about the script. Maybe the writer has even made some money on an option. Nevertheless, even though the script is admired, it's not made into a film. That's what happened to scripts such as *The Electric Horseman, Unforgiven,* and a number of other great ones. If you're not willing to be in the game for the long haul, this isn't the business for you.

How to Keep Your Query Letter out of the Round File and Your Project on Their Mind

People often come to screenwriting with a literary mind-set. They've written short stories or novels and believe a manuscript is always submitted with a query letter attached, or a query letter is sent asking the agent or publisher to request the manuscript. A query letter offers a bit of description about the project, in the hope that it will convince someone to ask to see it.

Should you send a similar letter to a Hollywood agent or producer? It's a toss up, a 50/50 chance that someone will read the letter at all. I'm of the mind to advise you to not send a letter at all, to call instead, or e-mail, but every time I think the query letter is completely dead with regard to effectiveness in Hollywood, I hear of someone who sent in query letters and got good responses.

If you do write a query letter, you need to keep the following elements in mind:

➤ *Who* you're writing to. *Never* send a "To Whom It May Concern" letter or any letter that looks like it has gone to several people. Find out who the person is who receives scripts, learn how to spell that person's name, and use decent stationery.

➤ *What* you're trying to sell. Get right to the point. Say what your script is about.

➤ *Why* you chose to write to them, indicating that you've done some research (and you'd better have really done it).

➤ *Who* you are. If you have any credits at all, any particular qualifications for writing your script, any prizes for your writing, or whatever, say so succinctly.

➤ *When* you will be available to talk about the project, if someone is interested? If you'll be in the city soon, say so. If you work during the day and can give out your work number, do so. If you have a cell phone, provide that number. People in Hollywood pick up the phone. The younger generation also fires off e-mails (and so do some older folks). Try to be as "reachable" as you can without sounding desperate.

It's Not for Us

Do not waste your money getting a query letter to anyone overnight or by special delivery, or use any kind of special envelope to make it get noticed. It won't help. In Hollywood, scripts are sent by messenger from place to place. How letters arrive doesn't matter—they just go in the pile.

How long should your letter be? A page or less (preferably less). I don't care what you're selling or how much you have to tell them. If you can't write it in less than a page, you need an editing class. I doubt that 1 person in 10 will read a query letter longer than a page. The average agency—particularly any agency listed in well-known contact books such as the *Hollywood Creative Directory*—gets *thousands* of query letters every year. Forget tricks, chocolates, and dancing delivery people—It's been done.

I suppose that if you delivered your letter dancing naked, it might get more noticed, but it might also get you arrested. Keep the letter less than a page, say what you have, and tell when and where to reach you. And ask whether a printed script or an e-mailed script is preferred. Oddly enough, some people will read an e-mailed script these days.

Okay, here it comes, the sample query letter. I'm not going to get cute with you because I don't think that you should try to be cute. Charming, maybe. Smart, sure. Not cute.

I will assume that you are sending your letter on nice stationery.

It's a small touch, but if you have printed stationery or something that comes off your printer that looks professional, you're better off. It at least shows that you're spending some money in an attempt to be professional.

Should you compare your movie to some others, as we've discussed earlier in this book? You know, *Men in Black* meets *The Perfect Storm* or something (assuming that your script is about aliens trying to take over Earth by creating superstorms, with only a couple government agents able to foil the plot.). No, you should not—not in a query letter. They see that kind of comparison all day long. They're sick of it. Trust me on this.

Okay, here's a sample query for you, using a property of mine.

ME THE SCREENWRITER

Date

Sandra Somebody

The Beverly Hills Agency
555 Canon Drive
Beverly Hills, CA 90210

Dear Ms. Somebody:

For many single women, turning 30 can be a traumatic event. They begin taking stock of their lives, assessing their progress. Many are particularly concerned about their romantic life.

MIRABELLE FLOWERS is stuck in Gallup, New Mexico, wondering if her Prince Charming will ever arrive. The night of her 30th birthday, she's waiting for her oddball collection of friends to throw her a "surprise" birthday party in the roadside diner that she owns, when a stranger walks in who might just be that Prince Charming.

But there's a strong possibility he's an alien.

I read the *Spec Screenplay Sales Directory* and noticed that you've been particularly adept at selling romantic comedies like mine.

My script, *Walking After Midnight,* was a finalist in two national competitions and a semifinalist in two others as a stage play. People kept telling me that it should be a screenplay, so when two working Hollywood professionals told me that in one week, I sat down and wrote the script.

You can reach me at the number or e-mail below, at your convenience. I hope you'll take a look at it.

Sincerely,

Me the Screenwriter

Address
Phone number
E-mail

I know your next question: "How long should I wait after sending my letter before I follow up?" That's easy. Don't. If you don't hear from your addressee, you're not going to hear. Cross that name off the list and move on to the next. Oh sure, your letter might get lost in the mail, but that's doubtful, at least in the United States. If you're convinced that this simply is the perfect agency or production company for you, and if it has been six weeks or more, you might post a very short, polite follow-up—even a postcard—but don't get your hopes up. Just send the letter and hope for the best. If you don't get the best, find it elsewhere.

Hollywood Heat

Although I later interviewed him for *Boy's Life* magazine, I had no idea how many people wanted to contact Steven Spielberg until the first time I sent a query to his production company, Amblin, located on the lot at Universal Studios. I got my letter back with a stamp that basically said, "We don't know you, so we won't even open your letter." That had never happened to me before. I quickly discovered that it is a standing policy at top Hollywood companies.

Sooner or later, if you keep at it, you'll strike gold with a query. Don't get too excited, though. They still have to like the script. If they're an agency, they have to sell it.

The Telephone as Weapon of Choice

Although it might seem intrusive to pick up the phone and call someone you don't know, you don't know Los Angeles. I can't tell you how many times I've seen people in Land Rovers, BMWs, or SUVs cutting through expressway traffic with one hand on the wheel and the other holding a cell phone to their ear. They might as well graft it to their ear, some people use the phone so much.

Personnel at many production companies change all the time. They move from one studio to another, depending on projects. They might even switch area codes. For your reference, 213 is downtown L.A. (not many production companies there). If a company is in Beverly Hills, that's 310. Hollywood is 323, and 818 is the San Fernando Valley (as in Burbank, where Warner Brothers and Disney are located). Normally, a production company will have an answering machine that will give you new numbers (including fax) but that does *not* record messages.

This means that you have to be willing to spend some money on long-distances charges, if you're calling from out of town. (Makes Internet phone calling sound better all the time.)

It takes some effort (albeit minimal) to get the post office to forward mail. There is no forwarding service for e-mail, unless a company has a Web page to update contact information. This is yet another reason why the telephone is the preferred way to contact people in Hollywood.

Skip's Tips

Many online services offer free trials. The *Hollywood Creative Directory* (www.hcdonline.com) also offers free phone numbers even after a free trial is over. When you know who you want to see your script, use free trials and free services to look up the phone numbers.

So here's the deal. Get your hands on some contact information from the myriad of sources available, and make some calls. Ask for a specific person, state who you are, and say what you have to offer, using a condensed version of the query letter. Ask if this person is willing to look at unsolicited material. If you get a cold "no," just politely say thanks and hang up. If that person says "sometimes" or gives you an opening, you'd better have a pitch ready. You'd better know the log line of your script cold.

If you get a pause on the other end and something like, "Hold on a second," that means one of two things: There's a rookie answering the phones who doesn't know the rules, or you've garnered someone's interest and that person wants to see if a higher-up or partner wants to hear about your screenplay. If, after hearing about it, the person says that he or she want to see your script, ask whether you should mail it or e-mail it. If it's by e-mail, all the better—nothing like striking while the iron is hot.

E-Mails and Other Specious Species

When e-mail was a relatively new item in Hollywood, people went crazy with the novelty of it. I sent an e-mail to a major producer, and she picked it up, I soon discovered, on the set of her movie in South Dakota. I was stunned when her assistant called me within an hour of my sending the e-mail.

Since that time (a couple of years ago), the bloom has killed the rose. People in Hollywood have suffered through the same e-mail abuse ("spam") as everyone else. They'll answer e-mail because it's quick, but some of them are *very* protective of their e-mail addresses. The main thing to know is that just about everyone I know in Hollywood has e-mail. They're checking it on their laptop, their Palm Pilot, and their desktop. They're swapping e-mails all day long, some of them. (You don't get phone neck from typing e-mails on a keyboard.) I still think that e-mail is *very* effective in getting someone to read your screenplay, though. You just need to know a very simple trick:

326

The subject line of your e-mail must compel them to open the message.

I do *not* mean using ALL CAPS. That's considered shouting in cyberspace and is very rude. I'll personally delete almost any e-mail from anyone with an ALL CAPS subject line. Older folks seem to love to use it, though, so I'll pause for a second to see who the e-mail is from; if I recognize the sender, I'll take a look.

You need to remember that viruses are sent via e-mail attachments these days, so never, ever, ever, send someone an attachment with an e-mail. Just don't do it. If that person has any sense at all, he won't open it. You'll have to get into communication with him first, and have him expecting an attachment.

Don't use subject headers such as "The Greatest Script on Earth." That one will be deleted. Using the example of my script, I'd use something like "Is Her Prince Charming an Alien?" I'd hazard a guess that would prompt someone interested in that type of material to open the e-mail. If so, I would continue the text of the e-mail as if the subject header was the first line. Something like:

> **It's Not for Us**
>
> Just as with e-mails, some companies can be sticklers about receiving faxes from people they don't know. There's a legal reason for it. Fax machines keep records of numbers they send a fax to, and these records can be used in court to prove access. Don't send a fax unless you know that it's okay to do so.

That's what Mirabelle Flowers is wondering on the night of her 30th birthday as she waits for her friends to show up to throw her a "surprise" birthday party ....

(Note: These italics are merely for emphasis. Use only plain text in e-mails, even if you have HTML capability. The recipient might have text-only e-mail, and your emphasis and fancy graphics will be lost on them and might cause a receiving problem.)

Then I'd explain who I am, tell why I picked the agency or production company, mention something about myself if there was anything I felt worth mentioning, and then close. If I had a Web page where the entire synopsis could be read, I might list the URL in a "signature" line below my name. I would keep the entire e-mail to no more than 10 to 12 lines. If someone has to scroll down the screen very far to read what you've sent, my feeling (based on experience) is that he probably won't. I would also add a line toward the end that "I hope this is no intrusion, and please accept my apologies if it is. This is a one-time mailing."

E-mail is a part of life now, particularly in Hollywood. The good thing about it is, it doesn't have to be answered immediately. It's not as intrusive as an unexpected fax, and it's as easy to trash as a mailed query letter. You need to be able to deliver your message effectively in a short space, though. Look at it this way—it offers you more chances to practice saying the most with the least words. That's something that always benefits a writer.

Last but not least, save copies of your e-mails with full headers (those things that give a unique signature to each e-mail message—check your software program help area or manual). I hope that it never happens to you, but you might need them as evidence later.

The Gatekeepers Know All the Tricks: The Usual Channels Are There for a Reason

I ran into producer David Permut a long time ago, when he was producing *Blind Date*. A script of mine impressed him, and I was invited to his offices to pitch. His assistant at the time, Katie Jacobs, has since gone on to become a major Hollywood player, as have many other people who have worked for Permut.

Similarly, when I first met producer Jennie Lew Tugend, she was the point person for producer/director Richard Donner, right after he made *Superman* but before he made *Lethal Weapon*. Her comments were always insightful, and we've remained friends ever since.

Both Jacobs and Tugend were development people then, the folks who (if they liked a query or a pitch) were the first ones to read a script. Over the years, despite a few (emphasis on few) instances of rude front office personnel, I've noticed two things:

➤ Smart development people become smart producers, often rather quickly.

➤ Writers who circumvent the existing structure are screwed because the producer will give the script to his reader first.

Perhaps because the Joseph Campbell myth structure is so well-known in Hollywood these days, the people who are the "threshold guardians" of agencies and production companies are looked upon as opposing forces that one must conquer. The exact opposite is true. In many classic stories, the first threshold to new and unknown territory is passed by providing the guardian with a secret password. In your case, that would be your very good screenplay. You must impress the development person.

And what happens if the development person or reader likes your script and checks "consider" or even the rare "recommend" on it? Well, unless the producer gave it to them to read, the development person "found" your property. If it goes into production, that person is likely to make a lot of extra money and get an "associate producer" credit. And guess what? Suddenly this person is not a development person any more. Now he or she has a higher position in the company and is on the way to being a producer.

So, if you talk to someone in development who sounds cross, that person has either had a hard day or doesn't like your pitch. Don't worry about it. Just wish him or her a good day and go on to the next one. You might be talking to someone who will be an important producer some day.

Before becoming a successful writer, I made a living doing word processing for law firms and working as a legal secretary. Maybe that's why I never saw receptionists and readers and development people as the first line of defense to breach on my way to winning the war of Hollywood. I could truly empathize with their long hours and short pay.

I also observed over the years that many people I'd met in development were now producing movies. Being nice is good business, to say nothing of good living. Like I've said before, generally, the nicest people in Hollywood are the ones at the top. It doesn't hurt to practice now.

How the Internet Is Changing the Access Codes

By the time you read this, I estimate that there will be several hundred production companies with Web sites. Who knows, there may be thousands. After all, in the *Pacific Coast Studio Directory,* the longest-running contact publication in the business, more than 3,500 production companies are listed in the Los Angeles area alone. Some of the production companies, such as Centropolis (www.centropolis.com), have Web sites only to show off their products and provide public relations stories; they specify that they will not accept material submitted via the Web site. Others, such as Nicolas Cage's Saturn Films (www.saturnfilms. com), started off actively looking for material via the site and have since scaled back.

Some companies have affiliated with Web sites that they know will draw in writers and accept material via those sites. A good example is Hollywood Literary Sales (www.hollywoodlitsales.com), a site put together by Howard Meibach, the author of the *Spec Screenplay Sales Directory.* Black & Blu Entertainment and the Steve Tisch Company were, at the time of this writing, aggressive in seeking material via this Web site. At the top of the page, the site proclaimed: "The people behind such films as *Forrest Gump, I Know What You Did Last Summer, Risky Business, Donnie Brasco,* and *Wild Things* have joined us to help turn your stories into movies."

Skip's Tips

Development people read a lot of scripts on weekends, trying hard to find a movie worth making. If they don't find something good sooner or later, they're out of a job. Use an old trick. Call them on Monday morning after 10:00 before their boss arrives. If they didn't find anything on the weekend, they're more likely to want to talk to you.

Skip's Tips

You can look up the street address, phone number, and e-mail contacts of just about any company with a Web site via Network Solutions, at www. networksolutions.com/cgi-bin/ whois/whois, or Register.com, at www.register.com.

Here's a trick. Many companies have registered domain names but do not maintain Web sites. They merely use the domain name to set up e-mail addresses. Or, they might have a Web site but not list e-mail addresses. However, if you know only *one* e-mail address within that company, you can figure out the listing of other names. For example, if you know that John Smith is jsmith@warner.com, it's likely that Mary Smith is msmith@warner.com. Just a little tip.

There are too many to even begin to list them all here, but the good news for writers is that even top agencies are now experimenting with accepting queries via the Internet. Others who go there first, such as Hart Literary Management, a company run by Susan Hart, have used the Internet to build a business. Hart signed up clients all over the world while a manager, and now she has her agent's license. She has set up projects at major networks and major production companies, even though she lives two hours away from Los Angeles. Not bad, doing business in your pajamas, if you want! See her site at www.silcom.com/~tibicen.

I have a giant chapter in my *Writer's Guide to Hollywood* about Web sites, and I was years ahead of most people in Hollywood advocating the use of the Web. Suffice it to say that the Web has revolutionized this business and will continue to do so in the future. It may make lasting changes in the way Hollywood does business, from top to bottom. It's an exciting time to be a screenwriter, wherever you live, thanks to the World Wide Web.

Flesh-and-Blood Contacts Are Still the Most Sexy

Let me make this as short and sweet as possible: The best way to gain access in Hollywood is *in person*. If you don't live in southern California, get there, at least for a big event. Have some business cards ready. Make sure that you're well-groomed and that your breath doesn't smell, and start meeting people.

Hollywood Heat

I have a good memory for faces and names, but once it failed me. I was at a party in the Hollywood Hills when I handed a beer from a refrigerator to a guy behind me. We got to talking and I asked him his name. "Peter" was all he would tell me, even though I asked his last name. Finally I realized that I was talking to Peter Yarrow of Peter, Paul and Mary (a folk group before my time). It was the first in a long list of celebrities I met who introduce themselves only by their first name. Keep that in mind in Hollywood.

In showbiz parlance, meeting people in a large gathering is called "working the room." Most people will have business cards, but some might have only their name and phone number (that's considered chic by some). The secret is simple: be yourself and don't push it. If they like you, it might lead to something. You might even make a friend. If there's no chemistry, move on. Good luck!

The Least You Need to Know

➤ If you're not willing to be in the game for the long haul, this isn't the business for you.

➤ The most effective query letter is less than a page long and tells people what you're trying to sell right up-front.

➤ Other than person to person, the telephone is still the preferred means of communication in Hollywood.

➤ When you call a production company or agency, ask for a specific person, state who you are, and say what you have.

➤ The secret of an effective e-mail query is that the subject line of your e-mail must compel someone to open the message.

➤ The development person you try to circumvent today could be the producer you try to sell to tomorrow.

➤ A great number of top production companies and agencies have Web sites now, and some are set up to accept e-mail queries.

➤ In a people business like Hollywood, the very best way to gain access is *in person*. If you don't live there, get there.

Chapter 28

Plotting Your Screenwriting Career

In This Chapter

➤ Your next script

➤ L.A. or not?

➤ The big picture

➤ Agent myths

➤ Somebody who knows somebody

➤ Effective post-screenplay resources

When you get to the point at which you can write a competent script, start with a great premise, create a tight plot, develop compelling characters, don't overwrite dialogue, and put interesting twists into scenes, you might be ready for Hollywood. Hopefully you've done a lot of reading and have seen a lot of films, because successful screenwriting is not so much a craft learned as one absorbed via the osmosis of immersion in great stories.

I know of one currently very successful screenwriter who was a lawyer. Interestingly enough, a lot of lawyers do very well in Hollywood as writers and then move on to being writer/producers or writer/directors. This one, a friend of a friend, rented the top 50 movies of all time and got the scripts for each of these films. He went about it in the way a lawyer does exhaustive "discovery" before a trial. He sat down and watched all the movies, scripts in hand. I thought that was a tremendous approach. He virtually absorbed great movie stories and put himself in the mental mind frame of the most successful screenplays in cinema history. I'd like to do that myself some time.

You not only need a great screenplay to break into the film business, but you also need dedication to learning.

You also need someone touting your writing, even if it's not a professional agent or manager. I know of another writer who finally broke in after his wife took over as his manager and began making phone calls for him. After a couple years of part-time effort, she made a deal for him, and he's been working constantly ever since. Hollywood is a small town. When you get known, everyone wants to know you.

When to Start Your Next Script

If you've completed your first script by the time you get to this chapter, I'd hazard a guess that you'll make it as a screenwriter, at least in some capacity. Screenwriters who work a lot write fast, and they write well. They are brimming with ideas.

Shortly before completing this book, I spoke at a writer's festival in Colorado, where I was approached by the wife of a man who said he had a great story. Could he e-mail me? Certainly, I said, I'm always happy to help other writers. The day I got home, I had three disjointed e-mails from this guy that didn't say what he was trying to tell me. Finally, I dug out of him what he wanted—help with a book he'd written that he thought could also be a screenplay. I asked him to tell me more about it. He asked how he could be assured I wouldn't steal his idea. I replied that I had 50 projects of my own, and I was pretty certain that they were all as good as his, whatever it was. And I let him go because I could see that he was a neurotic person with only one desperate story to tell.

It's Not for Us

Never settle for "good enough." Make each script the absolute best that it can be. The more you write, the better you'll get, but if you don't maintain high standards for yourself—such as a movie you'd pay to see—your chances of impressing others are lessened.

If you sell your first script, or if your first script impresses someone but that person doesn't want to buy it, the first question you'll have to field will be, "So, what else you got?" (Probably those exact words.) If you're serious about screenwriting, you'll think of it like going on a major expedition. You'll want to be as well-equipped as possible.

I think that you should have at least three fully worked-out scenarios from which to pick your next script, if not a dozen. I mentioned earlier in this book that prolific writers throw away ideas or even whole scripts, or shove them in a drawer somewhere until a time when they're in a position to use them. You really must think in terms of quantity, chaff to sort through to get to the wheat.

After you've rewritten your first script and made it as perfect as you can, and after giving yourself a pat on the back and a break to rest, you should begin your next script. You might think of trying a different genre with your next screenplay. If you're a versatile writer, that makes you more desirable. Most screenwriters are not that versatile, though, and Hollywood will try to pigeonhole you into one category. Having several different samples in different genres gives you some leeway on what that category turns out to be.

Hollywood Heat

Hollywood, particularly television, can be amazingly lucrative. A show that runs for three years usually makes millionaires out of the writer/producers involved. Unfortunately, the schedule is deadly, and values can get distorted. I've known top TV people who are multimillionaires, but they work like madmen and seem personally emotionless—it all goes into the scripts. And I personally knew a TV producer who got fired from his million-dollar-a-year job after a fit of pique and, not long afterward, committed suicide. If you think that you're going to take off in Hollywood, you'd do well to get your personal life very well grounded first.

A saleable screenplay might not print out from your computer until your third or fourth try. Unfortunately, you have to write better when breaking in than you do once you're established. You have to write something really great, something that stands head and shoulders above other scripts, to break in. So, get used to having time blocked out in your schedule to study the craft and another block in which to write. I have paying projects stacked up, one after another, and most working writers I know do, too. As soon as this book is done, I'm finishing another for a TV executive and then am doing another one for a publisher. After that, I finally get to do another screenplay. Get used to being able to maintain a schedule like that, and you'll be ready for it when you break in.

Do You Need to Live in L.A.?

Although I know people who do not live in Los Angeles yet sell screenplays (even their first screenplay), I can't imagine not living in southern California while trying to make it in Hollywood, at least for a year. Besides, where else can you brush up against movie legends, or even break bread with them as an unknown? Despite my own ups and downs and heartbreaks in Hollywood, the good has far outweighed the bad.

One day I parked my car at the curb to have breakfast at Nate 'n Al's Deli in Beverly Hills, and Fred Astaire turned the corner and said good morning to me. Another time, my wife and I were in Century City when Burt Lancaster sauntered by, grinned broadly, and said hello. My mother and stepfather were visiting from out of state, so I took them to dinner at the world-famous Magic Castle in Hollywood. Danny DeVito stopped at our table and pretended to be maître d', asking if our meal was okay that evening. That same trip, I got my mother an NBC sports jacket and took her backstage to meet one of the stars of her favorite sitcom. Amazing stuff.

Skip's Tips

If you want the shortest route to making it in Hollywood, bring some skill other than writing, and go to work for a production company. You'll make 10 percent less than comparable jobs in other industries, but you'll get to know people. Use the Internet for job information. For example, try www.showbizjobs.com.

Oh sure, you're thinking, he's been in the business a long time, so he knows people. While that's true, the real point is that this is where the stars, producers, directors, and studio people live. If you're out and about in certain areas, you'll see them going about everyday life. It's not hard to say hello or strike up a conversation. It really isn't. I met director/producer Richard Donner by saying hello in a grocery store parking lot.

As mentioned previously, great seminars take place in southern California all the time. The Learning Annex also offers classes for less than $50, taught by top industry people. There is always something going on that can forward your career. And tell me where else in the world you can be skiing in the morning and surfing in the afternoon, and then see a movie at the magnificent Mann's Chinese Theater in the evening, or even a screening of a new film at a movie studio.

Do you need to live in L.A.? Only if you want a career. Even if you can give it only six months, I urge you to try it.

The Big Picture Is Not Just a Movie

Most people I know think too little of themselves, and they have myths built up about Hollywood. Maybe that's because actors on a movie screen are five times larger than the normal person. Or, they read tabloid stories and books about the seedy side of the entertainment business, which, frankly, can be a veritable garden of weeds at times. Lives can indeed get destroyed, but the last time I checked, there was a major heroin problem in Plano, Texas, a town north of Dallas where I used to live.

If you show up in Los Angeles on impulse, knowing no one, you have my sympathies. Remember, this is show *business*. It's a billion-dollar business that dazzles people around the world. Despite the glitter tales, the people that I see make it have a well thought-out plan from which they work. They don't depend on a muse, a stroke of luck, or a pot of gold at the bottom of the Hollywood sign. They methodically go about trying to make a career work. Even then, in the darkest hour before their dawn, they're prepared to pack it in. Michael J. Fox had sold his furniture and was ready to go back to Canada when he got the part on "Family Ties" that made him famous. I've personally been homeless in Los Angeles, with no job and sleeping in my car. It can be tough.

You can get around the troubles with a plan. If you live in Southern California, you probably already know what to do. If you don't, you might want to do something like the following:

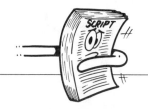

It's Not for Us

Never rely on any single person's advice about breaking into Hollywood. What is true for that person is only his or her reality. Others may have had exactly the opposite experience. For example, some will tell you that the Writers Guild Agent list is no good, while others will get agents using it. Go for a consensus opinion.

1. Find a way to give yourself at least six months. If you have a full-time job that provides a good living, see if you can take a sabbatical. Three months isn't enough. Within six months, you should be able to know whether you want to pursue Hollywood.

2. Arrive with a good, dependable car, or the funds to buy one. Los Angeles has recently opened a reliable subway system and has decent buses, but you need a car. See the L.A. Traffic Report at www.lk.cs.ucla.edu/LK/Presentations/facultylecture/canned-html/LARoad.html.

3. Expect to pay a lot of money for rent—Not as much as New York, but more than most parts of the country. For an idea about rent, check the *Los Angeles Times*. The online version is at www.latimes.com.

4. Working professionals (working east to west toward the Pacific Ocean) tend to live and congregate in Burbank, Los Feliz, the Hollywood Hills, North Hollywood, West Hollywood, Santa Monica, and Venice. To get a good idea of what's going on among young professionals in Los Angeles, read the *L.A. Weekly*. The online version is at www.laweekly.com.

5. Use every contact you have to get help setting you up in Los Angeles—friends, relatives, alumni associations, fellow workers. Have a written plan in hand when you meet people who are working in the business. Offer to buy them lunch or breakfast to get their advice on your plan. Rely heavily on getting advice; people love to give it as long as you are appreciative and not too pushy or dependent.

6. As soon as you arrive, spend some time learning where writers spend time. You can attend events at the Writers Guild of America and Directors Guild of America, whether you are a member or not. The same goes for the Academy of Motion Picture Arts & Sciences and the Television Academy in North Hollywood. It amazes me that some people are here for a year or more before they know that.

Script Notes

Humility is a word that has only this to do with screenwriting: There are a lot of talented writers in Hollywood. If you arrive thinking that you're the most special scribe since William Shakespeare and that your writing doesn't need improvement, you're destined to land face first in mud. Learn humility, and keep learning.

7. Be a friend. You'll find there are many more like you in Hollywood, and they appreciate just having someone to have coffee with and commiserate. Friends help friends in this business, sometimes over more talented people. That's just how it is.

8. Give freely of your time. I know people who have gotten hired by production companies after walking in and offering to read scripts and offer opinions for free. Others volunteer for worthy causes and meet people. Familiarity breeds trust in this business.

9. Keep a sunny disposition, and don't get down on yourself. Be sincere and persistent, no matter what. There are too many people ready to put you down; don't do their job for them.

For someone on a six-month mission to make it in Hollywood, I suggest that you divide your time into: writing, meeting people, learning the town (and I don't mean only the geography), and having fun. I look at the big picture, and I'm in the game for the long haul, but I've met some of the best people when simply enjoying myself.

The WGA Agent List and Agent Myths

The Writers Guild of America West maintains a list of agents from across the United States who represent film, television, and interactive writers. It is freely available to anyone, WGA member or not. Beyond the contact information, the Guild does not offer any help in finding an agent. Some people will tell you that the WGA agent list is worthless and that the only agents on the list who will look at material from new screenwriters aren't worth having as an agent, anyway.

At one time I might have agreed with that advice, but not anymore. Take a look at the list online at www.wga.org/forwriters_index.html, or call the Guild's Agency Department at 323-782-4502 to get a printed copy. Because I'm at least partially familiar with every agency on the California list, I feel safe in saying that it's really a good list these days. You get only the name, address, and phone number, but every agency listed conforms to the WGAw "no fees" policy, which stipulates that no agent listed charges a "reading fee" or any other type of fee to read your material.

You have to read the WGAw list carefully. The Guild provides a legend that indicates which agencies will consider new writers and which ones will consider writers "ONLY as a result of references from persons known to it." When you winnow the list down to the ones that consider only new writers, let's just say that you're mostly not dealing with the top agencies. Just about any agent, however, is better than no agent.

This is precisely why you need to meet other writers, and attend events mentioned previously.

You need to know a few other things about agents that I haven't already mentioned. First, they're busy, and they don't want to waste time trying to figure out whether someone is worth representing. If they are successful, they have a stable of clients who are working regularly, and they concentrate on those writers. If someone whose opinion they respect refers someone, though, they will take the time to study that person's work.

Next, most writers I know get as much work on their own, if not more, than their agents do for them. That goes for book writers as well as screenwriters. Agents are good at making sure that contracts benefit the writer and at getting more money, particularly enough to cover their agenting fee.

Last but not least, agents at the big agencies—Creative Artists, International Creative Management, the William Morris Agency, and United Talent Artists—won't be interested in you until you've made some noise on your own. That usually means a screenplay sale. The only way around that is if someone already a client, or if someone whose opinion is respected by an agent at one of those agencies refers you, or by winning a major contest such as the Nicholl or the Chesterfield.

Skip's Tips

If you're moving to Hollywood from some other city, you might contact your local newspaper about providing stories or interviews with celebrities. If a celebrity knows that a story will be published, he or she will often talk to you. It's bad form to try to hit someone up about your screenwriting, but asking for advice politely could lead to something down the road.

Skip's Tips

Your area code is something that people pay a lot of attention to in Hollywood. If you don't live in the 213, 323, or 310 area codes, you might get a grimace at a party. The 818 area code (where I live) is acceptable enough but not as hip. It's just geographic desirability, nothing more, nothing less.

When you first start out in Hollywood, you're better off contacting independent production companies directly to get them to read your material. Keep trying to meet working writers, and ask them to read and refer you (while offering to do something for them in exchange). Don't think that an agent is your instant ticket to success. Until you make a sale, and even well after that, the primary burden will be on you, so get used to it. I hope that you get lucky and find that perfect agent right away, but for most writers, that isn't what happens.

Somebody Who Knows Somebody— How It Usually Works

I continually hear this phrase—"He (or she) knew somebody." Well, how does anyone know somebody? The best way is an introduction. The second is a social occasion. The next is a public event where you know that you have at least a shared interest. Last but not least is simply introducing yourself and asking for a few minutes of someone's time.

I was standing in a photocopy shop in Sunset Boulevard one day waiting for some copies when I noticed that the fellow next to me was looking over some copies about something to do with playwright Tennessee Williams. Without really looking at the man closely, I remarked that I'd interviewed Mr. Williams once for a magazine and found him to be a gracious, interesting interview. Then I made eye contact with the other fellow and realized that it was distinguished English actor Michael York. Like most celebrities, he was uncomfortable at being approached with little hurrah, but being the gracious man that he is, York had a bit of a conversation with me about the tribute that he was participating in for Williams.

I later learned that he had starred in an original Williams play on Broadway. Being the bold person that I am, I asked York (who has over the years become a congenial acquaintance) if I could send him a screenplay of mine sometime. It turned out that he and his wife had recently moved to Los Angeles from Monaco, and he said he'd be happy to read something. He gave me an address and, amazingly enough, optioned the first thing I sent him. As these things go, the project never got off the ground, but I've found him and his wife, Pat, to be two of the most pleasant people I've met in show business.

Sometimes you are simply physically close to someone. I met a lady named Loretta Crawford because she lived in the apartment below me in Los Feliz. I discovered that Loretta had been married to a fellow named Henry Crawford in Australia, at a time when almost all Australian filmmakers were learning their craft at Crawford Film & Television. She had a company called The Australian Connection that helped Aussie showbiz people get a toehold in Hollywood. She knew everyone from Australia, it seemed: Mel Gibson, Olivia Newton-John, Peter Weir. She called me one day and said that she was shooting a music video of a group that she thought had a lot of potential, Men at Work. Not long after that, they were dominating the music charts.

Hollywood Heat

I briefly dated a girl one time who beat out 250 other actresses to win a part on a high-profile network TV show. It didn't take me long to find out that she was a heroin addict. The last time I saw her, she was appearing on *Inside Edition* complaining about a person who supposedly ruined her career, when I knew very well that only she had done it. Showbiz tolerance of self-abusive people grows less with passing years, particularly when problems become public. Read *You'll Never Eat Lunch in This Town Again,* by Julia Phillips, and you'll see what I mean.

Neither of the people I've mentioned knowing ever led me to lucrative deals, but that's okay. I was simply trying to illustrate that if you are in the right areas of Los Angeles, you're bound to meet people. It's not some magical kingdom where serfs (writers) aren't allowed to meet the royalty working in the business.

There's one more thing: Talented people can sense other talented people. They really can. I've seen it happen over and over. People at parties tend to gravitate toward other people of like mind. If you're upbeat, sincere, and genuinely interested in others, it comes across. While I know that it's hip to be cynical and full of sharp quips as a screenwriter, most of the successful ones I know don't sport all the attitude.

Writer's Guide to Hollywood and Other Effective Post-Screenplay Resources

And now it's time to say good night. We're at the end of our show, and we hope that it's been as much fun for you as it has been for us. We really meant that. I'd like to say thank you on behalf of the group and myself, and I hope that we passed the audition. (I stole that from John Lennon, in *Let It Be.*)

I spend too much time helping other writers. I know, because friends are selling screenplays for more than a million dollars, and I'm not living in a house in Pacific Palisades or the Hollywood Hills like they are. But every time I hear a writer say that I've helped, often from around the world, I can't help but grin. I hear from my brothers who live in Southern California about aspiring writers they meet who have read my *Writer's Guide to Hollywood Producers, Directors, and Screenwriters' Agents* (Prima Publishing 1999) and had glowing things to say about it. Having my family proud of me is reward enough.

I know that I've mentioned my other Hollywood book a lot herein—perhaps too much to suit you, and I apologize if that's the case. I feel, however, that it's really the best reference guide to screenwriting resources on the market. Shortly after finishing this book, I'll be doing a third edition, which will be bigger and better than the first two and will offer advice on things that I haven't mentioned before, such as making your own digital movies. If you're interested, for anyone who has a copy of any of my books, I offer a free monthly e-mail newsletter. When I first hear from people, I send them all the back issues, which at this point total more than 150 pages. E-mail me at skip_press@ excite.com or skippress@earthlink.net if you want to be on the list.

I sincerely hope that I've provided you with the tools to embark on a fulfilling and lucrative screenwriting career. If I have helped you, let me know. If you have ideas about other things you'd like help with, let me know that as well.

And so we fade out, leaving you to fade in, with pictures that thrill and dazzle us all. Write on, screenwriter!

Skip's Tips

Another post-screenplay book that I highly recommend is K Callan's *The Script is Finished, Now What Do I Do?* (Sweden Press Inc., Box 1612, Studio City, CA 91614, phone 818-995-4250, fax 818-995-4399, www. swedenpress.com). You probably know Callan—she played Superman's mom on the TV series *Lois and Clark*.

The Least You Need to Know

➤ When you sell or make an impression with your first script, the next question will be, "So, what else you got?"

➤ You have to write better when breaking into Hollywood than you do when you're established.

➤ After you've rewritten your first script and made it as perfect as you can, take a break; then start another one, preferably of a different genre.

➤ For most people, it's advisable to live in L.A. for at least six months to get a screenwriting career started.

➤ Screenwriters need to look at the big picture and be in the game for the long haul if they expect to make it.

➤ The Writers Guild of America West agent list can be helpful in finding representation, but you have to read it carefully.

➤ The big agencies won't be interested in you until you've made some noise on your own, meaning a sale.

➤ Writers first starting out in Hollywood are better off contacting independent production companies directly.

➤ My *Writer's Guide to Hollywood Producers, Directors, and Screenwriters' Agents* is the best reference on screenwriting resources on the market today.

➤ You'll make your own luck, but good luck, anyway!

Index

THE COMPLETE IDIOT'S GUIDE TO

| Arts & Sciences | Business & Personal Finance | Computers & the Internet | Family & Home | Hobbies & Crafts | Language Reference | Health & Fitness | Personal Enrichment | Sports & Recreation | Teens |

IDIOTSGUIDES.COM
Introducing a new
and different Web site

Millions of people love to learn through *The Complete Idiot's Guide*® books. Discover the same pleasure online in **idiotsguides.com**–part of The Learning Network.

Idiotsguides.com is a new and different Web site, where you can:

- Explore and download more than 150 fascinating and useful mini-guides—FREE! Print out or send to a friend.

- Share your own knowledge and experience as a mini-guide contributor.

- Join discussions with authors and exchange ideas with other lifelong learners.

- Read sample chapters from a vast library of *Complete Idiot's Guide*® books.

- Find out how to become an author.

- Check out upcoming book promotions and author signings.

- Purchase books through your favorite online retailer.

Learning for Fun. Learning for Life.

IDIOTSGUIDES.COM • LEARNINGNETWORK.COM

Copyright © 2000 Macmillan USA, Inc.